About Island Press

Island Press is the only nonprofit organization in the United States whose principal purpose is the publication of books on environmental issues and natural resource management. We provide solutions-oriented information to professionals, public officials, business and community leaders, and concerned citizens who are shaping responses to environmental problems.

In 1999, Island Press celebrates its fifteenth anniversary as the leading provider of timely and practical books that take a multidisciplinary approach to critical environmental concerns. Our growing list of titles reflects our commitment to bringing the best of an expanding body of literature to the environmental community throughout North America and the world.

Support for Island Press is provided by The Jenifer Altman Foundation, The Bullitt Foundation, The Mary Flagler Cary Charitable Trust, The Nathan Cummings Foundation, The Geraldine R. Dodge Foundation, The Charles Engelhard Foundation, The Ford Foundation, The Vira I. Heinz Endowment, The W. Alton Jones Foundation, The John D. and Catherine T. MacArthur Foundation, The Andrew W. Mellon Foundation, The Charles Stewart Mott Foundation, The Curtis and Edith Munson Foundation, The National Fish and Wildlife Foundation, The National Science Foundation, The New-Land Foundation, The David and Lucile Packard Foundation, The Pew Charitable Trusts, The Surdna Foundation, The Winslow Foundation, and individual donors.

COMMUNICATION SKILLS

F O R

CONSERVATION PROFESSIONALS

Never doubt that a small group of thoughtful, committed citizens can change the world. Indeed, it's the only thing that ever has.

—*Margaret Mead*

COMMUNICATION
SKILLS
FOR
CONSERVATION
PROFESSIONALS

Susan K. Jacobson

ISLAND PRESS
Washington, D.C. ♦ Covelo, California

Library of Congress Cataloging-in-Publication Data
Jacobson, Susan Kay.
    Communication skills for conservation professionals / Susan K. Jacobson.
        p.   cm.
    Includes bibliographical references (p.   ).
    ISBN 1–55963–508–8 (cloth). — ISBN 1–55963–509–6 (paper)
    1. Communication in nature conservation.   I. Title.
QH75.J335   1999   99–18532
333.7'2'014—dc21   CIP

Printed on recycled, acid-free paper

Manufactured in the United States of America
10 9 8 7 6 5 4

Contents

Acknowledgments

I am grateful to the scores of conservation professionals who shared their exciting stories with me for this book. I thank Mallory McDuff, Susan Marynowski, Andy Lyons, and Gary Appelson for their valuable assistance and contributions to various manuscript drafts. Kerry Carlin, Jodi DiCamillo, Geof Gowan, Nicole Howard, Christian Newman, Ligia Rocha, and Kristy Wallmo enthusiastically critiqued early versions of chapters 1 and 3. The U.F. Department of Wildlife Ecology and Conservation provided a collegial home for my research. I thank Alison Gilcher and Jessica Sarduy for excellent secretarial and computer help, and Ellen Main for editorial assistance. I appreciate the encouragement and expertise of Barbara Dean, executive editor, and Barbara Young-blood, developmental editor, of Island Press. I owe special thanks to my father, Perry Jacobson, who read a draft of the book and wrote "ouch" next to turgid prose. My mother, Betty Jacobson, encouraged my early interest in the toads and worms in our mulch pile and instigated my lifelong love and work for nature. I thank my husband, Jeff Hardesty, for sustenance during the writing process. Proceeds from the sale of this book will help support conservation activities.

Introduction

Florida—I sat in a darkened room with one hundred neighbors whose homes were threatened by flooding. Representatives from the water management district were attempting to placate fears of more flooding. After a preamble by the program director, the district scientist shuffled to the front of the room to put our minds at ease. He put three illegible diagrams on the overhead projector in rapid succession. Binoculars might have made the print readable. He explained probabilistic theory in relation to a five-hundred-year flood event in such a way that even my fellow Ph.D.'s in the room missed his point. He mumbled about aquifer recharge, wetlands restoration, some hydrological jargon, and sat down.

The crowd got ugly. My normally civil neighbors raised their voices and accused the district of incompetence in dealing with their flooded yards. Yet, the district was not guilty of incompetence in hydrological monitoring, but rather of failed communication. The opportunity to explain watershed management or make a pitch for wetlands conservation was lost. A few simple communications skills could have prevented the disaster. The scientist could have asked himself, "What is my message? Who is my audience? What vocabulary will they understand? Can they read my diagram from the back of the room?" This small, but real-life, example underscores the need for communication skills, whether you are protecting endangered species, managing landscapes, or restoring ecosystems. Conservation and resource management problems cannot be solved without effective communication.

This book is meant to guide the student, scientist, manager, and professional in achieving conservation goals through better communications. Whether in the form of talking to the public or the press, devising a special event, training volunteers, or raising project funds, conservation involves people. An understanding of human interactions and dynamics is critical for effective conservation work. This book provides an introduction to communication processes—marketing and mass media, citizen participation, public information, environmental interpretation, and conservation education activities.

Advice and ample examples provide readers with the skills needed for successful communication.

Chapter 1 introduces the communication process and ends with examples of successful campaigns, from bear hunting to Smokey Bear. Chapter 2 explains the golden rule for effective communication: know your audience. Guidelines in this chapter cover a variety of research techniques, from quantitative surveys to qualitative observations, for designing conservation communications programs. These first two chapters set the stage and provide the background for the remainder of the book.

Busy professionals may wish to turn to chapter 3 first, because it outlines the steps for developing a communications campaign. The chapter discusses how best to frame your message and strategically select from a wide range of media and activities to accomplish your conservation goals. Chapter 4 focuses on using mass media, from simply giving an interview, which is not so simple if you do it well, to writing news releases and holding press conferences. Chapter 5 provides many examples, from parks to zoos, for developing interpretive media for conservation. Chapter 6 focuses on long-term conservation education strategies. Chapter 7 completes the communication process by providing program evaluation techniques with which to determine your success or identify steps toward improvement.

A valuable component of the book is the many examples, guidelines, and planning tools provided for all sorts of communications. From the U.S. Fish and Wildlife Service to The Nature Conservancy, and from Adirondack Park to Yellowstone, strategies and materials that worked for other resource managers and conservation scientists may work for you, or may stimulate your creative spirit. I intend for this book to be used as a cookbook: You need to prepare a public talk—look up "recipes" for successful presentations in chapter 5. You want to notify the press about a conservation issue—turn to examples of news releases in chapter 4. A group of students is arriving at your site tomorrow morning for an educational outing—chapter 6 provides a menu for a "gourmet" experience. It's not hard.

My hope is that this book will help conservation scientists, managers, concerned citizens, and students to more effectively communicate their knowledge and concern about the environment. Our wildlife and wildlands depend on it.

Chapter 1

COMMUNICATIONS FOR CONSERVATION

Save the manatees.

Only YOU can prevent forest fires.

Reduce, reuse, recycle.

Conservationists beseech the public to save, conserve, or restore plants, animals, and ecosystems. This chorus of warnings and pleas is part of the communication process aimed at changing people's conservation awareness and attitudes, and, ultimately, their behavior.

Conservation goals focus on biological problems, but solutions lie with people. Conservation communications recognizes the central role people play in all nature conservation efforts. Conservation strategies must increasingly focus on communications designed to affect people's beliefs and behavior toward nature. Use of public lands and natural resources is a political, and therefore public, decision. For example, rearing endangered Florida panthers in captivity is a biological challenge. Yet, the public decides whether to allocate required funds, reintroduce additional panthers in Florida, or conserve land needed to sustain the large carnivores. The panther's fate depends on how managers communicate with public groups and decision makers to raise concern and support for panther conservation.

Lack of an effective communications strategy doomed the panther recovery program goal of reestablishing panthers in northern Florida. Twenty-six animals were experimentally released in Osceola National Forest to test habitat suitability for reintroduction. The experiment was a biological success—the habitat was suitable. Yet, poor communications by the agencies fueled local landowner opposition and curtailed future recovery efforts in north Florida.[1]

Think of a difficult conservation problem you have encountered. More than likely, people are part of the problem and communications will be part of

1

the solution. Effective communications are essential for influencing conservation policy, changing people's behaviors, garnering funds, or recruiting volunteers. On a broad scale, the fate of our wildlands and natural resources depends on effective communications for a variety of audiences in diverse settings.

Why Communicate?

We all communicate virtually all the time whether we are conscious of it or not; even a lack of communication is communication. To carry out successful conservation programs, we must better understand and begin addressing the void in effective communication of conservation goals. The U.S. Fish and Wildlife Service recognized this need in their 1997 National Outreach Strategy: "It is our job to speak up for the wild creatures that cannot speak for themselves. To be effective, we must do so in a way that engenders public understanding and support."

Recent trends emphasize the need for conservation communications. For example, the number of constituents, or stakeholders, of public lands and natural resources is increasing. As a result, conflicts in land management continue to grow in concert with demands of diverse interest groups. Imagine the varying viewpoints on a proposed wildlife refuge from the following stakeholders: landowners concerned with property rights, politicians concerned with votes, business people concerned with the tax base, hunters concerned with access, preservationists concerned with protecting the ecosystem, animal rights activists concerned with individual animals, and parents concerned with outdoor recreation opportunities. Stakeholders are diverse and their concerns often overlap and conflict.

Some public opinion trends show promise. Interest in and concern for wildlife and the environment are increasing. Recent polls show high levels of support for environmental protection and wildlife conservation. For example, a Times Mirror Magazines poll found that 60 percent of U.S. citizens felt that environmental protection was more important than economic development when compromise could not be found.[2] The National Opinion Research Center found that 61 percent of respondents recognized that humans are the main cause of species extinctions.[3] In a similar poll, *ABC News/Washington Post* revealed that 70 percent of the public thought that the government had not gone far enough in protecting the environment.[4]

These findings may reflect our increasing exposure to conservation issues. Information is available through print media, radio, television, the Internet, satellite, cable, and other communication technologies. Images of oil spills coating baby seals, or unemployed loggers posed with their families are beamed instantly into living rooms or downloaded to home computers. Yet, people know little about conservation. Researchers have found that the views of most Americans are based on limited ecological understanding, and that concern for wildlife is largely confined to attractive and emotionally appealing species. Public opinion about the environment is a mile wide and an inch deep. Scientists bemoan "a citizenry that is emotionally charged but woefully lacking in basic ecological knowledge."[5]

If conservation efforts are to thrive, communication initiatives must build on existing positive attitudes to expand the public's narrow focus and limited knowledge. Improved ecological understanding should inform public decisions and actions. Communication efforts can enhance all aspects of this transformation.

Conservation organizations and natural resource agencies rely on good relations with the public. Opinions and actions of concerned individuals and groups influence environmental agendas and the survival of these institutions. Organizations and agencies must be sensitive to their many audiences. The goals of most wildlife agencies and organizations in the United States include the need to communicate with their wildlife-oriented constituencies. For example, one of The Wildlife Society's four principal objectives is "to increase awareness and appreciation of wildlife values."[6] Yet, resource managers often have considered public information and education programs superfluous.

Only recently have conservation professionals tested the use of public communications as a tool to meet specific natural resource goals. For example, to better manage park visitors, researchers compared the influence of interpretive techniques on the attitudes of visitors to Ohio state parks.[7] They found that both brochures and personal interaction with park staff increased visitors' knowledge and concern about park management objectives and problems such as illegal tree cutting, wildflower picking, and trapping of animals.

Communications efforts can succeed where regulations or disincentives for negative behaviors have failed. Managers at Tortuguero National Park in Costa Rica trained local guides to keep ecotourists from disturbing nesting sea turtles.[8] Their management goals were achieved through the use of a communications program for tourists, rather than through heightened enforcement or increased physical barriers, which were not feasible in the park.

As a conservation professional, your communication skills must include the ability to market your organization's products—its mission, policies, services, and goods. Marketing entails sparking public interest in the objectives of land management and environmental initiatives. Communicating with the public and decision makers helps increase their long-term support and leads to appropriate behavior and sound conservation policy. Like two sides of a coin, institutional goals must be integrated with the public's concerns; likewise, institutions must influence public opinion to support their conservation mission. Researchers have shown that appropriate communications can shift public support, improve pro-environmental behavior, reduce vandalism, decrease poaching, increase effective carrying capacities, and influence policies and decisions that affect public lands and natural resources.[9] Can you afford not to communicate?

What Is Communication?

Communication is a process of exchanging ideas and imparting information. It involves making yourself understood to others and understanding others in return. If you send a message—verbal, visual, or written—that the intended receiver does not understand, communication has not occurred. Consider the conservation campaign message, "It's good to protect biodiversity." The Nature Conservancy discovered that this simple message was not compelling to the public. Based on research with small focus groups (discussed in chapter 2), half the audience had no idea what biodiversity was and the other half provided mostly erroneous definitions. Yet the participants did reveal that they perceived value in nature conservation and concepts like the "web of life."[10] The Nature Conservancy had three options: change their message, target a more knowledgeable audience, or educate their constituents. Their situation demonstrates how much effort is needed to understand target audiences and the likely impact of messages and products; otherwise, time and resources are wasted. No wonder public relations is a multibillion dollar industry in the United States.

Communication involves both interpersonal processes, such as personal interaction and conversation, and mass media approaches, such as newspapers, magazines, radio, television, telephone, mail, books, films, mobile exhibits, billboards, and extension publications. It also involves electronic media such as the Internet and satellite conferences. The public receives much of its environmental information through mass media channels. A survey of teenagers in England, the United States, Australia, and Israel revealed that mass media—radio, television, and the press (but not school!)—were students' most important sources of information about environmental issues.[11] Although these mass media are our primary source of information in the technology age, interpersonal and hands-on activities can be effective in influencing attitudes and behaviors. Selecting the appropriate communications method based on your audience and the goals of the communication effort is critical. The theories and approaches that are the basis of good communication are described here and throughout this book and apply to all forms of communications for conservation—speeches, press conferences, interviews, public events, descriptive brochures, interpretive trail signs, and educational program designs.

Communication Theory

Much of communication theory is derived from disciplines such as psychology, sociology, and anthropology. A quick foray into this arena demonstrates the complexity of devising effective communications. An understanding of the many detours inherent in the communications process helps in successfully navigating toward conservation goals.

Early models illustrate communication as emanating from a source (fig. 1.1). The source sends a message through a medium, such as a poster or television program, to a receiver who responds and decides what action, if any, to take.

This simple model ignores the noise that distorts many messages. New communication models include an encoding stage, in which the original message is translated and conveyed to the receiver via a channel, and a decoding stage in which the receiver interprets the encoded message and responds (fig. 1.2).[12] Both encoding and decoding are critical stages in the communication process. The channels selected for your communication may be interpersonal, through speeches and participatory demonstrations; electronic, through cable and airways; or in print, through newspapers and books. The channel you select will affect the encoding and decoding of your conservation message.

Gatekeepers regulate the flow of information from source to receiver. Different channels have different gatekeepers. Suppose you speak to a reporter about your organization's new project to save endangered orchids. The reporter encodes your message in the form of a newspaper article. A gatekeeper in the form of an editor must accept the story for publication. Perhaps the last three paragraphs will be cut due to a shortage of space. The receivers, individuals perusing the paper over their morning coffee, will decode the article based on their own experience—why should orchids interest them? If you do not catch their attention, they will not read it.

Feedback, in the form of action from the receivers, allows the source to adjust the message; thus receivers become senders if their response is captured in some way. However, sources must be listening in order to modify their communications on the basis of the receivers' feedback. An agency that fails to respond to constituent anger about changes in a hunting policy will have more problems than an agency that listens and understand the needs of all its constituents. Researchers in upstate New York found that the communication process in itself—whether through individual conversations, group surveys, or a citizens' task force—improved satisfaction with the wildlife management agency, regardless of the management outcome.[13] Public agencies, fueled by

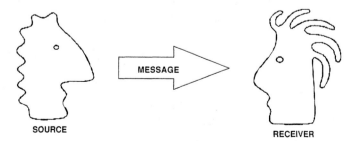

SOURCE   RECEIVER

FIGURE 1.1. *Simplified model of the communication process.*

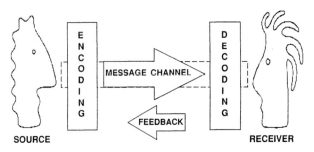

FIGURE 1.2. *Current models of communications reveals the complexity involved in delivering a conservation message.*

tax dollars, must respond to public wants and needs. Unless an agency or organization understands its diverse clientele and aligns its products and services with public desires, the agency and its mission are doomed.

Elements of Communication

The vital elements of the communication process are the source, encoding, message, medium, decoding, receiver, and feedback. An understanding of these components can help you design effective conservation communications programs. Failure in any step of the process destroys the entire effort. Ensuring that each component is appropriate for your situation is one key to success.

The Source

The source of the message is the central person, organization, or agency doing the communicating: an agency director gives a public speech on management changes, a ranger leads a guided hike, or an organization publishes a fund-raising brochure. The source knows how it wants the message to be received, yet it can't guarantee how the receiver will interpret it. During a speech, the speaker's body language, voice tone, and vocabulary influence how the audience receives the message. Understanding the concerns and vocabulary of the audience can greatly enhance communication efforts by targeting the message to the audience's characteristics and needs. Chapter 2 discusses methods of collecting information in order to target specific audiences.

Encoding

Once the message leaves the source, it is translated, intercepted, truncated, or passed on unscathed through encoding. Many factors affect the process of encoding a message. News media have gatekeepers such as reporters, photographers, editors, and others who select, change, or screen messages. The encoding of messages is subject to numerous breakdowns from the source or gate-keepers. A message will not be encoded well if the source obscures it with scientific jargon or offensive language.

Other gatekeepers controlling the encoding process include information officers and public relations staff within government agencies and private organizations. An interview or coverage of a speech may be encoded by media editors, whose interests and priorities are different from those of the source. Gatekeepers may give little attention to topics of concern to your cause. Radio coverage may change your message by playing only a ten-second sound bite from a longer interview. A biologist studying endangered manatees was disappointed when his only quote in a radio interview was an offhand remark he had made about the granting agency, whereas the point he had wanted to make was that speeding boats kill manatees.

Controversial issues, such as "the Spotted Owl versus the timber industry," are much hotter subjects for media coverage than basic ecological information, such as the range contraction of a rare butterfly. Ecological data are rarely deemed newsworthy. One of the few times that the Everglades' unusual geology appeared on the front page of a Florida newspaper was in the summer of 1996. The day after a Valujet plane crashed into south Florida's "River of Grass," a detailed, full-color diagram of the Everglades' vegetation and soil layers accompanied the news.

Words selected for a message also influence audience perception. The term "wise use" to a member of the Wise Use Movement may emphasize immediate resource exploitation; "wise use" to a preservationist might mean protecting natural resources for future generations. The term "sustainable development" also has been interpreted in different ways by various agencies. Phrases like "property rights" or "safe drinking water" arouse audiences' emotions and therefore their perceptions of the message.

The Message and the Medium

Once the source's ideas are encoded or translated, they are transmitted in the form of a message. Messages can be carried to a variety of audiences via many channels:

- speeches
- conversation
- demonstration
- direct mail
- telephone
- exhibits
- guided programs
- newspapers

- magazines
- news releases
- broadcast reports
- World Wide Web
- face-to-face meetings

What medium works best for the job? You must choose the medium that will *effectively* reach the greatest percentage of the target audience. Different channels offer different advantages. The mass media play a powerful role in setting the public agenda and reinforcing opinions. However, more detailed publications or interpersonal methods are generally needed to change an audience's fundamental knowledge or opinions. For environmental issues, source credibility is important. Most readers will scrutinize an advertisement by an oil company regarding the status of the Arctic National Wildlife Refuge differently than an announcement by a government agency or environmental organization.

Target audiences can be segregated by factors such as age, education, occupation, or geographic location. Using a variety of media may be the answer to effectively reaching each audience. From personalized techniques such as speeches or direct mailings to mediated approaches such as placement of messages in newsletters or specialized magazines, different audience characteristics call for different media. The use of more than one channel increases the likelihood of reaching a greater audience and reinforces the message. When selecting media, conservation communicators must evaluate such factors as potential impact, production expense, cost of dissemination, audience size, frequency, and sustainability.

The content of the message, its medium, and its source all influence the perception of the message. Simple messages are most easily understood.

"Where's the beef?" was a popular slogan for Wendy's fast-food restaurants. It made a short, simple point. The ads did not ask, "How much ground tenderloin do you get in a bun from our competitors' restaurants?"

"Only YOU can prevent forest fires," is unambiguous on a poster with Smokey Bear dousing a campfire.

Messages dealing with more complex issues may be harder to transmit to the public. The concept of prescribed fire as a management tool goes against many people's early indoctrination by Smokey Bear. In a survey of citizens living in northwest Florida, only 12 percent knew that regular fires are a natural process maintaining their local, native pine forests.[14] In contrast, 98 percent of U.S. citizens could identify Smokey Bear in a survey conducted by the Forest Service.[15] Chapter 3 discusses how best to frame your message and strategically select media to most effectively reach your target audience.

Decoding

After a message is transmitted, it must be decoded by the receiver before a response or action is taken. Like encoding, the message is again translated, this time into terms the receiver understands. In decoding the message, many factors affect receiver comprehension. If the receiver is tired or busy, the message may be perceived in a different way than if the receiver is alert and focused. Past experiences and current attitudes will slant the reception of the message. Both proponents and opponents of a proposed forest reserve may hear arguments for *their* cause from the very same speech or message. A politician's remark that "government needs to ensure the sustainable use of land" may cause reserve proponents to think the forest will be preserved for future generations, while opponents may think the statement means maximum yield of forest products to benefit people today. Receivers decode a message depending on their own perceptions and values. Everyone has personal biases and receives messages differently. Understanding these differences is key to effective communication and is discussed further in chapter 2.

Language is important in the decoding process. If the message is unclear or the receiver translates it differently, then his or her response may not match the intended outcome. Semantics, or the use of words, can change the image of an event. Compare the images that the words "seal harvest" versus "seal slaughter" evoke in a layperson. "Deer culling" versus "deer hunting" is another example. While the same number of animals may die in the same way, the words create different impressions of the event. Communicators must choose their words carefully.

In addition to semantics, symbols are important in conveying a message. Symbols have been used traditionally for positive persuasion; for example, American flags and bald eagles conjure up nationalistic feelings in the United States. Advertisers use symbols of the "wild" to sell everything from cars to cologne. Numerous car models are named after wild animals—cougar, mustang, pinto, jaguar—and are photographed atop a western butte or in a red rock canyon. Environmental organizations also make use of symbols in their logos and images, as in World Wildlife Fund's charismatic panda and the leaping antelope of the Wildlife Conservation Society.

Commercial companies use symbols of nature to ameliorate bad press about oil spills or toxic waste. Power companies and natural resource industries try to offset public perceptions of negative environmental impacts by advertising in magazines that target environmentalists. A multinational company dealing in forest products recently ran a full-page ad in *Sierra* magazine. Under a photograph of a forester working in a lovely forest canopy, was the following quote by the forester: "We need to take care of the forest and the things that live here. Out here, you understand that the forest is more than just trees. And that caring for the wildlife that lives here is important. To all of us."

For the company, the price tag of over $20,000 to place an ad in *Sierra* was off-set by the positive public relations that the nature symbols and language were expected to evoke.

Receiver

If a tree falls in the forest and no one hears it, does it make a noise? This conundrum has a parallel in communications. If a message doesn't reach the intended receiver or if it fails to elicit the desired response, does it matter if it made a noise? The results of any communication can vary, from not affecting the receiver, to creating awareness in the receiver, to shifting the receiver's attitude, or, more rarely, to stimulating or changing the receiver's behavior.

The receiver often is a targeted or specialized audience, such as outdoor recreationists, wealthy urbanites, or middle-aged males. Chapter 2 describes processes for identifying and targeting audiences, which can then be broken into subgroups (segmented) using a variety of characteristics. Sociodemographic information, psychological profiles, consumer behaviors, geographic residence, and a host of other variables can be used to differentiate receivers to tailor the message to their specific needs.

Early theories of mass communication held that an organization sends a message to the media for delivery to the masses.[16] But this theory did not explain the observed reality. For example, a newspaper editorial supports Candidate A, yet Candidate B wins by a landslide. Obviously, many factors influence people's choices and decisions.

Later communications theories portrayed information diffusing through society from opinion leaders to informed people, and then to uninformed people. Researchers claimed that ideas were like ripples emanating from a rock thrown into a pond. Ideas spread in concentric circles from great thinkers to disseminators to politically active people and finally to those who are politically inert.[17] This diffusion theory assumes opinion leaders have greater influence on the public than do mass media. Subsequent research has found that people who are most likely to act on new information or adopt new ways of thinking generally travel more, are better educated, have higher income, and have more memberships in organizations. Studies of how ideas diffuse through society show groups of early, average, and late adopters of information.[18] Knowledge of your target audience can facilitate diffusion of conservation ideas to the most critical members. This will improve the likelihood of getting the response you want from your audience.

Feedback

Was your message received as intended? Did you increase your audience's awareness about a conservation issue, shift their attitudes, or change their behaviors? Feedback tells you whether your communications program worked and how it could be improved. Methods of collecting feedback range from formal before-and-after surveys to direct observations of the target audience or their impacts on the environment. To measure the effectiveness of a communications program to conserve a rare plant, you might count new members joining your organization, funds donated to purchase lands, or legislators' votes to pass protective measures. You may also assess levels of public awareness after your campaign, or the status of the plant population after a certain time period. Chapter 7 discusses methods of evaluation to provide you with the feedback you need in order to achieve your conservation objectives.

Communications Programs

Communications programs strive to create messages that solve problems or fulfill needs of their audiences. To succeed, organizations and agencies must understand and respond to their audiences' existing behaviors. Some communications programs target a broad audience with a public awareness campaign, such as providing information about recycling to all homeowners in Colorado. Other programs target groups practicing specific behaviors that the organization wishes to change, like providing grizzly bear hunters with information about hunting practices. To assess the nature of communication needs for a conservation effort, organizations and agencies must ask five questions as illustrated here by a program to promote male-selective harvests of grizzly bears in Canada's Yukon. [19]

Example: A Communications Program for Grizzly Bear Hunters

This program was developed as a communications approach to bear conservation by Yukon's Department of Renewable Resources. A shift to male-selective harvest of grizzlies would reduce the number of female bears killed and would thereby help to increase the grizzly population.

1. What stakeholder groups are involved in the issues to be communicated?

The audience should be defined using socioeconomic, psychographic, or demographic analyses to gain insight into the nature of the audience, their needs and interests, and their behaviors.

The target audience for grizzly bear hunting was identified as the outfitters and guides in the Canadian Yukon. Big-game outfitters from twenty concessions provide guides for the approximately 480 hunters who arrive each year to hunt six species of mammals, including grizzly bears. Past efforts to prevent the unintentional over-harvest of grizzly bears included a 3:1 incentive scheme (a system that limits hunters to shoot three males or only one female per quota) to provide an economic rationale for harvesting male as opposed to female bears. After four years of the incentive program, however, an evaluation had showed that the economic incentive had failed because the proportion of females in the harvest was unchanged. In addition, all outfitters in the evaluation had requested materials to train their guides to selectively hunt male bears—to quickly tell males from females.

2. For each audience, what conservation actions are desired?

The objectives must be specified regarding the expected changes in audience knowledge, attitudes, or behaviors that will result from the communication program. These objectives must be measurable in order to later determine if your communication program or method worked.

The agency wanted to intervene in the hunters' behaviors to promote the conservation of female bears. The apparent lack of knowledge about how to avoid shooting female bears guided the development of the following objectives for the educational program:

- Hunting guides will gain knowledge and skill at identifying male and female bear characteristics, resulting in passing up bears likely to be female.
- The proportion of female bears killed will be reduced from 38 percent to 25 percent or less.
- Outfitters will be provided with a tool for evaluating guide competence in identifying the sex of distant bears.[20]

3. What messages must be sent?

The interests, needs, and motivations of the stakeholder groups must be addressed. Specific motivational factors must be selected to appeal to members of the target audience.

The most critical message for the Yukon communication campaign was information that gave guides the ability to judge the sex and age of a grizzly bear. A constraint to the program was the initial skepticism among outfitters and guides that morphological characteristics of female bears could be judged at a distance. Thus the stakeholders were motivated by convincing evidence of the ability to sex bears from a distance. The message the agency used took advantage of motivational factors for the outfitters and guides, including the symbolic value of the bear as a lone, powerful, wild figure, an image researchers had found appealed to their audience. In addition, it was discovered that outfitters were not interested in cooperation between concessions due to competition for clients. Thus the educational messages had to incorporate the outfitters' interests in restricting information flow between concessions or competing guides.

4. What channels will most efficiently result in the desired behaviors?

The media that will most efficiently, effectively, and economically deliver the message to the audience depend on which stakeholder groups are involved.

The educational media chosen for the Yukon program included five products for use in training the guides and outfitters:

- a videotaped workshop with a respected Alaskan master bear guide that convincingly demonstrated to outfitters that guides could judge bear age, sex, and weight, and lead clients to kill only male bears
- a twelve-minute video provided to outfitters for training guides in the use of observational tools based on body proportion for identifying male versus female and young bears
- a sixty-minute video quiz with drill and practice sequences to allow guides to practice their identification skills and outfitters to evaluate their guides' abilities
- an adhesive sticker that pictured an adult male bear and listed its characteristics, which could be stuck to packs or gear for quick reference by the guides
- a twenty-four-page booklet titled *Hunt Wisely: A Guide to Male-Selective Grizzly Bear Hunting*[21]

Video was selected as the primary medium due to the need to show animal movements and behavior and the ease of distributing videos to outfitters who were dispersed during the hunting season. Also, the videos enabled outfitters to maintain control over the training of their guides, a critical factor given the intense competition among outfitters. Imagery in the videos was selected to be consistent with symbolic values—such as wilderness, power, aggression, and danger—that guides and outfitters often like to attribute to grizzly bears (and perhaps to themselves).

5. How will the organization or individual know if the method worked?

Program planners should define the desired results and methods that will be used to evaluate program success *before* the program is implemented. The results of a communication program often are specified in terms of numbers participating, changes in behavior, and impacts on the environment. They reflect the objectives established in the second question listed here.

The initial goal of the Yukon communication program was to decrease the proportion of females killed from 38 percent to less than 25 percent. The data from the first two years were promising with a decline to 26 percent in 1990. The project director speculated that initial enthusiasm for the program, based on new knowledge and skills, coupled with the expectation of greater revenues, contributed to the decrease in the proportion of females killed.

This example illustrates that a well-designed communications program can motivate behavior change. Programs that carefully target their audiences can improve public knowledge and values regarding conservation issues, reinforce positive social norms, teach new skills, and foster support for conservation laws and policies.

Communications and the Public

"I felt sure that it was just a public relations problem that only needed a public relations solution," Richard M. Nixon wrote about the Watergate break-in.[22] Obviously, a good public relations campaign did not rescue former President Nixon, but communications efforts can help address many serious problems. Strangely, the natural resources community often underplays the significance of communications programming and undersells its programs and goals. This lack of attention to communications and public relations can sink an otherwise sound conservation ark.

The public plays a pivotal role in the success or failure of conservation efforts. Public influence is especially prevalent in controversial conservation issues such as reintroductions of rare predators. In the case of reintroduction of the gray wolf in Yellowstone National Park, biologists working with the recovery plan concluded that "many recovery issues are perceptual, having more to do with deeply held personal values about the government, outside influences, people's relationship to 'nature,' and the political role of special interest groups than to wolves themselves."[23] In essence, researchers could spend years studying the biology of gray wolves in preparation for reintroduction, but recovery efforts would collapse without adequate public support. In such cases, failure to accurately assess and target public opinions can result in opposition to conservation initiatives and costly political battles.

Public relations is defined as "the management function which evaluates public attitudes, identifies the policies and procedures of an individual or an organization with the public interest, and plans and executes a program of action to earn public understanding and acceptance."[24] A "public" refers to any group of people who share a common interest. Hunters, bird-watchers, business owners, local legislators, and landowner groups each may have a different interest in a new wildlife refuge. From the duck habitat conserved, to the tourism dollars generated, to increased property values, each public is concerned with the development of the refuge. Their opinions express their individual attitudes about a specific subject such as the wildlife refuge.

Public opinion is the aggregate of many individuals' opinions, although how individuals respond to a particular issue may vary. People with strong opinions petition resource agencies, lobby legislators, picket, boycott, write letters to the newspaper, and distribute press releases. These types of actions can result from positive or negative attitudes about conservation.

Influencing Attitudes

Attitudes are predispositions to think in a specific way about a specific subject, mediated by the situation. A homeowner might think recycling is good for industry but too time-consuming to bother with in her own household. Hence, she votes for legislation mandating recycling for business, but may be too lazy to recycle her soda cans.

People hold a positive, negative, or neutral attitude toward a particular issue. Most people (the silent majority!) are neutral or don't care. A small percentage will express strong support or opposition. People whose attitudes can be influenced most easily are those who hold a neutral view or just do not care. Influencing people who strongly oppose a subject is difficult, while reinforcing someone who already agrees with an issue or individual is easy. The success of communications lies primarily in winning support from the vast majority of the public sailing in the apathetic doldrums. Clear, targeted, and persuasive communications can make a neutral person aware of an issue and foster a positive opinion.

Social psychologists have noted that opinion is usually determined by self-interest. A communication will affect public opinion primarily if its relationship to the audience members' interests is clear.[25] A conservation organization wishing to influence public opinion must ask, "What's in this for the individuals whose opinion we are trying to change?"

People are motivated by various needs and desires. The psychologist Abraham Maslow developed a hierarchy of people's needs, or drives. His theory states that people will first fulfill their physiological needs for food and health as well as safety and security. Human needs then progress to personal drives for a sense of social belonging, self-esteem, and, ultimately, self-actualization (fig. 1.3).[26] As people satisfy one level of needs, they move up the hierarchy. Maslow believed that fewer than 10 percent of people satisfy all their needs and become self-actualized. Knowing where your target audience fits in this hierarchy can help you develop appropriate messages to influence their attitudes. A wildlife refuge offers recreational opportunities that may appeal to someone seeking to meet needs for esteem or fulfillment, while opportunities for hunting could appeal to needs for food or safety for subsistence hunters or

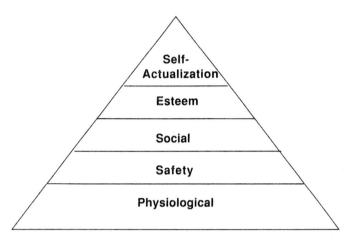

FIGURE 1.3. *Maslow's "Hierarchy of Needs" helps explain human motivations.*

a sense of belonging or esteem for sport hunters. Framing messages to appeal to people's specific needs can reinforce positive attitudes about your conservation agenda.

The values and uses to people of ecosystem services can be viewed according to Maslow's hierarchy of needs. These values are useful for communicators to employ when trying to promote conservation of natural systems. People's basic physiological and security needs are fulfilled when natural systems provide material goods such as food, clothing, shelter, water, and medicine. Also basic are the life support or ecosystem services that natural systems provide, such as clean water, degradation of wastes, and natural pest and pathogen control.

Nonmaterial uses of natural resources and ecological systems address people's higher needs for a sense of belonging, esteem, and fulfillment. These include the value of nature for religious beliefs and ceremonial uses, spiritual and aesthetic uses, scientific and educational uses, and, of course, physical and emotional recreation. For some people, preserving or delaying the use of natural systems for future generations also may meet their need for fulfillment.

Although some argue that nature has values independent of human needs, most people find it difficult to relate to an argument for the intrinsic value of natural systems. The belief that nonhuman species and ecosystems have values unrelated to human well-being is rare, although perhaps more prevalent among readers of this book. Communicators must deal with the real needs and desires of their target audiences if they expect to achieve their conservation goals.

Over the years, researchers have developed lists of values that all people seek. Political scientist Harold Lasswell lists eight base values.[27]

Power: the ability to make decisions that affect your life
Enlightenment: seeking knowledge
Wealth: ownership of resources
Well-being: pursuit of health, safety, and comfort
Skill: pursuit of proficiency in an area
Affection: friendship, love, or loyalty
Respect: recognition from others
Rectitude: pursuit of religious or moral standards

People seek to gratify these desires, but similar to Maslow's hierarchy of needs, different needs are pursued more vigorously at different times. Communicators must understand, for example, that some individuals may *perceive* that the Endangered Species Act or other environmental regulation threatens their base values of wealth or power. Conversely, an intact forest that harbors endangered species may satisfy individuals' base values of well-being or wealth. Communicating how conservation initiatives satisfy basic human values is one key to effective programming.

In general, public opinion about environmental issues waxes and wanes. Events and personalities change the agenda regularly. Toxic waste spills stimulate concerns about pollution; record hot temperatures increase speculation about global warming trends. Events can move public opinion more readily than mere words, as when the nuclear power accident at Pennsylvania's Three Mile Island in 1979 helped rally opponents of nuclear power. Multiple deaths of endangered manatees in Florida during the summer of 1996 raised interest in establishing manatee reserves. Events such as these stimulate emotional responses in the public. Scientists have found that the brain's limbic system— the center of emotional activity—can overpower its rational capacity. Thus trial lawyers seek to manipulate the emotions of jury members by introducing graphic, emotional evidence whenever they can. Timing communications programs with external events can reinforce your conservation message.

Influencing Behavior

Many conservation communications programs aim to affect long-term behavior—a difficult task. Researchers debate the influence of people's knowledge and attitudes on their behaviors. Increased awareness of a conservation problem in no way guarantees meaningful behavioral changes in support of conservation. Conservation educators initially suggested that the learning process necessary for conservation action progresses from ignorance, to aware-

ness, understanding, concern, and, finally, to action.[28] Following this awareness-to-action model, communications programs should first deliver information to increase knowledge and shift attitudes about a conservation problem,
and then seek to influence future behaviors.

However, changing behaviors related to environmental protection is
extremely complex. The consequences of conservation problems are often
long term, and delayed or intangible benefits provide little incentive for people facing urgent day-to-day concerns. Many conservation problems seem
national or global in scope so individuals feel they can do little to help. Personal actions fail to have noticeable effects because of broader political and
economic factors. People often misbehave *despite* knowledge of the environmentally correct thing to do. They do not recycle; they poach wildlife; they do
not carpool; they harvest trees unsustainably. Simply giving people new information will not necessarily lead to behavior changes. People might be aware
of the problem, but may not have the knowledge, motivation, or skills to identify viable alternatives to their current behaviors.

Recent studies of environmental behavior reveal factors that affect conservation action. Educators believe that environmental behavior depends on
cognitive factors, such as an individual's knowledge of environmental issues
and action strategies, and skills in performing conservation-oriented activities.
Personality factors, such as the degree of responsibility and commitment felt
toward the environment, attitudes toward the environment, and perception of
the ability to affect change also influence an individual's intention to act in an
environmentally responsible manner.[29] Obviously, if individuals do not believe
that they can make a difference, they will be unlikely to act.

Marketing specialists use psychological factors to predict behavior change.
They examine an individual's perception of benefits and barriers to practicing
a new behavior.[30] Marketers believe you must offer people a benefit they want
in exchange for their behavioral change. In other words, the benefits must out-
weigh any costs of engaging in a new behavior. Other researchers focus on
social influences or norms regarding the new behavior.[31] The individual's
intention to behave in a certain way is mediated by anticipated responses of
parents or friends. All of these factors can influence a person's desire and ability to act in accordance with the objectives of your conservation program.

Social psychology research has unearthed a variety of theories with which
to analyze human behavior and behavioral change. This work has influenced
communication techniques and our understanding of effective communication processes by showing that shifts in attitude are not a necessary prerequisite for behavioral change. The relationship between attitudes and behaviors
can be weak—teaching people that many cavity-nesting birds eat insect pests
is easy, but convincing people to leave dead trees standing in their yards for
these birds to nest in is another matter. Regardless of their positive opinions
of cavity-nesting birds, most homeowners chop down "unsightly" snags.

Some research suggests that changes in knowledge, attitudes, or behavior can occur in any order.[32] Psychologists note that if you change people's behavior they may subsequently change their attitudes in order to justify that behavior. Persuading a person to pet a snake at a reptile show, despite a dislike of snakes, can inspire both an interest in herpetological information and an attitude shift in favor of snakes—"Oh, they really aren't slimy!" You also can use information to shift attitudes in favor of not killing snakes, for example, by increasing audience knowledge about the benefits of snakes as rodent predators. In other cases, you could use existing positive attitudes to encourage individuals to seek information or change behavior. People who view themselves as conservationists could be convinced to learn more about the role of snakes in the food web or to write a letter to a legislator urging protection of an endangered snake species.

In sum, communication programs may follow a variety of strategies to achieve the goal of changing behaviors in favor of conservation. Programs may increase influence their audience's knowledge about the environment and engender attitudes and behavior that can promote environmentally responsible actions in the future. It follows that techniques for conservation communications must be multifaceted to influence knowledge, attitudes, and behaviors.

Example: Campaigns to Influence Public Attitudes and Behaviors Regarding Fire Prevention and Fire Prescription

Let's look at two communication campaigns that address the issue of fire, one to prevent wildfires and one to support prescribed fires. These two campaigns present contrasting approaches to influencing public awareness. The success of Smokey Bear is a public relations legend. So far attempts to reeducate the public to embrace prescribed fire as a management tool have been less successful.

Only YOU Can Prevent Forest Fires

The Smokey Bear forest fire prevention campaign waged by the USDA. Forest Service is one of the most successful and enduring public relations campaigns ever created (fig. 1.4). The success of this campaign has inadvertently fueled our cultural myth that all fire is bad.

The Smokey Bear campaign was organized during World War II after a Japanese submarine shelled the Southern California coast. The fear that future enemy attacks could spark widespread forest fires motivated forestry officials to cultivate the support of the American public in preventing wildfires. Our national forests were seen as natural resources that protected

FIGURE 1.4. *Smokey Bear is recognized by the majority of U.S. citizens.*

watersheds needed for urban water supplies. They were rich with wildlife and were valuable timber resources. Perhaps more important at the time, the deployment of people and resources to fight fires would detract from the war effort.

The War Advertising Council participated in the tremendous effort to spread the word of fire prevention through a variety of activities. These focused on messages such as "Careless Matches Aid the Axis," giving a nationalistic flair to fire prevention. Advertising materials included ten million cards, five million air raid warden leaflets, two million bookmarks, one million cigarette cases, twenty thousand trolley car ads, five thousand billboards, ten thousand posters, and a series of radio spots.[33] The State Forestry Associations joined in the development of a "Wartime Forest Fire Prevention" effort with the Forest Service and the Advertising Council.

In 1944, Smokey Bear was developed as a symbol for the communications campaign. He stood upright to demonstrate good campfire practices. He sported an appealing expression and wore a ranger's hat. In 1947 an advertising firm created the slogan, "Remember, only YOU can prevent forest fires." In 1950 a real bear was rescued from a forest fire in New Mexico. He was christened Smokey and sent to the National Zoo in Washington, D.C.—a living mascot for fire prevention. Smokey received over thirteen thousand letters a week, prompting the Postal Service to give Smokey his own zip code. Smokey also became an animated television show and millions of children signed the Smokey Bear pledge or filled out forms to become Junior Forest Rangers.

Since its conception, the Smokey Bear campaign changed public opinion using a myriad of public relations materials to convey its famous message. The communications efforts have been aimed at children as well as adults who were reached through strategies such as annual posters that were appropriate for all ages.

In one study, 95 percent of people surveyed could finish the sentence when given the first words of Smokey Bear's slogan, "Remember, only YOU . . ." The same survey found that 98 percent of the respondents could identify Smokey Bear from his picture.[34] The campaign was so successful from the start that the Smokey Bear Act was passed in 1952 to license Smokey's image for the Forest Service.

One way the Forest Service measured the campaign's effectiveness was to compare acreage burned before the campaign to postcampaign forest fire figures. In 1942, over ten million acres (4 million hectares) of wildlands were burned. In 1981, only three million acres (1.2 million hectares) were burned, representing a savings of more than $20 billion for U.S. taxpayers, according to the Forest Service.[35]

The problem with Smokey Bear's message was, ironically, its success. As our knowledge and understanding of the natural world expands, how do we modify such an effective and ingrained public relations message to better reflect reality? The concept that fire is essential and natural in many ecological systems may seem ludicrous to people raised on Smokey Bear.

When Fire Is Good

Fire, because of its power to destroy as well as restore, is a controversial management tool. At the same time that prescribed fire has become more common in forest and wildlands management, more people are settling in forested landscapes and are being exposed to the potential risks and benefits of fire. As a result, fire policy decisions have a strong social component. Public ignorance about the ecological role of fire in natural systems adds fuel to the conflict. Public communication campaigns could lead to greater public understanding and acceptance of prescribed fire and to more meaningful public participation in fire policy debates.

For example, a shift toward ecosystem management at Eglin Air Force

Base in Florida, home to the largest contiguous longleaf pine forest left in the southeastern United States, has changed field practices that affect recreationists and neighboring citizens. Restoration of fire-dependent pine ecosystems has entailed increased prescribed burning and more summer (growing season) burns. While prescribed burning can accomplish management objectives, smoke and temporarily denuded landscapes engender negative attitudes where the public lacks understanding of the benefits of fire. In a 1993 survey of Eglin's neighbors only 12 percent of the public knew that regular fire was a natural and necessary process in maintaining native pine forests.[36] Obviously a public communications program must accompany plans to ignite more than 50,000 acres (20,000 hectares) annually under Eglin's new management plan.

Prescribed fire education programs have been initiated in many places in the past two decades, since fire policies shifted direction in the 1970s. Early communication efforts tended to be local and scattered throughout the United States. They were seldom coordinated efforts among land management agencies.

In some areas, both prescribed burn and let-burn policies on public lands have been enveloped in controversy. Often, the only information readily available to the public is through mass media, which can distort reports and invoke controversy. The attitude of most reporters toward the 1988 Yellowstone fires was that all fires are bad and that the government should smother them as soon as possible. News reports consistently said that fires "destroyed," "blackened," and "devastated" an area, rather than "covered," "swept," or "cleansed" it, as biologists would have preferred.[37] The media fed on the dramatic visual images of the Yellowstone fires. Agencies also were partly to blame for misleading the public: each fire-management unit was colored entirely black on official maps, fostering the public misconception that most of the park had burned, when many areas within those units were completely untouched by the spotty fires.

Press reports of wildfires that swept over 500,000 acres (200,000 hectares) in Florida during a summer drought in 1998 indicated that fire prescription advocates have made progress. Local press coverage mentioned that prescribed fires could have saved the scorched towns from the blaze had they been implemented on a regular basis in the past. A decade after the Yellowstone fires the front page in one Florida paper read: "Florida can learn from fires: Yellowstone Park's comeback is a sign of things to come." The story quotes ecologists calling the fire a cleansing agent. It reports that fire is "vital, even necessary, for Florida's piney woods."[38]

Obstacles to Acceptance of Prescribed Fire

A number of obstacles to implementing prescribed fire policies relate directly to the need for effective public communications. These barriers include:

- misunderstanding on the part of the public and some agency personnel of the ecological effects of fire, coupled with inadequate feedback on the positive results of prescribed fires;
- public fear of fire and lack of public information about smoke, danger, and other immediate effects of prescribed burning;
- adverse effects of fire on public aesthetic and recreational values and lack of public preparation for postfire vegetation and wildlife recovery;
- lack of public confidence or trust in agencies that have been inconsistent in fire management;
- successful Smokey Bear fire prevention campaign that portrays fire as destructive and dangerous;
- media misinterpretation of prescribed fire practices;
- disjointed information due to a lack of interagency coordination and cooperation in fire awareness programs; and
- lack of a prescribed fire information program that is effective, coordinated, and targeted to key audiences.[39]

Communications for Fire Prevention versus Fire Prescription

The Smokey Bear campaign employed a number of effective communication strategies that led to its phenomenal success. Where Smokey Bear delivered a simple and effective message with flair, prescribed fire education programs often lack appeal or are poorly coordinated. The ecological complexity of prescribed fire makes it even more critical to employ effective communication techniques. A few of the strategies followed by fire prevention and fire prescription proponents in efforts to promote their cause are listed here, and the relative success of the campaigns employing these strategies is compared.

Coordinate across Agency Borders

FIRE PREVENTION. The Smokey Bear campaign was an early collaboration between the U.S. Forest Service, National Association of State Foresters, and the National Advertising Council. This cooperation allowed for both national and localized approaches and audiences, as well as a consistent message.

FIRE PRESCRIPTION. Most efforts have been local and uncoordinated until recently. Prescribed fire education programs are scattered throughout many regions of the United States and are not coordinated between land management entities. While researchers emphasize that effective prescribed fire education programs must address local conditions to targeted audiences, they also emphasize the great need for a well-organized, consistent, nationally coordinated prescribed fire education effort.

Evidence of agency cooperation is growing. For example, Florida has been divided into three prescribed fire councils, composed of agency, industry, and landowner alliances.[40] These alliances promote understanding of prescribed fire among the general public, new Florida residents, and landowners adjacent to prescribed burns. In addition, the Florida Division of Forestry has teamed up with the U.S. Forest Service to produce publications such as the booklet, *The Natural Role of Fire*.[41] Florida has a clearly legislated prescribed fire policy and a statewide training program for certified prescribed fire managers to promote safety and reliability among agency and private burners.

Develop a Long-Term Campaign Using Repetition and Continuity to Deliver the Message

FIRE PREVENTION. Smokey Bear celebrated his 55th birthday in 1999. His face and slogan are widely recognized and continue to be used on Forest Service publications. Smokey Bear paraphernalia has become "collectible."

FIRE PRESCRIPTION. Efforts to educate the public about prescribed fire did not begin until the policy reforms of the 1970s and increased prescribed burning in the 1980s. Coordinated, long-term efforts are needed to effectively educate the public. The National Wildfire Coordinating Group now has a prescribed fire working team that collaborates with the prevention, education, and communications team to develop a national education strategy. This will address the role of fire in resource management in the wake of the 1995 Federal Wildland Fire Policy and Program Review.[42]

While public acceptance of fire has increased in the past few decades, knowledge lags. The best communications messages for prescribed fire build on existing positive public attitudes and emphasize that fire[43]

- improves scenic beauty and recreational values, after a short period of temporary degradation
- is a natural ecological process in forest systems, enhancing forest health
- results in low wildlife mortality and improved wildlife habitat

- results in the ecologically sound removal of dead vegetation to prevent wildfire
- historically, was often of natural (lightning) origin rather than arson or carelessness
- can be effectively and safely controlled
- results in temporary smoke and low risk, as opposed to heavy smoke and significant risk to property and public safety
- matches a prescription for specific ecological or economic benefits, assuring the public that prescribed fires match stated agency objectives

The challenge is to translate this information into easily digested sound bites and thoughtful public education materials that can be repeated over the long term.

Use a Charismatic Spokesperson/Mascot

FIRE PREVENTION. Smokey Bear was created to be appealing and to be able to demonstrate campfire techniques.

FIRE PRESCRIPTION. Prescribed fire education programs have not adopted a mascot. In a few instances, Smokey Bear has been recruited as a spokesperson for controlled fires to offset his earlier indoctrination of the public against fire. For example, a coloring book for children takes advantage of Smokey's fame.[44] A boy is illustrated looking at a Smokey Bear poster. The boy says, "Smokey Bear has really done a good job of preventing forest fires."

An adult replies, "He really has, Rusty, but there is a type of fire that actually helps some of our trees, plants, and wildlife—it's called prescribed fire!"

Use a Catchy Motto or Slogan

FIRE PREVENTION. "Only YOU . . . " The simplicity of Smokey's message—that fire is bad and should be prevented, and the dramatic visual images that accompanied that message—burning, smoldering forest with vulnerable, cute animals, contributed to the pervasive public and political focus on fire's detrimental effects.

FIRE PRESCRIPTION. Prescribed fire educational programs are more complex and subtle than the simplified Smokey Bear fire-prevention campaigns. Prescribed fire education must relay a message about the various benefits and problems with fire, the positive ecological effects of fire, and the dynamics of forest ecosystems.

Some prescribed fire brochures have addressed the ecological role of fire. A brochure produced by the Forest Service tried a catchy title: "R$_x$ Fire!" This draws the obvious analogy to fire as a doctor's prescription to forest health. The cover page reads: "As a doctor prescribes medicine for an illness, Forest Service managers sometimes prescribe fire to improve the health of our southwestern forests."

Target Audiences Effectively

FIRE PREVENTION. Education efforts have been aimed at both children and adults, using everything from cigarette cases and nationalistic slogans targeting men to Smokey Bear cartoons and pledges for children.

FIRE PRESCRIPTION. Programs to date have mostly used brochures and educational booklets aimed at adults. Children are less frequently targeted. Campaigns have not capitalized on knowledge of audience sociodemographic or cultural backgrounds, and mass media or electronic channels have not been exploited to their fullest.

Seek Business and Industry Support and Cooperation

FIRE PREVENTION. Congress removed Smokey Bear from the public domain in 1952, restricting its use to agency educational efforts. But in 1974, in response to growing illegal use of the popular symbol, Congress amended the law to allow licensing of Smokey Bear products by the chief of the U.S. Forest Service. The licensing program insures appropriate merchandise and messages for all products, as Smokey Bear is only to be used for forest fire prevention programs and has never been used for product endorsements or other commercial purposes. Licensing is a minor source of revenue for forest fire prevention programs, garnering only $40,000 in 1996, but in the same year over $30 million worth of free advertising on television, radio, print, cable, and computer media was donated to the effort through the Ad Council.

FIRE PRESCRIPTION. Agencies have seldom collaborated with business or industry, and educational campaigns have been mostly a governmental effort. The new ecosystem management movement is leading to more public–private cooperation for landscape-level management, and may result in broader educational programs partly supported by the private forest industry.

Because the public everywhere needs to be informed about the benefits of prescribed fire, managers and communicators must become more informed about actual public knowledge. Is the public willing to accept new fire practices, and what are their perceptions of the various impacts of these fires? Improved social data about knowledge and attitude levels of key audiences, such as recreational users, area citizens, and neighboring landowners, can provide a basis for designing public communication programs and a baseline for monitoring changes in public awareness over time.

Public–private partnerships also can help produce fire information programs to educate mass media representatives. The disaster-mode coverage of fires in the past leaves the incorrect impression that fires destroy everything and that fire policy has no ecological basis. Industry and public land managers employing prescribed fire can work together in counteracting this image. Some progress has been made. Media coverage of the two thousand separate conflagrations in the 1998 Florida fires included quotes from biologists bemoaning the prior lack of prescribed fire and emphasized the many positive benefits of prescribed burning to Florida's forests.

Incorporate Evaluation into the Program

FIRE PREVENTION. The Forest Service monitors actual improvement on the ground by an annual count of human-caused fires and by public recognition of Smokey Bear. In the last twenty years, rates of human-caused fires have fallen 40 percent. Before the 1944 invention of Smokey, 80 percent of forest fires were caused by humans—that number has been reduced to 29 percent.[45] The Forest Service measures audience familiarity with Smokey Bear every ten years. Recent public surveys have shown over 80 percent recognition rate for Smokey—lower than Santa Claus, but higher than the U.S. president.

FIRE PRESCRIPTION. Recent research on the effectiveness of prescribed fire education programs also has shown positive results. Educational programs employing brochures, mass media coverage, and other tactics have been effective in improving public knowledge and support of prescribed fire in Arizona, Florida, Montana, and Wyoming.[46] Evaluation research also has shown that direct experience with prescribed fire or burned areas, participation in outdoor recreation, and residency near a natural area are factors leading to increased knowledge and heightened acceptance of fire.[47] Based on these studies, it seems that, as information and experience with the benefits of prescribed fire increase, more public support for prescribed fire will follow.

Last Words

The need for effective communications for conservation continues to grow as public interest in the environment increases and conflicts in land management expand. Communications involve sources, messages, media, and audiences. Recognizing these elements is key to developing communications programs, whether for grizzly bear hunters or the public affected by fire management schemes. For conservation organizations and natural resource agencies, an understanding of their audiences' conservation knowledge, attitudes, and behaviors draws a target for formulating successful messages and using the best media for reaching their audience. Research has shown that communications are most persuasive when they

- come from several, highly credible sources (credibility = trustworthiness, expertise, and power)[48]
- have a simple message that is easy to understand and relates to the audience's everyday life
- arouse personal relevance and involvement in the conservation issue

The remainder of this book provides communications background, examples, ideas, and activities through which you can achieve your own conservation objectives.

Chapter 2

RESEARCH FOR CONSERVATION COMMUNICATIONS

The Species Survival Commission had an unfortunate experience in reintroducing crocodilians into the Orinoco River, in Venezuela. It was a costly exercise to breed and reintroduce the animal, but there was no communication with the local people about the scheme before it began. Afterwards, it was discovered that the community had been trying to get rid of crocodiles and did not want them in the river. As soon as the crocodiles were released they were killed.*

Although the researchers understood crocodilian biology, their project failed because they ignored the communications process. An understanding of the audience is critical to all conservation programs. Without knowledge of constituents' needs and concerns, conservation programs are doomed.

Audience research forms the backbone of a conservation communications program. The body of your activities is built around it. Research allows you to discover your audience's

- interests and needs regarding products and services
- knowledge of and attitudes about your conservation issues
- background characteristics such as age, education, gender, and occupation

Audience research helps you orient your conservation program to meet your audience's needs and to market the products of your organization. Research allows you to assess alternative communication channels and mes-

---

*IUCN, The World Conservation Fund. 1997. World Conservation 1/2:53.

sages for building support for a program or influencing audience behaviors. Research also provides baseline information for the evaluation of your communications and conservation efforts.

Imagine going on a blind date. (You, of course, look terrific.) With interest, you assess your date's physique, wardrobe, and body language. Your initial conversation may be awkward, centering on jobs, hobbies, or your families. Your mutual goal is to discover common interests and desires so that you can carry on a conversation or form a relationship. Although at a more calculated level, communications research has similar objectives—the systematic collection and interpretation of information to increase understanding of the needs and desires of an audience. Research unearths the interests and backgrounds of the audience. This information is needed to develop effective conservation communications strategies and to later assess the impact of your activities.

Like your assessment of your blind date, audience research involves observation, questioning, and collection of background information. The techniques of audience research include surveys, interviews, meetings, direct observation, census reports, Internet sources, case studies, and networks with organizations that already serve the audience.

Audience Research Goals

Research begins by examining the current situation; the audience's background, interests and attitudes; and the program's resources and constraints. This information is used for strategic planning of conservation communications programs. When a program is complete, your audience research allows you to determine if the program has accomplished its objectives. As you evaluate the effects of your program, you then can decide what actions to take next.

Strategic research allows you to

- Define constituent audiences or stakeholders. Common interests, needs, and behaviors are revealed so that you can effectively communicate with your audience.
- Determine message strategies for target audiences. Factors to consider in selecting the communications media are revealed. These include accessibility of the audience, regions and populations reached, and appropriateness of the communication medium to both the public and the message.
- Establish benchmarks for implementing the communication plan. This will define who will be reached by your program, how many, at what rate, and with what effect.

Evaluative research allows you to

- Evaluate the effects of your activities. Research conducted before and after your program will reveal if your objectives have been achieved and if you had unanticipated or secondary impacts.

- Assess the need for additional programs. Research results will indicate if your program should be modified, expanded, continued, or cut.

A typical research agenda for a communications program includes defining target audiences based on your program goals. You then collect baseline data to identify your audience's needs, interests, and behaviors. Based on the results of your strategic research, you develop the communications program and evaluate its success. Examples in this chapter and chapter 3 demonstrate how strategic audience research is used to design an effective communications program. Evaluative research is discussed in chapter 7.

Defining Target Audiences

Knowledge of your audiences, also called stakeholders or publics, is vital in designing messages and selecting media to produce an effective program. All audiences are different. The "general public" does not exist. Rather communicators must identify different segments of the public they wish to communicate with, a process that advertisers call market segmentation. Advertisers divide the general public into small, homogenous segments based on relevant, distinguishing characteristics. Examples of market segments might be Asian American teenagers who watch television or retired women living in urban areas. Marketing theorists develop long lists of segmentation categories based on demographics, values and lifestyles, geographic regions, and consumer behaviors. Marketing programs can then be profitably targeted to specific audience segments—lipstick ads can be placed in women's magazines and ads for aftershave in magazines targeting men.

Conservation communicators also can be more effective by dividing their audiences into segments according to specific wants and needs, interests, habits, or other useful characteristics. To succeed, messages must be directed to your target public. Knowing the media habits of your audience is one obvious way to target a message. An article in the *Washington Post* may effectively reach policy makers' eyes, but few rural landowners may ever read it; an article in a farming newsletter would better target the latter audience

Analysis of audiences or stakeholder groups can be done in many ways. Marketing analysts use demographic studies to identify potential audiences. Knowledge of audience age, sex, occupation, residency, education, and income can help you predict consumption patterns, media habits, and values and attitudes toward the environment.

A typical conservation organization or agency needs to be able to communicate with many publics, each with its own self-interests, desires, and concerns. These include internal publics such as other employees or advisers (fig. 2.1).

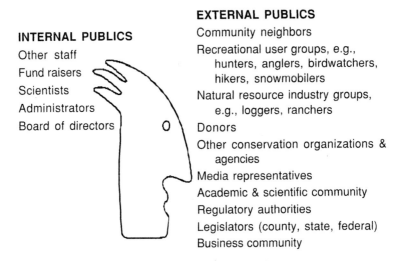

EXTERNAL PUBLICS
Community neighbors
Recreational user groups, e.g.,
  hunters, anglers, birdwatchers,
  hikers, snowmobilers
Natural resource industry groups,
  e.g., loggers, ranchers
Donors
Other conservation organizations &
  agencies
Media representatives
Academic & scientific community
Regulatory authorities
Legislators (county, state, federal)
Business community

INTERNAL PUBLICS
Other staff
Fund raisers
Scientists
Administrators
Board of directors

FIGURE 2.1. *Typical publics of an environmental organization or resource management agency.*

External publics, whether hunters or legislators, are a more diverse group whose support must be won and maintained. Proponents, opponents, and neutral members of target publics must all receive appropriate information, based on two-way communication.

By knowing your audience, you can infer what motivates members to support your conservation activities. Audience research shows that people join organizations or support causes for a variety of reasons. These include material, social, and political incentives. If the objective of a communication campaign is to increase membership or bolster support for a cause, knowledge of these incentives can be used to craft an effective strategy. Each incentive appeals to different motivations of your audience.

Material incentives provide products or services that have monetary value. For example, the World Wildlife Fund offers a panda-emblazoned backpack to new members along with their annual report with conservation news. The Audubon Society provides members with a glossy bimonthly magazine. In 1996, the Florida Wildlife Federation decided to test Audubon's motivational approach by offering a magazine incentive. The FWF sent out a trial magazine and survey to 230 randomly selected members from their 11,000-member list in order to see if this product would induce them to pay more money for membership or would attract new members. Analysis of the results made them drop the magazine publication. According to FWF president Manley Fuller, "The numbers did not add up. We figured to make the venture feasible, we would need to generate over $35,000 for the magazine to go to all the members. The members sampled were not willing to pay so much! Audience research is critical for small non-profit organizations like us because we always have to watch the bottom dollar."

Social incentives provide intangible social rewards, such as the congeniality or prestige associated with belonging to a group. The National Wildlife Federation woos wealthy donors with a plea to "Join a rare group of people in the Rara Avis Society, a group of 'rare birds' who are proactive and concerned enough about the environment to leave donations to NWF in their wills." The Wildlife Conservation Society offers their members tours to exotic destinations. Many local environmental groups or chapters offer monthly meetings, presentations, field trips, and other social events.

Political incentives provide satisfaction to people who have contributed to what they deem a worthwhile cause, even if members contribute nothing but their money or name. These incentives help reinforce an individual's self-identity. Some people join organizations to gain a sense of political efficacy through the belief that their contributions make a difference in providing for the collective good. For example, lobbying efforts on behalf of environmental legislation attract individuals to join the Natural Resources Defense Council. Studies of environmental groups, such as the Sierra Club, show that members join for political reasons. Many local groups go beyond social engagements and offer opportunities for members to get involved in lobbying for conservation initiatives or promoting clean-ups in nearby parks or rivers.

Identifying Audience Knowledge, Interests, and Attitudes

An understanding of your audience's baseline knowledge is a prerequisite for creating effective conservation messages. The controversy in the Pacific Northwest surrounding conservation of old growth forests and endangered Spotted Owls offers an eye-opening example. Some westerners framed the conservation debate as fueled by extremist groups that cared more about varmints than human needs. Audience research revealed that only 8 percent of the people understood why habitat loss was a cause of species extinction.[1] Some people believed that spotted owls were simply being stubborn by refusing to move from old growth forests to other places where they would cause less trouble.[2] Obviously, messages framed for an uninformed audience must address their present knowledge and beliefs.

Research also reveals audience attitudes toward your conservation concern. Many factors influence the formation of environmental attitudes. Researchers have shown that socioeconomic characteristics, such as high income or education levels, often correlate with certain attitudes toward the environment. Stephen Kellert, a sociologist at Yale University, developed a typology of environmental attitudes (box 2.1). He used this to determine socioeconomic factors in the United States that correlated with certain attitudes. He found neg-

Box 2.1. Kellert's typology of people's attitudes
toward nature

Utilitarian: Practical and material exploitation of nature

Naturalistic: Direct experience and exploration of nature

Ecologistic-Scientific: Systemic study of structure, function, and relationship in nature

Aesthetic: Physical appeal and beauty of nature

Symbolic: Use of nature for language and thought

Humanistic: Strong emotional attachment and "love" for aspects of nature

Moralistic: Spiritual reverence and ethical concern for nature

Dominionistic: Mastery, physical control, dominance of nature

Negativistic: Fear, aversion, alienation from nature

Source: Kellert, S. R. 1996. *The Value of Life: Biological Diversity and Human Society.* Island Press, Washington, D.C.

ative and utilitarian views of wildlife are most common, particularly among groups with the following characteristics: lower socioeconomic levels, elderly, rural, and engaged in natural resource–dependent occupations.[3]

Studies such as these are gems to conservation communicators. Understanding public attitudes can help you polish specific messages to attract your audience and achieve your program objectives. A good example is an effort to communicate with local hunters about the problems caused by feral hogs on a public reserve in Florida. Managers emphasized that hogs damaged regenerating forests and competed for food with other game animals (of particular concern for hunters!). The managers did not focus on their own concern about hog damage to endangered plant species. These managers understood their audience and used a utilitarian message rather than an ecologistic one to target their rural hunting public.[4]

Researchers have discovered that people's appreciation of wildlife is restricted to large, charismatic mammals.[5] Many conservation organizations have made use of this knowledge in designing their logos as seen in the World Wildlife Fund panda, the Wildlife Conservation Society antelope, the Defenders of Wildlife wolf, and the Marine Mammal Center seal.

The Xerces Society, an organization dedicated to invertebrate conservation, funded a study that revealed that few people care about invertebrate animals or understand their ecological value. People only like invertebrates with unusual aesthetic or practical value, such as butterflies and bees.[6] The Xerces Society wisely selected an attractive butterfly for their logo.

The research findings of social scientists emphasize that family backgrounds influence environmental attitudes. Parents pass on to their children experiences, organizational memberships, tastes, political affinities, and values. Psychologist Martin Fishbein developed the theory of reasoned action to explain some of these influences. It is based on the assumption that people will act in a manner according to how they believe people of influence (often family members) would behave in a particular situation.[7] In developing appropriate messages, communicators can use this information as well as data about their audience's attitudes toward current issues or policies. For example, state agencies wishing to promote hunting as a recreational activity could focus on current hunters and their younger relatives. Having an older family member who hunts is closely correlated with children who hunt.

Public concern for conservation issues waxes and wanes, making it necessary to analyze an audience in terms of their current interests in an issue or problem. Communicators must determine which interests motivate a particular group. People often cannot be segmented into just one interest group. At times, individuals may qualify as members of the public on both sides of an issue. In balancing pros and cons of an issue like snowmobile regulations, some people may be both skiers and snowmobilers and have specific, yet different, desires regarding snowmobile regulations in particular regions. Research on your target audiences will unearth such complexities and suggest the appropriate media and messages for addressing them.

Research also will reveal the breadth of your audience. For example, stakeholders supporting the establishment of a new wildlife preserve outside a rural town may include

- owners of businesses who will benefit from increased tourism to the area
- residents in the vicinity who believe habitat protection will increase their property values or who worry about increased noise, litter, or crime
- hunters who plan to hunt ducks in the area
- bird-watchers and other visitors who wish access for recreation
- regulatory agency staff responsible for managing the area
- elected officials who worry about a potential loss of tax revenues or whose political future may be influenced by this decision
- members of environmental organizations interested in land protection
- scientists interested in ecosystem health or research opportunities

These groups are important from a communications standpoint because their opinion will influence the eventual outcome of the decision to establish the reserve and its land management policies. Audience research provides you with data to make the transaction less objectionable to opponents and more savory for supporters. Preserve supporters could work to minimize specific concerns of stakeholder groups in a number of ways. If research findings indicate resident opposition is due to perceptions of potential criminal activity or increased trash associated with the establishment of the preserve, proponents could guarantee a security force for those worried about crime and a maintenance crew for picking up litter. They could present data from case studies from other regions regarding the positive effects of a wildlife preserve on property values and other benefits from conservation. They might advocate setting up a business bureau to ensure their community benefits from the tourism impact.

It is important for conservation communications programs to have clear goals. If the establishment of the reserve is the objective, then that is the measure of success: will the politicians implement it? If the long-term aim is conservation, then activities besides reserve establishment, such as ordinances or voluntary easements, also should be explored. Communications can help sell the various options to adversaries. One objective may be to create awareness among the majority of the county residents of the unique biodiversity in the area. Surveys of residents before and after the communications program could be used to develop targeted communications campaigns and to measure increased awareness. After completion of the communications program the agency can undertake evaluative research to decide if the objectives were achieved, if the program was worth the cost, and whether communication strategies should be modified for future campaigns.

A variety of data collection tools can be used to reveal the knowledge and attitudes of people toward your conservation agenda. These include interviews, surveys, workshops, focus groups, panel discussions, public meetings, and conferences. Unobtrusive measures such as observation of your audience, content analysis of documents, readability studies of your materials, naturalistic inquiry, and analysis of similar cases allow you to study the problem with minimal influence on the audience. These methods can be used not only to better understand the target audience but to test assumptions about techniques, media, materials, and messages for the audience. These methods are described in detail in the remainder of the chapter, but first an example from Guatemala demonstrates the use of several research methods for designing a communications program for a park audience.

Example: Strategic Research for Conservation Communications at Tikal National Park

Conservation communicators at Tikal National Park in Guatemala used several research methods to plan a communications program.[8] The audience targeted by a new park communications program included local visitors and populations in surrounding areas. No activities had addressed these potential audiences in the past; nor was any information concerning local ecology and resource management available to the park's visitors (numbering about fifteen thousand domestic visitors and seventy-five thousand foreign visitors annually in the 1990s). Tikal was an ideal site for public communications because of its abundant and easily seen wildlife, famous archaeological attractions, accessibility, and cultural diversity (fig. 2.2). Park managers were eager to better understand their local audience and to select appropriate communication approaches to use.

Park staff, in collaboration with several organizations,[9] selected research tools to use in identifying program constraints and resources and determining priority issues to communicate. The team conducted interviews, reviewed materials from similar programs elsewhere, held participatory workshops with audience members, and conducted surveys as part of their strategic research for the communications program. Each of these research techniques proved useful in planning the communications program.

Interviews

In-depth interviews with administrators at Guatemala's park and resource management agencies, meetings with ten conservation and development organizations active in northern Guatemala, and informal discussions with local school teachers and health practitioners provided background information on park management and interpretive needs. The interviews allowed replication of successful approaches developed by area organizations and avoided duplication of effort.

Document Review

The team gathered conservation education materials developed for a variety of audiences in other regions of Guatemala. Reviewing these documents helped the team to understand appropriate materials and content areas.

Workshops

To identify specific audience needs, the team designed a participatory community workshop to determine local interests and attitudes toward the natural and cultural resources of the area. Over 150 community residents attended the two days of discussions, interactions, and games, which were designed to reveal the knowledge and attitudes of the participating men, women, and children. These exercises were filmed in order for the park staff to review and discuss the community input after completion of the workshop.

Surveys

Another assessment activity involved conducting oral surveys of Guatemalan visitors to Tikal Park. These surveys identified visitors' needs and concerns

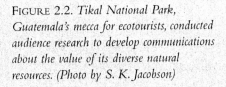

FIGURE 2.2. *Tikal National Park,
Guatemala's mecca for ecotourists, conducted
audience research to develop communications
about the value of its diverse natural
resources. (Photo by S. K. Jacobson)*

regarding local natural and cultural conservation. Over one hundred visitors were surveyed. The questionnaire determined current activities at the park as well as their information needs and interpretive media preferences. Sociodemographic questions about visitor backgrounds and education levels also helped guide the design of materials.

The audience assessments, together with park management objectives, formed the basis for the development of initial communications and interpretation activities. Park visitor questionnaires revealed that the majority of visitors preferred interpretive trails and children's guidebooks, while films were least in demand. Local visitors also reported a strong preference for information on Mayan cultural history and local natural history. The participatory workshop revealed a keen local interest in traditional and sustainable forest product use, and enthusiasm for youth opportunities to participate in an outdoor learning experience.

Based on the results of the audience research, three initial activities were developed targeting local visitors and residents. These included designing (with the help of local residents) a full-color brochure and poster for Tikal describing the natural and cultural history of the area; a park interpretive trail with signs highlighting medicinal plants, useful forest products, and general ecological principles; and a community eco-camp program—a four-day educational experience for local youths that included lectures, songs, games, and guided trail walks that explored the park's rich natural and cultural history.

Strategic audience research requires a number of qualitative and quantitative methods for collecting data. At Tikal Park, in-depth interviews were employed to gather information from specific experts and relevant groups, while surveys conducted by natural resource staff collected broad-based input from visitors. Participatory workshops provided a forum for input from a variety of individuals and local stakeholders. The various research tools available for gathering data are described in more detail in the rest of this chapter.

Research Methods

To ensure that research findings are valid and to increase confidence in the results, strategic research often combines a number of data collection techniques to capitalize on the strengths of each approach and to minimize the weaknesses inherent in single strategies. In addition to multiple methods, strategic research can combine multiple data sources, perspectives, and investigators to cross check data for accuracy. The ability to incorporate relevant information into the development of a communications program enhances decision making about program design.

Available research techniques offer distinct advantages and disadvantages when used to guide communications programs for conservation. Qualitative approaches, such as group interviews and workshops, use small, information-rich samples selected purposefully to allow an in-depth focus on issues important to communicators.[10] Quantitative approaches, such as a survey of a randomly selected sample of a population, can allow generalization of the results to the whole population. Knowledge of the range of qualitative and quantitative tools available for gathering data results in more efficient and effective development of conservation communications.

For guiding communications programs, all research methods require that their measurement techniques are reliable, valid, and useful.

A reliable measurement instrument consistently conveys the same meaning and will dependably reap the same results if it is measured again. This means, for example, that a test of audience comprehension of a brochure on prescribed fire will get similar scores if the sample is retested.

A valid instrument accurately measures the information that it is supposed to measure. For example, a survey that asks people about their attitudes toward wolves should not actually be measuring their attitudes toward the resource agency implementing the wolf project.

A useful instrument is affordable and easy to administer, score, and interpret. For example, data collected using an observational checklist will only work if trained data collectors are available to conduct the study.

When used carefully, a variety of research methods, from surveys to observation have proven reliable, valid, and useful in communications research. Comparisons among various data collection methods have found that, if data are collected systematically, results are often similar. For example, researchers in northern New York compared three methods of gathering input from the public on the subject of deer management:[11]

- unsolicited input in the form of written correspondence, telephone calls, office visits, commentary during public meetings, public hearings, and stakeholder group meetings;
- a systematic questionnaire that contacted stakeholders by mail or phone and surveyed their attitudes and opinions; and
- a citizen task force formed with a group of representative stakeholders that attended monthly meetings to reach a consensus on deer management objectives.

At the end of the study period, all three methods resulted in similar recommendations. However, the survey and task force techniques involved more stakeholders in the decision-making process. The researchers noted that these may have proved more successful than the unsolicited input if the decision to be made had been more controversial.

Audience research techniques cover a variety of approaches to suit a program's needs, budget, and time. The following techniques are described below:

- Surveys
- Group interviews and meetings
- Observational techniques
- Document reviews and content analysis
- Case studies
- Visual techniques
- Participatory rural appraisal
- Naturalistic inquiry

Surveys

A survey is a systematic way of collecting information, from a sample of people, that is used to make generalizations about a target population. Survey research is commonly used to measure public attitudes and knowledge, and to identify who a target audience is, where they live, and what their concerns are.

Understanding audience opinions and attitudes toward conservation issues skyrockets your chances of successfully reaching your audience with appropriate programs. Surveys are useful both for collecting information on broad societal issues, like spending money on endangered species conservation, and for detailed site or program-specific problems, like the design of interpretive brochures for visitors to a park. Surveys also have limitations. They require time and expertise to develop. Their results can be subject to misinterpretation depending on how questions and response categories are designed. The data are limited in scope, often omitting underlying reasons or specific behaviors that are of real interest to communicators. Despite these constraints, a well-designed survey can be a great tool for gathering information about conservation knowledge and attitudes from a broad range of individuals.

Many books have been written on developing and conducting surveys. The following suggestions for questionnaire design are culled from a variety of sources.[12] These seven steps will help you climb the ladder to successful program results.

1. DEFINE YOUR SURVEY OBJECTIVES. Before you begin, it is important to define the specific objectives of your survey. Survey results can describe:

- the social and political make-up of your target audience;
- where audience members get their information;
- audience opinion about current issues, such as new ecosystem management strategies;
- how the audience prioritizes conservation problems;
- compromises people may be willing to make on environmental or economic issues;
- what your audience knows, for example, which specific aspects of ecosystem management are not understood by park neighbors; and
- how your audience will react to a new policy or communications campaign message.

Survey research gathers these different types of information to help explain the basis of your audience's opinions and attitudes, and to provide insight into which communication approaches and conservation messages should be successful. Careful determination of the objectives of your survey will shape it to get the information you need.

2. SELECT A SAMPLE FROM THE TARGET POPULATION. Most surveys follow a sampling procedure to gather representative information from the target population. The target population is all the people in your particular audience. The population may be residents of a specific town or state, hunters or bird-watchers, or people in a specific age group. Asking questions of the entire population (a census) usually is not feasible, so data are collected from a much smaller number of people. An appropriate sample size must be selected from the population so that you can reliably generalize your results to your entire target audience. Sampling procedures depend on the population of interest and your available resources.

Usually the ideal method of sampling is random sampling, also known as probability sampling. Random sampling allows you to make generalizations about the whole population. In a random sample, all members of the population have an equal chance of being selected. Election polls use random samples. To assess the popularity of TV shows, the Nielsen ratings survey a sample of four thousand homes across the United States to represent all television viewers.

In nonprobability sampling, the probability of selecting any one individual is unknown, and you are more likely to unintentionally bias your results. Nonprobability sampling includes data collected through volunteer phone-ins, or by leaving a stack of surveys near a meeting-room door. Interviewing only people who are interested in an issue or who are easily accessible is also nonprobability sampling. These types of data may be useful for certain purposes, but the results cannot be generalized to a larger population as random sampling allows.

To conduct a simple random sample you must have a list of all members of the population. Then you select members at random, which often means assigning each person a number and then picking numbers randomly out of a hat or random number table. Systematic random sampling uses a random starting point and selects every nth person on a list. Although it is less reliable than true random sampling, it is often cheaper and easier when using a long list, such as a phone book, as a sampling source. A stratified random sample is used to survey different strata of the population. For example, if an agency wants to know if people's ages are correlated with different views toward logging or controlled burning, they can purposefully sample young, middle-aged, and elderly populations for comparison.

A sample provides an accurate representation of the opinions of your target population without having to contact every member of that group. Your sample responses will give you the opinions of the larger group within a certain degree of confidence and a certain rate of error. After conducting a survey on wolf conservation using a random sample of the target population (say, landowners in Montana), you may conclude with 95 percent certainty that 60 percent (plus or minus 4 percent error) of the population supports your wolf reintroduction program.

The sample size is based on the laws of probability. The size of the population is one factor that influences the size of the sample needed. Pollsters recommend samples of four hundred to five hundred for most major mail or phone polls, and a sample of two hundred for small target populations.[13]

3. DEVELOP THE SURVEY. Stick to the goals of your study. After listing potential survey questions, weed out irrelevant ones. The shorter the survey, the more likely respondents will be to complete it. The questions and the design

of your survey can affect audience responses. The following tips will help you get useful information:

- Make a list of all the topics you need to cover, then organize them logically. Generally, opinion questions go first, then knowledge questions, followed by sociodemographic questions. The sequence of your questions can bias results; sensitive questions should always go last. Commonly, surveys move from more general questions to more specific ones.

- Make each question concise and clear. Bad questions may be poorly worded, too broad, ambiguous, assume too much of the respondent, use unfamiliar vocabulary, or use words that might bias respondents. An example of a poorly worded item from a survey of recreational visitors to the forests at Eglin Air Force Base is: "I am satisfied with the information and services from Eglin's Natural Resources Division." Respondents in a pilot test were asked to agree or disagree with the statement. The pilot test revealed, however, that respondents were not sure what they were agreeing to. The wording was bad because it included two topics—a double-barreled statement. For the final survey, this item was divided into two. One question asked about personal services and the second about publications. This clarified in each case that the satisfaction referred to one specific product provided by the Natural Resources Division.

- Pilot test the questionnaire using open-ended questions with your target population before constructing close-ended responses. For example, "What types of outdoor recreational activities did you do in the past year at Eglin?" was presented as an open-ended question in a pretest of the Eglin survey; the respondents could write in any response they wanted. In the final survey, this was transformed into a close-ended question where the respondents were constrained to choose from a list of seventeen activities that had been most often cited in the pilot survey. Open-ended questions in telephone and personal interviews allow you to probe more deeply. You can ask, "What do you mean?," "Could you be more specific?" or, "Anything else?"

- Pilot test the revised survey with enough members of the target population (usually ten to twenty) to eliminate any vague, biased, objectionable, ambiguous, or confusing questions. Give the survey to respondents exactly in the manner you plan to administer it in the future. You can check their responses and additionally ask them if all the questions and directions were clear.

- Test your method for coding and entering data with the pilot responses. Modify your coding method if necessary.

- Provide a brief but persuasive introduction to entice people to complete the survey. Stress why the study is useful, why their participation is important, and that their answers are confidential. Appeal to their interests. The Eglin mail survey was prefaced with the following: "Thank you for taking time to answer this survey. . . . Your response will help us to improve recreational activities for you. . . . "

- Revise and retest again if problems occur. Researcher Kellert, in his survey of public attitudes toward wildlife, tested over 1,500 questions and conducted five to seven pilot tests for each of his four questionnaire sections.[14]

4. CONDUCT THE SURVEY. Examples of mail, telephone, and personal surveys are described in the next section.

5. ENCOURAGE A HIGH RESPONSE RATE. If you follow effective techniques, response rates can be as high as 60 to 70 percent for mail surveys. Response rates are generally higher in telephone and personal interviews. The bias caused by nonresponses is often the greatest source of error in surveys. For example, hunters who hunt unsuccessfully might be less likely to complete a hunter survey. Thus the sample would overrepresent successful and satisfied hunters. A number of techniques can help improve response rates. These include: showing written or verbal appreciation; offering tangible awards, such as posters, postcards, or cash; making the questionnaire interesting; making the work appear brief; offering copies of results; minimizing mental effort needed; eliminating embarrassing questions; and providing up to three call-backs for telephone surveys and two to three reminder postcards and/or follow-up letters for written surveys. You also should contact a small sample of individuals who did not respond to your survey. Questioning them will help you understand some of the nonresponse bias that was introduced.

6. ANALYZE THE DATA. Survey results often are summarized using descriptive statistics, such as percentages and averages. For example, survey data revealed that only 56 percent of recreational users and 38 percent of neighboring citizens knew that fire benefited native plants on Eglin Air Force Base. Computer spreadsheet programs easily calculate means and ranges from survey data. Specialized statistical software can do more complex analyses to allow you to draw conclusions about what the population as a whole thinks, to compare the knowledge or attitudes of various subgroups, or to determine how strongly variables are related to each other. For example, the difference in knowledge levels about fire and native plants was statistically significant between recreational users and neighboring citizens at Eglin. If the task seems daunting, survey data entry and analyses services can be hired through a market research firm, accounting office, or university research service.

7. USE THE DATA. Information about respondents' knowledge, attitudes, activities, behaviors, and media preferences should directly help you select and

FIGURE 2.3. *Survey research provided data to guide the creation of signs about ecosystem management on Eglin's golf course. (Photo by S.K. Jacobson)*

design appropriate messages and media channels. The survey of recreational visitors to Eglin revealed that hunters and anglers held more negative views about the conservation of endangered species than did hikers and picnickers. Their lack of support stemmed from a perception that the endangered species conservation programs compete with, detract from, or interfere with hunting and fishing programs. A targeted fact sheet was prepared to address their concerns. A study of the outdoor activities of Eglin military leaders revealed that 51 percent played golf for outdoor recreation. This information was used to develop conservation communications for this audience. Interpretive signs about ecosystem management were nailed to water coolers on the base's golf courses where the audience recreated (fig. 2.3).

Mail Surveys
Conducting surveys by mail permits wide geographic coverage and large sample sizes. Mail surveys are advantageous because their confidentiality helps promote honest replies. This method also eliminates interviewer bias, a problem encountered when conducting face-to-face interviews. Mail surveys are relatively inexpensive and convenient compared to phone surveys or personal interviews. They require fewer staff and less organization. They also allow more complex questions to be asked than with phone surveys because the respondents read the questions at their own speed.

The main disadvantages of mail surveys include the inability to clarify or ask follow-up questions. As for all survey methods, the questions must be clear and pretested with the audience before conducting the survey. Mail surveys also suffer from a large number of nonresponses—refusals to complete a survey. The response to mail surveys is only about 30 percent if no reminder mailings are sent. High levels of nonresponse introduce bias: what are the opinions of the 70 percent of the sample that did not fill out a survey? However, with follow-up and reminder letters, response rates of over 60 percent can be expected.[15] A further disadvantage of mail surveys is that you have no control over who actually fills out the survey—man, woman, teenager, or retiree—and this could bias your data.

A recent addition to mail survey techniques is the use of electronic questionnaires. This mode offers great simplicity in disseminating questionnaires and analyzing results. E-mail is a convenient way to reach a large number of people without much effort or cost. Questions can be precoded so that responses easily transfer to a spreadsheet or database for immediate analysis. E-mail surveys have the same disadvantages as traditional mail questionnaires, with the added constraint that your target audience must all have access to electronic mail.

Example: Mail Survey of Public Opinion Conducted by the Natural Resource Branch of Eglin Air Force Base

Located in the Florida Panhandle, the half-million-acre Eglin Air Force Base encompasses the Southeast's largest remaining longleaf pine forest. The objective of the first phase of the communications program was to identify and better understand the recreational users and neighboring citizens of Eglin. The new ecosystem management plan included various human uses of the forest, but departed from traditional management on the base in that it focused on entire systems, rather than a particular species. The public needed to have input and to be educated about the adoption of this new and different management approach. Natural resource managers at Eglin wanted to establish a common understanding about ecosystem management among constituents with different knowledge levels, attitudes, and values, and to build support among their diverse publics.

Data collected through survey research were integrated with ecological information to enhance management efforts at the base. Researchers designed a survey to assess knowledge and attitudes of recreationists and neighboring citizens.[16] The size and geographic range of the populations being studied were large, so a self-administered mail survey was used for data collection. To maximize the response rate, two copies of the survey and a reminder postcard were mailed to the sample over a six-week period. Once an individual responded, no further mailings were sent. The response rate was over 60 percent and high enough to generalize to the target populations. The results of the surveys were used to develop effective methods of communication about the principles of ecosystem management for these audiences.

The survey was composed of twenty-five opinion and attitude questions, fourteen awareness and knowledge questions, and twenty-seven sociodemographic questions. Examples of these three general categories of survey questions are given below.

Opinion and attitude questions measure the beliefs and feelings of the subjects. Respondents were given an incremental scale (called a Likert scale after the researcher who invented it) to record their opinion. Respondents were asked to check one response for each statement such as:

- How would you rate the health of Eglin's forests this year as compared to past years?

___much better ___better ___no change ___worse ___much worse

- Recreation should be allowed on Eglin regardless of negative impacts to wildlife.

___strongly agree ___agree ___no opinion ___disagree ___strongly disagree

Awareness and knowledge questions measure the respondents' awareness or understanding of specific issues.

- Ecosystem management focuses on conserving more native plants and animals than previous management programs.

___true ___false ___don't know

- The most widespread tree on Eglin is the

___red oak ___longleaf pine ___shagbark hickory ___loblolly pine ___don't know

Activity and sociodemographic questions ask people what activities they participate in and what their backgrounds are. To determine what types of media may reach a potential audience, you must ask questions concerning media use and news sources.

- What is your main source of environmental news?

___television ___radio ___newspaper ___friends ___family ___co-workers

Open-ended questions, in which respondents can list any response, also are useful.

- What types of outdoor recreational activities did you do in the past year at Eglin?

Demographic questions ask about sex, race, education, occupation, and characteristics such as place of residence and income level.

- What year were you born? ___
- What formal schooling have you completed?

___some high school ___high school diploma ___some college or vocational school

___college degree ___graduate or professional degree

The responses to questions such as these provided useful data for Eglin managers to understand their audience's communication needs. Note that some background questions, such as queries into income levels or age, may be sensitive issues for some respondents and should be placed near the end of the survey with a reminder that all answers are confidential.

Telephone Surveys

The design and implementation of telephone surveys is similar to mail surveys, but with some added benefits. Telephone surveys offer the ability to earmark a specific sampling unit or member of a household, such as man versus woman or employed versus retired. Although complex questions are difficult to ask, open-ended ones are effective and follow-up questions are easy to incorporate. A primary advantage of telephone interviews is the speed with which they can be conducted. Public opinion polls that appear daily in places like the front page of USA Today quickly survey 1,500 citizens by telephone. Phone interviewers do not influence respondents as much as personal interviewers. Respondents cannot see the interviewer's reaction over the phone, nor make judgments about what the interviewer might want to hear based on visual cues.

Telephone surveys also have disadvantages. Sampling from telephone directories introduces biases as it discriminates against people with unlisted numbers, outdated listings, nonworking numbers, and, of course, the 5 percent of the United States public who do not own phones. The complexity of the questions that can be asked is limited because respondents cannot grasp or remember a lengthy inquiry.

Example: Telephone Survey of Public Knowledge and Opinion About the Reintroduction of the Florida Panther

The reintroduction of the endangered Florida panther depends not only on biological research to ensure the survival of the remaining fifty or so panthers, but also acceptance of reintroduced panthers by local landowners. To study the feasibility of reintroducing Florida panthers into north Florida, state and federal wildlife agencies introduced twenty-six cougars, as surrogate panthers, to see if they could find adequate food and shelter. A small, but vocal, group of landowners in the region opposed the panther reintroduction and generated tremendous media coverage.

A University of Florida survey helped elucidate the real feelings of north Florida residents.[17] A random telephone survey of three hundred area residents revealed that the majority of the public supported panthers and their reintroduction into the area. When asked, "Do you support or oppose reintroducing panthers into the Osceola National Forest region of north Florida?" 75 percent of respondents said that they moderately or strongly supported the program. The results of this and other questions about panthers and their habitat revealed a high level of support in the region for panthers and other wildlife. This information helped put the minority opposition to the panthers into perspective and will be used in further assessing the efforts of the reintroduction program. Some of the questions from the survey are presented below with the interviewer's scripted responses and prompts included.[18]

"Hello, my name is Patti Cramer, and I'm working in conjunction with the University of Florida. Am I speaking with an adult of the home?

"We are conducting a survey on people's opinions and knowledge of wildlife conservation. We are not selling anything. This is more of an opportunity for you to have input into how the state manages your natural resources. This survey is part of an educational program that is sponsored by the University of Florida, a private company, and the Florida Advisory Council on Environmental Education.

"In order to be most accurate, I need to speak with the adult living in your household who had the most recent birthday. It's necessary for me to speak with that person in order to make an accurate survey." [Note: This helps randomize the respondent within each household, rather than biasing the interviews toward homemakers or retired individuals who may be more likely to answer the phone. If the correct person is not home, a time to return the call is arranged.]

If the correct person answers, "Would you be willing to spend about ten minutes with me to talk about wildlife-related issues in your area?"

If yes, "Thank you for your time. You do not have to answer any question you do not want to answer. There will be no association with your responses and your name. And there is no compensation for participation in this survey." [Note: If the respondent is reluctant, the interviewer offers to call back at a more convenient time and asks who to call and at what time.]

[After three general questions about wildlife in the area]:

4. Are you aware that panthers exist in Florida?

___ 1. Yes
___ 2. No—[Interviewer response: "Well actually there are wild panthers living in Florida."]

5. What general region of the state do you think panthers live in? [check all that apply]

___ 1. None
___ 2. Statewide
___ 3. North Florida
___ 4. Central Florida
___ 5. South Florida

6. Overall, do you support or oppose efforts to save the Florida panther from extinction? [prompt for degree]
___ 1. Strongly support
___ 2. Moderately support
___ 3. Neither support nor oppose
___ 4. Moderately oppose
___ 5. Strongly oppose
___ 6. Don't know

7. Were you aware that state and federal government agencies are considering a program to reintroduce Florida panthers into the Osceola National

Forest/Lake City region of north Florida to help reestablish panther populations?

___ 1. Yes

___ 2. No

8. Do you support or oppose reintroducing panthers into the Osceola National Forest region of north Florida? [prompt for degree]
___ 1. Strongly support [go to question 9]
___ 2. Moderately support [go to question 9]
___ 3. Neither support or oppose [go to question 11]
___ 4. Moderately oppose [go to question 10]
___ 5. Strongly oppose [go to question 10]
___ 6. Don't know [go to question 11]

9. What is your main reason for supporting panther reintroduction?

[write response on sheet]_____

10. What is your main reason for opposing panther reintroduction?

[write response on sheet]_____

[Questions 11 to 13 continue to probe opposition to panther reintroduction.]

14. How would you agree or disagree with the following statement: "I favor the reintroduction of panthers in my county or surrounding counties." Would you:

___ 1. Strongly agree
___ 2. Moderately agree
___ 3. Neither agree nor disagree
___ 4. Moderately disagree
___ 5. Strongly disagree
___ 6. Don't know

15. I'm going to read you a question, and I want you to tell me if it's true or false. "Protecting panthers can serve to preserve natural habitat."

___ 1. True
___ 2. False
___ 3. Don't know

16. One of the ways proposed to protect wildlife habitat is to offer farmers and other landowners incentives or benefits or rewards to manage and protect their lands for wildlife. How helpful do you think the following incentives will be in encouraging landowners to manage their land for wildlife? [Response selection: 1 = Definitely, 2 = Probably, 3 = Maybe, 4 = Probably not, 5 = Definitely not, 6 = Don't know.]

Incentives:
A. Tax breaks
B. Public recognition for landowners
C. Greater cooperation from regulatory agencies

After some additional questions about land ownership and habitat protection, the interviewer says: "Great, we're just about through. The final few questions are for background information and are used to help analyze the results. We will be talking with three hundred people in this survey, and all information you give me can in no way be directly connected to you."

This is followed by sociodemographic questions regarding residence, education, race, occupation, income, and age. The interviewer records the sex of the respondent and closes with: "That is the end of the questionnaire, thank you very much for your time and cooperation."

Personal Surveys

Personal (face-to-face) surveys provide immediate data regarding attitudes toward an environmental issue or a communication strategy. Surveys conducted as personal interviews can be structured, strictly following a preset interview format, or unstructured, loosely following a discussion guide and allowing the respondent to digress from the questions. Personal surveys allow the interviewer to ask for clarification and to probe into reasons behind answers given. The interviewer also can look for visual as well as verbal responses. Thus personal surveys can provide more in-depth information than written or telephone surveys. Longer questionnaires, of over an hour, can be administered using more complex questions, including open-ended questions. Interviewers can probe deeply into issues to glean a full understanding of the attitudes and concerns of the audience.

Another advantage to personal surveys is that people are more likely to agree to participate. It is easy to throw away a mail survey or hang up on a telephone call. It is harder to evade a person standing in front of you. Additionally, the personal approach allows the researcher to ask people why they decline to participate. This helps identify any bias resulting from nonrespondents. Personal surveys also increase the likelihood that all questions will be answered.

The disadvantages of personal surveys include problems with biased answers due to unknown influences of the interviewer. Respondents may give answers they think the interviewer wants to hear or may react to the interviewer's facial expression or body language. Interviewers, themselves, could distort the answers when recording them. Logistical requirements for personal surveys are often more arduous than mail or telephone surveys, requiring more resources, people, and training to conduct interviews, especially for surveys with large sample sizes.

Example: Personal Surveys with Residents of Machililla National Park

In preparation for developing a public communication program for Machalilla National Park in Ecuador, researcher Elba Fiallo interviewed residents in five communities surrounding the park.[19] The interviews measured residents'

- attitudes toward the national park's and their perception of its benefits
- knowledge about conservation issues and the park goals
- changes in natural resource use after the establishment of the park
- relations with park employees

Representative questions Fiallo asked respondents about their relations with the park staff included:

1. How often do you receive a visit from park staff? [If receives visit, go to question 2; if not, skip to 3]
2. For what reasons do park staff visit you?
3. Do the park staff do any helpful or good activities for you? [If yes, go to question 4; if not, skip to 5]
4. What kind of activities?
5. Do the staff engage in any activities that negatively impact you? [If yes, go to question 6; if not, skip to 7]
6. What kind of activities?
7. What work do the park staff do?
8. Do you think the park staff are necessary?
9. Would you consider the park staff your friends?

The interviewer asked sixty-three questions of each respondent. In addition to asking about relations with park staff, respondents were asked about the impacts of the park on their personal lives and the natural resource base, their perceptions of the park and conservation, and sociodemographic questions about duration of residency, size of household, income, and education levels.

Fiallo interviewed ninety people over a three-month period. The most surprising result for the park managers was that poor relations between park employees and community residents were the main reason for distrust and distaste for the park. Sixty-two percent of the residents interviewed reported poor relations with park staff. The interviews provided data that identified specific management problems and local perceptions about conservation. Responses to the interviews provided a beacon to guide park plans for a public outreach program. The survey also collected baseline information to compare with people's attitudes after a public outreach program was implemented.

Group Interviews and Meetings

Resource managers and conservation communicators can learn about their target audiences by holding group meetings. Focus groups, public meetings, advisory committees, meetings with stakeholder groups, and community forums can provide information for designing new programs and fostering audience support. Group meetings, of course, are not solely for data collection purposes. They are increasingly used by resource agencies to inform and build approval for decisions, as well as involve the public in the planning process. Many public agencies initiate communication strategies to encourage public involvement throughout program development. A number of techniques enable the public to participate in decision-making processes for conservation and provide communicators with valuable data for designing programs.

In general, conducting a meeting with members of the public requires you to:

1. establish the objectives of the forum or meeting;
2. develop an agenda, specific interview schedule, or group process guidelines;
3. select a group (some groups may already exist, such as hunt clubs or bird-watching groups, others will need to be attracted);
4. provide incentives for participation;
5. make arrangements for gathering;
6. record data from meeting, often with audio- or video-tape;
7. transcribe and analyze the data; and
8. use the results.

Like any research method, careful planning and appropriate logistical support make group approaches most effective. The application of these general principles to several different formats for group meetings is discussed below.

Focus Groups

Focus groups are a useful data collection tool with which to explore general attitudes, motivations, and behaviors of your audience. Focus groups are used during the design and development stages of a program to receive feedback from a specific target population about ideas and communication approaches. Communicators use focus groups to

- obtain background information about people's perceptions of a specific topic;
- generate ideas or effective approaches for introducing a new service, product, program, or organization; and
- stimulate new research hypotheses or interpret previous results from quantitative research.

A focus group consists of an interview with a homogeneous group of seven to twelve individuals who share some key characteristics, such as age, race, occupation, or interests. They are interviewed in great detail about a single topic, and usually receive a small payment for their participation.

A moderator facilitates the focus group meeting using an interview guide. A good moderator leads the group through a discussion without influencing the spontaneity, honesty, and content of the responses. Respondents interact with each other as well as with the interviewer, potentially stimulating new ideas or insights. The session is videotaped for review and analysis. Marketing research firms additionally conduct focus group interviews behind one-way mirrors to observe group responses and dynamics unobtrusively. Focus groups allow you to probe deeply into people's perceptions concerning the conservation topic of interest. Participants' responses and interactions provide data for making decisions about your activities and approaches. Focus groups are relatively inexpensive and produce results quickly.

Focus groups also have limitations. Their data are sometimes difficult to analyze, group discussion may be difficult to control, and the interviewer needs careful training. Also keep in mind that results from focus groups cannot be extrapolated to the entire population.

Example: Focus Group Exploring Children's Attitudes Toward Hunting

The International Association of Fish and Wildlife Agencies (IAFWA) used focus groups to assess attitudes of children toward hunting. The results were used to help guide the development of their "Hunting As a Choice" educational campaign. Supported by the U.S. Fish and Wildlife Service, this program hoped to encourage children's interest in hunting. The agencies were concerned because numbers of hunters are declining and hunters' license fees provide funding for many wildlife management programs of state agencies. Jodi DiCamillo, project coordinator, explains that her agency used focus groups "as an exploratory technique to find out more information about our broad and somewhat unfocused topic of kids' perceptions of and interest in hunting. The focus groups helped us to identify relevant factors about kids and hunting and led us in the right direction for designing materials to reach this audience."

Her team conducted five focus group interviews in cities across the United States. They hired a market research firm in each city to recruit focus group participants, provide a suitable room, pay cash incentives ($30–$50, depending on the city), and serve refreshments to participants and observers. The objectives of the focus groups were to discover what messages would work with children to promote an awareness of hunting, stimulate interest in a hunter education course, and identify types of media effective with this age group. The interview guide for the focus groups included seven specific areas that the agency wished to learn about:[20]

1. *Introduction of participants:*
   Name
   Age and grade
   Sports and activities in which they are involved

2. *Attitudes toward outdoor activities:*
   Fishing
   Watching wildlife
   Hunting

3. *Attitudes toward hunting:*
   What do you think about hunting?
   Do you hunt or know someone else who does?
   Why do people hunt?
   Why do or don't you hunt?
   Is it cool to go hunting?
   What do you and your friends think about hunting and other kids who hunt?
   What do your parents think of hunting? If you wanted to go hunting, would your parents allow you?
   Who would be allowed to take you?
   Would you like to try hunting if someone showed you how? With whom would you like to go?
   What do you think it would be like? What do you think people do when they hunt?
   Who would want to show you how to hunt?

4. *Message testing to promote a tolerance and understanding of hunting:*
   Next, I'm going to read to you some reasons why some people think it's okay to hunt. Let's talk about what you think about each of these.

   - Message 1: People used to hunt a long time ago when they were still living in caves. People who hunt are just doing what their ancestors did.

   - Message 2: In the old days, you had to hunt to get meat. You couldn't buy it in a grocery store.

   - Message 3: Some people who hunt can't afford to buy meat; they need to hunt to feed their families.

   - Message 4: Lots of animals eat other animals. Mountain lions eat deer and wolves eat caribou. When humans hunt, they are like these animals and are only acting as part of the food chain.

   - Message 5: Make an educated decision! Check out hunter education. If you had to develop a commercial to get kids interested in hunting, what would you say in it?

5. *Promoting an interest in hunting and hunter education:*
   Why do some people hunt?

   - Some kids like to hunt because they can hang out with their dads and moms and other family members.

   - Some kids like to hunt because they like to camp in the woods with their family.

   - Some kids like to hunt because it's challenge—sneaking up on an animal without letting the animal know they are there.

   If you were interested in hunting, should you have to take a
   hunter education course?
   How would you find out more about the course? Do they have them
   near here?
   What would your parents think if you asked them if you could attend
   a hunter education course?
   Would they let you? Would they help you?
   Do you think taking a hunter education course would be fun? What
   could they do to get you to take a course and make it fun?

6. *Sources of information:*
   Have you ever seen or heard anything about hunting? Where?
   Does anyone famous hunt? What do you think of these people?

Have you ever talked about hunting in the classroom? What did you hear and learn?

Do you have any classes at school on the environment?

7. *Review of pilot materials:*

The facilitator shows the children messages in some pilot brochures and a video script called "Let's Look at Hunting." Participants discuss what they like and do not like about the materials.

Through the interactive group process, the results of the focused discussions revealed the attitudes of the children toward hunting, as well as their sources of information about hunting. The focus groups also served as a forum for testing agency messages designed to encourage positive attitudes toward hunting and hunter education. One result from the focus groups revealed the children's negative impressions of an animal mascot that a state agency had used for years. The children found the squirrel character to be "dumb and boring," according to DiCamillo. The findings helped IAFWA tailor their "Hunting As a Choice" project to effectively reach their target audience of 10–12-year-olds. Based on the focus group results, the communication medium selected was a computer game and World Wide Web page that children could view easily on school or home computers.

Public Meetings

A number of group techniques allow agencies and organizations to collect information about their audiences and to involve the public in making decisions about conservation initiatives. It is important to distinguish between involving the public in making a decision, collecting baseline information for making future decisions, and simply informing the public of a decision already made. The first two techniques include two-way communication methods such as public hearings, meetings for community residents or specific stakeholders, informal contacts with agency officials, workshops, and citizen's advisory committees. One study on public participation in deer management decisions found that group methods like citizen advisory councils resulted in outcomes similar to those of agency decision makers, but with the added advantage of a more knowledgeable and supportive public.[21]

Research also suggests that input from a variety of people, including management, staff, and external stakeholders, produces higher-quality decisions. Collective decisions generally better address the needs of the audience, are more accurate, and are more creative than decisions made by an individual or single viewpoint.[22] Public meetings and workshops can facilitate citizen input, promote a two-way dialogue, and disseminate ideas about issues and programs.

Not all group meetings are useful for audience research. Officials must be committed to determining public needs and responding to these needs if the interaction is to truly incorporate participants' opinions in the decision-making process.

The typical structure of a workshop divides participants into small groups to address specific issues or concerns. The format consists of an orientation phase where agency staff describe the purpose and procedures of the workshop and provide background information needed to meet the workshop goal. This is followed by a group activity or working period where participants perform an assignment that results in a specific product. Generally a group discussion follows that allows participants to discuss, evaluate, and prioritize recommendations.

The advantages of group techniques are the sharing and stimulation of ideas, facilitation of consensus among different stakeholders, open access for the public, and low cost. The disadvantages include the time demands, the need for a skilled facilitator for most methods, the potential for just a few people to hog the discussion, and the risk of unresolved conflict among participants. Other disadvantages of group meetings are that participants are chosen or self-selected and may not represent the larger community. Consequently, researchers cannot draw broad conclusions from the individual participants and workshop results.

Several data collection strategies involve small groups or expert panels in processes to identify problems, opportunities, priorities, and methods for reaching broader audiences. Popular techniques include simple brainstorming groups, Nominal Group Technique, the Delphi Technique, and a combination of the latter two techniques known as the Improved Nominal Group Technique. These four types of group processes are discussed below. The steps for planning a group meeting are similar for all the techniques (box 2.2).

Brainstorming

Brainstorming generates ideas through individual input and group interaction. A brainstorming session involves developing a problem statement, such as, What are the most important problems we face with visitors to our park that our communications program must address in the next three years? Initially, no criticisms are made of the ideas generated and participants are encouraged to dream up creative solutions regardless of constraints, and to combine or improve ideas that are listed. A recorder writes ideas on a board or flip chart until all the participants' imaginations are exhausted. Next, the group assesses the ideas, assigning them priority or value.

The advantages of brainstorming include social interaction that often produces cohesiveness within the group, development of a group consensus, and an emphasis on completing the task. Brainstorming requires little time or expense, but gives you a broad view of a specific conservation problem. Disadvantages of this technique include the need for an experienced facilitator to

Box 2.2. Planning checklist for holding a group meeting

1. Discuss meeting with administrators, collaborators, sponsors, and target audiences

2. Identify meeting goals

3. Select type of meeting

4. Determine budget, funding sources, and sponsorships

5. Identify potential participants and their needs

6. Choose time and duration

7. Select meeting place
   Central location?
   Public transportation access?
   Suitable parking?
   Safe area?
   Adequate facilities?
   Rental fee?

8. Review meeting space needs
   Total number of people expected?
   Seating arrangements for general and discussion sessions?

9. Select meeting leader

10. Select facilitators, speakers, or additional guest presenters
    Instructions provided to them for meeting times, duties, and
       compensation?

11. Develop the agenda
    Questions or discussion guide?
    Complete schedule planned?

12. Develop background information materials
    Information to be provided:
       Graphics identified?
       Written information completed?
    Distribution methods:
       Copies reproduced?
       Materials sent to participants before the workshop?
       Graphics to be used in oral presentations?
       Display equipment ordered?
       Graphics to be used in discussion groups?

13. Publicize the workshop
    Methods selected?
    Preparation and distribution?
    Incentives for participation?

14. Make meeting arrangements
    For the general session:
        Set-up and clean-up arranged?
        Lecterns, chairs, tables obtained?
        Speaker system obtained?
        Computers/projectors/screens obtained?
        Space for wall displays?
        Registration table/space?
        Personnel for registration?
        Refreshments?
        Name tags obtained?
        Room arrangements made?
        Audiovisual equipment set up?
        Ventilation/heating adequate?
    For discussion sections
        Easels/ blackboards obtained?
        Supplies (paper, chalk, erasers, felt tip pens, thumb tacks) obtained?
15. Orientation for facilitators or discussion moderators
    Orientation meeting and materials prepared?
16. Recording the proceedings
    Methods to be used?
    Personnel/equipment obtained?
17. Meeting-day schedule
    Start/stop on time?
    Breaks included as planned?
    Time allowed for participants to give feedback or evaluation of
    workshop at end?
18. Identify follow-up activities
19. Using and disseminating the results
    Analysis of results:
        Reporting format for decision makers?
        Reporting formats to the public?
        Reporting formats to the media?
20. Meeting evaluation
    Recommendations obtained from participants, presenters,
    collaborators, and sponsors?
    Feedback incorporated for future programs?

Source: J. A. Braus and M. C. Monroe. 1994. *Designing Effective Workshops: EE Toolbox-Workshop Resource Manual.* School of Natural Resources and Environment, University of Michigan, Ann Arbor; James L. Creighton. 1980. *Public Involvement Manual: Involving the Public in Water and Power Resources Decisions.* United States Department of the Interior Water and Power Resources Service. U.S. Government Printing Office, Washington, D.C.

ensure audience participation. Even with a good facilitator, peer pressure or the dominance of only a few participants can lead to mediocre results.

Nominal Group Technique

The Nominal Group Technique is a structured approach to a brainstorming session. It was designed based on research that suggests that individuals generate more creative ideas and information when they work in the presence of each other but do not interact. According to researchers, people in groups are more likely to react to each other's ideas than come up with new ideas or consider new dimensions to a problem. Participants in the Nominal Group process instead react to a specific topic or problem that is introduced by a facilitator. Each participant writes all his or her ideas or responses on a notecard.[23] The ideas are collected by going around the group until no more ideas are forthcoming. Next the ideas are presented verbally or visually. Each item is clarified and discussed. Choosing a course of action or prioritizing the ideas or options is the next step. This involves clarifying goals, listing alternative options, assessing costs, and ranking and selecting the best choices. This method generates a high-quality list of options from which to choose.

Participants can rank or vote on the importance of the concerns identified. This method can be reiterated several times to further expand the discussion and clarify opinions. Finally, the votes can be weighted and assigned values. If carefully planned, the entire process can be performed in one meeting of two to three hours.

Like the brainstorming process, this technique generates many ideas in a short period of time. In addition, the Nominal Group process solicits the full range of individuals' thoughts and concerns and gives all participants an equal opportunity to express opinions and ideas in a nonthreatening setting. This is particularly important for groups composed of people of different backgrounds and experiences.

Delphi Technique

The Delphi Technique is more structured than the Nominal Group Technique. It uses a series of questionnaires and summarized feedback reports to solicit opinions. This approach is useful for many of the same things as the Nominal Group process: generating and clarifying ideas, reaching consensus, prioritizing, and making decisions on alternative actions. Unlike the Nominal Group process, responses using the Delphi Technique are often anonymous and the group is selected based on expertise of the individuals.[24]

The technique is particularly useful because you do not need to gather the group to meet. Instead, you select a panel of experts for your particular topic, such as a strategy for a new resource management plan, and send the panel members an open-ended questionnaire about the issue under study. You tabulate and aggregate their initial responses and positions on the topic. For the next round, you send all the responses (which are usually kept anonymous) to the panel and ask them to rank priorities of the initial responses using a rating scale. Again, these responses are tabulated and sent back for review. Panelists clarify reasons for disagreement, reevaluate options and provide additional ratings in an attempt to reach a consensus. The final result is a ranking of the priority issues and concerns of the "experts." This technique distills expert opinion on a specific topic. It allows participants to remain anonymous and share information free of social pressures. The technique can be particularly useful for reaching consensus among groups hostile to each other. Disadvantages with this technique include the difficulty of getting responses in a timely manner, confusion among experts about specific vocabulary used, or misunderstandings about written responses. The technique also prohibits personal dialogue or rapport from developing among participants.

Improved Nominal Group Technique

The Nominal Group and Delphi Techniques are combined in the Improved Nominal Group Technique (INGT). This approach combines an initial written exercise to gather ideas anonymously followed by a meeting to discuss ideas and build a consensus. These steps enhance the generation of creative ideas, include social interaction with lower pressure to conform, and focus on task completion.[25] The results of the INGT are generally high quality. This technique takes advantage of several aspects of group dynamics:

1. Groups are more effective if they have an opportunity to think, write, and reflect before being forced to choose an option.
2. Productivity in decision making by groups increases when a focus or specific question is identified.
3. The collective memory and knowledge of a group surpasses that of any individual.
4. Group members can piggyback on the ideas of others to produce more creative and useful suggestions.[26]

The disadvantage of the INGT technique is that the process demands a high level of training for the facilitator.[27]

Example: An Improved Nominal Group Technique for Obtaining Public Input in Watershed Management[28]

A regional office of the Water and Power Resources Service (WPRS) of the U.S. Department of Interior held workshops in four counties as part of a study to determine future water needs for the area. The desired product was a set of scenarios about future development and water needs.

Prior to the workshops, meetings were held with stakeholders in each county to solicit recommendations for a balanced slate of individuals to participate in the workshops. The agency was anxious to get representative input from as many stakeholder groups as possible. Before the workshop, a workbook was prepared to introduce the study, the planning process, the workshop agenda, and a summary of basic human, agricultural, fish and wildlife, and industrial water needs. A pilot test of the workshop was conducted with internal planning staff to discover which portions of the workshop seemed effective and which needed modification to avoid potential landmines. The dry run also allowed the staff to test their workshop facilitation skills.

Each workshop was a full-day event, held in the seat of each county. Approximately 150 people participated in the first round of four workshops, and over 250 people attended a second round of open workshops and evening meetings. The agenda of activities for each workshop follows.

Opening

An opening session described the study, planning procedures, future public participation activities, and workshop procedures. Teams were assigned using a counting-off system to insure that participants of a single interest would not gather together on a team.

TEAM ACTIVITY 1: Identifying Factors That Affect Development

TIME: 30 minutes

Teams were asked to brainstorm a list of factors that would either encourage or inhibit future development in the area. Participants were not concerned with the value or importance of each factor at this time.

TEAM ACTIVITY 2: Evaluating the Importance of Each Factor

TIME: 45 minutes

Teams were asked to select the three factors that would be most significant in affecting development in the four-county region. Remaining factors were assigned to high-, middle-, and low-impact categories.

Team Reports

Team spokespersons reported on their results.

Lunch

Team reports were consolidated. Themes were proposed for further development in the afternoon session.

Discussion

Proposed themes were discussed with the groups, and additions or changes were made. Once the themes—(1) human, (2) agricultural, (3) wildlife, and

(4) industrial water uses—had been selected, teams were assigned one of the themes.

TEAM ACTIVITY 3: Developing an Alternative Futures Scenario

TIME: 1 hour

Teams were asked to develop a scenario describing the future development of the county based on their assigned theme. The scenario was to include details about population centers, agriculture, and industry so that water demands could be estimated.

TEAM ACTIVITY 4: Estimating Water Needs

TIME: 30 minutes

Teams developed estimates of the amounts, quality, and location of future water needs based on the scenario. A list of potential water supply sources was provided.

Final Reports and Discussion

Each team reported on their scenarios and their estimates of water needs. The group was allowed to ask questions, point out invalid assumptions, or propose additional things that should have been included in the scenarios.

Hand-in Workbook and Workshop Evaluation

Participants received a "Hand-In Workbook" which allowed them to comment on the workshop. The "Hand-in Workbook" asked questions such as:

- Were there factors that you consider to be of greater or lesser importance than did your team? For what reasons?
- Were there other themes you would like to have seen used as the basis for developing scenarios? For what reasons?
- Do you believe the scenarios accurately reflected the themes on which they were based? What changes would you suggest?
- In your opinion, did the water demands developed for each scenario make sense? What changes would you make?
- Are there any other items you would particularly like us to examine as part of the study?

The "Hand-in Workbook" also allowed participants to rate each scenario on two 9-point scales:

- I believe the likelihood of this alternative future actually occurring is: (1= extremely unlikely to 9 = very likely)
- If this alternative future occurred I would feel: (1 = very unhappy to 9 = very pleased)

The "Hand-in Workbook" also contained a workshop evaluation form, and asked participants to suggest individuals who might serve effectively on an advisory committee for their county.

The agency planning staff were satisfied with the process and output of the workshops. The workshop evaluations included in the "Hand-in Workbook" indicated that the participants were happy with the workshop format and felt that it had provided them with ample opportunities to participate and express their points of view. The planning staff reported that the scenarios developed based on the public comment were comprehensive, detailed, and useful for making the projections of future growth needed for the study. The workshops not only allowed the public to feel consulted but contributed to completing the planning tasks.[29] Careful planning and selection of an appropriate group technique helped lead to the success of the workshops in incorporating stakeholder needs and concerns into management plans.

Observational Techniques

Systematic observation provides a variety of methods for collecting useful data for a program and unobtrusively monitoring a situation. Observational methods range from simple checklists to hiring experts to make professional judgments. Observations may be quantitative or qualitative.

Quantitative measurement instruments include recordings or checklists of audience behaviors. For example, observations of the actions of crowds at a zoo exhibit can identify exhibit components that effectively captivate visitors. Observations of role playing, rating scales, simulation games, and experimental choice situations devised by the researcher also can provide quantitative information.

Qualitative observations involve keeping an account of anecdotal records and incidents that occur or recording detailed field observations describing the situation to be addressed. Observers usually attempt to be invisible—drawing as little attention to themselves as possible from the people being observed. Participants in an activity also may serve as observers; for example, staff may assess other participants' activities during a program. Observations may be short or long term—from one intensive hour to selected observations spanning more than a year.

Although observations can be a reliable (unbiased) and valid (reflecting the actual situation) method of research, they are not used regularly as the sole data gathering technique. Observational data often are combined with results from other techniques, such as interviews and case study analyses, to provide a richer and deeper view of a problem.

The difficulties of appropriately training observers to record and interpret observational data are the main disadvantages of this method. Like other methods, you must clearly define the objectives of the study, the population sample, and the unit of analysis in order to collect data from which you can draw conclusions. Examples of observational data collection techniques are described below.

Quantitative Observations

Quantitative observations depend on carefully defining clear and distinct behaviors to be observed. Researchers design checklists prior to the study for recording whether a characteristic or behavior is present or absent. Rating scales can indicate the degree of an action, while frequency and duration counts record the time involved. Quantitative observations are generally made for short periods of time, called interval sampling. They can define what activities your target audience is engaged in at a particular setting, like a nature center, and how often and long members spend in certain activities.

Studies of visitors to exhibits and museum displays often use the technique of unobtrusively observing visitor activities. Time spent examining a display, conversations about the exhibit, and movements and behaviors on a trail can all be used to infer visitor interest, success of different types of communication materials, and content areas that should be appropriate for the target audience. Because few standardized procedures exist for observations, the checklist or measurement instrument must be pilot-tested under field conditions. If more than one observer is used, careful training and testing of observations helps ensure that data are collected in a consistent manner. When conducting observational research, you also must guard against influencing the behavior of the observed.[30]

Example: An Observation Checklist for Visitors to a Museum

Observations of museum visitors reveal that most visitors spend little time at most exhibits. The challenge for museum display designers is to hit the visitor with a quick dollop of enticing information, not a full course meal all at once. Observations of visitors can help reveal common elements among successful exhibits and suggest effective techniques to incorporate into new exhibit designs. Museum program administrator at the Florida Museum of Natural History, Betty Dunckel Camp, says they test and review all their exhibits using observational assessment techniques. Their front-end evaluation of visitors' needs and interests helps ensure more effective programs. Visitor tracking and timing observations on prototype exhibit panels help to get the kinks out of exhibits as they are being planned. This approach optimizes the amount of information and appropriate content of each exhibit based on visitor needs. The museum's observation checklist is used for evaluating new exhibits and includes the following questions:

- How many visitors walked up to the exhibit?
- How many visitors appeared to read the exhibit sign(s)?
- Of those visitors who walked up to the exhibit, how many used the exhibit?
- How long did they spend at the exhibit?
- How many of those that used the exhibit used it correctly?
- Of those who did NOT use the exhibit correctly, what were they doing wrong?

Qualitative Observations

Direct observations are a qualitative technique for collecting in-depth information about audience actions and program impacts and activities. As a researcher, you must decide what to observe and what data to collect in order to meet your program needs. This method requires well-trained observers and a large investment of time to observe and interpret findings accurately. The technique is an ongoing exercise where the observer continuously collects and analyzes data. New questions often arise during the course of data collection.

A disadvantage of this method is the bias potentially introduced by the observer. This method also does not identify causative relationships or allow one specific conclusion. Rather, a number of explanations for a phenomenon are often the result. The final product is a report that allows the reader to enter the situation and understand what was happening through the descriptions of the observer. Combined with other research techniques, this method can provide specific and useful information for program design.

Example: Qualitative Observation Techniques to Improve a Recycling Program in a National Park

An observational method of analysis was used to evaluate a recycling project that used large signs and recycling bins to encourage people to separate garbage in two public parks at the foot of the Washington and Lincoln Memorials in Washington, D.C.[31] The purpose of the observations was to assess the existing recycling program to determine why it was unsuccessful and to make recommendations for improvement.

Four observation areas were delineated:

- by a concession stand near an attractive signboard on the importance of

recycling and a clearly marked container for plastic, glass, and aluminum recycling, along with a traditional garbage can;
- at a congested bus stop with the recycling signboard;
- by a second concession area with multiple garbage receptacles, the recycling signboard, and a rest area for visitors; and
- on a street corner, not served by the concession stand, but with a recycling container and a traditional garbage can.

Existing Program

Each sign made three points. First, it pictured glass bottles, plastic bottles, foam cups, and aluminum cans and their placement in bins separate from other garbage, with an illustration of two children using a recycling container. Second, it illustrated the technology of recycling. Third, it indicated how much garbage is produced near the memorials every week.

The recycling containers displayed a recycling symbol and were labeled Plastic, Glass, Foam, and Aluminum Only, with two symbols indicating that hot dog and potato chip wrappers were not to be thrown into the can. The garbage bins were a different size from the recycling containers and were labeled Trash Only.

Program planners had hoped that the large, new signs and the availability of recycling trash containers would lead to a high level (80 percent) of proper disposal of recyclable drink cups and other products. The observational research would assess the results and would help indicate problems and alternative solutions.

Methods

Observations were conducted for two days, one on a weekend and one during the week, for two periods of sixty minutes each. Teams of two or three observers worked at each site for a total of twelve to fifteen hours. Observers were trained for one hour on how to observe and record data.

Results

The observers found that most people ignored the expensive signs and did not recycle properly. The contents of the bins showed that cups clearly marked as recyclable were almost evenly distributed in the recycling and nonrecycling containers.

One conclusion was that people come to the memorials to have fun, not to recycle. They expected to see signs with information about the monuments they had come to see, not signs about recycling. Another conclusion was that there were too many types of garbage bins and too many conflicting labels that led those people who tried to recycle to make mistakes or give up.

Finally the information program was designed to reach everyone entering the area, but only 2 percent of the visitors bought an item that could be recycled. Based on these observations, the researchers concluded that the general approach of public signs was a hit-or-miss strategy that missed more often than it hit.

Using the Observational Findings

The researchers suggested a new strategy.

- A clear goal would be set: 90 percent of recyclable cups would be placed in a recycling container.
- A specific target audience would be identified: all individuals purchasing recyclable cups at the concession stand.
- Containers would be standardized to more clearly distinguish between garbage and recycling containers.
- Signs would be replaced by a training and incentive program for sales staff at the concession stands. They would be trained to provide a simple verbal cue to every customer buying a recyclable cup to instruct, remind, and thank people for recycling that cup. Staff would be given a small financial reward every day the recycling goal was met.

Based on the results of audience research using direct observation, this new program strategy significantly improved recycling around the memorials.

Professional Judgment

Professional judgment is the observation and assessment of a program or activity by an expert in the field. Professional judgments are based on an intuitive assessment of the quality of a program and its impact on the audience. Using either informal criteria or formal standards, the experts make observations, then answer questions or write a report on their impressions. A variation of this approach is to invite peers from other institutions to observe your program and make suggestions. The advantages of using these techniques include the immediacy of obtaining results and the ease of implementation.[32] Some of the disadvantages, such as inherent biases of the observer, can be overcome by having more than one expert and by clearly defining the criteria and relative importance of various factors that require judgment. Professional review is a useful technique for improving a communications program.

Example: Peer Teaching Review at the University of Florida

To improve the teaching performance of professors in the Department of Wildlife Ecology and Conservation and other units at the University of Florida, a peer teaching evaluation was designed. Four "peers" (other professors in the department) observe the professor teaching a class, and review the course materials and student evaluations. The peer review team's individual observations and recommendations cover three main areas and are summarized in a final report that is used by professors to improve their teaching styles and course content:

1. Classroom context and organization
   • Organization
   • Presentation
   • Rapport
   • Credibility/Control
   • Content
   • Interaction
   • Active learning

2. Course materials
   • Texts
   • Supplemental materials
   • Evidence of professional development

3. Summary of student evaluations

Document Review and Content Analysis

Volumes of information are available to help conservation communicators conduct audience research. Documents and records provide a historical perspective from which you can identify patterns or current environmental trends. These data are inexpensive and usually easy to obtain. Libraries offer a wealth of information, and, increasingly, the Internet offers a storehouse of databases for public use. These records can provide specific information for a given region, such as population density, age and sex distribution, and employment rates. U.S. census data reveal socioeconomic backgrounds for any geographic area.

Census data were used in a study of residents living near Blackwater State Forest in western Florida. The census data available at the public library revealed that the populations in the four-county area had a median age of from 32 to 38 years and that 77 to 94 percent were Caucasian. This represents an older, less ethnically diverse community than many other Florida counties. Unlike south Florida where interpretive materials for recreationists in the state forests may be bilingual to effectively reach Hispanic populations, Blackwater's local audience did not require multicultural materials.

Documents from local newspapers to chamber of commerce data provide clues about the political outlooks and conservation history of an area. Publications from conservation agencies or organizations in the region may offer communications materials that have already been tested to some degree with the public. The Internet offers general information about an audience and specific materials from hundreds of environmental organizations. Review of these documents can help prevent replicating failure or reinventing the wheel.

Combining document review with personal interviews with staff and communicators in other organizations is especially useful for organizations initiating programs. This approach makes use of existing data that can be secured at low cost with minimum expertise. It offers an easy way to monitor changes in a community over time. The disadvantage of archival data, however, is that records can be incomplete, outdated, or inaccurate. Bear these disadvantages in mind as you use data collected from a variety of sources, which can include:

- Government archives
- Annual reports
- Institutional or organizational records
- Minutes of meetings
- Maps
- Photographs
- Polls
- Sales records
- Media stories
- Chamber of commerce records
- Voting records
- Information from youth and civic organizations
- World Wide Web pages

Content Analysis

One method used to quantify document reviews is content analysis. Content analysis is an objective description of the content of communications, which can include written documents as described above, and also video, songs, or visual materials. Content analysis involves coding or classifying communications based on established categories. To conduct a content analysis you must

1. Define the population to be studied
2. Determine the sample
3. Isolate the unit of analysis
4. Code the data
5. Conduct the statistical analysis
6. Use the results.[33]

Materials such as program documents, annual reports, strategic plans, periodicals, and correspondence provide resources for data collection. For example, materials for conservation education can be assessed using content analysis. Researchers used content analysis in an evaluation of environmental education curriculum guides for elementary schools. An analysis of seven hundred individual lessons revealed that the majority of materials emphasized basic ecological knowledge and excluded environmental problem-solving, consumer behaviors, and natural resource management issues.[34] Environmental educators can use this information to devise new, more hands-on curricula.

Content analysis also is used to record the frequency of press coverage of a specific topic, such as mention of an ecosystem management plan after an agency has sent out news releases announcing the plan. Analysis of the content and placement of a subject within the newspaper, the number of people reached, and the conservation messages expressed, as well as the attitude toward a topic, management issue, or organization can be systematically analyzed.[35]

Example: Content Analysis of Public Response to a Resource Management Plan

Resource managers use content analysis to evaluate public input they receive for making management decisions. After soliciting public comment, content analysis provides a format for the written responses to be systematically categorized and analyzed. George Stankey, a research social scientist with the U.S. Forest Service, described the typical use of content analysis to assess public attitudes about management of the Mission Mountains Primitive Area in Montana.[36] The Forest Service distributed a booklet outlining five management alternatives and asked the public to express their support or opposition to the various alternatives and to comment about other relevant management issues. The five management alternatives were: (A) wilderness, (B) backcountry, (C) wilderness and backcountry combination, (D) wilderness classification with major boundary adjustments, and (E) management for maximum public access and optimum resource management.

The Forest Service received five hundred letters. These were coded into six categories that included:

1. respondent's preferred alternative (A, B, C, D, or E);
2. reasons for support of or opposition to each alternative;
3. specific details about unacceptable alternatives;
4. respondent background regarding special interest groups, such as affiliation with an environmental organization or forest products industry;
5. respondent's residence; and
6. indication of whether or not respondent had visited the Mission Mountain area.

Responses to each category were further subdivided. For example, reasons respondents gave for supporting a given alternative were coded into twelve subcategories:[37]

1. Personal interest
2. Concern for future generations
3. Educational/scientific value
4. Scarcity value
5. Vital for mental well-being
6. Unique environment
7. Spiritual/religious values
8. Value as wildlife habitat
9. Best economic use of area
10. Means of preventing further cutting or general destruction of forests
11. Preventing damage normally accompanying "mass recreation" such as litter
12. General aesthetics

The Forest Service staff spent about one month condensing and synthesizing the five hundred letters. They created a series of tables that permitted administrators to quickly evaluate public opinion about the decision to be made. The respondents overwhelmingly selected alternative (A)—Wilderness, and their comments provided useful background information for designing and targeting communications to this audience.

Case Studies

Case studies investigate a program or situation within its real-life context. Case studies can be used to gather information about the background, current status, and interactions of audience and program. Case studies use multiple sources of evidence and often require multiple methods of data collection and analysis. They allow interpretation of a specific situation as an immediate "snapshot" or over a longer period of time. While a case study may provide insight into other situations, you cannot generalize the results beyond the specific context. Case studies lack the scientific rigor of quantitative methods or controlled experiments, yet if done with care, they can provide an excellent understanding of the complex nature of a particular situation.

The procedure for conducting a case study is straightforward:[38]

1. Identify the objective of the investigation.
2. Outline the scope of your study.
3. Determine appropriate measurement tools based on efficiency (i.e., budget and time) and efficacy (i.e., data will tell you what you need to know).
4. Analyze the data.

5. Interpret the results.
6. Make recommendations or decisions based on your findings.

Your particular situation will dictate the data collected for a case study. Research on audiences and programs using a case study approach often incorporates data from multiple sources, such as observations and interviews with a review of documents and archival records. These data are then organized and categorized to provide a historical and multidisciplinary context for understanding the situation. The final case study report attempts to describe all relevant aspects of the individuals, organization, or program examined. Evidence for conclusions drawn should be clear, and any alternative explanations should be included. The report also should elucidate how other situations are similar to or different from the case described.

An example of a case study is provided in the appendix. It describes the public relations program that accompanied the reintroduction of the gray wolf into Yellowstone National Park. Resource managers recognized that public sentiment would influence the success of this controversial project. The case study reviews communication methods and techniques used by the U.S. Fish and Wildlife Service and shows how public relations were handled in this particular situation. Although the case study focuses on communications surrounding wolf reintroduction, it also may offer insights into aspects of the program that are similar to other communication challenges, such as reintroduction of panthers in Florida, grizzly bears in the western United States, or bobcats on Georgia's barrier islands. As the wolf reintroduction continues to be embroiled in controversy, the case study findings can help communicators set a new course for smoother sailing in the future.

Visual Techniques

Drawings, maps, and other visual tools are useful when determining audience or individual perceptions of a conservation problem in cultures with visually oriented traditions, with children, and with almost any group for the sake of variety.[39] Drawings produced by individuals that highlight conservation problems or solutions can facilitate discussion, as well as enable comparison with later drawings. In one case, Brazilian children's drawings of a rainforest before their visit to a national park depicted elephants, giraffes, and other exotic animals. After their park visit, they drew native fauna.[40] Park staff used the drawings to assess the impact of their program.

Maps produced by community members are a useful tool for monitoring land use changes and perceptions of land use change.[41] Maps drawn by different groups of people can serve as baseline and comparison data, and can be contrasted with purchased maps or aerial photographs. Mapping exercises are useful in long-range land-use planning, particularly when used in conjunction with a workshop approach.

Example: Visual Techniques Used for Conservation Planning

Maps played an important role in involving community members in the design and designation of the Community Baboon Sanctuary (CBS) in Belize.[42] Working with local farmers, the sanctuary was established in 1985, and extends along a 19-mile (30-kilometer) stretch of the Belize River in central Belize. The primary goal of the project is the protection of the threatened black howler monkey (*Alouatta pigra*), known locally as a "baboon." Protection of the monkey's tropical forest habitat is the key to protection of the species. The CBS organizers targeted landowners that practiced subsistence farming to join the sanctuary and voluntarily protect monkey habitat on their property. The challenge in planning this project was to develop a conservation program that would integrate the culture of the local farming community, as well as recognize the constraints placed on subsistence farmers (fig. 2.4). Land management plans were developed through collaboration with each farmer or family involved.

The main management objective was to establish a continuous forest corridor along the river, thus providing the howlers with adequate forage among the mosaic of successional forest patches. The protection of this riparian land also would improve agricultural land use by decreasing soil erosion along the riverbank. The use of aerial photographs and individual plot maps was instrumental in communicating these benefits to farmers. Using aerial photographs, survey records, and natural landmarks, landownership maps were developed in consultation with twelve landowners. This information allowed for the development and public presentation of twelve individual management plans, followed by a voluntary pledge to uphold a conservation plan for each property. Subsequent expansion included additional landowners in seven neighboring villages. The maps and photographs provided visual reference points to aid the understanding of cumulative effects of individual land management practices. These impacts would have been hard to "see" in any other way. In this case, a picture was worth a thousand words.

FIGURE 2.4. *Development of the Community Baboon Sanctuary included a new museum and nature trails to attract tourists to the community. Sanctuary manager Fallett Young gives a guided forest tour. (Photo by S. K. Jacobson)*

Participatory Rural Appraisal

The participatory rural appraisal technique (PRA) has mainly been used in developing countries and grew from efforts to involve local citizens in conservation and development decisions. PRA techniques combine a slate of approaches and methods that enable local people to share and analyze their knowledge of environmental conditions, and to prioritize and plan future actions.[43] The PRA team relies on local expertise to define the current situation as well as to envision a preferred future situation. Through workshops, field studies, and meetings, the facilitators of the PRA work with community members to construct accurate documentation of the environmental, social, political, and economic resources and constraints of the community. Through this interactive process, conservation and development priorities and an action plan are developed.

The difficulties of this method are many. The facilitators must be carefully trained and should represent several disciplines with diverse expertise. Participatory methodology requires experience and skills in program design, communications, facilitation, conflict resolution, and, sometimes, cross-cultural understanding.[45] The community also must accept the team socially and culturally. Lastly, the results of the PRA depend on the priorities of the community, which may not always coincide with a conservation strategy.

Example: A Participatory Rural Appraisal for the Pululahua Reserve in Ecuador[45]

The Pululahua Geobotanical Reserve, created in 1966, is a state protected area 20 minutes north of Quito, the Ecuadorian capital, in the Andes Mountains. Pululahua is a small farming community located deep inside a 3-mile- (5-kilometer)-wide, extinct volcanic crater. The spectacular geology and patches of cloud forest, as well as a variety of orchids and wildlife rarely found near Quito, make Pululahua an important conservation site and a uniquely accessible tourist destination.

The Quito-based conservation organization EcoCiencia proposed the establishment of a reserve interpretation program based on Pululahua's natural and historical attributes. EcoCiencia had found it difficult to learn about the community's own perception of conservation and development problems and did not know if their proposal would be welcomed. Thus the group sponsored a participatory rural appraisal to obtain a better picture of the community's realities and interests.

The PRA team's objectives included:

• identifying and prioritizing the problems of the community and arriving at viable solutions to problems of highest priority, and

- integrating the participation of EcoCiencia into the PRA framework in order to build a communication bridge between the community and the outside agency.

A four-person PRA team carried out six activities. These resulted in a community map, data collected from ecological transects of farms and forests, a history of the community, a seasonal farming and labor calendar, a diagram of institutions central to the Pululahua's community, and trend diagrams of several variables mutually chosen by the team and participants. Results indicated, among other things, that the community structure and their relationship with government agencies was weak. During the final assembly, community members prioritized problem areas and voiced their priorities. Their primary concern was the difficulty of getting their produce to the market from the crater floor. Additional meetings with engineers were needed to explore efficient ways of getting agricultural products out of the crater without damaging the environment.

Although the initial PRA did not produce a viable action plan, which would be the anticipated outcome of a typical PRA, the results were useful for organizing future interactions. The team prepared the proceedings of the PRA and distributed copies to key members of the community and organizations with development interests in Pululahua. This example demonstrates that participatory methods may not always facilitate an organization's short-term conservation objectives, but can provide open dialogue needed for long-term sustenance of a conservation program.

Naturalistic Inquiry

Naturalistic inquiry represents the collection of a range of people's perceptions about a situation or experience. Naturalistic inquiry is conducted in the natural setting of the program or activity. The evaluator, rather than a questionnaire or survey, is the instrument that gathers the data. This is done using interviews, observations, and unobtrusive monitoring techniques. Data are collected until the information obtained becomes redundant, or similar, from a number of sources. The data and results are discussed and verified with the participants to enhance confidence in the validity of the findings. The results are presented in an evaluation or as part of a case study report.

Naturalistic inquiry is also called a qualitative, interpretive, ethnographic, or responsive study. These terms refer to a methodological approach to research that emphasizes a nondirective, participatory format using qualitative methods.[46] The basis for a naturalistic inquiry is an in-depth interaction with the audience. This approach can provide managers or conservation communicators with valid information for planning and developing programs.

Naturalistic inquiry offers a way to explore the complexity of the impact of a conservation program or service. The evaluator listens to the perceptions and interpretations of the audience and staff and verifies the findings with stakeholders of the program or service. A disadvantage of this technique is that it is not generalizable to other programs or settings; the findings are specific to the time, participants, and context. Yet, this method offers insights that may be transferred to other programs operating under similar contexts.

Example: Naturalistic Inquiry for Improving an Outdoor Camp Program[47]

Researcher Lorraine Smith spent ten weeks conducting a naturalistic inquiry at a resident outdoor camp. The purpose of the study was to understand the nature of the resident camp experience as perceived by the counselors. The objective was to clarify the present status of the program and then develop ideas for better achieving the intended goals of the program.

Following a naturalistic inquiry approach, Smith continuously observed the camp setting and activities. Her primary data collection method was a series of in-depth interviews with the camp counselors and directors. She analyzed documents such as personnel policies and program operating procedures. Follow-up interviews to verify her findings were conducted ten weeks after the camp season ended. Smith produced a comprehensive report describing the staff experience. She summarized her field notes into a series of forty-two findings aggregated into six categories. The categories were administration, program areas, campers, other staff, environmental conditions, and the individual counselor. The results present the staff's perspectives on their experience at the camp, including the factors that contributed to their satisfaction, dissatisfaction, and the overall meaning of the camp to them. A few of her findings are presented here.

Based on interviews at the beginning of camp, Smith described the goals and expectations counselors held of the camp administration:

- To be accessible and communicative,
- To provide dependable leadership, and
- To offer advice and feedback concerning performance.

Further into the summer, a description of the staff's concerns about the camp's administration emerged from the counselors' interviews:

- The director's expectations of staff performance were never clearly communicated.
- The director's expectations of counselor roles were unrealistic.

At the same time, most staff evaluated their experiences positively:

- Staff generally had a personally successful summer.

(continues on p. 82)

TABLE 2.1. *Relative strengths and weaknesses of audience research techniques*
(● = high, ◐ = medium, ○ = low)

	Identifies target audiences	Determines attitudes and opinions	Simple to use	Generates new ideas	Promotes interaction among target audiences	Provides generalizable results
SURVEYS						
Mail	●	●	○	○	○	●
Telephone	●	●	○	○	○	●
Personal (face-to-face)	●	●	○	◐	○	●
GROUP INTERVIEWS						
Focus groups	●	●	●	◐	◐	○
Nominal group techniques	●	●	●	●	◐	○
GROUP MEETINGS						
Citizen advisory committee	○	○	●	●	●	○
Public hearing	○	○	●	●	○	○
Workshops	○	●	●	●	●	○
Informal contacts	○	○	●	○	○	○
OBSERVATION						
Quantitative observation	●	○	○	●	○	●
Qualitative observation	●	○	○	●	○	○
Professional judgment	○	○	○	●	○	○
CONTENT ANALYSIS	○	○	○	○	○	●
DOCUMENT REVIEW	○	○	●	○	○	◐
CASE STUDIES	○	○	◐	●	○	○
VISUAL TECHNIQUES	○	○	○	○	○	○
PARTICIPATORY RURAL APPRAISAL	●	●	○	●	●	○
NATURALISTIC INQUIRY	●	●	○	◐	●	○

Requires expertise in facilitator	Requires high costs	Requires long time	Requires many staff	Biases audience reactions	Provides in-depth contextual data	Involves audience in decision making	Requires data base
●	●	●	○	○	○	○	●
●	●	○	●	○	○	○	●
●	●	●	●	◐	●	○	●
●	◐	○	○	○	●	○	○
●	◐	○	○	◐	◐	◐	◐
○	○	●	○	●	○	●	○
●	○	○	○	●	○	○	○
●	○	○	○	●	○	●	○
○	○	○	○	○	○	○	○
●	◐	◐	◐	○	●	○	○
●	○	◐	◐	○	●	○	○
●	◐	○	○	●	◐	○	○
●	○	○	○	○	○	○	●
○	○	○	○	○	○	○	●
◐	○	○	○	○	●	○	●
◐	○	○	○	●	◐	○	○
●	●	○	●	○	●	●	○
●	○	●	○	○	●	○	○

- The campers were the main means by which staff felt rewarded.
- The campers were an important factor leading to staff satisfaction.

Staff dissatisfaction stemmed from several perceived problems:

- Staff experienced difficulties within their program areas;
- Quality time available to spend with campers outside program and general camp commitments were lacking.
- Days off did not help staff feel positive, enthusiastic, or refreshed upon returning.[48]

This selection from the forty-two findings by Smith offers a vignette of the kinds of information that can be gathered through naturalistic inquiry. The full evaluation report provided the camp directors with a vivid picture of what had occurred at their camp that summer. Camp administrators used the information as a blueprint for planning and improving future programming.

Last Words

"If the people want rock and roll, don't make them polka." Understanding audience needs and desires is critical for effective communications. A variety of research methods are available to help you make decisions about your communication needs. Quantitative methods, such as survey techniques, are useful for minimizing bias in data collection and allow you to generalize your results to the greater population. Qualitative data often offer more in-depth insights into the problem. They are useful for framing issues and explaining observed phenomena. Qualitative techniques are often used for pretesting communication strategies and validating quantitative research approaches.

Time, staff, and budgets limit communications research. You must ask yourself three important questions: What do I want to find out? (the research question); What do I need to know to figure it out? (the data); and How will I use this information to come up with the answer? (the analysis). The answers to these questions will dictate which methods will be most useful. When possible, use more than one data source in order to strengthen and provide multiple perspectives on your conclusions.[49] Known as triangulation, using several sources of data, multiple collection methods, and several researchers, helps provide high-quality results, because the process involves a variety of perspectives and participants.

Table 2.1 identifies the relative strengths of the research techniques described in this chapter. All research methods introduce inherent biases. Without research, however, identifying and communicating with target audiences becomes a guessing game. If you guess wrong, or you do not even bother to guess, as with the crocodile reintroduction in Venezuela, your program has little chance of success. Audience research for communications is key to effective programming to achieve conservation goals.

Chapter 3

DESIGNING A PUBLIC COMMUNICATIONS CAMPAIGN

If you want to move people, it has to be toward a vision that's
positive for them, that taps important values, that gets them
something they desire, and it has to be presented in a compelling way that they feel inspired to follow.

—*Martin Luther King Jr.*

Dr. King "moved" people through his communications and actions. Although
your program goals are different, the fundamental goal—moving people—is
the same. Just as public communications activities were key to the civil rights
movement, they also are key to a successful business, government agency, or
nonprofit organization. This chapter offers a how-to approach for planning a
public communications campaign for conservation.

Careful planning can help you make a wave, maybe even a tsunami, to
move people toward your cause. The goals of most communications programs
are to increase public awareness, reinforce favorable opinions or neutralize hostile ones, or promote positive behaviors. Communications strategies provided
in this chapter include the activities of the Save the Manatee Club in Florida
and urban forestry initiatives in Ohio. Direct mail efforts to protect New York's
Adirondack Park, a special event planned by The Nature Conservancy, and the
use of environmental marketing to sell cosmetics are just a few of the examples demonstrating possible communications strategies. These are part of the
arsenal as you wage campaigns, discussed later in this chapter, of political
action, public information, promotion, organizational development, environmental interpretation, or conservation education.

Systematic planning, implementation, and evaluation are the foundation

---

Box 3.1. A communications campaign involves careful planning, implementation, and evaluation

Planning
- Review organizational mission and goals
- Identify target audiences
- Determine specific objectives
- Identify resources and constraints
- Assess potential approaches and activities

Implementation
- Pretest tools and messages
- Develop and implement selected activities
- Monitor and complete the communications program

Evaluation
- Compare results with the objectives
- Make decisions regarding program changes and continuation

---

of effective communications campaigns (Box 3.1). A campaign begins by identifying your communication needs, objectives, and target audiences. You weigh possible strategies based on your resources and constraints of time, money, and staff. The campaign proceeds from a series of decisions about the structure, operation, and assessment of your program. The planning process provides information for making decisions about the nature and scope of your actions. Implementation involves pilot testing strategies and monitoring the ongoing operations. Continuous assessment allows you to modify activities based on timely feedback and new information. Evaluation of products and outcomes tells if your tactics worked. It allows you to make decisions about the fate of the program—whether it should be continued, cut, or expanded. Following a systematic approach helps avoid problems such as targeting the wrong audience or using an inappropriate message or medium. Most conservation concerns are urgent. These guidelines will help you avoid wasting time on ineffective programs.

Planning

Planning starts with a review of the mission of your organization or agency and the goals for the communications campaign. With this foundation you can identify target audiences and develop objectives for each audience. Based on the audience and objectives, you devise specific activities to attain your goal. An inventory of your resources in terms of staff, materials, and funds shapes the design of realistic activities. The entire planning process assesses and then narrows the menu of activities, media channels, and messages for the communications campaign.

A number of approaches can be followed in the planning process, but all of them include the development of goals, objectives, and actions in response to conservation issues important to your organization. By determining each element of the campaign, you can design an effective plan from start to finish.

Review Your Organizational Mission

The mission of an organization is its reason for existing. A mission statement articulates the guiding principles for the organization's actions and long-term goals. Organization staff must ask themselves, "Who are we, what do we do, and why?" The answers will circumscribe the range of activities and opportunities to be pursued in a communications campaign. A mission statement ideally includes the audiences or customers to be served, the needs of those audiences, and the means by which to serve those needs. The mission statement provides overall direction in light of audience needs, the organization's resources, and external constraints and opportunities. Like a beacon in the night, it illuminates your path so you can get where you want to go. Without a clear mission, you risk stumbling in the darkness of an ineffective campaign.

Here are some examples of mission statements from conservation agencies and organizations. Some (even of large organizations) neglect to completely answer the who, what, and why of a good mission statement, but they may give you ideas for your own.

The mission of the National Wildlife Federation: "To educate, inspire and assist individuals and organizations of diverse cultures to conserve wildlife and other natural resources while protecting the Earth's environment to promote a peaceful, equitable, and sustainable future."[1] Their work ranges from advocacy and litigation for conservation policies and protection of special places to science-based education programs for all ages, including a campus ecology program. Their Corporate Conservation Council promotes dialogue with corporate business executives.[2]

The Save the Manatee Club mission: "To provide public education, conservation and advocacy for the endangered manatee."[3] Former Florida Governor Bob Graham and singer Jimmy Buffett established this member-based organization in 1981 to halt the demise of these aquatic mammals. The activities of the Save the Manatee Club are discussed later in this chapter.

Wilderness Southeast's mission: "To develop awareness, appreciation, understanding and enjoyment of the natural world, and to instill in our travelers a sense of environmental stewardship." This ecotourist company leads groups into the Okefenokee Swamp, the Everglades, and other wilderness areas.

The Nature Conservancy's mission: "To preserve plants, animals and natural communities that represent the diversity of life on earth by protecting the lands and waters they need to survive." TNC's activities span land purchase, resource management, policy, and public education programs.

The Biological Resources Division (BRD) of the U.S. Geological Survey's mission: "To work with others to provide the scientific understanding and technologies needed to support the sound management and conservation of our Nation's biological resources."[4] The BRD statement also identifies partners and obligations: "[T]he BRD has a unique capability to integrate the work of many scientists in diverse locations so that difficult issues and widespread problems can be broadly addressed. This special role, coupled with obligations to the biotic resources of federally managed lands, defines the essence of Federal science as it pertains to the BRD."

These mission statements summarize reasons why each group exists. A proposed activity that does not help an organization achieve its mission should probably not be undertaken.

Determine Your Goals

The mission of your organization leads to a set of goals that describes the desired outcomes of your organization's activities. Goals focus the broad mission statement into more concrete and action-oriented activities, such as a public communications campaign. The goal of a business firm is to serve its customers in order to earn a profit. Similarly, the goals of nonprofit organizations are to provide goods or services to specific or general audiences with the greatest efficiency and least cost.[5] The very survival of nonprofit organizations and government agencies ultimately depends on their meeting the needs of the audiences they serve. Local, state, and federal agencies manage natural resources to serve the public good. Goals of conservation organizations and agencies may be to protect an endangered species, sustain game species, conserve a parcel of land, manage a reserve, or restore a forest. All of these goals implicitly define associated target audiences and specific goods and services to be provided.

Goals generally address problems. Conversely, identifying problems is a good way to formulate goals. An analysis of the context and situation helps determine the specific conservation problem or opportunity to be addressed. One of the Save the Manatee Club's goals, for example, is the recovery of manatees in the wild. The more clearly the problem is stated, the more targeted a goal will be. The problem, "Manatees are an endangered species," is less helpful for identifying potential communications-based solutions than: "Collisions with motorboats cause manatee deaths in Florida." This problem statement helps to identify a specific goal: "Reduce boat collisions with manatees." It also helps identify specific audiences, such as boat owners, marina operators, or water management district regulators (fig. 3.1).

Most conservation organizations have a number of goals. For example, the California Wilderness Coalition, an alliance of individuals, businesses, and eighty conservation groups has four goals:

FIGURE 3.1. *Save the Manatee Club uses signs in its efforts to reduce boat collisions with manatees. (Photo by Carol Lippincott)*

- To create a grassroots activist network throughout California
- To ensure that critical wildlands in California are defended from immediate, short-term threats
- To achieve long-term protection for wildlands through promotion of wilderness legislation such as the California Wilderness Act of 1984, and as the Wildlands Project affiliate in California
- To serve the California conservation community in a coordinating and leadership capacity[6]

Identify Target Audiences

The most important ingredient of any communications strategy is the selection of the target audiences or stakeholders. You must know how the audiences are connected to the problem, what actions you wish them to take, and their current experience and knowledge of the problem. Your strategy depends on an understanding of the target audience's awareness, attitudes, or behaviors that must be changed, and the communications techniques that may potentially accomplish your objectives. Knowledge of audience demographics, lifestyles, media use, and other factors (discussed in chapter 2) will help you select appropriate communications approaches and define specific objectives.

Define Objectives

While goals are broad, objectives are specific and measurable. Thinking at both levels helps you form a bridge from the mission statement to the activities you eventually carry out. A goal can be dissected into measurable objectives for each target audience. Later these objectives can serve as benchmarks for measuring a program's performance.

Communications objectives may be related to changing a target audience's knowledge, attitudes, or behaviors. Commercial advertisers view objectives in the form of a staircase leading up to their goal of selling their product. The first step is building consumer awareness—the consumer's ability to recognize and remember the product. The next step piques the consumer's interest and desire to learn about some of the features of the product, and to evaluate these attributes. The remaining steps lead to the consumer's first purchase, and if all goes according to plan, the repeated purchase and continued use of the product.

This same process can be duplicated in conservation communications where each objective may focus on one or several of these steps. An initial message may try only to increase awareness about an issue, service, or product. A further objective may focus on increasing concern, and a final objective may encourage conservation action. Remember, however, that increasing general awareness about a problem or product does not necessarily guarantee action (chapter 1).

To determine if your communications objectives are met, they must be measurable. Often objectives specify the number of people that will display the desired concern or behavior and the dates by which these changes will be achieved (e.g., a 10 percent increase in visitors to a wildlife reserve per month, or one hundred new donors to a conservation organization in a year). All objectives should identify the audience, the desired effect, and the time frame for a communications strategy to be implemented and the results attained. When objectives are measurable, the results can be compared with anticipated outcomes to judge success and make decisions about program continuation. To be measurable, objectives must be carefully formulated to specify the expected outcome. For example, the Save the Manatee Club (SMC) may identify objectives to increase public knowledge, build positive attitudes, or focus on specific behaviors their target audiences must practice.

SMC objectives related to the *knowledge* of their audience could include increasing the percentage of people who

- can identify manatee habitat
- are aware of boat-related manatee mortality
- are aware of precautions to take to reduce mortality or conserve manatee habitat
- are knowledgeable about the location of well-populated manatee habitats

SMC objectives related to the *attitudes* of their audience could include increasing the percentage of people who

- are concerned about manatees
- want to reduce boat collision mortalities in manatees
- think it is good for people to change their boating behaviors to help conserve manatees
- desire to support manatee protection legislation

SMC objectives related to the *behaviors* of their audience could include increasing the percentage of people who

- buy a product, such as propeller guards for their boats
- give up an undesirable behavior, such as touching or feeding manatees
- adopt desirable behaviors, such as slowing their boats in manatee habitat or no-wake zones
- donate money or time to the SMC

SMC behavioral objectives for specific audiences will be more defined.

- Legislators: voting for more stringent protection for manatees or to appropriate funds for conserving their habitat
- State agency regulators: reducing boat speeds in the ten waterways most populated by manatees
- Marina owners: posting no-wake zones near critical manatee habitats

To make these objectives measurable, the SMC would need to specify the numbers or percentage of audience members that will exhibit the new understanding, attitudes, or behaviors. Without specific measures, it would be difficult for the SMC to track their progress and evaluate their activities.

Inventory Resources and Constraints

A realistic view of the resources and constraints of time, personnel, and money provides the ingredients for the strategic menu. Constraints limit the activities you can consider. For example, television ads may be beyond your budget, periodic newsletters may be too sluggish for your scheduling needs, or lack of staff may turn a special event into a nightmare. Time, staff, and money are often limiting.

Timing of your various activities may need to relate to the annual calendar, seasonal occurrences, school schedules, or special days. Other activities may be required at a moment's notice to respond to an unexpected opportunity or problem. Many actions may just need to follow a chronological order. No matter what the timing, the schedule for any activity requires careful planning to provide sufficient hours and days to successfully complete each task.

Staffing requirements must be realistically gauged. Who will do what? If many people are needed to help with events, where will they come from? Staff niches can be filled by volunteers from the community, Scouts or club members, interns from local colleges, or temporary hires. Each alternative has advantages and disadvantages and will require additional resources for training or stipends.

Accurate knowledge of the funds needed versus the funds available is critical to planning a communications campaign. Resources must be allocated efficiently, with a focus on priority activities. In one year, four companies

(Procter & Gamble, Philip Morris, General Motors, and Sears) spent over $1 billion each to communicate with their U.S. consumers through advertising activities.[7] Obviously communications budgets for environmental organizations and agencies are orders of magnitude lower. The Florida Game and Freshwater Fish Commission allocated $205,000 in operating expenses for their public nongame wildlife education efforts in 1997.[8] The Save the Manatee Club spent $117,208 on membership services in one year, and The Nature Conservancy spent $6,200 on one public event, the Tiger Creek Jubilee, in central Florida.

How much money should be spent on communications with the public? Some private companies spend a percentage of their sales on their advertising budget, whereas others match their competitors' advertising levels. The most effective method is to determine your communications objectives, identify tasks to accomplish the objectives, and determine the costs of these activities. If your budget is too small, consider substituting alternate activities, redefining the objectives, or finding partners to share the costs. If enough funds are not available, you may be able to get donations of money, goods, or services in support of the campaign. Often fundraising may be an objective in itself.

Select Activities and Messages

The final stage of the planning process identifies activities to be implemented to meet the objectives for each target audience. The activities must be attuned to the situation and will depend on the results of your inventory of budgets, personnel, time frames, and other constraints and opportunities. Your own experience and observation of effective campaigns of other nonprofit, as well as for-profit, endeavors can provide a wellspring of ideas for specific activities.

For example, if you are embarking on a communications campaign to protect an endangered species, you may review the actions and message content of the Save the Manatee Club's efforts. The annual report of the SMC records their activities. Their annual budget of $745,368 included expenditures for the following activities: education ($280,451), conservation ($180,372), membership services ($117,208), manatee merchandise ($35,602), volunteer services ($13,907), and advocacy ($9,954).[9] Activities of the public awareness program of the Save the Manatee Club targeted boaters and property owners, tourists and manatee viewers, the Florida public, teachers and students, and policy makers.

For boaters and shoreline property owners SMC

- produced two thousand waterway signs to alert boaters to the presence of manatees. The free signs were distributed to Florida shoreline property owners through Florida Marine Patrol offices.
- funded a study that demonstrated that manatee speed zones do not depreciate property values, as some critics had charged.

For tourists and manatee viewers SMC

- cofunded with the U.S. Fish and Wildlife Service a manatee information radio station in Crystal River, Florida, instructing people how to behave around manatees at this popular viewing area

For the Florida public SMC

- sent six thousand press kits about manatees to local, state, and national media
- recorded public service announcements for radio and television with singer Jimmy Buffett and with Spanish singer Willie Colon for south Florida audiences
- answered an average of four thousand calls and thousands of letters per month requesting information on manatees
- coordinated a volunteer manatee sighting network in order to assist research and management plans

For teachers and students SMC

- provided free manatee education packets and staff interviews to students and teachers
- distributed the videotape *Manatee Messages: What You Can Do!* to schools in Florida, and manatee coloring books to educators
- offered free in-service training programs for teachers, and volunteer speaker programs for school classes and community groups in Florida

For policy makers SMC

- served on Florida's Manatee Technical Advisory Council, making recommendations on manatee issues to state government
- provided comments on permit applications for marine events and coastal development
- filed legal challenges against development projects that would have potential adverse affects on manatees and manatee habitat
- hired lobbyists in Tallahassee to represent SMC during state legislative sessions
- encouraged grassroots support for legislation like the Manatee License Plate Bill [10]

The SMC continues to develop new strategies and activities on behalf of the beleaguered manatee. Whatever your objective, activities that worked for a similar target audience—interpretive signs, volunteer presentations, media events, silent auctions, political advocacy, or schoolyard ecology programs— may work for you. On the other hand, don't be afraid to try something new. Fresh approaches may succeed because they attract greater media coverage. Sometimes using the mass media to reach multiple audiences or key decision makers may be your most effective strategy. Consideration of the following seven criteria can help you make decisions regarding the activities and messages to use:

1. The background and habits of the target audience
2. Attributes of the message [Does it require background knowledge, maps, graphics, color, or sound?]
3. Urgency of the message [Do you need a response today or next month?]
4. Complexity of the message [Is a thirty-second sound bite adequate for the message or is a lengthy educational publication necessary?]
5. Frequency of the message [Is repetition needed regularly, seasonally, infrequently? Do new people keep joining the target audience?]
6. Personnel required [Is staff time available for personal contact, developing materials, providing outreach activities, interfacing with media, or training volunteers?]
7. Cost [How many of your target audience can be reached, for how long, with what detail, at what price?]

Once you select appropriate activities and media channels, you will need to craft effective messages. Again, understanding the target audience is the key to success. Ideally, an activity and message should appeal to the self-interest of the audience. Consider how an activity, message, or product can increase public recognition, individual profit, favorable attention, or ego satisfaction for members of your audience. The message must focus on identifying the benefits of your organization or the goals that you think are important to the target audience in deciding to adopt a new idea, behavior, or product. The Sierra Club sells calendars, but purchasers are buying not only an organizing tool, but also aesthetic pleasure, and the feeling of helping a good cause. After uncovering the essential human needs or desires lurking under a conservation product, the communicator's task is to reveal the product's benefits, in addition to its features.

In commercial advertising, messages consist of both information and persuasion. For example, in selling a product, marketers provide information about the product name, its benefits, features, and price. Persuasive elements of the message incorporate tactics such as fear, sexiness, or humor to influence their customers. Marketers make good use of our knowledge of human motivations, such as the hierarchy of needs outlined by Maslow (chapter 1) to target needs and desires of their audience. This persuasive component helps sell everything from detergent to beer. Surprisingly, many environmental organizations provide only information and neglect to include persuasive arguments in their messages.

Persuasive arguments can work for conservation causes. Environmental organizations may exploit public fear by emphasizing the negative effects of not heeding their message. The Natural Resources Defense Council (NRDC) exhorted the public to call their congressional representatives and senators to support new air quality standards proposed by the Environmental Protection Agency (EPA). If the new standards don't pass, claimed their ads, "we're left with the current inadequate standards. That means more loss of life every year, and tens of thousands of people—mostly the very young and the elderly—ending up in the hospital." NRDC was successful in generating a groundswell of comments in support of the new standards during the EPA public comment period. "Thousands of people supported the new standards. Many of them were NRDC members who responded to our appeals and called EPA by phone directly. Hundreds more visited the NRDC Web site and then sent e-mails to EPA supporting the new standards."[11]

Positive persuasion focusing on ego gratification or sex appeal also can be effective. Sex appeal sells more than just toothpaste. Environmental organizations employ this tactic when they imply that the audience's attractiveness will increase by heeding their message. A controversial animal rights organization, People for the Ethical Treatment of Animals, used this technique in their "Turn Your Back on Fur" antifur campaign. This campaign was launched in 1996 with a staged media event in Times Square and a full-page ad purchased by the organization in *USA Today.* At the event, models dropped their "unsexy" fur garments on a stage behind a banner, giving the appearance of being nude (fig. 3.2). This event generated print media coverage through the national wire services, and television news coverage on major networks and shows such as *Hard Copy, E,* and *Access Hollywood.*

FIGURE 3.2. *People for the Ethical Treatment of Animals designed an ad to catch the reader's attention and demonstrate that it might be sexier not to wear fur. (Photo by Judson Baker, Boss Models— The world's first fur-free modeling agency; courtesy of PETA)*

More subtle appeals to ego gratification can be seen in conservation fundraising communications. The National Wildlife Federation entices readers to join their Rara Avis Society, described as an exclusive and exciting group of people—"rare birds"—who make donations to NWF in their wills. The literature for joining the group mentions the "tremendous feeling of satisfaction from investing in the conservation of America's wildlife for future generations." Other benefits include personal invitations to a private reception with NWF's president, complimentary newsletter, and a certificate "suitable for framing."

Humor or excitement also appeals to the public by implying that a product or service is more fun than the alternatives. Humor can be used to lighten critical messages or catch an audience's attention. In an advertisement appearing in the January issue of their magazine,[12] The Nature Conservancy presented a tongue-in-cheek list of suggested New Year's resolutions. The ad, displayed on a scrap of paper, read:

> *My New Year's Resolutions*
> 1. Get in shape
> 2. Take more hikes
> 3. Eat more fruits and vegetables
> 4. Include The Nature Conservancy in my will
>
> A Bequest to The Nature Conservancy will make you feel great, too!

In another conservation campaign, The Nature Conservancy designed posters to adorn the walls of ships that ferry hordes of visitors to Block Island off the coast of Rhode Island. One poster to encourage protection of rare plants found on the island, reads in bold, black print: "TO YOU IT'S A MOUNTAIN BIKE. TO THEM IT'S A STEAMROLLER." An illustration of some smashed yellow flowers is followed in small print by: "No, we didn't flatten this beautiful Bushy Rockrose, one of the 40 rare or endangered species that flourishes on the fragile ecosystem of Block Island. And if you call us . . . we'll show you how you can bike, hike and explore this extraordinary island without plowing into the Rockrose, too."

Implementation

Once your audiences, objectives, and potential activities are planned, you are ready to pre-test and implement your campaign.

Pilot Test the Activities

Just like a rehearsal before a theater production, trying out your activities before implementing your communications campaign allows you to fine tune your performance or postpone opening day while changes are made. This is called pilot testing the activities. Pilot tests involve subjecting a small group of the target audience to your planned activity or materials. Pilot tests answer questions such as:

- How do members of the audience react to the activity?
- Which alternative versions of the activities are most successful?
- Does the activity communicate the appropriate message to achieve the objective?
- What feedback do people give about the activity?

Pilot tests are conducted before a program is implemented fully. They help ensure that the activities are effective and allow you to make needed changes before the expense of implementing the entire program.

Methods for collecting data about an activity include focus groups or surveys with members of the target audience similar to those described in chapter 2. For written materials, you can use simple approaches such as portfolio tests. This entails placing the new materials in a folder, alone or with other materials, and asking the test subjects from the target audience for their reactions. The audience can relay their impressions of the materials using ratings or scales (such as *very attractive—attractive—neither attractive nor unattractive—unattractive—very unattractive*). Once feedback is obtained, the activity or materials can be revised, if needed, and pretested again before the campaign is carried out. Pilot testing ensures that the best activities are implemented.

Pilot tests are critical for most communications activities. The Florida Wildlife Federation (FWF) avoided financial heartache by conducting a pilot test. Before the FWF embarked on a new magazine for its members, they wisely pilot tested it. They sent a sample of three hundred members a trial magazine issue with a written survey. The survey asked the members what they liked most and least about the publication, and how much they might pay to receive such a magazine. Based on the negative responses to the survey and the high cost of the project, the FWF rejected the entire activity of publishing a magazine.[13]

Program Operations

Thoughtful planning, from developing goals and objectives to identifying resources and constraints, provides the wood and fire for your campaign blaze. Program implementation is like tending a fire, adjusting the fuel load to get the heat you desire. During implementation you develop a final schedule, budget, and staff duties to ensure your program will run smoothly. The establishment of a system for monitoring program operations ensures that the activities you selected will continue to achieve your objectives. Monitoring tells you when to add more logs or to throw a bucket of water on your blaze.

The following is a hypothetical example of the planning and implementation of a local organization's communications campaign. Although this illustration involves a small club, the same principles apply to the largest conservation organization.

Example: Program Planning and Implementation of the Orange County Nature Club

Mission: Protect the biodiversity of Orange County through citizen initiatives to preserve natural areas.

Problem: The Orange County Nature Club was suffering from declining membership, primarily due to lack of new recruits.

Goal: Increase membership, particularly among young people in this university town.

Target audience: College students

Objectives:

- Audience knowledge—within three months increase awareness by 25 percent among college students about the opportunity to join the Orange County Nature Club.
- Audience behavior—to increase membership by seventy-five new student members within three months.

Target audience research: Through an informal focus group conducted with current student members of the Orange County Nature Club, the following information was gleaned:

- Students joined the Orange County Nature Club mainly to take advantage of the monthly field trips and the chance to meet local environmental activists.

- The time and place of the monthly meetings was convenient for students and did not pose a barrier to joining.

- Student interest probably would come from majors in zoology, wildlife, botany, and forestry.
- Audience media habits included reading the free school newspaper and listening to the local rock radio station.

The Orange County Nature Club staff also reviewed other organizations' marketing attempts that focused on their target audience—students. They observed a campaign initiated by a local shopping mall to attract more college students to its shops. The mall's effort included drawings for repeat shoppers for free merchandise, such as movie tickets, T-shirts, and gift certificates. The mall also expanded its traditional advertising media to include posters on campus, college radio, movie theaters, and a Web site.

Potential messages: The Nature Club developed several persuasive messages for their membership campaign. For example, membership in the Orange County Nature Club will allow students to:

- meet new people and participate in exciting field trips [motivation: sex appeal, social appeal, and fun]
- help save the planet [motivation: ego-satisfaction]
- prevent the surrounding environment from deteriorating [motivation: fear].
- meet people in your field who may be good professional contacts [motivation: personal gain]

Potential activities: A number of communications activities were selected to target the college audience. These included:

- Biweekly advertisements in the college paper for three months. This would cost $2,352 for quarter-page ads ($392 per issue).
- Daily advertisements on the local rock radio station. The radio station agrees to air the thirty-second ad for free as a public service announcement, but the frequency and time of airing cannot be guaranteed. Because student schedules are often unusual, the lack of exposure during prime time is not considered a problem. It beats the alternative of paying $48 for a thirty- or sixty-second spot during prime time.
- Distribution of one free Orange County Nature Club newsletter and membership application to every environmental science major. Printing an eight-page newsletter, from camera-ready copy, for 1,500 students in the departments of wildlife, zoology, botany, and forestry costs $368.
- Visit by guest speakers to student environmental clubs (two/month): eighteen hours of volunteer staff time.
- Raffles held at monthly club meetings. Prizes include free nature club T-shirts and movie tickets donated by the local theater.

Resources and Constraints

Time: The membership committee wants results within three months.

Personnel and schedule: Six volunteers each commit up to two hours a week. The volunteer communications committee designs the radio and newspaper ads within two weeks. Staff work with the newspaper and radio sales office to complete and air the ads. All materials are pilot tested with current student members.

Projected budget: $2,720. To save money, the newspaper ads run for only two weeks. To assess the immediate impact of the ads, the targeted student audience is contacted using informal phone interviews. Additional funds for continuing the ads is allocated based on this evaluation. In addition, Nature Club members prepare a press release about their monthly meeting and invite reporters from the student paper to attend a news conference. A free newspaper article about the event brings more attention about the club to its target audience.

The Orange County Nature Club found that a variety of communications activities are available to inexpensively promote their mission and goals.

Evaluation

The Nature Club's campaign should not end with the implementation phase. Of critical interest is whether more students became aware of the Nature Club. Did club membership increase? Evaluation should occur throughout the life of a communications project. The planning and implementation processes can be carefully assessed through continuous review of goals and objectives and pilot tests of media and messages. Once the activities are executed, the results must be evaluated to see if your intended objectives were achieved.

After any communications program, conservation organizations must ask:

- Are there changes in audience knowledge, attitudes, or skills?
- Are there long-term changes in resource use or participant behavior, or is there increased concern for environmental management or conservation legislation?

Evaluation tells you if the program is worth the time, money, and resources. Is it cost-effective? Does it need modification? Should it be continued? Should the approach or message be adapted for other campaigns?

Program outcomes may be immediate or long term and expected or unanticipated. A number of evaluation techniques are available to assess the products of your programs. The evaluation of your products includes observing post-program changes in the target audience or the conservation concern and making decisions regarding the continuation, expansion, or deletion of your program. Many of the research techniques discussed in chapter 2 provide baseline information for making before and after comparisons. You also can design controlled experiments where, for example, radio ads are used in one market and newspaper ads are used in another. Results can then be compared to test the efficacy of different media. Results often are evaluated in terms of changes in public awareness, attitudes, or behaviors, and cost-effectiveness and efficiency of the program. The evaluation phase of program development is essential to long-term success. Chapter 7 discusses evaluation methods in detail.

Communication Strategies and Actions

As shown in box 3.2, potential activities for communications campaigns fall within five broad categories: political, informational, promotional, organizational, and educational and interpretive.

The following descriptions will assist you in choosing the best activities, based on your constraints, opportunities, and target audiences. If some approaches seem too expensive or labor intensive, consider forming partnerships with other organizations or industry groups with common interests. Knowledge of the myriad approaches available is helpful in brainstorming strategies for your own goals and objectives. Activities for communications with the public and decision makers fall within the general areas of political action, information dissemination, promotion and marketing, organizational development, and educational and interpretive programs. Examples of each are described below.

Political Activities

Garnering political action in support of your organization or mission involves a variety of possibilities, each with its own procedures. You can use communications in many ways to harness government support. In these types of campaigns, the target audience consists of politicians or other government officials. The key to success in building political support lies in ensuring that the activity is in the politician's self-interest. The action should promote the official's political agenda to a segment of his or her constituency. If the action is obviously in the public interest, sponsorship should be easy to find. If it is controversial, constituents will need to be visibly supportive of the action. A few examples of political or official actions in support of conservation causes are presented here.

Official Proclamations and Legislation

A phone call to the mayor's or governor's office will provide you with the procedures for drafting and submitting an official proclamation, such as "adopt-a-tree day," "eagle week," "John Muir highway," or whatever promotes your particular cause and links to other activities in your strategy. A draft of the proclamation can be provided to the policy maker's staff for feedback and approval.

Box 3.2. A sampler of communication strategies and actions

Political Activities
- Official proclamations and legislation
- Lobbying
- Indirect lobbying
- Public hearings
- Special-issue stamps

Public Information Activities
- News or media conference
- Personality appearance, spokesperson tour
- Speakers bureau
- Information booths and exhibits
- Contests
- Billboards and posters
- Special events

Promotional Activities
- Public Service Announcements and community calendars
- Spectacles
- Marketing activities
- Drama and the arts
- Fund-raising
- Research findings
- Community relations

Organizational Activities
- Establishing an organization
- Building partnerships
- Meetings, conventions, and seminars

Educational and Interpretive Activities
- Classes and presentations
- Production of posters
- Publication of brochures
- Audiovisual materials
- Tours
- Exhibits
- Websites

A city, township, county, state, province, legislative body, governor, or president can make proclamations. Proclamations of support by a local government body can help give greater prominence to a conservation concern.

A proclamation should include descriptions of

- who or what is to be commemorated and the thing (day, street, park, etc.) being proclaimed
- any pertinent background about the subject
- how the subject of the proclamation relates to the city, county, or state
- why the subject of the proclamation is important
- the current status of the subject

Example: A Proclamation Promoted by Earth Day Organizers in 1996 and Approved by the City Council of Saint Paul, Minnesota

The City of Saint Paul

Proclamation

Whereas, Earth Day is an annual opportunity to remember that all of us depend on the Earth for our well-being and our survival; and

Whereas, all people benefit by slowing down the rate at which we deplete the Earth's natural resources; and

Whereas, the City of Saint Paul is committed to keeping its house in order to develop a sustainable environment and economy, making our City facilities more energy efficient, recycling, making City operations more effective by using fast, no-cost communications methods and adding vehicles that use efficient alternative fuels to the City fleet;

Whereas, the City has also worked hard to clean up contaminated land to prepare it for economic development and to separate storm and sanitary sewer systems to make our river cleaner; and

Whereas, we all need to join together to improve the environment in our region; and

Whereas, Monday, April 22, 1996, is the Twenty-sixth Earth Day;

Now Therefore, I, Norm Coleman, Mayor of the City of Saint Paul, do hereby proclaim Monday, April 22, 1996, to be Earth Day in the City of Saint Paul, and encourage all City employees and citizens to make one extra gesture to help this effort.

Proclamations help draw attention to a cause and can lure local media interest. Issues of broader concern may warrant having a document read into the Congressional Record of the U.S. Congress by convincing a member of your state or district legislative delegation to request it. The document should have some public interest, or be in the interest of a segment of a legislator's constituency. Reprints of the proclamation are valuable for publicity when distributed to the press afterward.

A bill also can be drafted, reviewed by an attorney, and submitted for consideration to a legislator. If a bill is in the public interest, lawmakers may bring the bill to Congress. The nonprofit organization Save America's Forests promoted the *Act to Save America's Forests* in 1997. It proposed a ban on clearcutting on all federal lands and called for the end of logging and road building in the last core areas of forest biodiversity—defined as ancient forests, roadless and watershed areas, and over one hundred "special" forests. SAF helped draft the bill with Congressional sponsors from New Jersey, California, and New York. According to executive director Carl Ross, "The Act to Save America's Forests couldn't pass in 1997 because of the make-up of Congress, but we're building support for future passage of the act."

Lobbying

Lobbying provides information to lawmakers that influences them for or against something. Individuals and organizations use this technique to inform legislators of their conservation concerns and their views on pending bills. The term "lobbying" originated from the practice of talking to legislators in the lobby outside their chamber. Sophisticated lobbying now goes way beyond a chat in the hallway.

Although lobbying is a form of free speech, federal and state laws govern lobbying activities, registration, and reporting. The Internal Revenue Service also restricts lobbying by tax-exempt organizations. If your group is legally unable to lobby in its own name, volunteers who agree with your cause may lobby as individual citizens. Also a variety of activities that are not considered lobbying, such as sending briefing papers and other informational materials to policy makers, can help communicate to politicians about favorable public opinion supporting legislation.

Lobbying is one of the main functions of some organizations. The Center for Marine Conservation (CMC) has lobbyists and a legal staff that advocate protection of marine ecosystems, such as the Florida Keys, the central California coast, and Puget Sound. They attempt to have special areas designated as National Marine Sanctuaries or protected areas. CMC also lobbies to improve marine protection measures through the Clean Water Act and other ocean and coastal laws.[14]

The Florida Audubon Society produced a Citizen's Guide to the Local Government Comprehensive Planning Act. The purpose was to help citizens participate in the process of developing local land development plans and regulations. The authors, attorneys Casey and David Gluckman, offer the following tips for effectively lobbying public officials. As attorneys, they also point out that verbal persuasion is much more cost-effective than a legal battle. Here are their rules for effective lobbying:[15]

MEET IN PERSON. Face-to-face contact is the strongest type of communication, and often is how business gets done. Prepare for the meeting or hearing in advance. Make sure you are certain of the points you want to make and can provide whatever back-up evidence is available. If you can't visit with the elected official immediately, a personal letter followed by a visit also can be effective. The Gluckmans suggest sending telegrams or overnight letters to add a sense of urgency to your correspondence.

DRESS PROFESSIONALLY. Your neat, clean appearance will make an important first impression. The Gluckmans generally recommend "overdressing" in business clothes.

BE BRIEF. Explain the purpose of your visit and your main points and supporting data in a well-organized manner. Emphasize your "take home message" succinctly. Spend no more than 15 minutes, or if you have been allotted a certain amount of time, do not exceed it unless the official encourages you to do so. Bring visual aids like photographs or maps to add interest to your discussion, but only if they emphasize your presentation and your key point.

BE FACTUAL. Tell the truth. Present the facts in an accurate and sincere manner. Overwrought, emotional outbursts seldom further your cause.

BE CREDIBLE. Explain both sides of the issue. Raise your opponents' concerns and explain why they are not valid.

BE PLEASANT. Officials will be more likely to talk to you and help you if you show good humor. Don't publicly argue with officials. "Discuss" disagreements, don't create embarrassing confrontations that won't further your cause.

LISTEN CAREFULLY. Good lobbying requires good listening skills. In a personal conversation, acknowledge what the official says to you. Say something affirmative like, "That's an interesting point," to signal your attentiveness. Empathize with the official's position, wants, and needs. Know your audience, and your point of view will be better received.

MAKE ADVANCE CONTACT. Talk to officials before a public meeting occurs. Often decisions are made *before* the public hearing occurs. Influence the decisions before minds are set. In fact, for organizations that regularly lobby lawmakers, establishing long-term relationships are one key to success.

DELIVER YOUR MESSAGE PERSUASIVELY. In making a public presentation, make eye contact with public officials. Practice in advance so you do not feel compelled to read your statement. If you've done your homework, you will have the facts and the main points you want to make at your fingertips.

PROVIDE SUMMARY DOCUMENTS. Provide a summary or short fact sheet that you can leave with the official. It should state the issue, present your position, and outline the reasons for your position. Make documents clear, complete, and brief. In Florida, citizens can ask to have materials entered into the public record at local commission meetings. If lawsuits ensue, data in the public record can be used as evidence in a legal finding.

If you feel hesitant about approaching your legislators, here's what Susan Hughes, a participant in the National Audubon Society Lobby Day writes about her experience with grassroots lobbying for their Population and Habitat Campaign:[16]

> Lobbying doesn't take a long time and you don't need to memorize reams of data to do it. Sometimes it's efficient to say, "I'm here because I feel strongly about this issue. I have studied it sufficiently to know that I am convinced that action X is the correct one because not doing X will have a detrimental impact on birds, wildlife, and habitat, and these are things about our world that are deeply important to me, and my family, and the people I know and care about. I have some materials here that will provide you the details, and if you want more information, just call me and I will make sure you get the information you need."
>
> If you have never lobbied or visited with your elected officials, you should give it a try. Start at home with a visit to a local official or to one of your national representatives during an at-home time. That may help you feel more at ease. Take someone along. That always helps, because you can share duties and back one another up with information to make sure all the crucial points get covered. . . . The most important thing is to express informed concerns validated by personal commitment. That's something each of us has.

Indirect (Grass-Roots) Lobbying

Organizations also can influence the legislative process by organizing voters to bring pressure to bear on a legislature or rule-making body. In their fight to "Save Kanapaha Prairie," a local homeowner's association collected over two thousand signatures for a petition to their county commissioners who were to vote on whether to allow a large housing development on the prairie. The homeowners won their battle with a 3–2 vote of the commissioners.

In the summer of 1997, World Wildlife Fund (WWF) generated over nineteen thousand signatures on a petition to President Clinton urging him to take a stand against whaling, which WWF says has almost tripled in Norway and Japan since 1992. The petition urged the president: "Whales have no voice to speak for their protection in the world's policy arena. You can speak on their behalf."[17]

As part of their 1995 battle to get Congress to repeal, or President Clinton to veto, the timber salvage rider, the nonprofit Save America's Forests (SAF) started a "Repeal the Rider" campaign that reached over a million people. The timber salvage rider, attached to the 1995 Recisions (budget-cutting) Act, allowed accelerated salvage cutting of timber on federal lands and suspended all environmental laws or citizen challenges to the cutting. SAF sent out thousands of packets with information and sample petitions to members and prospective members, urging them to write letters to Congress. SAF leaders also spoke on hundreds of radio programs. Finally, a full-page letter was printed as an ad in a national magazine, urging President Clinton to demand repeal of the rider by threatening a veto. The effort was initially unsuccessful, but supporters of timber salvage later were unable to gain enough support to renew the rider, which expired at the end of 1996. "The timber salvage rider became one of the most unpopular environmental actions of the Clinton administration," said coordinator Carl Ross. "Creating so much national attention and causing the rider to expire was a great victory for us."[18]

Public Hearings

Public hearings give citizen groups still another opportunity to communicate with the public or public officials. Here your objectives may be twofold. First, to get your views before the regulatory agency or legislative body holding the hearing. Second, to get your views to the general public through the press. The following suggestions were published by the U.S. Environmental Protection Agency Office of Public Affairs to help maximize benefits from participating in a public hearing.[19]

Before the hearing

1. Make copies of your easy-to-read typewritten statement.
2. Prepare an advance press release (see chapter 4). Send the release and a

copy of your full statement to the press the day before the hearing. Be sure both the release and the statement are marked "Advance Copy—Not for release until. . . ." [Insert date and time when you expect to present the statement].

3. If possible, deliver the release and the statement personally to your press contacts. If you can't, call and tell them the release and statement are on the way. Don't waste the reporter's time by trying to discuss or read the release or statement over the phone—unless you are asked to. This advance work reminds the press that the hearing is coming up. If they cannot cover the hearing themselves, at least they have your statement.

At the hearing

1. Have enough copies of your prepared statement for each member of the committee, board, or commission conducting the hearing, plus some extras for their files. Have copies for the press too, along with your press release.

2. When you're called to testify, be brief, no more than four or five minutes, but request that your full statement be included in the hearing record.

3. Begin with your name, address, title or group affiliation, and cite other groups, if any, that support your position and have asked you to say so.

4. Tell why you support—or oppose—the subject under consideration. Give facts to back up your position. Don't make charges or accusations you cannot prove.

5. If appropriate, explain how the issue and the costs and benefits affect public interest.

6. If you have several speakers, avoid repetition unless special emphasis is desired. Have each cover a different point, or approach the problem from a different aspect.

7. Speak clearly—loudly enough to be heard, slowly enough to be understood, but quickly enough to hold attention.

8. Be prepared to answer questions—to explain your position, to explain the nature of your group, how your group's position was reached (executive board vote, membership meeting, mail referendum, etc.). If you don't know the answer to a question, say so. Don't bluff. Offer to get the answer and send it in for the record. On rare occasions, a committee member may attempt to rattle, confuse, irritate, or intimidate you. Don't let yourself get confused, angry, or nasty.

9. Try to have many supporters attend the meeting even though they will not testify. Casually mention their presence in the audience in your opening remarks. [Have them raise their hands or stand up.] Some call this "packing a hearing." Others call it "showing strength and support."

Numbers reinforce your stand. An indication of the broad support can sway legislators as well as public opinion.

10. Listen carefully to other statements presented, especially by the opposition. Make note of factual errors or new ideas or proposals, for you may be asked to comment on what other witnesses say. If so, don't attack the opposition or make personal remarks.

11. Respect the right of others to disagree with you. Do not applaud or show disapproval of any speaker.

12. If you have written statements of community leaders or other organizations that support your position but could not attend the hearing, ask that the statements be included in the record.

13. Thank the committee or board or commission for giving you the opportunity to testify.

After the hearing

1. Promptly prepare and submit answers to any questions you were asked but could not answer at the hearing. If you think any comments made by the opposition were factually incorrect or need rebuttal, prepare and submit a supplementary statement for the record. But don't rehash what was said in your original statement.

2. If your press contacts wrote or broadcasted stories containing your views, call them, congratulate them on their good reporting, and thank them for the coverage.

3. Don't complain to the press if your views weren't included in their coverage, if you think the coverage was bad, or if you think you were misquoted.

4. A few days after the hearing, consider sending a letter to the editor (see chapter 4) for publication, referring to the hearing, and try to point out what the public can do to help.

5. Inform your own members about what happened at the hearing through your organization's newsletter, or send a special letter to all members with copies of press clippings, if any.

Building support for your views by testifying at a hearing or by submitting a written statement before the deadline for comments is one useful strategy to affect local conservation problems."[20]

Special-Issue Stamps

Stamps honoring contributions to American life may be proposed to the Citizen's Stamp Advisory Committee of the U.S. Postal Service. The Postal Service produces a brochure describing the procedure for proposing stamps. Anything can be commemorated, from a landmark court decision to a prominent

FIGURE 3.3. *Special stamps were produced in Pakistan to raise public awareness for endangered Siberian Cranes.*

person. The most celebrated stamps of 1990 originated as an attempt to call attention to the danger of unsustainable whale hunts. The effort grew into a block of four marine mammal stamps, jointly issued by the U.S. Postal Service and the former Soviet Union. The stamps featured killer whales, dolphins, sea lions, and sea otters. The main constraint to this activity is a three-year lag time between the time a subject is nominated and a stamp is made. Also, the Postal Service receives over forty thousand proposals a year, further reducing your chances.

In other countries, it may be easier to have the stamp of your dreams issued. In India, the International Crane Foundation worked with other organizations to convince the postal service to issue a stamp of the endangered Siberian Crane to commemorate an International Crane Conference held in Bharatpur. Within a few years, postal authorities in all four countries represented at the conference and within the range of Siberian Cranes (Pakistan, China, Mongolia, and Russia) were persuaded to issue similar stamps (fig. 3.3).[21]

Public Information Activities

Media conferences, special events, and a variety of other techniques can help you deliver conservation information to your audience. From a poetry contest to a billboard, the following examples successfully spread a conservation message. The use of mass media for conservation is described in detail in chapter 4.

News or Media Conference

A news conference announces significant news to the mass media. A knowledgeable spokesperson for your organization announces timely information about a new conservation program, new director, new scientific finding, or new angle on an old issue. When The Nature Conservancy brokered a multi-partner ecosystem management program for almost a million acres of coastal forests in the Southeast, the federal, state, and private landowners held a joint media event to announce their new partnership. They invited over fifty media representatives from local television, radio, and newspapers. Partner spokespeople delivered a carefully scripted message designed to accurately describe the partnership goals and to allay any fears of private property owners in the region. Chapter 4 describes the mechanisms for staging a news conference.

Personality Appearance, Spokesperson Tour

Some organizations select a celebrity or expert to represent and disseminate information about their organization, product, or service. Resource management agencies sometimes use experts to rally the public to their cause, while environmental organizations have successfully employed celebrities. The success of the Save the Manatee Club was in part due to singer Jimmy Buffett's widespread popularity. The Sea Shepherd Conservation Society has garnered public support from musicians and movie stars like Mick Jagger, Julian Lennon, Steven Seagal, Cher, Pierce Brosnan, and Woody Harrelson.

The Center for Wildlife Information in Montana got a boost from retired General Norman Schwarzkopf, the popular U.S. military leader, nicknamed "The Bear," who was photographed holding a teddy bear in a bunker during the 1991 Persian Gulf War. Schwarzkopf is now the national spokesman for grizzly bear recovery efforts of the Center for Wildlife Information. During a June 1997 visit to Yellowstone National Park to see how military technology such as Global Positioning Systems can be used to track grizzlies, Schwarzkopf said, "I'm very much interested in anything having to do with grizzly bears in the Lower 48. I want to see them survive as a symbol of the American wilderness."[22]

A number of environmental groups rely on celebrity figures to lend their names to a project to pique the media's and the public's interest. When the African Wildlife Foundation was in the midst of a public education campaign against the ivory trade to protect endangered elephants, its campaign theme was incorporated into a *General Hospital* soap opera episode. One of the show's characters was working to stop the slaughter of elephants.

Many celebrities record public service announcements (PSAs) for good causes. Robert Redford spoke out about energy conservation in a PSA for the Safe Energy Communication Council. When some of Co-op America's more conspicuous members—the rock group R.E.M.—were interviewed for a *Spin* magazine article about the band, R.E.M. members mentioned in detail their admiration of Co-op America's work. Another musician, Dan Fogelberg, conducted a concert tour in which he promoted the importance of becoming a member of the Wilderness Society, and the need to fight for the society's causes.[23]

Speakers Bureau

Organizations and agencies can provide experts, trained employees, or volunteers to speak at programs of clubs, service organizations, and schools. This provides valuable publicity for the sponsoring organization and offers vital information to interested audiences. Reaching out to the public through organized presentations and lectures allows organizations to make direct contact with specific groups. Docent programs at zoos often bring live animals and slide-shows to schools. The outreach program for the Weeks Bay Estuarine Research Reserve in Fairhope, Alabama, reached 1,600 local members of civic organizations, clubs, and church groups in 1997 through presentations on coastal habitats and the estuarine environment. About half of these presentations were conducted at the Weeks Bay educational center, while staff attended functions such as the local Kiwanis Club meetings for the other half. A dozen volunteers work in the outreach program and are responsible for attending regional events, like the Annual Arts and Crafts Festival, in order to educate visitors through a booth that provides information about the Weeks Bay reserve.

Many speakers bureaus are dependent primarily on volunteer staff, since this activity can be labor intensive unless the target audience is small. The Carolina Raptor Center in Charlotte, North Carolina, conducts programs that take birds, such as red-tailed hawks and great horned owls, into the schools and to other organizations. Staff and a dedicated cadre of volunteers offer live performances on topics such as Raptors and North American Culture, Amazing Adaptations, and Predators from the Sky. With their Wild Wings traveling program, staff members take the birds on the road for a week, stopping at schools across North and South Carolina. In 1997, the Carolina Raptor Center reached 29,802 people through its speakers bureau.

Information Booths and Exhibits

This activity allows you to dispense information to a group of people gathered in one location. Depending on the occasion and expected crowd, this can be a good way to interact with a target audience. Exhibits, or kiosks, can be designed to travel from event to event. These are popular among both state agencies and nongovernmental organizations (NGOs) to raise public awareness about their mission or specific activities. Events that allow such exhibits include fairs, art shows, outdoor concerts, conventions, and national or regional meetings.

The Partners in Flight program of the Florida Game and Fresh Water Fish Commission sets up a kiosk at state fairs and meetings (see fig. 5.3). Joni Blakeslee, the agency's education specialist, describes the exhibit:

> The objective of the table top exhibit is to increase citizen involvement in the conservation of neotropical migrant species.

The exhibit introduces Florida as an important stopover area for migrants and suggests actions each individual can take to help these birds survive. I believe attractive art is the key to piquing people's interest in an exhibit. If they only read the bold print they will still walk away with some knowledge. Narrowing down to "sound bite" information for this exhibit was quite a task. For people interested in more detail, additional information is available in handouts that accompany the exhibit.

Four Partners in Flight educational exhibits were designed, produced, and distributed for display at festivals and presentations. In one year, the exhibit was displayed at the following events (number of people reached in parentheses): League of Environmental Educators of Florida Conference (300), Native Plant Conference (425), Mt. Dora Garden Festival (1,500), Homosassa State Park Visitor Center (10,000), Department of Education's Environmental Education Fair and Symposium (200), Leadership Ocala Community Service Fair (150), Project WILD teacher training weekend (90), and Song Day Festivals (1050).

"The cost of the exhibits ($1,030, including use fees for the photographs), was kept at a minimum by doing some leg work myself. Since most of the cost in exhibits is the designing stage, I wrote the text, priced materials, found the photographs, and had them enlarged. I worked with a local sign shop who produced the vinyl lettering and assembled each panel," explains Blakeslee.

Contests

Competitions to establish the best, biggest, fastest, ugliest, or most beautiful "whatever" can inspire interest among audiences. Awarding a prize for the best nature poem or artwork can help increase public awareness about the mission and activities of your organization. Competitions for designs for logos and T-shirts help involve the public in an entertaining way.

The Nature Conservancy promotes an annual "Wildlife and Wild Places" photography contest in their magazine, *Nature Conservancy*. In their recent contest, over two thousand hopeful photographers entered over ten thousand photos. Winning photographs were reproduced in the magazine and prizes awarded by sponsoring businesses.

The International Rivers Network (IRN), a California-based nonprofit organization, links human rights with environmental protection to promote sound river management. They developed the River of Words Project with former U.S. poet laureate Robert Haas. This national initiative sponsors an environmental poetry and art contest for children on the theme of watersheds. A fifty-page curriculum guide combines the arts with natural resource conservation issues and is distributed to schools and libraries. In 1998, over ten thousand schoolchildren entered the contest (fig. 3.4). Each year eight national

FIGURE 3.4. *Winning poetry and art entries in the River of Words competition form an exhibit that travels to public libraries and schools.*

grand prize winners and one teacher-of-the-year are selected to attend ceremonies in Washington, D.C.

Mt. Kinabalu National Park in Malaysian Borneo sponsors an arduous run up Mt. Kinabalu (13,455 ft./4,101 meters) every year. The race attracts residents from surrounding villages to compete in the grueling run or to cheer their friends. The contest brings a different clientele to the park on an annul basis and promotes interest and good will locally.

Billboards and Posters

A wide range of media from billboards, which many environmental groups shun, to signs or displays in airports, health clubs, subways, or buses can be used to spread a conservation message. These are often low cost, but the message must be simple. This medium does not allow much detail and people frequently only glance at the material. Signs are often hit-or-miss and do not generally allow you to target a specific audience.

A good example was given earlier in this chapter of the series of conservation posters placed on ferries to Block Island, Rhode Island. The Nature Conservancy designed the posters in an effort to mitigate the environmental impact of the hordes of tourists. One poster depicting some small beetles, simply said: "To you it's a morning jog. To them it's a cluster bomb."

FIGURE 3.5. *A highway billboard advertises the protection of the Florida panther, funded by the Florida Advisory Council for Environmental Education. (Photo by the Florida Advisory Council for Environmental Education)*

The Florida Advisory Council on Environmental Education provided a $73,000 grant to the Florida Outdoor Advertising Association, Inc., to implement a statewide public advertising campaign promoting the protection of the Florida panther and awareness of the Florida panther license plate (fig. 3.5). Money raised from the panther license plate helps fund nongame wildlife programs in Florida. The campaign bought space for two years on 270 billboards throughout the state. Done partly as a public service by the association, the billboards had a total value of $300,000.

Special Events

Celebrations can mark a special day, week, or month to recognize a memorable time such as an anniversary, a national activity such as Arbor Day, or a naturally occurring event such as spring wildflowers, fall bird migrations, the solstice, or a full moon. The evening of the spring equinox is celebrated at Florida's Kanapaha Botanical Gardens with wandering musicians and guided walks in the full moon. The moonlit evenings include music, refreshments, and telescopes for astronomical observations. Paper lanterns and floating candles are set up throughout the gardens to guide visitors along the paths. In addition, the gift shop profits from selling glow jewelry for patrons to wear during the evening event. Over one thousand visitors attend the event, many of whom are new to the gardens. Director Don Goodman says, "These events are principally fund raisers for operating revenue, and to provide us with increased exposure to the community. We know that people wait for these events because our phones start ringing off the hook a few weeks before the full moon."

A profusion of fall wildflowers after a summer prescribed burn stimulated Morningside Nature Center in north Florida to offer weekend wildflower walks for the public. Color photographs published in the local paper helped draw a crowd to visit the city park and hear about the benefits of prescribed burning to native plants.

Events also can be planned to attract media coverage and generate publicity. For example, groundbreaking activities for a new building can be cause for media attention and can help to get the word out. With this goal, target audiences include the participants in the event and also the people who will receive the message via the evening news or the local paper.

Example: Planning a Special Event, the Tiger Creek Jamboree

The Nature Conservancy in Florida planned a special event to communicate with the public. The following plan was outlined by Tricia Martin, Community Relations Manager for The Nature Conservancy in Florida. The Tiger Creek Jamboree celebrated the twenty-fifth anniversary of TNC's Tiger Creek Preserve, a 4,700-acre parcel of unique scrub in central Florida.

Objective of Event
To introduce new audiences to The Nature Conservancy and the Tiger Creek Preserve.

Audiences
- TNC volunteers and members
- Neighbors
- Families and retirees that have had no previous contact with TNC
- Partner organizations

Messages to Communicate
- TNC preserves biodiversity
- TNC is a good land manager
- TNC is a vital member of the community
- Florida's ancient scrub is a fascinating ecosystem that must be protected

Media
- Exhibits
- TNC literature
- Naturalist-led hikes and hayrides
- Free lunch

Desired Behaviors of Audience after Attending Program
- Support Tiger Creek Program
- Become members and financially support TNC work
- Speak well of TNC in the community
- Volunteer for TNC

Time Constraints
- Planning for the twenty-fifth-anniversary celebration started in May 1996, eight months before the January 1997 Jamboree.
- Printed materials were needed by mid-December.
- In September, advance publicity began by placing announcements in other organizations' publications, such as local Audubon chapter newsletters and native plant society bulletins.
- Date planning completed: mid-November

Planning Requirements for Individual Activities
- Parking: select lots, draw map, plan for overflow parking.
- Site preparation: recruit six volunteers to set up.
- Volunteer coordination: Check-in station, colored T-shirts for easy identification by visitors.
- T-shirts: one design for volunteers, one for sale to visitors.
- Music: Country music station (WPCV of Lakeland) recruited.
- Food: Provided by Woody's Bar-B-Q.
- Guided hikes: TNC partners and regional office staff asked to lead the guided hikes.
- Games for kids: "Scrub Species in Jeopardy" (game already developed by TNC staff).
- Guided hayrides: Commissioned from local farmer.
- Displays: Subjects will include bird census program results; rare plants and monitoring program; prescribed fire program; endangered gopher frogs at TCP; hydrological monitoring description; and a Wildlife Corridor map that recognizes TNC partners and celebrates the more than 200,000-acre (80,000-hectare) corridor of which Tiger Creek is a part.
- Nature artists exhibit entitled "Conservation on Canvas": Local artist

Tom Freeman will set up an easel and paint a local scene while his nature paintings are displayed for sale.

- TNC information booth: T-shirt sales and membership information.
- Partner organization booth: Florida Trail Association will provide its own materials.
- First aid: ask local Emergency Medical Service volunteers to attend.
- Photography: David to take photos, try for someone to take video coverage.
- Clean-up: between 5 P.M. and dark; recruit eight volunteers to work with four staff.
- Volunteers: training and orientation arranged for the week before the event.

Results of the Special Event

Seventy-one volunteers donated a total of 397 hours to the Jamboree. TNC was successful at generating in-kind services and moderately successful in obtaining donations for the Jamboree. TNC received the support of two corporations: $500 donated from the Florida Power Corporation and $150 from a local bank. Individual donations totaled $370. A number of organizations donated in-kind services, such as a barbecue restaurant and two radio stations. Merchandise sales totaled $925. Garden Club donations came to $225. Total expenses, including the Conservation on Canvas exhibit were $6,200.

Staff counted 1,305 participants; more than double the number anticipated. Martin could not attribute the popularity of the event to any one thing. A number of factors contributed, including free food, good media coverage, and beautiful weather (fig. 3.6).

FIGURE 3.6. *Free food, music, and other attractions offer incentives for the public to attend a conservation event. (Photo by S.K. Jacobson)*

Some visitors walked almost a mile to get to the event. The old-time nature of the event also appealed to people—some waited for two hours to go on a hayride. People also picked up printed material on Tiger Creek and TNC. On the day of the event two people became TNC members and six people completed volunteer information forms. After the event, TNC received additional phone calls and visits from people wanting to learn more about Tiger Creek and TNC. TNC staff also observed more hikers at the preserve in subsequent weeks.

The staff also learned from the event and made the following recommendations for future events:

- Plan to accommodate larger crowds, seek additional sponsors early in the process, and involve the local audience in planning the event.
- Provide a TNC contribution bucket and make membership booths, brochures, and TNC merchandise more visible.
- Post signs regarding pets, trail trampling, and other regulations.
- Develop a visitor survey to gather specific feedback.

Promotional Activities

Promoting your conservation cause requires careful planning and creativity. Agencies seldom contemplate advertising and marketing their products and services, yet conservation objectives can often be furthered by just such an approach.

Public Service Announcements and Community Calendars

Print and broadcast media in most areas regularly include calendars listing community events. To spread the word about your activities, send the editor a brief press release about your special event—outlining who you are, what the event is, where and when it will take place, and why it is significant. If you can provide the paper with a photograph or artwork to publish in the newspaper calendar of events, more people will notice your activity. For radio and television coverage, provide a completed, professional-quality audio- or videotaped public service announcement (PSA) with the help of a supportive recording studio. Chapter 4 provides guidelines and examples of advertisements and PSAs.

Spectacles

Creating a spectacle at the correct time will attract media coverage. Activists protesting a proposed dam or clear-cut forest have suspended themselves from construction sites and trees with the hope of appearing in the paper or on television to publicize their cause. Lofting colorful banners has served a similar purpose. For example, in 1989 a New York barge and its load of garbage was rejected from ports around the world and forced to return to its home harbor. Greenpeace activists swam to the barge and unfurled a banner reading Next Time Try Recycling. International media broadcast photos of the event.

Environmental activists in Arizona dramatized the relationship between the state's environmental regulators and an incinerator company by dragging a bed to the steps of the Capitol and putting effigies of the government officials and alleged polluters in bed together. The activists threatened to remain "until the government gets out of bed with the polluters." Television stations broadcast updates from the bed.[24] To protest an operating incinerator in Greenpoint, New York, the New York Public Interest Research Group put up signs along part of the famous New York marathon route in Greenpoint. The series of signs asked: "Are you breathing more heavily? Do you know why?" The signs pointed out local pollution problems and brought their cause to runners and media alike at this highly visible event.[25]

A visual replica of a problem or threat—of endangered species like blue whales or environmental threats like toxic waste—can increase awareness among the public that views it and often attracts media attention to reach a much broader audience. Protesters in Utah opposed a proposed nuclear waste storage site by "dumping" a 20-foot- (6-meter) tall inflatable radioactive waste barrel on the Capitol steps.[26] The environmental organization Earth First! has received tremendous publicity for its activities, from tree sitting to road blockades, publicizing the need to protect natural areas. Their dramatic exploits often attracted media attention where more staid approaches had received less coverage.

The Ancient Forest Rescue Expedition of the Northwest Ecosystems Alliance (NWEA) hauled an enormous old-growth log around the nation on a flatbed truck to educate the public about the continued logging of old-growth forests in the northwestern United States. The log truck took four tours across the country. In the spring of 1991, the tour carried a 7-foot-wide by 28-foot-long, (2-by-8.5 meter) 730-year-old Douglas fir log. "Each day involved one or two press conferences—usually at a truck stop and a final venue, such as a museum or university—and an evening show, including slides, speeches, and music," said NWEA's Mitch Friedman. "The actual shows drew between five and one hundred people or more, thousands saw us on the highway and at truck stops and mall parking lots, and millions saw us on TV and in newspaper photos and articles" (fig. 3.7).

In 1993 the tour went across the country under the auspices of the Western Ancient Forest Campaign. Karen Wood, who led the trip on its final 1993 leg from Washington, D.C., to Olympia, Washington, says, "The log had an instant, strong, and hopefully abiding impact on all the people who came to

FIGURE 3.7. *The Northwest Ecosystems Alliance toured the United States with an old-growth log to draw attention to unsustainable logging practices. (Photo by Daniel Dancer)*

see it." She explains that people in the West often take ancient forests and big trees on log trucks for granted. "Anywhere else in the country, people are appalled. We need to get the information to them about what is really happening—what 'old growth' really means. The log was the most effective tool I've ever been able to use at accomplishing that."

Marketing Activities

Organizations can match their products with the needs of their target audiences. T-shirts, guidebooks, photographs, notecards, and calendars are all familiar products for sale by environmental organizations. They help advertise the organization, raise funds, and build membership through incentives like gifts or member discounts.

For example, the National Wildlife Federation (NWF) has an entire catalog of products that complements their membership and other fundraising efforts by reaching two million active customers and millions of nonmembers each year. Because the organization is nonprofit, all catalog items must be related to the NWF mission. The order form tells customers about NWF and invites them to become members. "Every catalog item is reviewed for accuracy by a naturalist and reviewed for its mission-related content by a lawyer to insure that this activity maintains our nonprofit status," explains NWF's

Susan Boghosian. The catalog includes computer items, gifts, apparel, and children's toys. Boghosian says that catalog sales support NWF by both generating revenue and providing mission-related information to new audiences. She mentions some other ways that NWF promotes their catalog sales: "We've begun to participate in some catalog showcases in magazines. We've also recently done a press kit for our business-to-business card catalog and sent it to business publications around the country. We've done the same for our regular catalog, and have gotten a lot of free publicity that way."[27] The National Wildlife Federation's 1997 Annual Report noted that 39 percent of their 1996 income ($37.2 million) came from the sale of "nature education materials," which included catalog sales as well as sales of publications and other materials.

The "adoption" of various endangered species or parcels of land for a fee can provide funds for an organization as well as opportunities for providing scientific information to the public. The Caribbean Conservation Corporation (CCC) has provided endangered sea turtles for adoption through their Tortuguero Sea Turtle research program. Every turtle is tagged with a unique number to enable researchers to track its fate. Conveniently, these numbers can be used to give each person who donates $25 or more a unique turtle for adoption. The donor receives a personalized adoption certificate, tag information on his or her specific turtle, an information packet, and a sea turtle distribution map. Higher-level donors receive gifts such as a pewter hatchling turtle key ring, logo T-shirt, books about turtles, or a sterling silver logo lapel pin. CCC adopts out about one thousand turtles each year. Revenues are used to fight development in sea turtle nesting beaches, advocate for policies to prevent sea turtle deaths from fishing and ocean garbage, and prevent water pollution.

Many environmental and conservation organizations offer a variety of products, services, personal opportunities, and social goods to the public. Marketing involves communicating the benefits of your products or services to the public in an effective manner.

Example: Marketing Products and Services by Urban Foresters in Ohio[28]

Urban forestry programs in Ohio have recognized that in addition to their traditional role of planting and maintaining public trees, citizen awareness and participation are key to their successful operation and financial support. Forester Sievert cites the many benefits of public support and participation in urban forestry programs.[29] Homeowners take better care of city trees on their property if they feel they have an investment in them. Enlisting volunteers can decrease costs and increase the reach of municipal tree programs. Public support can translate into a lobby for sustaining budget allocations during times of fiscal austerity.

Urban foresters have used a variety of approaches and activities to increase public participation and support of shade tree programs in Ohio's cities. Some programs are intended to increase awareness while others provide enhanced community services. Media coverage of the various activities has helped maximize their impacts by reaching many taxpayers, not just those involved in the programs. Sievert believes city tree programs get short-changed during budget appropriations because residents are unaware that their tax dollars are needed for tree programs.

The following activities have been implemented in Ohio to increase citizen awareness and support for shade tree programs:

- City officials hold meetings at local homes to let property owners choose tree species to be planted in their neighborhood.
- On Arbor Day, potted dogwoods are distributed to all first- and fifth-grade students. Additional trees are given away at home football games, and local merchants display promotional tree-friendly messages on their signs.
- An adopt-a-tree program encourages participation in street tree planting programs. The city provides trees and planting expertise to individual residents, while the residents pay a small administrative fee and care for the new trees. The financial and labor investment creates an incentive to care for the new trees.
- Residents are mailed informational letters prior to any tree planting near their property. A second letter is mailed after the tree planting to solicit care for the tree and seek support for the program in the form of letters to the city council or contributions.
- For a contribution, citizens may have a memorial tree planted in the village square, or new parents can receive a seedling to mark the birth of their child.
- The city provides live Christmas trees to residents who make a contribution to the program. The live trees are then planted in city parks after the holidays. Free cuttings from American Holly trees also are provided for making holiday decorations.
- Local merchants help grow trees near their businesses and organize pruning parties to maintain their trees. Merchants are interested in beautifying their shopping area.
- Community civic organizations, like the Kiwanis Club, purchase

seedlings for the city nursery and participate in tree planting projects. Participation from community groups such as Boy Scouts is solicited for special tree planting events. This reduces costs and allows a greater number of trees to be planted. Scouts earn badges for their work.

- For a nominal fee citizens are allowed to remove fallen park trees to use for firewood.
- Local nurseries and garden centers contribute to a brochure on municipal tree policies and a self-guided tour of city trees. They receive free advertising in return.
- An annual Arbor Day award is given to an individual who has made significant contributions toward beautifying the city. Local media publicize the award ceremony at City Hall.

These activities demonstrate that communicators should never underestimate the value of ego gratification in serving people's needs. In addition to highlighting the aesthetic and economic benefits of the city tree programs, Ohio's municipal foresters have effectively used communications and marketing techniques to reach their target audience—the taxpayer and legislators—and gained support for their programs. It's no wonder Ohio has received more "Tree City USA" awards than any other state.

Drama and the Arts

A demonstration of how a product or process works can attract public interest, while dramatic performances appeal to audience emotions. The Atlantic Center for the Environment sponsors community theater along the Atlantic coast in Canada. Children dressed as endangered sea birds, such as puffins and murres, role-play sea bird conservation. This involves and educates adults vicariously through helping their children rehearse and watching them perform.

The theater group, Human Nature, has produced two musical comedies to help audiences examine the relationship between humans and nature. They designed their first play, *Queen Salmon,* to address the demise of king salmon in their Pacific Northwest watershed, where habitat has been destroyed by shortsighted forestry and planning policies. The play became a rallying point for their local community and instigated the formation of the Mattole Watershed Alliance to begin to change logging standards and sport fishing regulations. David Simpson, the playwright, said *Queen Salmon* was supposed to entertain, yet at the same time he notes, "The dramatic form is a great vehicle for presenting the many conflicts and points of view of people in our community interacting with the natural resources. Theater can create a scenario to show people how they can live and work and even laugh together."

The value of using music and art to influence people's attitudes toward nature has been recognized for a long time. A recent example is a compact disc entitled *Earthbeat!* that contains performances by country singer Hank Williams Jr., Dan Fogelberg, and Canadian singer Bruce Cockburn. According to a newspaper report, the CD tries "to inspire passion for forests and nature that newspapers, policy makers, lobbyists and bureaucrats may not be able to. . . . The music isn't fair or objective, but art never was supposed to be."

"Art is supposed to entertain, inspire and motivate," says coproducer of the CD, Darryl Cherney. "Music is sugar-coating for the truth pill. It reaches the heart, and usually the heart is more open to new ideas than the mind."[30]

Fund-Raising

Organizations often must design activities to raise money from foundations, the public, or corporations to help supplement a meager communications budget or raise money for specific activities. Activities such as public events, direct mail appeals, and grant proposals to foundations can help support conservation initiatives and communicate their goals.

Conservation groups commonly use fund-raising dinners, musical events, walk-a-thons, silent auctions, and other events to raise money for specific causes. For example, the Wildlife Conservation Society (WCS) regularly sponsors fund-raising dinners and talks featuring presentations by their prominent conservation scientists. On a recent fund-raising tour in California, WCS scientists Margaret Kinnaird and Tim O'Brien gave presentations at the California Academy of Sciences and attended receptions for smaller groups of high-dollar WCS donors.

WCS director of support Geoffrey Mellor, admits these activities are not the most efficient way of raising money, "But it keeps our visibility high," explains Mellor. "It brings in new blood to our membership and lets the public see what conservation is all about."

In order to be effective at fund-raising presentations, Mellor counsels that speakers must be dynamic, like Kinnaird and O'Brien. He coaches WCS scientists to

- be concise and adhere to time limits.
- emphasize storytelling and anecdotes.
- let the wildlife generate interest.
- use good images/slides.
- show no more than a couple of data slides or charts.
- practice with fund-raising staff or friends.

Direct mail is another common fund-raising tool. Large organizations use direct mail to target specific people. Companies can provide advertisers with a mailing list of their target audience, from students living near a specific park to people who live in high-income neighborhoods. Many organizations will sell or trade their membership lists. For example, the Competitive Enterprise Institute, a conservative organization, purchased the membership list of the North American Association for Environmental Education in order to target environmental teachers. They sent their target audience a Free Market Environmental Bibliography that espoused their point of view.

Direct mail allows space for detailed information to reach a specific audience. A major problem is the tendency of many people to view this mail as junk. If marketing research can narrow down an audience to specific people interested in the message, this helps make the expense of postage cost-effective, and reduces the amount of paper waste.

Many environmental organizations solicit membership through the mail. Richard Beamish, former director of communications for the National Audubon Society, lauds the value of direct mail marketing for nonprofit organizations. He suggests that as long as 1–2 percent of the recipients of your mass mailing send you money and join your cause, you probably will recover your costs in the first year. Most new members will continue their support for an average of three years. Beamish emphasizes the importance of being selective in choosing your mailing list of prospective members.[31]

For example, the Adirondack Council in New York launched a successful mail campaign. They obtained the mailing list of the forty thousand subscribers to Adirondack Life magazine. Soon after a provocative article appeared in the magazine describing a developer's plans to alter the area's pristine landscape, the Adirondack Council sent a mailing to the magazine's subscribers encouraging the reader to join with them to permanently protect Adirondack Park from such threats. Three percent of the readers responded, netting 1,457 new members from this successful appeal.[32]

Generally a mailing includes a cover letter stressing the importance of the organization, its activities, and the urgency of the situation. A reply envelope is usually included. Some organizations also include other material such as a promotional gimmick that promises a free gift for those who join, a press clipping to add authority to the solicitation, a brochure that describes the organization in more detail, or reference to Web pages and Internet resources.

Many organizations depend on grants from foundations to fund conservation activities, including public communications programs. A list of over four hundred foundations can be found in The Environmental Grantmaking Foundations Directory.[33] Once you have identified foundations with goals and objectives similar to your own, a variety of sources can help with writing grant proposals.[34] The key to success is to understand the interests of the funding source and to make sure that your project directly matches the foundation's focus.

From a communications perspective, the foundation is your target audience and you must address their needs and concerns. The following are a few tips for writing effective grant proposals:

- Plan ahead. Many granting cycles, from your initial query to a decision on your request and receipt of the check, take from six to eighteen months.
- Follow the proposal guidelines precisely. Ensure that all components of the proposal requested by the foundation are clearly marked and organized. A clear description of the project generally includes an introduction, significance of proposed work, timeline, products to be delivered, evaluation, and budget.
- Make contact with the program officer. Your professionalism and enthusiasm for the project should be evident by your careful research on the foundation and your detailed knowledge of your proposed initiative. People give to people.

Research Findings

If controversy surrounds an issue, scientific documentation of facts or evaluation of research results can be useful in answering misinformation and gaining publicity. Scientific findings can be summarized for policy makers and presented as fact sheets to media representatives to promote a conservation initiative (see chapter 4).

Florida Defenders of the Environment (FDE) used research findings in their effort to restore the Ocklawaha River. Part of the river was dammed many years ago in an attempt to build a cross-Florida barge canal. Although the canal project was halted long ago, the Rodman reservoir remains a controversial water body, a favorite bass fishing place to some and an ecological disaster to others.

Florida Defenders of the Environment has a unique board of directors composed of scientific experts. Instead of giving money, their board is encouraged to donate scientific expertise during environmental battles. During the 1990s, the campaign to drain the reservoir and restore the free-flowing river accelerated, and FDE's scientific experts and additional biologists were called upon to provide supportive information for the political battle. Their volunteer board, composed of attorneys, economists, and biologists, presented legal briefs, ecological data, and economic analyses to support river restoration.

"These expert findings helped influence and educate policy makers, state agency staff, and the public on lots of often complicated issues regarding the restoration of the Ocklawaha," says Gary Appelson, project director of FDE. "Expert advice from the private sector, inserted respectfully, forcefully, and professionally into the process as early as possible, clearly has the potential to influence policy further down the road."

Community Relations

When an organization or its employees participate in activities that benefit the community, good publicity is generated. Activities like sponsoring an environmental event specifically for a nursing home or a disadvantaged youth program foster relationships with other groups and organizations, and link conservation organizations to the community. The IPE Ecology Institute in Brazil built good will for the Poco de Antas National Park through their work with local teachers and students. When a forest fire threatened the park, community members came to the rescue and fought the wildfire.

Businesses are often more clever than conservation organizations at using people's interest in the environment to sell their products. Companies increasingly promote their "environmentally friendly" products in public relations campaigns. The following example illustrates how natural resource agencies and organizations might better capitalize on community interest in the environment.

Example: Madison Avenue's Approach to Marketing the Environment—Estee Lauder's "GREEN" Cosmetics[35]

Madison Avenue markets the environment more successfully than many environmental groups. A typical marketing strategy for a new line of cosmetics usually includes gorgeous models posed in glamorous settings and expensive promotional ads in slick magazines and television. It's not exactly a strategy congruent with an environmental message. A leader in the cosmetics industry, Estee Lauder waged an environmentally focused public relations effort to promote a new line of cosmetics. The environmental orientation translated into overwhelming sales for their cosmetic line, Origins.

Origins is a "totally new concept in skin care, color, and sensory therapy," according to Rebecca C. McGreevy, senior vice president of public relations. Designed without animal ingredients and with recyclable, green packaging, Origins represents a business success story based on consumers' interest in the green movement.

"We wanted to be environmentally responsible," said William Lauder, vice president/general manager of Origins and grandson of Estee Lauder. "But we realized that being green could not be our sole reason for being. What's more, we believed that simply slapping a 'Now Recyclable' banner on your package doesn't make you green. True green is a special sensitivity that must permeate every aspect of your marketing platform and actions."

Recognizing their consumers' expectations for Estee Lauder products, the team at Origins introduced the line in thirty upscale department stores nationwide. Advertising involved a simple product shot that appeared in the Sunday *New York Times Magazine* and *L.A. Style*. The marketing strategy used consumers' desire for a commitment to the environment to enhance product sales.

Product Development

The cosmetics industry often is a target of criticism because they test their products on animals or use harmful chemicals. The Origins skin care products touted their use of plant extracts instead of ingredients derived from animals. All testing was conducted with human volunteers, instead of animals. The packaging reflected the environmentally conscious image Origins wanted to portray, as all products are shipped in recycled cardboard boxes and all printed materials use recyclable papers and soy-based inks. Every Origins location also included a recycling bin with compartments for recyclable materials.

Target Audiences

Marketing a cosmetic product with an environmental message requires identification of specific target audiences in order to effectively communicate the link between the skin care products and an environmental commitment. The public relations campaign for Origins focused on three target audiences: the media, upscale department stores, and consumers. Initial publicity activities designed for these audiences are outlined below.

The Media
- Detailed press briefings were held at Lauder headquarters to introduce the product to editors of national magazines. At these briefings, beauty and fashion editors heard in-depth product information from Origins' marketing and research team.
- The public relations managers met with key members of the local press before presenting Origins to leading department stores nationwide.

Department Stores
- Origins' public relations team introduced the product to executives at the leading department stores.
- The Lauder family members hosted breakfast presentations at department stores to introduce the product to executives at individual stores.

Consumers
To target the consumer, the marketers for Origins launched environmental events in collaboration with community organizations. Such special events served to connect the product to both the community and the

green movement. The events publicized the product to the consumer but also included the media and department stores as target audiences. The publicity efforts included the following events:

- "Run for the Earth," a collaborative effort with Nordstrom's Department Store in Santa Barbara, featured a half marathon and family 5K fun run. Five dollars from each entry fee went to a fund to repair damage from the 1990 Santa Barbara Painted Cave fire, which destroyed thousands of acres of forested lands. Each runner received a T-shirt with the Nordstrom/Origins logo and a gift certificate. Race winners received a trip to Hawaii and entry into the Honolulu Marathon.
- A tree planting ceremony to reforest the area destroyed by the Santa Barbara Painted Cave fire.
- A tree planting program planned with California Re-leaf and Nordstrom South Coast Plaza to improve the quality of California air.
- Participation in Earth Day 1990 before Origins became an official company. Staff from Origins sold T-shirts and posters and raised more than $15,000 for Earth Day.

Evaluation

Evaluation is as critical to a corporate marketing program as it is for a conservation communications program. What has been the payoff from these "green" public relations efforts for sales of Origins? According to the public relations manager, the events fueled additional press about the product: "Press coverage continues to roll in every day."

For a corporate cosmetics giant, the final evaluation of a marketing strategy lies in product sales. Only one month after introducing the 155 product items, Origins sold out in several areas around the country. As sales exceeded the initial projections by 70 percent, distribution expanded beyond the original thirty stores around the country. One key to Origins' overnight success was tapping consumers' "deep concern for the environment communicated via solid public relations principles," claims the Origins team.

Organizational Activities

Strengthening existing institutions or forging new partnerships involves communication skills from start to finish. These types of activities help organizations achieve their conservation goals.

Establishing an Organization

Supporters of an organization can form a new group to expand their capacity and enhance cooperative efforts. Often these new entities can provide public outreach, bolster volunteer staff, and provide other resources not mandated or budgeted within the parent agency or organization. A formally instituted group often has more clout and can garner more resources than a loosely knit band of supporters.

A good example is the Friends of Acadia (FOA). Founded in 1986, FOA provides citizen support to preserve and protect Acadia National Park and surrounding communities on Mount Desert Island in Maine. The organization's operating philosophy is to:

- champion park interests to the National Park Service and other governmental entities
- represent park users for the betterment of the park and its operations
- raise private funds for projects in Acadia and for its enlightened stewardship
- promote conservation in border communities through programs and grants that complement park values
- promote volunteerism to meet park needs
- leverage funds to bring the highest conservation return per donated dollar
- operate as an independent, nonprofit organization in support of the park

In recent years, FOA raised $4 million in private contributions. This helped restore Acadia's historic carriage roads, provided direct cash grants to the park for vital but threatened programs, funded Acadia Youth Conservation Corps teenagers to work in the park, promoted ethical recreation through the Resource Sensitive Tourism program, and negotiated a historic timber moratorium on 1,600 acres of neighboring Schoodic Peninsula.[36]

Building Partnerships

Increasingly, organizations are teaming up with agencies and private industry to share resources and expertise. These alliances among groups that share similar goals or specific objectives can result in mutually beneficial programs. Partnerships for conservation between government agencies, nonprofit organizations, industry, and academia pool resources for accomplishing mutual goals. Partnerships increase efficiency by reducing duplication of effort and provide more creative solutions to problems by bringing people together with a variety of experiences and perspectives. Organizations have reported improved morale as a result of involvement in partnerships that offered new project opportunities for employees.[37]

The National Wildlife Federation (NWF) engaged in a month-long partnership with McDonald's fast-food restaurants in the United States. During the partnership, all fast food bags and cups were imprinted with information about NWF. With the information, consumers could send for one of two children's magazines published by NWF. This benefited NWF by providing broad national exposure to young people who were potential conservationists and supporters, while McDonald's benefited from showing their support for wildlife conservation.

Partnerships provide not only money but also a variety of tangible benefits from the relationship, including:

- Shared efficiency by pooling resources
- Increased effectiveness by combining knowledge and skills
- Innovative solutions by involving people of different backgrounds and experiences
- Increased public influence by pooling support
- Increased organizational morale from new contacts and synergism
- Reduction of duplication or waste
- Decreased conflict through long-term collaborations

Rich Baker, research coordinator for the Minnesota Natural Heritage and Nongame Research Program has formed partnerships with a number of public and private organizations to help achieve resource management goals. Baker credits these partnerships with infusing new resources and innovative problem solving into his program. A current partnership is providing the resources to study the small population of northern goshawks in Minnesota. Although goshawks are not yet a listed species in Minnesota because of a lack of data, the U.S. Forest Service has been concerned about the impact on timber sales should goshawks become listed.

Baker joined in partnerships with the timber industry (the National Council of the Paper Industry for Air and Stream Improvement) and the U.S. Forest Service. Together they jointly agreed on research priorities for the northern goshawk and the influences of forestry practices. They shared funding responsibilities and established shared goals. "Because they are buying into the planning, development, and implementation of the project, they are stakeholders in the results, and therefore, the conservation of goshawks. As partners, they remove themselves from an adversarial position and instead are pulling together toward agreed upon objectives," says Baker. "Overall, partnerships should be a win–win strategy."

Meetings, Conventions, and Seminars

Gatherings among colleagues or diverse groups foster the exchange of information and help build recognition of the host organization. Information can be disseminated to scientists, managers, business people, teachers, and other special-interest groups. The North American Association for Environmental

Education held their annual conference in Atlanta, Georgia, in 1998. It brought together over 1,200 teachers, scholars, park interpreters, museum exhibitors, curriculum designers, and others involved in environmental education to exchange experiences, learn new techniques, and make helpful contacts. For their $175 registration fee, participants selected from over 400 presentations, workshops, and field trips dealing with environmental education. The conference offered information in a variety of formats, including workshops, symposia, hands-on sessions, presentations, interactive discussions, and poster sessions.

Rather than organize their own conference, the Society for Conservation Geographic Information Systems (SCGIS), a small professional group of people who use GIS software for conservation purposes, meets annually on the weekend prior to the mammoth Arc/Info Users Conference (a popular GIS software package).[38] The main Arc/Info conference, which attracts over six thousand people, is held at the San Diego Convention Center. SCGIS rents a couple of lodges in a nearby state park for the forty to fifty people who attend their preconference meetings. This quiet atmosphere permits focused presentations, small-group discussions, and networking opportunities that would not be possible in the hustle and bustle of the main conference.[39] Other groups frequently piggyback onto larger conferences by organizing a session, symposium, or social events that cater to the "group-within-a-group." This strategy provides an opportunity for the group to meet, which would not otherwise be possible, and can be valuable for recruiting new members.

Educational and Interpretive Activities

In-depth communications to interpret conservation and educate the public run the gamut from colorful posters to year-long courses. Techniques and illustrations of a multitude of activities are provided in detail in chapters 5 and 6.

Classes and Presentations

Presentations on site or in schools or clubs provide extensive opportunities to interact with target groups and cover environmental material in depth. The North Cascades Institute offers a variety of seminars, courses, and field camps to teach about the Pacific Northwest environment.[40] Their natural history field seminars offer over seventy multiday adult seminars on Northwest natural and cultural history, from the ecology of salmon to Native American ethnobotany. Academic credit is available through Western Washington University. Their Mountain School provides fifth-grade classes with three-day learning adventures in the North Cascades. Teachers and parents camp with students as they learn about local geology, ecology, and culture. For adults over 55, the North Cascade Institute hosts Elderhostel programs. These one-week sessions enable seniors to explore the Puget Sound and Columbia River ecosystems.

Production of Posters

Posters that are eye-catching, attractive, and based on an organization's goals can be an effective way to increase visibility and transmit knowledge. Posters can provide a quick reference to wildlife species, endangered plants, or common insects. They can focus on an organization's objectives, a regional issue, environmental problem, or biodiversity. Some posters combine photographs or illustrations with text and an annual calendar to create a useful and educational tool for conservation. The environmental branch of the Florida Army National Guard publishes a calendar poster of their Camp Blanding reserve each year. Brilliant photos of representative habitats, plants, and animals illustrate their ecosystem management goals. Because the poster includes a calendar, it is tacked on the walls of many offices around the reserve.

In many tropical countries, conservation organizations produce posters to familiarize residents with endangered species, wildlife regulations, resource management needs, or new development policies. Biologist Margaret Kinnaird of the Wildlife Conservation Society designed and disseminated posters of the Sumba Island Hornbill, a rare and endemic bird in Indonesia.

According to Kinnaird: "The poster targeted villagers of the island of Sumba, a small island with about 300,000 inhabitants. The objectives were to appeal to their pride about having a rare bird found only on their island, increase their awareness concerning the ecological importance of the Sumba Island Hornbill, and of course to encourage people to conserve the birds and their habitat. With the help of the Indonesian Forest Department, we disseminated approximately two thousand posters to churches, village leaders, local hangouts (food stands, restaurants, airline offices), and government officials throughout Sumba provinces. We initially targeted fifteen villages near the newly proposed national park. The posters were so popular, that they ended up going everywhere."

Publication of Brochures

Brochures are typically produced to describe an organization's goals and activities for a broad audience. They can describe environmental management objectives, special facts about the agency or site, or details about an important conservation campaign. Text can be combined with graphics or glossy photos to produce a professional introduction to the organization. These are often useful for increasing membership or raising funds. A brochure is often the front-line information for an organization—the first thing a prospective member or supporter sees about your cause or learns about your site.

The Program for Studies in Tropical Conservation (PSTC) at the University of Florida is an interdisciplinary program that develops human resources and strengthens institutions in tropical countries through integrated research and training. The PSTC published a brochure to publicize their pro-

gram to students and garner support from foundation funds. Like most organizations' brochures it describes their mission, objectives, concrete examples of
achievements, past funding sources, and areas of funding needs. This small
group raised over $2 million in the past decade.

Audiovisual Materials

Slide-shows and videos can provide a visually compelling introduction to an
organization or its conservation message. They are useful in a wide range of
situations, such as visitor centers, table or booth public displays, conferences,
traveling exhibits, outdoor trails, auto tours, and special events. Audiovisual
materials can last from several minutes to several hours for a multipart series.
Their production cost has an equally wide range depending on length and
professional quality. They are especially useful for orienting visitors to a site or
to "bring" the audience to the site without leaving their offices, classrooms, or
living rooms.

Video images are effective in influencing people's lives because they sim-
ulate the real experience. The interpretation center for the Pacific Rim
National Park in Vancouver, British Columbia, focuses on the marine environment, especially on the whales that reside and migrate along their shore. At
their center, a half dozen videos are shown daily to provide in-depth views of
research on and conservation of whales and their marine ecosystems. The
videos expose visitors, who may not see a whale in the wild, to the whale's
beauty and fragile environment.

Tours

Visits and hands-on experiences are very effective in engaging public interest
in a site or subject. Research has shown that direct contact and exposure to
natural areas or special places often stimulates positive attitudes toward the
environment.

Rock Creek National Park in Washington, D.C., offers a variety of guided
tours to meet the needs of its largely urban audience. They have made a con-
certed effort to increase participation by offering activities geared to a wide
variety of interests and age groups. They use colorful titles and descriptions to
make their events sound appealing and employ several different media to promote their programs. Their Color-Search hike is a guided field walk that
focuses on coloration adaptations in plants and animals. Other tours include a
scavenger hunt for ages 4 to 10; the Spring Forest Hike, on which a ranger
expounds on the seasonal changes in forest ecosystems; the Herring Hike,
which focuses on the migration of herring up Rock Creek; and Flood! which
explores the many roles of seasonal flooding. By maximizing the diversity of
its tours, Rock Creek Park is able to maximize the size of its audience (and
public support) as well as capitalize on staff interests and expertise.[41]

Exhibits

Displays and exhibits are popular at parks, visitor centers, zoos, and agency public offices. Innovative exhibits have increased zoo visitors and engaged them in new learning experiences. The Bronx Zoo's World of Darkness teaches visitors about nocturnal animals while they watch bats fly and shrews eat dinner in a twilight setting. An Amazon rainforest exhibit graces the National Zoo in Washington. Children visiting the Roger Williams Park Zoo in Rhode Island crawl through tunnels and pop up into plastic bubbles to learn about prairie dog towns.

The Monterey Bay Aquarium touch tank attracts children and parents to handle starfish or pet a stingray. According to Jim Covel, interpretive program manager for the Monterey Bay Aquarium, this is one of the most popular exhibits for the 1.7–1.8 million visitors each year.

"The Touch Pool Exhibit is designed to provide a hands-on experience for visitors," Covel explains. "A place where they can have an intimate experience with some common marine invertebrates.

"A recent visitor survey rated this exhibit as one of the outstanding experiences for aquarium visitors. The visitors commented that the combination of a hands-on experience coupled with a friendly and informative person to facilitate the experience was particularly engaging and memorable. I'm not sure how much invertebrate information visitors pick up at this exhibit, but that's not really our objective. The real goal is to allow visitors a chance to get their hands wet, experience the medium these animals live in, and apply multiple senses to experience a plant or animal (look, feel, smell—we discourage tasting). We provide docents to ask or answer questions to help the visitor process the experience. In exit surveys over the years, visitors continually rate this near the top of their aquarium experience.

"The only concern visitors have expressed with the Touch Pool is an occasional question about the welfare of the specimens and the impact of people handling them. As a result, we have taken measures to provide close supervision over contact with animals and to keep the animals immersed at all times. Since these new practices were put into place, questions or concerns about the specimens are rarely heard."[42]

.Websites

The information superhighway has led environmental organizations and agencies into Internet tools and Web pages. One popular search engine listed over five hundred organizations and over 1,800 sites on environmental topics as this book was going to press. Due to the versatility of the Web, it offers an excellent medium for providing educational and interpretive resources. Web pages are relatively inexpensive to design and maintain and are discussed further in chapter 4.

One of the popular features of the World Wildlife Fund's Website are materials from their Windows on the Wild (WOW) educational curriculum.[43] Visitors to the Web page can take a biodiversity IQ test, explore an interactive map of ecoregions in the United States, order publications about biodiversity issues, or see sample articles from the WOW magazine.

Journey North is another environmental education program that reaches students and teachers through the Internet. The centerpiece of this program is an online database of student-submitted observations of seasonal events, such as monarch butterfly migrations in the spring or "first frost" in the fall. Their Website offers weekly challenge questions about each of the seasonal patterns the participating students monitor. Information includes background materials, lesson plans for teachers, and correspondence from collaborating field biologists who contribute satellite telemetry data from migrating whales, eagles, and caribou. By using the Web, Journey North has been able to reach 100,000 students, a number few other environmental education programs can boast.[44]

Zoos and aquariums with educational missions were among the earliest pioneers to offer interpretation resources via the Internet. In fact there are so many zoos and aquariums online that a site called Zoo Web has been developed just to keep track of them all.[45] Sites can range from simple pages with text and pictures, to more complex layouts with sound bites and interactive games, to video clips and "zoocams," which take a snapshot every few seconds of your favorite group of orangutans, falcons, sharks, or other popular animals.

Last Words

Your imagination is the only limit to designing communications activities that will "move people" to support conservation efforts. Following a systematic process of planning, implementing, and evaluating your program is critical. It helps ensure that the most effective activities are selected and that approaches appropriate for your target audiences are designed. This chapter provides a menu of communications activities, including informational, political, promotional, organizational, educational, and interpretive approaches. Unlike menus encountered in restaurants where chefs seldom share recipes, this chapter gives the recipes and lists of ingredients to help you in designing your own programs. Chapters 4, 5, and 6 provide the context and guidelines for creating your own materials and programs for mass media, environmental interpretation, and conservation education. Chapter 7 explains how to evaluate your results.

Chapter 4

Using Mass Media

Most ordinary reporters would practically cross the street to avoid running into an expert since they consider scientists to be unemotional, uncommunicative, unintelligible creatures who are apt to use differential equations and logarithms against them the way Yankee pitchers use fastballs and breaking curves.*

Conservation professionals and members of the press share this antipathy toward each other. Many conservation professionals fear a close encounter with a reporter, perhaps envisioning a *60 Minutes* interviewer barging into their office. Few conservation professionals appreciate how valuable media coverage can be for their program or cause. What they fail to realize is that they have the credibility to present information about many aspects of conservation to reporters who can then help present the ideas to the public. This chapter explores how you can use mass communications to amplify your messages through a variety of media approaches. Mass communications may be the ticket to reaching your conservation goals.

Mass communications involves transmitting conservation messages through newspapers, radio, television, and, increasingly, the Internet to achieve program objectives. This chapter offers tips for designing and presenting interviews, advertisements, news releases, public service announcements, press kits, and news conferences. World Wide Web sites and electronic mail also provide channels for reaching vast audiences. Specific guidelines for writing and speaking provide successful techniques for delivering your message using mass

---

*W. Burrows. 1980. Science Meets the Press: Bad Chemistry. *Sciences* (April):15–19; cited in D. Nelkin. 1987. *Selling Science: How the Press Covers Science and Technology*, p. 8. Freeman, New York.

media. Examples range from an innovative press conference staged by the National Wildlife Federation that focused attention on water pollution to a succinct news release by the U.S. Fish and Wildlife Service on the reintroduction of California condors. Every conservation organization and agency can benefit from the effective use of mass media.

Mass Communications

Mass communication touches almost everyone in the United States and much of the world. In the United States more than 95 percent of all homes have television sets, and over half a billion radios receive transmissions from almost ten thousand stations. More than 1,500 daily newspapers and hundreds of weekly papers and magazines are delivered to rural, suburban, and urban subscribers. Over sixty-seven million people now plug into the World Wide Web, and 78 percent of the nation's public schools are connected to the Internet.[1] Mass media are omnipresent.

Research on the impacts of mass media is extensive, but findings are not always unified. Most researchers agree that mass media shape the public agenda. The media generate public interest in an issue and, through daily exposure, can influence its importance. News stories stimulate discussion of an issue, particularly if the issue touches audience needs or concerns. This interpersonal communication in turn influences the public agenda.

Mass media further influence our social context. The development of public attitudes and behaviors is shaped by numerous social factors. The opinions of others influence individuals to conform to certain behaviors. For example, people are more likely to conserve energy when mass media messages suggest that others are conserving energy.[2]

Staff at conservation and resource management organizations are increasingly aware of the power of mass media and have become more interested and adept at harnessing it. They also are aware of the painful consequences of not using mass media. Imagine:

- What if you planned a special event or offered a program and nobody came?
- What if you took a stand on a controversial conservation issue and no one knew it?
- What if you designated new hunting or recreation regulations and the public was unaware of them?

Mass media are a necessary part of the existence of your agency or organization. Your ability to use mass communications will directly affect the success of your mission.

Many established conservation organizations have worked hard to cultivate their relationship with mass media contacts. According to a media relations manager of the National Wildlife Federation: "All the various aspects of the Federation depend on media, whether it's cultivating an atmosphere that's conducive to seeking out new donors and increasing name recognition, to influencing policy-makers, decision-makers, opinion-makers, and members of Congress on our positions on the issues. On the public affairs side, [mass media is critical] to educate, to achieve visibility for issues. . . . We view the media as a tool to achieve those goals."[3]

Mass Communications Approaches

A variety of mass communications approaches can convey your conservation message. Different types of media transmit messages of varying complexity and reach varying numbers and types of people. Your situation and message will dictate the right media for achieving your objectives. Typical mass communications approaches include:

- Interviews with the press
- Advertisements
- Public service announcements
- News releases
- Fact and tip sheets
- Press kits
- Press conferences
- World Wide Web pages
- E-mail lists

All of these approaches rely on the same four successive steps to any successful communications campaign:

1. Define objectives
2. Identify audiences
3. Develop and implement strategy
4. Evaluate results

Define Your Mass Communications Goals and Objectives

The overall goal may be to accomplish tasks associated with your organizational mission, such as gaining protection for a particular species or raising public awareness of an issue in order to influence congressional actions. Specific objectives can range from the modest act of transmitting information to an audience (i.e., individuals receive your message) to expecting significant changes in behavior (i.e., individuals act on message). The impact of a communications program can be broken down into five levels; each new level penetrates further than the previous one and as such is more difficult to achieve.

Members of the target audience progress from one level to the next as they: (a) receive the message, (b) remember the message, (c) believe the message, (d) intend to act on the message, and, perhaps, (e) act on the message.[4] Specific procedures for setting goals and objectives are described in chapter 3.

Identify Your Audiences and Craft Your Message

Determine who is important to achieving your goals. Who are the stakeholders, decision makers, and people that influence the decision makers? Determine their needs, concerns, and interests. What will motivate them to retain and accept your message, to change their attitude or behavior?

Develop and Implement a Strategy to Reach Your Audiences Through Appropriate Media Channels

Determine where your target audiences get their information. Ensure that your various media approaches enhance each other. For example, specialized newsletters for a specific audience might complement messages transmitted through brief radio spots.

Monitor and Evaluate Your Performance Against Your Objectives

Monitor your program and modify it accordingly as you go along. After the activity, assess the outcomes—press coverage, audience members contacted, impacts on natural resources, and so on—to determine what did and did not work.

Making Your Activities Newsworthy

Mass communications inform, educate, persuade, and, last but not least, entertain the public. Often a message must incorporate all four functions to be effective. A glaring example of the importance of entertainment is the most popular news story of 1995. The topic that received more coverage in the United States than any other was not a critical political, economic, or environmental issue. It was the O. J. Simpson murder trial, filled with drama, sex, and violence.

Using mass communications successfully requires an understanding of what makes your activities or events newsworthy. Your organization is newsworthy when you do things that are socially useful, fill a public need, and are interesting. Newsworthy activities are easy to identify, whether you are conducting and publishing a conservation study or protecting a species or parcel of land. Cluny Madison, public relations manager for The Nature Conservancy in Florida categorizes each activity to best present it to the media. "Is the activity environmental, business-related, scientific, or social?" asks Madison as she seeks to obtain media coverage. Here are some of her examples of Conservancy events that make news.

- Acquisition of a preserve (purchase, gift, bargain sale, trade)
- Launch of a fund-raising project or a capital campaign
- Preserve stewardship (work days, prescribed burns, habitat restoration)
- Establishment of a state heritage program or results of such programs
- Ceremonies marking donations, dedications, or transfers of preserves
- Successful completion of a fund-raising project or campaign
- Special events
- Corporate support of Conservancy projects and programs
- An unusual discovery on a Conservancy preserve
- Publication of Conservancy-related scientific news or research results
- Visits to preserves by schoolchildren, politicians, Rotarians, celebrities
- Speeches and personal appearances by Conservancy leaders
- Conservation awards to or from The Nature Conservancy

The first law of journalism is simply: Be interesting.[5] People will read or watch only what interests them, such as drama, sex, and violence. The topic must concern or touch the audience in some way. Capitalizing on the audience's self-interest—a quality called relevance—will increase the audience's attention. Media outlets try to understand their audiences' wants and needs. Their profit depends on addressing audience desires, which governs what they will publish.

A good example of addressing the self-interest of a target audience is a National Audubon Society press release announcing a new publication, *Banquet for Birds*. The booklet offered advice for attracting birds to homeowners' backyards. One tip was to leave a section of the yard unmowed to provide a meadow habitat for birds. The headline on the press release read: New Audubon Booklet Contains Good News for Lazy Homeowners. Subsequent paragraphs explained the publication, gave some examples, and told how to order the book. The press release and booklet were mailed to about 1,500 outdoor and garden reporters nationally. The article was printed by hundreds of newspapers. Over twenty thousand readers ordered the book.[6] Piquing reader interest by promising benefits to lazy homeowners (most of the audience!) was key to widespread coverage.

To be newsworthy, a story must appeal to people's needs, interests, and desires. Recall from chapter 1 the hierarchy of needs that motivate people. This theory argues that individual needs are met in a sequential manner, beginning with lower needs and moving toward higher needs.[7] The most basic needs are physiological, such as people's need for food, rest, and shelter. From a communications perspective, issues about basic resource use such as consumption of wild animals or plant materials may address this need.

Once basic physiological needs are met, people's need for safety is paramount—protection against deprivation, danger, and the unfamiliar. Stories about environmental health, water and air quality, safety, and economic impacts appeal to this need. Once these basic needs in the hierarchy are adequately satisfied, higher-order needs can be met by the individual, such as social needs and the need to belong to a group. Conservation issues that bring people together or affect their popularity address these needs.

Social needs are followed by a desire for self-esteem and status and a drive for recognition and respect. Appeals to beautify their surroundings or engage in leisure activities may satisfy this need, or may allow people to fulfill a sense of ethical responsibility. The final drive is the need for self-actualization. This is the continued development and self-fulfillment of an individual. The opportunity for personal growth, outdoor learning, or leadership activities speaks to this need. Once a need is satisfied, it no longer serves as a motivating force for action. For example, well-to-do suburbanites probably would not respond to an appeal to hunt to satisfy food needs because most are already well fed. Appeals to their need for social interaction or recreational desires would stimulate them more.

Cultivating Media Relations

Attractive and newsworthy material obviously is necessary for any successful communications program. Less obvious may be the need to make personal contacts to enhance the chances of getting your materials published. You can easily find out who handles your type of activities at the local newspaper and radio and television stations. For newspapers, this is usually the city editor or features editor, and for radio or television, the news director, public affairs director, or producer. Get to know them. Call them and make an appointment to tell them about your organization and programs. Provide them with written material and discuss the schedule of your upcoming events. All written and oral communications to papers or stations should be brief; the atmosphere in a newsroom has been described as controlled chaos.[8]

Follow-up phone calls to the correct reporter or producer help notify them that your story is on the way. Your call can help spark interest about the story concept. It allows you to answer questions or provide a phone number of someone who can answer questions. After an initial meeting, which gives a human face to your name and organization, most communications are conducted by phone or fax.

After your introduction, continue your contact with the press. Send them story ideas and press releases about your newsworthy activities two weeks in advance, or within a time frame they specify. Give them enough time to plan to cover your activity, but not enough time to forget it. Many editors are delighted to cover local stories, and it often helps if they have met the person listed on your press release. Reaching staff at large metropolitan newspapers and television stations is more difficult, and written communication may be all that is possible.

Developing a list of media representatives and keeping it current is one key to obtaining good media coverage. Some cities have published media guides developed by the local public relations association or the chamber of commerce. The press mailing list for the National Audubon Society consists of environmental writers, science writers, editorial page editors nationwide, and interested producers of radio and television networks, including public broadcast stations. The Adirondack Council in New York has a mailing list composed of major newspapers and news services of New York State, legislative correspondents in the state capital, and press outlets around the 6-million-acre (2.4-million-hectare) Adirondack Park.[9]

The media selection for your organization or agency should target media that reach *your* audiences, whether local, regional, national, or international in scope. These might include:

- Daily newspapers
- Suburban and weekly newspapers
- School newsletters
- Radio stations
- Television stations
- Cable television stations
- News wire services, such as the Associated Press
- Internet outlets, electronic bulletin boards, and mailing lists

Public relations staff at large conservation organizations cultivate relationships with specific reporters by regular phone contact or even occasional lunches. As the World Wildlife Fund's public affairs vice president explains: "We've done a lot of just going and having lunch with these people and getting a sense of what their interests and agendas are. . . . Often they are surprised because they see us purely as a wildlife organization and we're not. We're much more than that. So that has been helpful."[10]

The ability to develop personal, yet professional, relationships with reporters is important to conservation organizations. The Greenhouse Crisis Foundation serves as an example. The foundation's office manager lauds the personal contacts that President Jeremy Rifkin has made with reporters as being instrumental to getting news coverage. She explains: "He has contacts at every major media and they listen to him. He'll tell them about a story; if they think it's worth it, they'll run the story. . . . Mass mailing of press releases really doesn't accomplish much. What really does work for us is Jeremy personally calling. He knows them all, and they will come in and talk to him for hours, get all the information, and write a story. . . ."[11]

Mass Media Approaches

Once you have determined the human interest in your organization's program, developed the message, and cultivated appropriate media channels, you must now select mass communications techniques to accomplish your objectives, each of which has various functions and constraints (table 4.1). The remainder of this chapter describes these methods in greater detail for creating successful mass media communications.

TABLE 4.1. *Functions and constraints of various media for spreading your conservation message*

Functions	Constraints
INTERVIEWS	
Identify your organization as an authority	Advance preparation needed
Allow a personal appeal for a campaign or project	Difficult to arrange
Provide human interest	Requires good speaking skills
Provide wide exposure	
ADVERTISEMENTS	
Deliver a specific message	Expensive
Control the time, duration, and place a message will be seen or heard	Requires technical skill
	Delivers only brief, simple message.
PUBLIC SERVICE ANNOUNCEMENTS	
Advertise free activities, events, or materials	Little control over time, place, and duration
Highlight a conservation issue	Competition for space and airtime is fierce
Recruit volunteers	Need technical expertise to meet standards of press or broadcast station
Inexpensive exposure	
	Delivers only brief, simple message
NEWS RELEASES	
Announce hard news, such as an action, award, new study, or new leader	Competes for attention with other organizations
Alert the public to an event or benefit activity	News must have broad interest and be timely
Reach many media outlets and publics at once	Media contacts may not understand newsworthiness of issue
PRESS KITS, TIP SHEETS, AND FACT SHEETS	
Provide background information on a conservation project or issue	Must be up-to-date
	Seldom useful alone
Provide supporting material for reporters at a news conference	Audience must have prior interest to use fact sheets

Augment other media materials by providing specific descriptions of projects or activities	May provide an excess of information
Summarize data regarding conservation programs or events	

PRESS CONFERENCES

Break a news story quickly	Advance preparation essential
Provide information to many outlets if interest in story is already generated	Complex logistics
Garner interest if a participant in the event is a celebrity or local expert and has personal news value	Risk of low interest and turnout
	Requires public speaking skills
Announce significant news (e.g., dedication of new land, new conservation policy, corporate donation, or conservation initiative)	

LETTERS TO THE EDITOR

Clarify your position	Information can be viewed as biased or frivolous
Voice a disagreement with a newspaper editorial or community policy	
Thank community members	
Bring attention to a specific cause	

WORLD WIDE WEB SITES AND ELECTRONIC MAIL

Inexpensively reach a potenitally huge audience	Inaccessible to many people
Provide and update information quickly	Accuracy of information presented will be questioned
Make a lot of information accessible to interested viewers	Need technical expertise to set up Website
Distribute materials 24 hours a day	

Interviews with the Press

Most communications approaches discussed in this chapter involve active contact and wooing of the media. As a conservation professional, however, your first encounter with the mass media may be a request from a reporter for an interview about your program, agency, or organization. Although interview requests may not come at a convenient time, they *can* be manna from heaven for your conservation work, if you are prepared to take advantage of them.

Steps toward Successful Interviews

Like all aspects of effective communications programs described in preceding chapters, working with mass media involves setting objectives and understanding your audience. The following five steps pertain to interview situations with print and broadcast media. These steps will help you put your best foot forward at the interview, rather than stumbling through it.

DEFINE YOUR COMMUNICATIONS OBJECTIVES FOR YOUR INTERVIEW. Whatever the ultimate medium for your interview—newspaper, magazine, radio, or television—you must always keep in mind your communications objectives. In advance, you must determine one or two specific messages that are most important for achieving your communications goal. Keeping your objectives in mind will help you lead the interviewer to the specific target area or will help you make a beeline back if the questions wander off track. Messages might be:

- The Nebraska Conservancy is a good community member and a good land manager.
- The Texas Wildlife Commission's program will ensure good hunting for years to come.
- Better protection of endangered species now will give you more land-use options in the future.

KNOW YOUR AUDIENCE. Before participating in an interview ask in advance about the audience that will read, hear, or view your piece. The editor or producer of the paper or program will determine how much coverage to give you based on your ability to help him or her build and maintain the audience. Knowledge of the audience will guide your objectives and your presentation. Put your story in a context relevant to the audience. Emphasize values and results that resonate with their lives. For a specialist audience, such as scientists, obviously you will describe your work or program with different words and visual props than for a generalist audience. *Mass* media implies a diverse audience, but even mass media channels have varied audiences. For example, the audience of a pop radio show will be different from the audience of a public broadcasting station. An understanding of their backgrounds and common interests will improve your likelihood of success.

KNOW THE SITUATION. In addition to understanding the audience, learn about the interview format and the background of the interviewer. If the interviewer has little knowledge of your subject, you can plan in advance the detail and explanations that you will provide. Before you give the interview, monitor the paper or show. Study the editorial style of the program in advance. Does the interviewer regularly grill subjects, or is a friendly, conversational session more the norm? What is the tone and style? How long will you have? Will others with opposing viewpoints appear with you?

News interviews, feature interviews, and magazine interviews have varying time constraints. Reporters often have only a few hours to write a news article while magazine writers may have several months. The deadline for the interview, the time and amount of research needed, and the nature of the story will dictate the type of interview you experience.

KNOW WHAT YOU WANT TO SAY. Always keep in mind your specific communications objectives. Write out your messages in advance to help organize your thoughts. Memorize your key messages and practice saying them three or four different ways. If you have time, rehearse potential questions and answers with a colleague. Practice taking every opportunity during the interview to make your points or state your messages—don't be afraid of repeating them. Focus on components of the questions that allow you to deliver your messages.

In giving any interview, two rules apply. First, tell the truth. If you can't answer a question, or need time to compose an answer to a controversial question, offer to get back to the reporter later. Second, never say *anything* that you do not want published or aired. There is no such thing as "off the record."

OFFER BACKGROUND MATERIAL. Provide the interviewer with background information in advance of your appearance to facilitate their job. While not all interviewers will have the time or interest to take advantage of it, background material will help them prepare for an effective interview based on *your* agenda. Advanced preparation can help promote your cause. You can offer to provide a slate of suggested questions to the interviewer if it is an informal talk show and the interviewer is receptive.

News Interviews

News interviews are conducted under a tight deadline and usually over the telephone. By having all your facts and figures at hand and answering questions concisely and clearly, you can provide news reporters with a good interview. You can prepare for the interview by anticipating the kinds of questions that might be asked. Every reporter asks the five W's: who, what, where, when, and why. Be prepared to briefly answer these questions about your organization or conservation issue. Always remember your communications objectives—the one or two messages that you want to deliver about your project or position. To help advance your message, be prepared to give concrete and specific data and examples. Do not be vague. For example, the answer "250 hunters signed the petition" is better than "lots of people support us."

Also, be prepared to answer questions about controversial subjects or weaknesses of your program, but do not get bogged down in negative conversation. Remember to emphasize your objectives and positive messages throughout the interview.

Written background material supplied to the reporter in advance of the interview could include fact sheets about the program or issue and background documents about your organization. These materials will help them prepare the story. Offer additional materials or sources at the end of the interview and make sure you immediately carry through on your offer. A final tip: although most news interviews are conducted by phone, always be available for a face-to-face interview. The added personal contact helps get your points across and develops good press relations for the future.

Sometimes an interviewer is simply looking for a response to some national or regional event, new policy, or activity. He or she may be seeking a reaction to a specific incident, such as an oil spill; an issue, such as new property rights legislation, or a study result, such as new data regarding declining frog populations. Your response should be brief. Often you can anticipate this request in advance and have the perfect quote prepared. This kind of regular contact for quotes will happen more as you cultivate your media contacts.

Feature Interviews

Many of the guidelines for news interviews also pertain to interviews for feature articles in newspapers and magazines. Feature interviews often have more time to explore a topic. Feature writers seek lively quotes, interesting anecdotes and personalities, and unusual facts around which to build their story.

These interviews are more comprehensive than a news story. Reporters will be grateful for supporting materials—briefings, brochures, data graphs, and so on—that you can provide for background to the story.

Interviewers in general will probe to discover your program goals, obstacles you have faced, solutions found, and the roots of your activities. Some typical questions asked in a feature interview might include:

1. What are you trying to achieve?
2. What is the purpose of your program?
3. What problems have you had?
4. What obstacles do you still face?
5. How have you handled past (and future) problems?
6. When did your program start?
7. Who started it?
8. How did you get interested in it?

Often a reporter will ask you how you feel about something. The audience can relate to your experience when you use words expressing your reaction or opinion. Words like alienated, angry, relieved, amused, hopeful, and so on, help you share your point of view with the listener.[12]

Example: Quotes Excerpted from Interviews with Well-Known Conservation Professionals

Note how the speakers express themselves to help their audience relate to their concerns. They use metaphors and analogies to simplify complex ideas and relate scientific concepts to everyday life.

Interview question: "What are your goals as president of the Sierra Club?"

Adam Werbach, president, Sierra Club: "I'm halfway there. I have a two-year project—reinvigorating the grassroots momentum and trying to focus the [environmental] movement on winning, not just placing band-aids on everything."[13]

Interview question: "Currently, we use less than one percent of the world's species. Couldn't we just get along without 99 percent?"

Daniel Janzen, restoration ecologist, University of Pennsylvania: "You could get along without your color vision, sense of smell, taste. We can turn you into a vegetable, and you'll stay alive. That's not the route I'll take, or most people if they know they have an alternative. Someone who says he doesn't need that extra biodiversity is like the guy who says he doesn't need to know what classical music or folk music is because he's happy listening to advertising ditties on TV all his life. . . ."[14]

Interview question: "Can our world really be sustainable . . . what will the landscape look like?"

John Robinson, vice president, Wildlife Conservation Society: "Think of a jigsaw puzzle. Each piece [of the landscape] has different activities with differing levels of sophistication. But all the pieces relate together to work as one sustainable whole. If those pieces don't fit together, the whole thing doesn't work."[15]

Interview question: "Is there any way to renew the interest in the environmental movement?"

Edward Wilson, author of *Biophilia* and biologist, Harvard University: "What it takes is a crisis. Even a drunk driver will stop if he hits a telephone pole. We may have that crisis on hand with the current endangered species legislation. . . ."[16]

Broadcast Media Interviews

With broadcast media, the audience hears or sees you deliver your message directly. Radio and television allow you to emphasize your main points with audio and visual effects. Your intonation and speed of delivery, gestures, and appearance can enhance your message. The type of broadcast program will dictate the amount of "air time" you get. You may have thirty seconds to get your point across on an evening news broadcast or thirty minutes on a radio talk show interview.

Similar to print media, interviews for broadcast media require careful planning. You must predetermine your communications objectives and decipher the audience and format for your interview. Like observing videos of an opposing team before a football match, the best preparation is to listen to or watch the program in advance to get an idea of the structure and approach your interview will take.

News broadcasts are brief, and you will need to get your message across in a few select words. Public relations experts suggest anticipating questions you may be asked and imagining your reply in the form of a newspaper headline. Practice completely answering a question in ten to fifteen seconds. Use the questions you anticipate as launching pads for your one or two key messages. If the interview will be taped and edited, your replies must be self-contained statements that can be aired without any of your preceding or following replies. Make sure the kernel of your message is in each reply.

For longer interviews, it is necessary to decide your message, repeat it multiple times, and prove it with statistics and examples. Make your point with data and information that support what you have to say. Use a few good examples or analogies to vividly dramatize your point. Your audience will relate to your anecdotes. Stories are an effective method of ensuring your message is remembered. Politicians litter their campaign speeches with anecdotes and personal stories to help the audience relate to their message. You should too.

Your conservation message might be: "The Cambridge Watershed Society is good for the community and our environment." Your anecdote: "We invited students from three high schools to participate in our Charles River clean-up for a semester. Two hundred students learned firsthand about water chemistry and pollution control. Not only did the water quality improve enough to allow swimming in the river for the first time in thirty years, but teachers reported students' science grades were the highest ever. One young man told me that working with our organization made him realize he wanted to go to college to study the environment. Before our program, he was considering dropping out of school."

It is important to anticipate potential negative questions from the interviewer and be prepared with replies that focus on positive aspects of your message. *Do not state your opponent's message; restate your own message.* Sometimes acknowledging a criticism and explaining how it is faulty or how it is being addressed can be effective. Also, practice the art of interpreting questions broadly so that you can reiterate your message successfully.

No matter what the interview setting, try to relax. Pretend that you are in a neighbor's living room talking with friends. This also will help you project a friendly, yet professional, manner. Speak convincingly and sincerely. For a television interview, learn from the expression of television news anchors—note their open and friendly faces and consistent eye contact. During the interview, look directly at the person asking the questions, not at the camera. For longer television programs, you also can make use of color slides, simple charts, or other props to enhance your message. Prepare these in advance with the consent of the program director.

The broadcast studio also can give you tips about what to wear. For example, pastels and neutral colors look better on television than stark black or white clothing. Boldly patterned material or flashy jewelry distract the viewer. Men may wish to shave before they appear since television exaggerates five o'clock shadows. The camera also accentuates women's short skirts or low necklines. Studios often provide make-up services for both men and women because the lights and camera tend to blanch skin tones.

Few people are natural stars. Advance preparation, such as (a) deciding your message, (b) reviewing your subject thoroughly, (c) finding out exactly what the reporter wants, and (d) understanding the format of the interview, will go a long way toward a successful encounter. When time permits, practice interviewing and answering difficult questions with a colleague in advance. You could even videotape yourself answering questions to get ideas for improving your performance. Practice your message in 15-second sound-bites—use action verbs, pithy phrases, and vivid images. You should be able to boil your message down to one or two sentences and deliver it in one breath. For example, Marjorie Stoneman Douglas, a venerated crusader for the Florida Everglades, is remembered for this soundbite: "The Everglades is a test. If we pass it, we get to keep the planet."

Other examples of effective soundbites include:

"Cutting down the rainforest for money is like burning a Rembrandt to cook soup."

"If you care about clean drinking water, you'll help us preserve the Hardesty marsh."

Sometimes you may wish to decline giving an interview. Reasons for turning down an invitation include: the reporter or show has poor credentials, the approach is hostile and unlikely to generate positive publicity, or your story or cause is controversial or sensitive and the time is not right. Remember though, that you are passing up the opportunity to use the media as a vehicle to get your message to your audience. No matter how hostile a reporter might be, do not lose sight of your objective and message. It is usually better that you tell your side of the story than let someone else tell it for you, particularly if it is beamed into the living rooms of your target audiences.

Advertisements

Marketing your messages through advertising media can be expensive, but it enables you to reach large numbers of people. If costs exceed your budget, you may be able to have a public service announcement placed for free, as described in the next section. Expenses of advertising include hiring professionals to design and prepare the ad, as well as paying the television, radio, newspaper, or magazine for the time or space. The following communication channels for your advertisements offer varied advantages.

Television

Television advertisements communicate through pictures, motion, print, and sound. Producing and airing ads on television is expensive. A thirty-second ad on prime-time TV can cost $130,000. One minute of advertising during the Superbowl may reach 130 million people and cost $1.7 million.[17] Less expensive ads can be aired on cable TV or local access stations that reach a smaller, more segmented, audience. Networks like MTV, the Nashville Network, or Discovery allow you to more specifically target your message. As powerful as the sight and sound of television ads are, they expose the audience to a message for a very short time, and only simple messages can be relayed.

Radio

Radio offers only auditory stimulation, yet many more radio than television stations are available to broadcast ads. The diverse types of radio shows make it easy to target a specific audience. *Farm Radio Network,* local talk shows, *Physicians Network,* opera, or New Age music shows reach specific groups of people. Unfortunately, audiences often tune out advertisements, both literally and figuratively. Like television, it is difficult to convey complex messages in the short amount of airtime. Unlike television, however, radio can be an inexpensive medium for reaching your audience.

Magazines

The special interest subject areas of magazines provide an already targeted audience. Bird-watchers subscribe to *Audubon,* gardeners read *Organic Gardening,* hikers read *Outdoors,* and anglers read *Field and Stream.* If you are targeting young people, the top five favorite magazines for college students are: *Cosmopolitan, Sports Illustrated, Time, Rolling Stone,* and *Glamour.*[18]

Magazines offer color ads that can be eye-catching and might be seen more than once by the subscriber flipping through the publication or by more than one person in an office or household. Messages can be fairly complex and are read at the audience's leisure. Some disadvantages include the long lead time for magazine publication, the relatively high cost (a full-page ad in *Audubon* costs over $20,000), and the competition with other ads and articles for the reader's attention.

Newspapers

Newspapers can reach either national or local audiences. Ads can be placed quickly, and response is usually immediate. Ads in local newspapers are inexpensive, but national advertising is costly. A full-page, color ad in *USA Today* costs close to $90,000 during the week and $120,000 on weekends. A full-page, color ad in a local paper can cost about $4,000.

The Natural Resources Defense Council collaborated with the National Environmental Trust to place a full-page, color ad in *USA Today*. The purpose was to raise public concern about global warming during the White House Conference on Climate Change (WHCCC). The ad pictured a large, imitation weather map of the United States designed to look like the *USA Today* daily weather map. Bright orange and red colors depicted the average high temperatures predicted for the year 2197. Florida readers saw the daytime high of 120 degrees Fahrenheit (49 degrees Celsius), and south Florida was missing entirely (apparently submerged). Readers in Montana saw daytime highs of 100 degrees (38 degrees Celsius).

Outreach director of the National Environment Trust, Greg Macias, explains the logistics of the ad: "The advertisement cost roughly $68,000 for the full page. We ran it the same day as the White House Conference on Climate Change held at Georgetown University in Washington, D.C. The WHCCC was broadcast to over fifty satellite link-up sites across the country. Appropriately, while I do not have the actual weather page from that day in front of me, I remember it having a record or near-record high."

The advertisement received a lot of attention, according to Macias, who monitors their outreach activities. "The 'Weather Page' ad produced a spike in both our Web page visits and our toll-free number. The level for that first full week in October saw over 1,600 hits, about three times the normal traffic. Our toll-free number went from about fifty calls a week to over five hundred (box 4.1).

"Reaction to the advertisement varied. Most people wanted to know the sources of the potential changes, while a few resorted to simple name-calling. We later modified the 'Weather Page' to be used at information booths at Earth Day celebrations, concerts and other public events."

The weather map was just a part of NRDC's global warming campaign. They placed a series of advertisements over a six-month period. "NRDC spent nearly $250,000 on advertisements combating the misinformation being

Box 4.1. National Environmental Trust's Environmental Information Center

As part of a National Environmental Trust advertising campaign on global warming, a toll-free telephone number was used to provide information to audience members and to record the impact of their ads. You would hear the following script if you dialed their number.

Hello. Thank you for calling the Environmental Information Center Information Line. If you are calling about global warming, **press one.** If you are calling for information about hormone-disrupting chemicals in the Great Lakes region, **press two.** If you are calling for information about clean air, **press three.**

ONE

Thank you for calling Climate Countdown, a project of the Environmental Information Center. Over 2,400 scientists agree that global warming is occurring and that we should take measures to stop the pollution that causes it. You can help by joining a national network of individuals, organizations, and communities taking steps to protect the environment.

Global warming will have severe economic, health, and environmental impacts from the disruption of weather patterns, melting of the ice-caps, rising seas and oceans, reduced agricultural production, and the spread of tropical diseases. You can learn more about how global warming contributes to extreme weather conditions at www.eic.org.

World leaders will soon be meeting to discuss how we can stop global warming and cut the pollution that causes it. Climate Countdown will be engaging concerned citizens like yourself to take a stand against global warming. Please leave your name and address and we will send you further information on steps you can take to fight global warming and how you can become part of Climate Countdown. Thank you!

put forth by the coal, oil, and auto industries," says Lisa Magnino, communications director, NRDC–Washington, D.C. "A fortune for us, but a drop in the bucket compared to the over $13 million figure cited in the launch of the industry's Global Climate Information Project's advertising campaign against the United Nations treaty."

Magnino describes the progression of their advertising campaign as follows:

- *June 1997:* "In advance of the president's address to the United Nations about U.S. measures to reduce global warming, we took out advertisements on bus shelters near the United Nations, featuring a photo of President Clinton with the headline, 'Mr. President, You Can Stop the Hot Air.'"
- *September 18, 1997:* "In anticipation of the White House Conference on Climate Change, NRDC launched a month-long advertising campaign in the Washington, D.C., subway system. Ads featured a TV screen with a weather channel box and a house being swept away by a flood. The headline of the ad was 'Tomorrow's Weather Brought to You by Big Business.'"
- *October 1, 1997:* "New ads were run in Washington, D.C., San Francisco, Tampa, and St. Petersburg on CNN, *Headline News,* and Sunday morning talk shows. The headline: 'Sierra Club, NRDC, and EIC Respond to $13 million Industry Lies—Ad Campaign on Global Warming Set to Begin This Weekend.'"
- *October 29, 1997:* "*New York Times* op-ed page ad, 'Oil Money Throws the Earth Out of Balance.'"
- *November 11, 1997:* "*New York Times* ad rebuts the industry misinformation campaign and runs in the *New Republic.*"
- *December 1, 1997:* "On the first day of the Climate Change meetings in Kyoto, *New York Times* ad appears in special section on global warming, outlining NRDC's measures of success in Kyoto."
- *December 5, 1997:* "*New York Times* op-ed page ad asks the president to call for more flexibility in negotiations, to establish his legacy on environmental issues."

The NRDC carefully selected messages and media to hit their target audience. Seven steps can be followed to design an advertisement for any media.

1. Identify the ultimate action you want from the reader, viewer, or listener.
2. Identify your audience—who are the decision makers? Who influences the decision makers?
3. Identify needs/concerns/interests of your audience, and determine the primary motivations that will cause action.
4. Write the message.
5. Choose channels of communication based on where audience members get their information.
6. Select a believable spokesperson, if appropriate.
7. Package the message to raise an audience need, concern, or interest, then offer your product or organization as a means of fulfilling that need, minimizing that concern, or satisfying that interest.[19]

Additional guidelines for effective advertisements also pertain to public service announcements and are described in the next section.

Public Service Announcements

Newspapers, magazines, radio, and television stations air free public service announcements (PSAs) as a service to the community. PSAs allow you to reach an enormous audience with only the cost of production. The Federal Communications Commission defines a PSA as an "announcement for which no charge is made and which promotes programs, activities, or services of federal, state, or local governments or the programs, activities, or services of nonprofit organizations and other announcements regarded as serving community interests."

Because of the steep competition from all sorts of social and environmental groups, your PSA must be interesting, professional, appealing, and important to the community. PSAs also must conform to the technical requirements of the newspaper or broadcast station, such as column width or airtime.

Success in placing PSAs is directly related to your familiarity with the public service or advertising directors who schedule the announcements. Contact with these key people is important. Delivering the PSA personally allows you to meet the people who will decide the fate of your communications strategy. All PSAs should be labeled clearly, and proof of your nonprofit status (IRS tax-exempt letter) should accompany your PSA, along with a cover letter and background material. Remember to thank the paper or station for their assistance if they use your PSA. Let them know you appreciate the favor.

Tips for Writing a PSA

The key qualities that affect whether a PSA will be read or heard are the PSA's format, its ability to address the audience's basic needs and interests, and the freshness of the message.[20]

The following guidelines will help you create an effective PSA.

1. Decide on your message. State it in a simple declarative sentence.
2. Select a compelling soundtrack, photograph, or illustration for the PSA; an action shot rather than a static image is more powerful. Generally a single focal point—one illustration and headline—is better than broken text or multiple images.
3. Make sure all your critical information is included, such as your contact number or date of event.
4. Write a headline or opening statement to grab the audience's attention. Make your benefit to the audience known at first glance. Each audience member wants to know, "What's in it for me?"
5. Write a short first paragraph or dialogue focused on your strongest point

---

Box 4.2. Radio monologue for a public service announcement for the Connecticut chapter of The Nature Conservancy

PSA Text—25 seconds (background nature sounds)

"The Connecticut River. Home to bald eagles, rare orchids, and miles of magnificent scenery. Today, this habitat for wildlife and people is threatened. That's why the Nature Conservancy has launched the Connecticut River Protection Program, a bold, new effort to save the river's remaining natural areas. But time is running out. To find out how you can help, call the Nature Conservancy's Connecticut Chapter in Middletown at 344-0716."

25 seconds (If there is time, insert "That's 344-0716")

---

or appeal that is of interest to the audience. Several other appeals of diminishing importance can follow.

6. The final statement should stimulate the reader to act: call for information, visit your site, volunteer time, or make a contribution. Tell the audience exactly how to do it. Urge them to act immediately.
7. Make the text appealing and easy to understand. For broadcast media, advertisers recommend getting your message across by telling a story. For print media, your photograph or illustration should tell the story for you.
8. Be as concise as possible. For a thirty-second radio spot, only about seventy-five words or 150 syllables can be uttered (box 4.2).

The California field office of The Nature Conservancy developed a series of print PSAs as part of its "Sliding toward Extinction" campaign. With donated help from an advertising agency, they designed a PSA with an adorable portrait of a kit fox under the headline, "Now Disappearing at a Location Near You." The full-page PSA appeared in regional periodicals and in-flight magazines. The kit fox became the dominant image for their entire campaign. Figure 4.1 shows a print PSA produced by The Nature Conservancy for a national audience.

News Releases

News releases, also called press releases, are a device for sending your message to the public via the news media. News releases are short stories describing a newsworthy activity or event of interest to newspaper, radio, and television

In-formation Superhighway

Thousands of songbirds, shorebirds, geese and cranes crowd the flyways from South America to the Arctic every season. But the wetland rest stops they need to refuel along the way are disappearing. The Nature Conservancy has created an award-winning computerized network to help us guarantee sufficient "service stations" along these birds' travel routes. • Whether it's manatees in Florida, pine barrens in New York or quetzals in Costa Rica, The Nature Conservancy protects the lands and waters that rare species need to survive. A world that can sustain its wildlife will be a healthier and happier place for our children and their great-grandchildren.

Please join us. Call us at **1-800-628-6860**.

Help us keep our migratory birds and waterfowl from veering off the exit ramp.

Or write: The Nature Conservancy, Box PSA, 1815 N. Lynn Street, Arlington, VA 22209.   Sandhill Cranes. Photograph © TNC
Or visit our website at: http://www.tnc.org

The
Nature
Conservancy®

audiences. News releases can be in print, audio, or video format, but regardless of the medium, they should always be brief. Depending on the scope of your news and the objectives of your communications program, you can send news releases to local, state, national, or international newspapers and radio and television stations.

A Conservation International report evaluating their news coverage for one year reflects the importance of news releases in promoting their conservation efforts: "CI's media outreach effort . . . can be measured as a resounding success in three ways—quality and quantity of coverage, audience size, and financial value. The combination of extensive international newspaper, magazine, radio, and television coverage means that CI press releases regularly reach worldwide audiences of 100 to 200 million. This widespread coverage, plus good placement, translates into free advertising to CI worth between one million and five million dollars, depending on amount of electronic and international coverage. The added incalculable value of this 'free advertising' is that it is in the form of hard news, which is regarded by the public as a much more legitimate information channel than advertising."[21]

An example touted in CI's report was a press release they distributed about their debt-for-nature swap in Mexico. The swap was a strategy to reduce Mexico's international debt in exchange for governmental agreements to preserve its tropical forests. The story appeared in over two hundred U.S. papers, including the *New York Times, Los Angeles Times, Chicago Tribune, San Francisco Chronicle,* and *Boston Globe.* The papers collectively reached a circulation of twenty-five million readers. The British Broadcasting Corporation picked up the story and reached up to 220 million additional people worldwide. Conservation International estimated that the debt-for-nature swap story earned "free advertising" worth $175,000 in U.S. papers, $250,000 in U.S. radio coverage, and $200,000 in television coverage.[22]

CI's impressive coverage is not the norm. Your news release will compete with releases from other organizations and industries stacked on the news editor's desk. You will have to work hard to get your message out. It is important that your release is structurally correct and newsworthy.

News Release Structure

Audio and video releases require technical expertise and expensive equipment, so the following guidelines focus on news releases for print media, which anyone can do. Technical help for broadcast media releases can be hired or sometimes obtained as donations from advertising agencies.

The format of a news release for print media helps ensure that it is easy for reporters to use. Contacts, dates, and the five Ws—who, what, where, when, why—are carefully composed and structured for easy and attractive reading. The structure of a news release places the most important information, the five Ws, in the first, or "lead," paragraph.

The lead paragraph must capture the essence of your story and tell the reader something of value. It also needs to hook the editor so that your story will be printed. The remaining paragraphs flesh out the story by providing necessary details. The body of the story often uses quotes of the people involved to give the story a human element and to add interest.

The structure of a news release can be diagrammed as an inverted pyramid (fig. 4.2). Information that is least important is placed at the bottom, or end. Editors will cut the article from the bottom up to fit the space available. By placing key material first, you minimize the risk of losing it. The closing paragraph often describes the mission of your organization or agency; it often, but not always, will be cut. Mention your organization's name and location near the beginning of the story to ensure that it is included.

The headline of your news release should get the editor's attention while highlighting your message. Headlines must be accurate and brief, and they usually tell who did what. They may contain a humorous or dramatic statement to catch the editor's eye. The headline that you write for your news release is unlikely to be used by the paper. Its main purpose is to catch the editor's eye.

As you will note by perusing a newspaper, brevity is key. Sentences are short. Paragraphs also are short, made up of only a few sentences. News releases are seldom longer than one page.

Finally, whenever possible, a photograph or graphic should be included with the release to illustrate the story. One picture really is worth a thousand words—an intriguing, high-quality photo can help get your release published and will spark reader interest. Photographs of California condors were available to accompany a press release produced by the U.S. Fish and Wildlife Service (box 4.3).

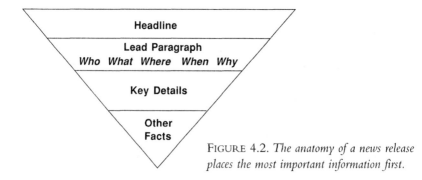

FIGURE 4.2. *The anatomy of a news release places the most important information first.*

Box 4.3. Press release by the U.S. Fish and Wildlife Service announcing the reintroduction of California condors

FOR IMMEDIATE RELEASE:
Contact: Ken Burton
Public Affairs Office
U.S. Fish and Wildlife Service
(address and phone contacts)

Six California Condors Are Released in Northern Arizona

Six California condors were released by the U.S. Fish and Wildlife Service and the Peregrine Fund from the Vermilion Cliffs of Northern Arizona today, the first time the giant birds have been seen in the skies of the American Southwest since 1924.

As staff members from the Arizona Game and Fish Department, the Peregrine Fund and the Los Angeles Zoo stood by on the Vermilion Cliffs, Interior Secretary Bruce Babbitt, using a hand-held two-way radio from a mile away, gave the order to release the birds, and biologists opened the pens.

The Arizona release, undertaken under provisions of the Endangered Species Act, placed the birds—part of a population of 120 left in the world—near the Paria Plateau, about 115 miles north of Flagstaff, Arizona, an area that once supported the condor. The rugged Coconino County terrain provides the necessary remoteness, ridges, cliffs, and caves favored by the carrion-eating birds.

"This is the kind of story that clearly demonstrates that the Endangered Species Act works and works well," said Babbitt. "In 1973, Congress gave us a charter to save animals and plants from extinction. And here is a bird that in the 1980s was on the very brink of extinction. Thanks to a lot of hard work and an excellent captive breeding program, we were able to restore a bit of balance. This is a success story that belongs to the American people."

The condors released today were bred in captivity in California at the Los Angeles Zoo and at the Peregrine Fund's World Center for Birds of Prey in Boise, Idaho. They were transferred in late October to the Vermilion Cliffs, where they have been kept away from people and allowed to acclimate to their new surroundings. Officially, they will be classified as an "experimental, non-essential" population under the Endangered Species Act, which allows the birds to be managed with fewer restrictions than those normally covering endangered species. The classifica-

(continues)

Box 4.3. (*Continued*)

tion also is designed to ensure that protected, reintroduced species are compatible with current and planned activities in the project area.

Peregrine Fund president William Burnham said he considered the experimental, nonessential designation a key to the condor reintroduction for Arizona and Utah. "This historic event is a result of cooperation between the government and the private sector to include the people of southern Utah and northern Arizona," Burnham said.

Authorities today closed about 10 acres of federal land around the release site, a temporary step that will remain in effect until the newly released birds have dispersed. If the initial release is successful, the Service will seek to release more condors over a period of years until there is a self-sustaining population of about 150 in the project area.

Nancy Kaufman, director of the Service's Southwest Region, which includes Arizona, said that "the condor success story is really more than a story about captive breeding. We have been able to raise these birds in captivity and conserve habitat at the same time. Captive breeding isn't the answer for every species, but it has worked well for the condor. The goal, of course, is to see the day when endangered species no longer have to be kept in zoos. Today, we made a major step in that direction."

. . . Adult condors weigh up to 20 pounds and have a wingspan of nearly 10 feet. In prehistoric times, the bird ranged from California to Mexico, across the southern United States to Florida and north on the east coast to New York State. The birds managed to maintain a strong population until the settlement of the West, when shooting, poisoning and egg collecting began to take a heavy toll. By 1987, the birds' population in the wild had dwindled to 7. In what was then a controversial decision, the Service decided to remove the remaining birds from the wild for captive breeding in a last-ditch effort to avert the condor's extinction.

Today, there are 120 condors in the world. In addition to the newly released Arizona birds, 20 are in the wild in California; four are in an acclimation pen in Ventana, California, and scheduled for release in January, 1997 and 90 are in captive-breeding facilities in California and Idaho. . . .

The U.S. Fish and Wildlife Service is the principal federal agency responsible for conserving, protecting and enhancing fish and wildlife and their habitats for the continuing benefit of the American people. The Service manages 511 national wildlife refuges covering 92 million acres as well as 72 national fish hatcheries. . . .

####

Writing a News Release

The following ten tips will help you write an effective news release:

1. KNOW WHAT YOU WANT TO SAY. Make an outline of the major points of your story and sequence them from most important to least important. Stay focused on your communications objective. If there is an action or behavior that you want from the reader, make sure your message states it clearly.

2. ENSURE THAT YOUR STORY IS NEWSWORTHY. Avoid propaganda. If your release reads like an advertisement, editors will ignore it.

3. KEEP IT SIMPLE AND DIRECT. The trend toward lower reading abilities and lowered appetites for reading among the U.S. public means your press release must use simple words and sentences to reach the reader.

4. KEEP IT BRIEF. A press release should fit on one or, at most, two pages (double-spaced). Additional information can be included with the release, in the form of fact sheets and background material. Use short words, sentences, and paragraphs.

5. EMPHASIZE THE HUMAN INTEREST. The story should be of interest to a wide range of people. Emphasize the readers' needs, concerns, and desires and make your message fill the needs or satisfy the desires. Self-interest compels attention. Remember that people find other people interesting. When possible, tell your message as a story and put people in it. Editors of local papers in particular must emphasize the local angle of a story. Your news release should be of interest to the paper's readers and relevant to their lives.

6. BE TIMELY. The release should arrive in time and not overlap with your prior releases. It also should be addressed to the correct media person (e.g., not someone who held the position a year ago).

7. ESTABLISH THE CREDENTIALS OF YOUR ORGANIZATION. Over time, your organization or agency should be viewed as a reputable and authoritative source. Success in having a release published depends on the media's belief that your release is factual and that your institution is trustworthy.

8. FOLLOW THE STANDARD FORMAT. The professional appearance of your press release in the form of legible type and proper style can help predispose the editor to react positively to its content. Typed on letterhead stationery, single-sided with ample margins, your release should be simple to read. The example in box 4.3 provides guidelines, with the release date, contacts, headline, and body of the text. Note that more than one page is indicated by writing "more" at the end of the first page, and the end of the story is demarcated with the symbol "####" or "-30-." Most importantly, proofread carefully, especially dates and correct spellings of names.

9. PROVIDE A PICTURE. Offer a photograph, map, or other visual aid to entice interest in your release.

10. WRITE WELL. The release should be clear, easy to read, and grammatically sound. Many books provide suggestions for writing well. *The Elements of Style,* written by E. B. White and William Strunk Jr.; *On Writing Well,* by William Zinsser; and *Write to Be Read,* by Benton Patterson, are some of the best. They remind writers of general rules to follow for creating a powerful piece. Some basic points include:

- Write with nouns and verbs. Adjectives and adverbs seldom add vigor to a story: "Bob yelled" is more compelling than "Bob said loudly."
- Use active, not passive, voice (e.g., active: "The park biologist darted the grizzly." passive: "The grizzly was darted by the park biologist.").
- Write simple, ordinary English. Avoid jargon and elaborate words (e.g., "use," not "utilize," and "now," not "at the present time").
- Avoid using qualifiers like "very," "rather," and "little." They sap strength from your statements.
- Be clear. As Mark Twain admonished: "Say what you propose to say, don't merely come near it. Choose the right word, not its second cousin."
- Relay your message using elements of interest to the reader.
- Be specific and provide details; do not be vague.
- Be concise. Short sentences and paragraphs are easier to read.
- Rewrite, rewrite, rewrite. Particularly when you are starting out, the wastebasket or delete key is your best friend.

Feature Articles

For longer articles and feature articles consider the advice of writing experts and present your conservation cause as a story. The formula for *Time* magazine's popularity involves telling the reader a compelling story. According to *Time*'s twenty-fifth-anniversary issue: "The basis of good *Time* writing is narrative, and the basis of good narrative is to tell events in the order in which they occur; in the form in which an observer might have seen them—so that the readers can imagine themselves on the scene. A *Time* story must be completely organized from beginning to end; it must go from nowhere to somewhere and sit down when it arrives."[23]

To make what you are writing interesting to the readers: (a) put specific people into the piece, (b) tell stories, and (c) let the readers see and hear the situation for themselves. Every feature or article must have ample amounts of the elements of good writing: anecdotes, quotes, and descriptive detail.[24] Good examples of feature stories appear in daily newspapers and national conservation magazines—read a selection of articles to get ideas about how to structure your own article. Alternatively, you can hire a freelance writer to develop a strong article for your organization or agency. Some writers can suggest appropriate publications or have relationships with newspapers or magazines that regularly publish their work.

Press Kits, Tip Sheets, and Fact Sheets

News releases can be combined with fact sheets and other materials in an attractive packet for the press. A press kit provides a news release outlining your main message or current issue along with detailed background information for reporters to use in writing their story. Press kits can be given to reporters attending a press conference or photo opportunity and sent to those unable to attend. They can be mailed to editors with a cover letter or tip sheet describing story ideas and providing contact information.

The Press Kit

Press kits can contain some or all of the following materials:

- Fact sheet providing background information
- Fact sheet or brochure about your agency or organization
- Photographs and biographical sketches of key people involved
- Reprints of articles and background material about your organization
- Photos or maps about your agency, conservation issue, or managed land
- Copies of speeches (if the kit is given out at a press conference)
- Camera-ready public service announcements

One or two samples of each are normally adequate and will not bury the reporter in superfluous detail.

Tip Sheets and Fact Sheets

Many large conservation organizations send letters to reporters with suggestions for story ideas. For example, staff of the Izaak Walton League of America distribute bimonthly tip sheets to reporters with short descriptions of five to ten story ideas. These are sent to about three thousand media outlets and contain information from the League on conservation issues, materials about relevant reports or resource kits, and updates on projects. "The tip sheets from the Izaak Walton League are particularly well-received among outdoor writers," media relations director Kristen Merriman says, "because of writers' regular need to fill up column space."[25]

Some organizations distribute directories to the media so that reporters working on stories can easily locate staff members for comments or data. The Center for Marine Conservation's directory provides a brief historical description of the organization with staff members listed by specialty. The thirty-six specialty headings range from beach cleanups and biological diversity to endangered species, coastal wetlands, sea turtles, drift nets, and the International Whaling Commission. Information on the group's field offices and some of its publications are also provided. The introduction advises journalists that they should "find this tool most helpful in their search for timely, factual information," and reminds them that CMC staff members "welcome your calls for authoritative information and comment."[26]

Fact sheets generally focus on a specific topic and provide details and statistics about an activity or issue. This information gives the press and the public a better understanding of a subject area in which they are already interested. The Caribbean Conservation Corporation designed a fact sheet about endangered sea turtles (box 4.4). They distribute the publication at press events and send it to people who request information about the organization.

Press Conferences

Press conferences will only attract the press if you have timely and newsworthy information. Press conferences may be appropriate for activities such as the opening of a new reserve or facility, presentations by a well-known spokesperson, activities at an unusual site, or introduction of a complex and compelling topic. If you are unsure whether your announcement warrants a press conference or will attract reporters, consider another mass media approach. Staging a press conference to which few reporters show up is worse than hosting a party that nobody attends.

The National Wildlife Federation holds news conferences to announce the results of major reports and studies that they have completed. One of their most successful press events occurred on Capitol Hill. The Federation hosted a reception to publicize a report on possible health hazards associated with eating contaminated fish from the polluted Great Lakes.[27] At the reception the Federation set up hors d'oeuvre tables of sliced fish from the Great Lakes, with signs beside each one warning that eating any of the food might be hazardous to one's health. The signs described various toxic chemicals that had been found in the fish. The graphic example of their scientific report stimulated high interest and news coverage by attending reporters.

Steps for Holding a Press Conference

1. Decide on a clear theme and message. Think about your audience—reporters and editors—and clearly define why the event will be newsworthy. The topic must be compelling to warrant press attention. Decide if your objective as well as your budget permits a field trip, meal, dramatization, or other activity.
2. Select a location that is important to your message and *convenient and*

Box 4.4. Excerpt from the Adopt-a-Turtle Fact Sheet distributed to the public and the media by the Caribbean Conservation Corporation

ADOPT-A-TURTLE FACT SHEET

Threats to Sea Turtles
- *Habitat destruction* is the biggest hazard to sea turtle survival. Important sea turtle nesting beaches throughout the world are being disrupted or destroyed by coastal development. Bright lights shining on the beach from shoreline buildings discourage turtles from nesting and often lure hatchlings away from the sea to their death. Ocean pollution, such as petroleum wastes and plastic, kills thousands of turtles every year. Many more drown after becoming entangled in commercial fishing nets.
- *Commercial exploitation* is a major reason for the dwindling number of sea turtles. Turtles around the world are hunted for their eggs, meat, and shells. Sea turtle products are still the most frequently seized contraband U.S. customs officials take from tourists returning from the Caribbean.

What is Being Done to Save Sea Turtles?
Your turtle adoption is an important part of our efforts to protect sea turtles from extinction. With your help we are:
- Conducting international scientific research and education programs to increase knowledge about sea turtles and the problems they face.
- Training local guides in Tortuguero, Costa Rica, to protect turtles and lead growing numbers of ecotourists along the Atlantic's largest green turtle nesting beach.
- Developing a management plan for Nicaragua's Miskito Coast Protected Area, the most important turtle feeding grounds in the Atlantic.
- Rallying support from the public and governments to protect sea turtles and the places they live.

Source: The Sea Turtle Survival League is a program of the Caribbean Conservation Corporation, located in Gainesville, Florida; used with permission.

accessible to reporters. Have a contingency plan ready in case of rain. Plan the arrangement of speakers, press, and materials in advance with the staff that will set up the site.

3. Choose a time and date to maximize press coverage. Generally weekdays before 3 P.M. allows reporters to file their stories before their daily deadline. Avoid public holidays and other big news days.

4. Develop press kits for participants and for reporters who are unable to attend the conference.

5. Order and check all the audiovisual equipment and back-up equipment in advance. Assign a technician to deal with lights, slides, sound, or other equipment. Prepare visual props for the speakers to enhance their points, if appropriate.

6. Schedule spokespeople and activities, usually to fit in a thirty- to forty-five-minute period. Designate order and time for presentations and a question period. One or two speakers are often optimal; five minutes each for four speakers is plenty. Plan more time for questions and answers than for the formal presentations. Decide on the main messages to communicate and think about answers to potential questions. Because Murphy's Law operates, arrange for alternate speakers and back-up staffing help.

7. About ten days in advance of the press conference, send out a media alert or advisory describing the conference: the purpose, who will speak, points to be covered, and planned activities. Stress the credentials of speakers and controversial or colorful subjects involved. Address the memo to specific reporters and editors by name, covering all media: print and wire services, radio, and television. Send out or phone additional guest invitations, such as to board members, supportive community leaders, or other appropriate individuals. Make reminder calls to reporters the day before the event.

8. After the conference, have spokespersons available to answer additional questions.

9. Make a transcript or audio- or videotape of the conference to share with additional audiences. Take photographs to use with future promotional materials or for later internal communications such as newsletters or annual reports. Send additional materials to any reporters that request them.

10. Look for coverage of the conference and evaluate its success. Learn from any mistakes to improve the process in the future.

Letters to the Editor

Research on newspaper readership shows that letters from readers are widely read.[28] Letters to the editor are an excellent device for commenting on conservation issues in the news and making a point about your program or activities.

Addressed to the editor, your letter should be brief and to the point. Your letter should state your opinion, give supporting facts and evidence, then suggest the conclusion and action you wish the reader to take.

Many papers have a limit of one hundred to four hundred words. Deliver your message succinctly. Keep in mind that both the Ten Commandments and the Gettysburg Address are under three hundred words. Brevity is best. A short letter—one page—will seldom be cut arbitrarily by the editor.

Letters should be clear and well written. Tirades and petty or personal-sounding concerns will not be published. Follow newspaper style, with terse writing and short paragraphs of only two to three sentences, for an effective letter. A compelling photograph can illustrate your point and catch the editor's and readers' attention. Often an illustration will help focus the eye on your letter before any others on the page.

Longer opinion pieces can be submitted as editorials or op-ed pieces (so-called because they often are published *op*posite the *ed*itorial page). Op-ed pieces can be up to seven hundred words in length. Talk to the op-ed editor before submitting your piece and see what interests and angles might be published. Cite your credentials for writing the piece. Remember all four functions of mass media—to inform, entertain, persuade, and educate—as you work on your piece. Facts are key, yet entertainment value will help ensure that editors print your piece and that readers finish reading it.

An op-ed piece by Dr. Gary Paul Nabhan, director of science at the Arizona–Sonora Desert Museum is shown in box 4.5. His editorial helped launch a campaign in 1996 to conserve pollinator species in order to protect rare plants and economically important food crops. The piece was released before Thanksgiving, providing a timely hook to snare editors and readers. Note how Nabhan appeals to the reader's *self-interest* in presenting reasons for conservation.

World Wide Web Sites and Electronic Mail
More and more people are turning to the Internet. A 1997 CommerceNet/Nielsen Internet demographics survey found that over 37.4 million adults in the United States and Canada use the Web, and the number continues to grow.[29] A study by the Georgia Institute of Technology found that the average age of Web users is 35 years; 69 percent are male, 83 percent are from the United States, and 64 percent access the Web from home.[30]

People use the Web for a variety of reasons. Collecting reference information is an important purpose for many users; 60 percent of Web users access reference material on a weekly or daily basis.[31] Education, entertainment, research, travel planning, and work also are common uses of the Web.

Box 4.5. Example of an op-ed piece published in over twenty newspapers by ecologist Gary Paul Nabhan, Sonoran Desert Museum

THE EMPTY TABLE: THANKSGIVING WITHOUT POLLINATORS

As I sit at the kitchen table, helping my family prepare Thanksgiving dinner, I think about the direct link between the cornucopia of foods we eat and the health of the farmlands and ecosystems from which they are derived. Not many people may recall this vital connection during our nation's Thanksgiving, but it is manifest in the many Native American and traditional foods we eat during this harvest feast. Now is a critical time to recognize "the forgotten pollinators" that will require further environmental protection if we are to continue this feasting.

Because of work I have done as a crop ecologist, I am often reminded of the many kinds of pollinators, which enable our farm crops to bear their fruits. And in this tragic year—which has witnessed more proposals than ever before to roll back conservation legislation and to cut the budgets of rural-based agencies—it is easy for me to imagine how any retreat from environmental protection may aggravate already serious declines in pollinators. This impending pollination crisis threatens to leave our tables empty for future Thanksgivings.

Can you imagine a Thanksgiving or Halloween without pumpkins? This year, for example, upstate New York suffered shortages of bees for what is normally a $13 million pumpkin crop. Droughts aggravated the growing scarcity of the native solitary bees that fertilize pumpkin blossoms and nest in woods adjacent to pumpkin patches. These squash and gourd bees are vulnerable to pesticide sprayings and to habitat loss. What will gutting environmental regulations do to the remaining bees? No pollinators, no pumpkin pies.

Bumblebees and leafcutter bees are among the many pollinators in cranberry bogs, where as many as 20 million flowers bloom on each acre. When there are not enough pollinators to go around, less than a third of these flowers develop into ripened cranberries. Pollination failure on blueberry and cranberry crops is not science fiction. In 1970, when widespread organophosphate spraying of spruce budworms wiped out native bees in forests adjacent to berry patches, yields plummeted. New Brunswick's blueberry harvest dropped from 5.5 million pounds in 1969 to 1.5 million in 1970, largely due to the poisoning of wild bees exposed to the organophosphate pesticide called fenitrothion. Bee populations did not fully recover for several years, causing a long-term decline of more than a quarter million pounds of berries per year, which cost farmers millions of dollars in losses. If we relax our laws mandating spraying setbacks adjacent to farmlands and near critical habitats for rare bees and their forage plants, we can say goodbye to cranberry sauce and blueberry muffins.

There are other traditional dishes that many of us associate with Thanksgiving or Christmas: green beans with sliced almonds, fig pudding, or roasted chestnuts. Some of these crops depend on domestic bees, others on wild bees and wasps, but all are vulnerable. Multimillion dollar almond orchards in California must already borrow mobile bee colonies from other states to help pollinate their flowering trees. Bees rented to pollinate Arizona's onionseed field can be easily killed by the incessant spraying for white flies, Africanized bees, and other pests. The green bee patches of upstate New York and the few remaining chestnut groves of Connecticut have been susceptible to contaminants produced by surrounding industries.

Yet when most people think of pollinators of food crops, they envision only the domestic honey bee, which today is in serious decline. Since 1990, we've lost nearly a quarter of all hives that formerly occurred in this country, thanks to parasites, diseases, pesticide poisonings, and Africanized bee invasions. My home state, Arizona, has seen a 44 percent decline in honey bee hives within the last year. And yet, one effort after another to support honey bees has dried up, even though these bees provide crop pollination services 60 times more valuable than the honey they produce. If we lost all honey bees in the United States without any wild pollinators taking over their chores, the resulting price increases for food in the U.S. would amount to 6 to 8 billion dollars a year.

No one believes that something so drastic might happen. That is because farmers still gain the free services of dozens of other native bees, bats, wasps, butterflies, and moths that pollinate American crops. These native pollinators—so essential to our Thanksgiving Day feast—may contribute between 4 and 6 billion dollars a year to the American economy! But they too are threatened by pesticides, habitat loss, and disease.

In order to keep fruits and vegetables on our plates, these wild pollinators need protected wildlands near croplands and reduced exposure to harmful insecticides. The next time that someone tells you that you must choose between a healthy economy and a healthy environment, invite that person over for a Thanksgiving dinner. Study what foods remain available only because of environmentally protective legislation—the Endangered Species Act, the Farm Bill, and pesticide controls. Habitat protection for pollinators is essential to our country's food security. Gutting environmental regulations is tantamount to eliminating the many foods otherwise destined for our Thanksgiving tables.

Source: Used with permission from Gary Paul Nabhan, Sonoran Desert Museum.

Capabilities of the Web

The Web can be many things to many people because it is such a versatile medium. Web pages can mix text, pictures, sound, and video clips. They allow users to give feedback (e.g., through surveys, online quizzes, feedback forms, database searches, order forms, games, and chat rooms) and download files such as documents, images, shareware programs, and games. As Web technology and software continue to improve, interactive features and true multimedia Websites will become more common and easy to create.

Anyone can create a Web page, and conservation organizations and agencies are increasingly making use of this medium. According to David Cappaert, former manager of the University of Michigan Environmental Education project (EE-Link), it makes good sense for an organization to distribute information over the Web. Reasons for using the Web include:

- The Internet is firmly established and will not go away.
- Electronic dissemination of information is cheap and independent of the number of "copies" distributed.
- The Internet is available globally and operates twenty-four hours a day.
- Distribution of information via the Web is efficient; users access information when *they* perceive it as valuable.
- Information is easy to update.

To use the Web effectively, you also must be aware of its limitations. Access to the Web will continue to grow, but a lot of people and places are not connected. Many schools, for instance, still do not have adequate computer facilities to take advantage of the Internet. Quality of information on the Web is another concern, in terms of both accuracy and relevance. Because anyone can produce a Web page, information is often suspect. Well-conceived Web pages can provide accurate and relevant information for an identified target audience, but only audiences that have reliable access to the Internet.

Example: The St. Johns Audubon Society Home Page

The St. Johns County Audubon Society (SJCAS) was the first Audubon chapter in Florida to go online with a Web page. According to vice president and membership chairman Roger Van Ghent, the genesis of the Web page stemmed from a desire to provide a versatile online resource to serve a variety of audiences. "Our Web page actually serves three target groups:

members of SJCAS, birders in general, and tourists coming to visit St. Johns County," says Van Ghent.

The Web page contains a wealth of information, including the SJCAS mission statement, upcoming events such as meetings and field trips, an online membership form, recent sightings and birding "hot spots" in St. Johns County, the county bird list, and selected articles from the group's newsletter. But, according to Van Ghent, the centerpiece of the Website is the photo section known as the Morgan Gallery.

"Two of our chapter members are excellent wildlife photographers, and we wanted to use our Web page to profile some of their outstanding bird pictures. We try to periodically add new pictures to this section to keep it fresh and exciting for our viewers." Van Ghent recommends incorporating a central theme or focal point, such as a photo gallery, into a Website in order to have a common reference point and maintain visitor interest.

To get new material for the Website, Van Ghent solicits contributions from the group's officers and other avid birders. He also works closely with the newsletter editor to select articles to put online and with the events coordinator to publish a calendar. In this way the Web page helps meet the challenge of keeping informed the over three hundred SJCAS members across the 2,500-square-mile (6,500-square kilometer) county.

In addition to reaching its own members, SJCAS hopes to join with other environmental Websites in St. Johns County in providing information for potential tourists to the county. "Our county has recently formed an ecotourism committee, and we hope to be part of the effort to provide environmental information on the Web. Already we've received e-mail from as far away as Ireland requesting information about natural resources in St. Johns County," states Van Ghent.

To promote the site, Van Ghent sent the Web address to the major search engines and exchanged links with other Audubon Websites. He published an article entitled, "Birding in Cyberspace," in the *Florida Naturalist* magazine of the Florida Audubon Society and always reminds people about the Website in the SJCAS newsletter and meetings. "Word of mouth has been an effective way to get the word out about the site," says Van Ghent. An automatic counter records visits to the Website. In the first year and a half the site was visited by nearly two thousand people.

For other groups contemplating starting a Website, Van Ghent offers the following words of advice, "First, be sure to have someone who understands and is willing to do the technical side. Once you understand this stuff, it's really not that hard or time consuming, and the software tools now available are making it easier every day. Also have a very clear idea of why you want to do this. What are you trying to communicate, and to whom? Then just get something going. Start small, have a core theme or message, and the site will evolve from that."[32]

Example: The Project WILD National Office Web Page

Project WILD is a national environmental education program that offers kindergarten through twelfth-grade activity guides available through teacher workshops. The project is implemented largely through state natural resource agencies, but is coordinated by a national office. The national office needed to create a Web page to serve as a clearinghouse of information about the program as a whole and link together individual state home pages, but had limited funds and expertise for the project. However, with creativity and partnerships, they were able to develop a first-class Web page at minimal expense. To host their home page, they turned to one of their organizational partners, EE-Link, an established Website for environmental education resources. It was easy and inexpensive for EE-Link to create a new directory on their Web server to host Project WILD's Web page. To develop the Web page, they looked for HTML experience in a short-term intern. When their intern left, they tapped into the local school system. All high school students in Montgomery County, Maryland, are required to perform 60 hours of community service for graduation. A few calls to guidance counselors and computer science teachers at nearby high schools resulted in several inquiries for the position from highly qualified "whiz-kids." The high school student who ultimately took the position completed his community service requirement and gained valuable work experience, and the Project WILD office developed their home page without adding another burden to their staff.[33]

Planning Your Website

The World Wide Web is popular with users and communicators alike, in large part, because it can be inexpensive relative to other media. The cost of setting up a Web page can be divided between developing and maintaining the content of the Web page, and renting Web server space with an Internet service provider.

Thorough planning of the content and appearance of your Web page will help produce a satisfactory result the first time around. Although Web pages are by nature dynamic and readily changeable, every alteration requires time and attention that collectively can add up to a major effort.

CONTENT. Similar to print media, the biggest decision when developing a Website is what to include. Careful consideration of your communications objectives and your Web audience will provide insights into what information should be provided. A quick tour of the Web reveals some common purposes and content of Web pages:

- general information about an organization (mission statement, main activities, contact information, annual report, long-range plan);
- announcements of special events, volunteer or job opportunities, and campaigns;
- schedules of ongoing programs and activities;
- information about publications and services offered by the organization;
- topic-specific information for specific audiences, such as homeowners, students, bird-watchers, or teachers;
- interactive features such as quizzes, guided tutorials, games, and feedback forms;
- photographs and graphics;
- search capabilities that allow users to find specific information on your page; and
- links to similar Web pages elsewhere on the Internet.

Almost anything can be put on a Web page, but it is important to focus on the main objectives that will be achieved by establishing a presence on the Web. Make sure your bells and whistles enhance your message. Also, be cautious about posting information that needs to be frequently updated. Schedules, prices, newsletters, and other time-sensitive special announcements all have to be edited or deleted on a regular basis. Unless someone on your staff has the time to spend on these tasks, it might be better to say "call or write for more information." No information at all is better than misinformation.

DESIGN. There are many books and Internet listings on designing Web pages. Good ideas can also be gleaned from other Web pages—make a mental note whenever you see an attractive Web page that might inspire your design. A few basic tips from Webmaster Andy Lyons would include the following:

- Don't put too much information on one page. Too much information will take longer to load and increase the likelihood that your reader will become impatient and leave your site. Large items should be broken down into smaller pieces and put on separate pages.

- Make your Web pages inviting. Many Web users are surfers; if you want to keep their attention, you need to give them something attractive to look at. Nothing is more boring than plain text on a dull gray background. It is easy to add color, horizontal rules, bold headlines, and graphic images to your pages. Engaging Web pages are especially important when you are trying to reach certain audiences, such as children.
- Be wary of large graphics or sound files. Large images can be frustratingly slow to load, a constraint that is especially limiting when you are trying to reach people who access the Web via a home computer modem or from overseas. If you are going to work with images, learn the tricks on how to keep them as small as possible to minimize downloading time.
- Develop a visual theme and use a standard page layout. People will not always visit your site through the introduction page, so using a consistent color scheme and layout will immediately allow users to recognize when they have landed in your site.
- Provide a menu navigation system at the bottom or side of every page. This will help people navigate through your site.
- When converting existing brochures, pamphlets, newsletters, or reports to the Web, do not simply transfer the file; the grouping and presentation order in a printed document is rarely the most effective structure for a Web page. Sections may be too long for a single Web page, layout might not be reproducible, or smaller pieces of information might become hard to find in the Web version. Organize it so that your readers can locate and get to the information they're interested in as quickly as possible.
- Do a keyword search on "HTML style" on any search engine (such as Yahoo [http://www.yahoo.com]) to find additional online resources for developing Web pages.

Example: Document Dissemination by the Illinois Department of Natural Resources on the Web

Many organizations have documents they want to make available to people who visit their Web page. Materials might include application and order forms, informational brochures, fact sheets, references, lesson plans, or directories. The Illinois Department of Natural Resources makes documents available for downloading from their Website. Their seven-eight-page conservation education catalog, entitled *Conservation Education in Illinois: A Sourcebook for Educators,* describes hundreds of free or inexpensive conservation education materials available from Illinois state agencies and natural resource organizations. The materials listed in the catalog include booklets, posters, videos, pamphlets, lesson plans, and fact sheets.

The catalog is available for anyone to download as a PDF file,[34] twenty-four hours a day, 365 days a year, and at no cost. According to Web development team leader, Shariq Ahmed, the Internet has allowed the Department of Natural Resources to disseminate conservation information faster and cheaper than ever before. In the first few months of their Internet operation, about forty-five catalogs were downloaded monthly, while about 250 printed copies were distributed over the entire period. The Illinois Department of Natural Resources has hunting and fishing license registration forms available for downloading, as well as past copies of the *Ground Water Gazette* newsletter. Patrons also can download an application form to join the Access Illinois Outdoors Program, a program to provide access opportunities to urban outdoor enthusiasts while helping rural landowners supplement their income and improve wildlife habitat on their property.[35]

ADVERTISE YOUR SITE. Designing a fabulous Website does not necessarily mean that anyone is going to see it. You may expect great things when you hear figures such as "fifty million potential visitors to your home page are on the Internet," but the key word here is *potential*. Like any other promotional or educational activity, the message must be accessed by a recipient before any communication can take place. No message can be delivered if people do not know about your site.

People use four methods to find Websites: search engines, links on other pages, publications, and word of mouth. Your efforts to promote your Web page should target each of these methods.

Search engines such as Yahoo and AltaVista are popular among Web users because they are free and have millions of Web pages indexed. According to one study, 88 percent of Web surfers use search engines when looking for information.[36] Users can enter a key word or title and search for it through these services. Search engines also are popular with Web developers because they do not charge anything to add your Website to their catalog. However, these search engines will not come and visit your Website by magic. You must inform the search engines that your site exists and invite them to visit it. To make the task easier, several Websites can help you deliver information concerning your Web page to all the major search engines.[37]

One of the most useful features of the World Wide Web is the ability to put "hotlinks" on a Web page, allowing users to instantly connect to a related Web page that physically might be stored on a computer halfway around the world. Virtually all Web surfers navigate from Web page to Web page via these links, a behavior on which you can base your promotion efforts. Are there other Web pages on the Internet that deal with topics similar to yours? To find out, connect to one of the search engines and do a search for your topic. Many Websites have a page of "links" somewhere on their site to connect to related sites, and many Webmasters will be willing to exchange links with related pages. In addition you may be able to link to one of many online directories of Web pages that deal with your topic. For example, EE-Link is a large listing of environmental education–related Websites and is heavily visited by teachers and others looking for information on environmental education.[38]

Sixty-eight percent of all Web users also find Web pages through printed materials.[39] Newsletters, stationery, press releases, business cards, articles, advertisements, flyers—all forms of printed matter—can be effective means of spreading the word about your Website. Printed material is perhaps the best way to reach audiences that are not completely Web savvy.

Finally, you should not forget the oldest form of communication—word of mouth. Presentations, informal talks, conferences, telephone inquiries, and other occasions where you interact with your target audience are all opportunities to increase the exposure of your Website. Some organizations even announce their Web page on their answering machine or voicemail recording.

Electronic Mail

E-mail lists offer another means of maintaining contact with an audience. E-mail lists function in much the same way as their "snail mail" counterparts. Once a person has been added to the mailing list, they automatically receive e-mail messages from the list. In theory, anybody with an e-mail account could start their own mailing list by simply e-mailing messages to a group of interested people. However, this can become tedious, so most mailing lists make use of a special software program that automatically deals with such mundane matters as sending messages to all the list subscribers, and subscribing or deleting users as requested.[40]

Mailing lists can be open, allowing anyone to join, or closed, allowing the list owner to grant access to specific participants. Similarly, lists can be unmoderated to encourage discussion and allow anyone to post a message. Moderated lists allow the list owner to approve each message before it goes out to the subscribers. Some lists are low volume (one or two messages per week), while others can generate dozens of messages per day. Publications such as weekly newsletters or media releases also can be sent via e-mail.

Mailing lists have two distinct advantages over a Web page. First of all, once users subscribe, they will automatically receive messages from the list, without any special effort except checking their e-mail. In contrast, a person using the Web must actively seek out and find a Web page before they can view its contents. Second, because mailing lists are thematic in nature, you can assume that the subscribers are all interested in and receptive to the topic.

Thousands of mailing lists are in operation. Some mailing lists focus on a general topic that is of interest to a broad audience (e.g., syh-exchange focuses on schoolyard habitat-improvement projects), while other lists are more specific to a particular program or region (e.g., ZOOGNUS provides announcements for the National Zoo in Washington, D.C.). Some lists remain active indefinitely, while others are designed to be temporary, like those centering on an event like Earth Day or an environmental conference.

Mailing lists can be advertised with many of the same strategies used to promote a Website, such as search engines, links on other Web pages, publications, and word of mouth. You also can inform mailing list databases about your mailing list.[41] As you promote your mailing list, be aware of the fear many people have of getting swamped by too much e-mail. A good description of your mailing list will indicate approximately how many messages per day or week a subscriber should expect to receive.

Announcing a mailing list after a special event or positive experience, during that small window of opportunity when energy and motivation are still high, can be an effective means of maintaining audience involvement and participation. The closing words of every presentation, conference, or guided activity could include, "If you would like to stay informed on this issue, write your e-mail address on our mailing list sign-up sheet."

Example: The ZOOGNUS Mailing List from the National Zoo

To publicize the guest lecture series and other special events at the National Zoo in Washington, D.C., the zoo's Office of Public Affairs sends postcards to a "snail mail" mailing list. While this strategy was manageable at first, as the list grew from year to year the postcard system became increasingly difficult to maintain. "It took us two to three days to complete a mailing, and the fact that people move frequently without informing us created an extra burden of dealing with all the returned mail," says Margie Gibson of the National Zoo Office of Public Affairs. "We wanted to find a way to get in touch with people more quickly and efficiently."

Out of these difficulties the e-mail list ZOOGNUS (pronounced zoo news) was born. The purpose of ZOOGNUS parallels the purpose of the postcard system: to inform interested members of the public about the special guest lectures and other events at the zoo. Rather than completely replacing the postcards, ZOOGNUS complements and reduces the workload of the snail mail list. Established with only forty original subscribers, many of whom were zoo employees, ZOOGNUS grew to over six hundred subscribers in less than two years. During the same period of time, the postcard list dropped from about 2,000 to 1,500 people.

ZOOGNUS is periodically mentioned in the zoo's newsletter and magazine, and an e-mail sign-up sheet is made available at all lectures. Anyone who reserves a lecture seat via e-mail is sent instructions on how to subscribe to ZOOGNUS. In addition, the *Washington Post* and other local papers provide ongoing publicity about the lecture series and make reference to the mailing list in announcements.

"Because we already had access to an Internet server through the Smithsonian, beginning the list didn't cost us a dime," says Gibson. "The only expense has been the amount of time I've needed to run the list. But because it doesn't require a lot of time or know-how, it can basically be run as a one-person operation."

The majority of time and effort required to operate ZOOGNUS goes into developing the wording for the announcements, which has to be done anyway to design the postcards. "I still have to do something with the list about two to three times a week, because a lot of people need help subscribing or unsubscribing. Occasionally someone will try to send an inappropriate message to the list that has to be weeded out. But it has significantly cut back on the amount of time and expense required to send out mailings via the postcards, and is much faster for those six hundred subscribers," says Gibson.

Sending out lecture announcements over e-mail has had other benefits as well. "It's been a good way to tap into some of the professional organizations in town, such as the National Science Foundation, National Academy of Science, and The Nature Conservancy. These people are really tied to their e-mail, and whereas before it was difficult to get them to join the snail mail list, we've had good success getting conservation and science professionals to join ZOOGNUS." Gibson estimates 10 percent of the people on the list are professionals working in allied fields.

Gibson also appreciates the independence ZOOGNUS provides for crafting event announcements, "It's nice not to have to depend on someone else to get your message out, which often means further editing or shrinking it down. E-mail lists are fast and inexpensive ways to reach a potentially large number of people with very little effort."

Her advice for other organizations thinking about starting a mailing list: "Just do it. You don't have to be a computer genius to start one of these, and it's a great way to communicate with people."

TABLE 4.2. *Type and frequency of media activities of environmental groups (● = frequently [more than semiannually], ◐ = ocassionally [at least once a year], ○ = rarely to never)*

	Using tip and fact sheets	Hosting media roundtable sessions	Contacting editorial boards	Mailing letters to the editor; op-eds	Using celebrities at press events	Using paid ads	Using public service announcements	Using World Wide Web pages
African Wildlife Foundation	●	○	○	◐	◐	○	○	●
The American Forestry Association	◐	○	●	●	○	○	●	●
American Rivers	◐	○	◐	●	◐	○	◐	●
Center for Marine Conservation	●	●	◐	●	◐	○	◐	●
Coastal States Organization	◐	○	○	○	○	○	○	●
Conservation International	●	◐	◐	●	○	○	◐	●
Defenders of Wildlife	◐	◐	●	●	●	○	●	●
Earth Society Foundation	○	○	○	◐	○	○	○	●
Environmental Action	◐	○	○	◐	○	○	◐	●
Environmental and Energy Study Institute	○	●	○	◐	○	○	○	◐
Environmental Defense Fund	●	●	●	●	○	○	●	●
Friends of the Earth	○	◐	◐	●	◐	◐	○	●
Greenpeace	●	◐	◐	●	○	○	◐	●
The Izaak Walton League of America	◐	○	◐	◐	○	○	◐	◐

TABLE 4.2. (*Continued*)

	Using tip and fact sheets	Hosting media roundtable sessions	Contacting editorial boards	Mailing letters to the editor; op-eds	Using celebrities at press events	Using paid ads	Using public service announcements	Using World Wide Web pages
League of Conservation Voters	◑	○	◑	●	◑	○	○	●
National Audubon Society	●	◑	●	●	◑	○	◑	●
National Wildlife Federation	●	◑	◑	●	◑	○	●	●
Natural Resources Defense Council	◑	◑	●	●	○	◑	◑	●
The Nature Conservancy	●	○	◑	◑	○	○	●	●
Resources for the Future	◑	◑	○	◑	○	○	○	●
Sierra Club	●	●	●	●	○	◑	◑	●
United States Public Interest Research Group	○	◑	●	●	◑	○	○	
The Wilderness Society	●	◑	●	●	◑	○	○	●
World Resources Institute	○	◑	◑	○	○	○	○	●
World Wildlife Fund	●	○	◑	◑	◑	○	●	●

Source: After D. E. Faris. 1995. *Mass Media Strategies of Interest Groups: Profiles of Educational and Environmental Organizations.* Ph.D. diss., Columbia University; p. 95; and web pages of listed organizations.

Last Words

Mass communications are an essential tool for accomplishing the conservation objectives of many organizations. Table 4.2 outlines the major types of media activities of some well-known environmental groups. While all the listed groups use World Wide Web pages to broadcast their goals and activities, almost none resort to paid advertisements. Instead, a smorgasbord of press conferences, editorials, fact sheets, relations with media representatives, and public service announcements helps to get the conservation word out. The guidelines and examples provided in this chapter should help you make use of mass media to accomplish your conservation goals.

Chapter 5

METHODS AND MATERIALS FOR INTERPRETING THE ENVIRONMENT

I'll interpret the rocks, learn the language of flood, storm and the avalanche. I'll acquaint myself with the glaciers and wild gardens, and get as near the heart of the world as I can.*

Just as a language interpreter translates a foreign tongue, an environmental interpreter translates natural or cultural events into a form that average people can understand. Interpretation, for example, might involve translating the technical language of biology to a form that can be understood by nonscientists or children.

Interpretation takes place in parks, museums, reserves, extension sites, camps, aquariums, zoos, and other informal settings. Traditionally, interpretation is directed toward visitors to orient them and promote enjoyment and understanding of a site. From an exhibit showing "Bees Are a Farmer's Best Friend" to a guided walk through the afterglow of a prescribed burn, interpretive approaches can increase visitors' appreciation for your conservation efforts.

Defining Interpretation
Playwright and philosopher Freeman Tilden first defined interpretation in his 1957 classic, *Interpreting Our Heritage.*[1] Interpretation is a communication process designed to reveal meanings and relationships of our natural (and cultural) heritage to the public through firsthand experience with objects, arti-

---

*John Muir, Yosemite Valley, 1871. Cited in G. W. Sharpe, 1982. *Interpreting the Environment,* 2nd ed. Macmillan, New York, p. vii.

facts, and landscapes.[2] Tilden outlined basic principles of interpretation that have been a reference point for interpreters at parks and nature centers ever since.

The audience for interpretation is a moving target. Most people visit parks, forests, marine reserves, zoos, and nature centers for recreation, not necessarily to learn something. People use parks and forests mainly to hike, camp, fish, and boat. They visit zoos to picnic and be with family and friends, and secondarily to look at animals. *Learning* about the animals or forests is usually low on the list of motivations to visit these sites. Thus interpretive activities must be fun and perceived as a recreational activity.

Interpreters have learned this the hard way. For example, park interpreters at an Ohio State Park found that attendance on their guided hikes increased when they eliminated the words "learn" or "educational experience" from their advertisements for the hikes.[3] Visitors were on vacation; they did not want schooling. Research has indicated that visitors to a park are more likely to remember the food they ate or the gifts they bought during their park visit than any program or display.[4] This recreation or vacation mind-set helps define many attributes of interpretation. You must realize that you are communicating with an audience that can simply walk away at any moment.

Interpretation uses many approaches to communicate technical information to nontechnical audiences. Interpretive program goals are accomplished through print media such as signs, exhibits, brochures, and self-guided walks; personal approaches such as talks, presentations, guided hikes, public events, and tours; and public participation such as school and volunteer programs. Interpreters increasingly use mass media such as radio, television, film, magazines, and computer-based activities to reach their clientele, on site and at home.

Goals of Interpretation

As in formal education, interpretation seeks to convey core messages or information to an audience; however, interpretation differs from formal classroom teaching in several ways. It attempts to communicate meanings and relationships in a thematic and informal presentation, rather than by reciting facts. Interpretation also differs from formal teaching in that it generally targets a voluntary audience, people who are interested in self-improvement, entertainment, or simply passing time. Besides translating technical information, interpretation entertains and interests the target audience.

In the United States, all federal land management agencies, such as the Forest Service, Bureau of Land Management, Army Corps of Engineers, and, of course, the National Park Service, offer interpretive programs for the public. The National Park Service has a six-part policy for the objectives of their interpretive activities that support the agency and parks while enhancing visitor enjoyment and enrichment. Their interpretive objectives include:

1. *Information and orientation:* provide easy access to information needed for a safe and enjoyable park experience.
2. *Understanding and appreciation:* foster deeper understanding of resources and values of the park, its regional context, and the national park system.
3. *Protection:* offer a variety of opportunities to interact safely with and enjoy park resources while protecting the resources from overuse, damage, vandalism, and theft.
4. *Participation and skill development:* aid and motivate development of recreational skills.
5. *Dialogue:* provide means for communication of thoughts and desires among the public, neighbors, and park managers.
6. *Education:* provide interested users and educational groups with information needed to develop a thorough understanding of a park's resources, its regional context, and the entire national park system's significance and values.[5]

Resource management agencies have used interpretation as a tool to help people understand the processes and policies of management objectives. Interpretation adds value to public and private lands by increasing visitor enjoyment and support. Studies have credited interpretation with successfully decreasing vandalism, poaching of wildlife, and other destructive behavior such as littering, collecting souvenirs, or riding bikes on hiking trails. Interpretive approaches also have increased compliance with park and reserve rules, increased support for management practices such as prescribed burns and feral animal control, and public safety.[6] In order to accomplish these objectives, interpretation must be carefully designed to be entertaining and relevant to the audience.

Interpretive Programs and Characteristics

A good interpretive program provides the visitor with a full menu of self-guided and guided activities. Diverse activities offer educational and skill development opportunities for a wide range of audience members, from novice to experienced, hurried to multiple-day, first-time to repeat, and children to elderly. A broad approach is necessary to allow for differences in learning styles and recreational preferences among visitors. Table 5.1 summarizes the advantages of various interpretive approaches. Visitor centers and museums offer the most popular forms of interpretation. These passive or sedentary

TABLE 5.1. *Comparison of personal and self-guided approaches for interpretation* (● = *high,* ◑ = *medium,* ○ = *low)*

	Personal (e.g., guides)	Written (e.g., publications)	Audiovisual (e.g., films)
FLEXIBILITY	●	○	○
AVAILABILITY	○	●	◑
PERFORMANCE	● (variable)	●	●
LOW EXPENSE	○	◑	◑
ENTERTAINMENT	●	○ (visitor must read)	● (uses senses)
LOW MAINTENANCE	●	●	○
OTHER ADVANTAGES	Can target specific visitors	Has souvenir value	Can compare different times and places

interpretive activities draw a bigger crowd than hikes or other more active programs.[7]

Like any communication process, the audience dictates the message content and medium of interpretation. Because audiences for interpretation are voluntary, professional interpreters have refined several principles of interpretation to catch and keep the visitors' attention.[8] This "interpretive approach" emphasizes that effective interpretation must be entertaining, relevant, and thematic.

Making Interpretation Entertaining and Relevant

While pleasure and entertainment aren't the end goals of interpretive programs, they are a characteristic of programs that attract audience attention. Because interpretive settings are informal, the presentation or display must attract and hold the audience's interest. Information by itself is not interpretation. Making the information interesting is one way of making it entertaining. Revealing new meanings and viewpoints to visitors and provoking their interest in your story will enhance their understanding of your message. Delivering the message in an informal and fun manner creates an enjoyable atmosphere for learning.

In most settings, you will be competing with other noise and activities for the attention of your audience. Tricks to make interpretation entertaining include colorful signs, exciting graphics, moving images, a feeling of spon-

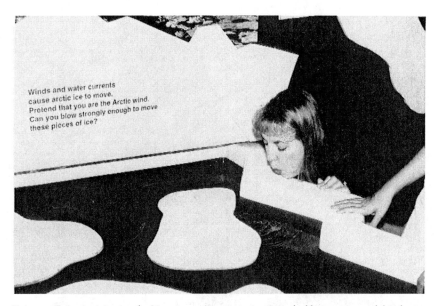

Winds and water currents
cause arctic ice to move.
Pretend that you are the Arctic wind.
Can you blow strongly enough to move
these pieces of ice?

FIGURE 5.1. *A visitor to the Vancouver Aquarium in Canada blows on a model iceberg to learn about the effects of wind and current. (Photo by S. K. Jacobson)*

taneity, game playing, hands-on activities, a conversational tone of voice, humor, use of the arts, and interaction with the audience (fig. 5.1).

Once an audience is attracted to an interpretive event or display, they must be enticed to stay. This is particularly important for informal interpretation, as most audiences are free to wander away if they lose interest. One sure way to hold an audience's interest is to relate the interpretive material to their lives and experiences. Analogies and comparisons can help your audience relate your message to their everyday lives. Visitors to the gibbon exhibit at the National Zoo in Washington, D.C., gaze up at a sprig of plastic fruit dangling about 13 feet (3 meters) overhead. The sign relates gibbon anatomy and adaptations (long arms!) to the audience, stimulating their curiosity with the question: "Why can't you reach the fruit?" An explanation follows, that if they were proportioned like a gibbon, they could (fig. 5.2).

Making the message personal is not hard. For example, to show a group of children that what they see on a forest trail is related to their daily life, you could prompt: "When was the last time you played baseball? Ash trees like this one are used to make baseball bats." As discussed in previous chapters, making interpretation relevant to the audience in this way is likely to increase their attention span, thus increasing the likelihood that your conservation message gets across. Specific techniques that interpreters use to make their presentations more entertaining and relevant, while conveying information, include:[9]

FIGURE 5.2. *The Gibbon exhibit at the National Zoo in Washington, D.C., piques visitors' curiosity with a bundle of plastic fruit overhanging the walkway. If a visitor was proportioned like a gibbon, he/she would be able to grab the fruit. (Photo by S. K. Jacobson)*

- Smile during personal presentations.
- Use active verbs in spoken or written text.
- Show direct relationships between causes and their effects.
- Link science to human history, e.g., tell how indigenous people or early explorers saw or used things.
- Link information to something the audience already knows and cares about.
- Get audience members to think about themselves and their own experiences as you relate new information to them, e.g., "How many of you have . . . ?" or "Think of the last time you. . . ."
- Relate material to audience members, their well-being and quality of life, and their values, principles, beliefs, and convictions.
- Use examples, analogies, and comparisons to convey ideas and meanings.
- Use visual metaphors to describe complex ideas.
- Use a vehicle such as exaggerated time or size scales to make your topic more interesting, e.g., "If we were small enough to crawl inside a bee hive, we would see a complex society."

- Use a ˋcontrived situation, e.g., have the audience imagine living before modern medicine to get them to think about medicinal plants.
- Use personification by presenting the point of view of an animal or object, e.g., narrate a program on watershed ecology from a duck's viewpoint, but be careful to delineate between fact and fiction.
- Use labels that include and support audience members, e.g., "All of us who care about saving endangered species. . . ." or "Parents who want to leave clean air and water for their children. . . ."
- Use "power" words recommended by advertising experts, e.g., *you, your, free, improve, new, guarantee, discover, health, save, money, safety.*

Organizing Interpretation around Themes

The organization or flow of an interpretive program is an important facet of attracting and holding an audience. The program must be not only entertaining and relevant, but also easy to grasp and follow. Effective interpretation presents a unifying theme or concept, rather than fragmented topics and ideas. Organization around a theme allows the audience to understand and remember your message with little effort. The important facts that support the theme and examples that illustrate it present your message in an easily remembered package. The introduction of a talk or the title of a brochure presents a theme and then organizes additional information around the theme. Audiences reading a U.S. Forest Service brochure on preventing forest fires understand Smokey Bear's simple theme: "Only *I* can prevent forest fires." This will help them remember to pour water on their campfire or snuff out their cigarette to help prevent fires.

The best interpretive exhibits or talks are concise and have a natural flow from subject to subject. To organize good interpretive programs, you should:

- Keep the main ideas to a manageable number; people are only capable of recalling about five different ideas at a time.[10]
- Tell or show the audience up front the theme and main points of the presentation, exhibit, or brochure to aid understanding and recall.
- Use headlines, title slides, pauses, or other mechanisms to physically separate the main ideas from each other.
- Attach subordinate information to each main idea so that it is not confused with another main idea.
- Ensure that the main ideas of each part of the program are clearly related to the overall theme.

Your interpretive ideas should be stated as themes. A theme is a central idea or major point of the interpretive activity. Developing a theme provides a clear organizational structure around which to build your supporting information. For example, the subject of an interpretive program might be "Forests." But if you were invited to a talk on forests, you would certainly want to know more about the theme of the talk before you decided to go. What is it about forests that you wish the audience to know or remember? Here are a few thematic titles about forests.[11] Note that themes are stated as complete sentences and reveal the overall purpose of the presentation, material, or activity in an interesting manner.

- Our Lives Depend on Forests
- This Forest Is Changing
- Trees Provide Oxygen for Us to Breathe
- Loss of Forests Harms Migratory Birds
- Fire Is a Natural Process in Pine Forests
- Smokey Bear Was Wrong
- Forest Soil Is a Living Thing
- The Forest Is Your Drugstore
- Forest Management Benefits People and Wildlife

Obviously, thematic titles are more interesting than the topic alone, and much more likely to draw an audience to an interpretive program or exhibit. In addition, if the theme title is repeated several times in an interpretive presentation, it is more likely that the audience will remember the main points of the program. After your presentation, audience members, when asked what your program was about, should respond with the theme.

Developing an Interpretation Program

As with other conservation communications efforts, developing an interpretive program involves planning, implementation, and evaluation phases. Components to consider as you develop your program are outlined below.

Planning Phase

Allowing for adequate planning is the best way to ensure successful interpretation as part of your overall conservation communications strategy.[12] The planning process guides the orderly development of the interpretive program in which you review and select from a variety of alternative courses of action to achieve your conservation goals.

The planning phase starts with an institutional review to determine and articulate why interpretation is needed and what goals within the mission of the organization it can address. From that foundation, you can construct the specific goals and objectives for the interpretation program.

After the need for the interpretive program and its objectives is established, planners must inventory and describe the interpretive resources and potential for the program. An inventory of biological and cultural resources will help you determine the resources and sites available for supporting the communications and for selecting major themes. These steps include inventories of:

- site accessibility, habitat types, unique features, demonstration areas for management or restoration, geological resources, scenic vistas, waterfalls, gardens, facilities and orientation areas (e.g., nearby sites interpreting related material, and key visitor contact locations, such as road intersections, boat launch areas, or campgrounds), and regional impacts based on traffic flow;
- facilities and services available and needed; and
- actions needed to minimize impact on natural or cultural resources and protect sensitive areas.

As in all communications programs, baseline information about the target audiences must be gathered to help you design appropriate program activities and materials, and for later program evaluation. These data paint a portrait of the potential audiences that includes:

- specific target groups;
- visitor motivations and perceptions;
- audience demographic characteristics;
- visitor orientation systems (previsit, onsite, postvisit);
- visitor use patterns (time of visit, seasonality); and
- mechanisms for audience participation in the planning process and in an ongoing advisory capacity.

Based on the resources and audiences, the design of interpretive materials considers questions of how, when, and where the interpretation will be conducted. During this phase, a thematic concept is developed for each area to be interpreted, including:

- interpretive theme for each individual site;
- site-specific objectives, content, and context;
- recommended interpretive media and services;
- preliminary program budgets and justification;
- draft design for interpretive activities; and
- flexibility to incorporate new materials and themes in the future.

Implementation Phase
In the implementation phase, the interpretation designs are pretested and the final designs are developed. The pretest involves evaluating a mock-up of the interpretive material with audience members by presenting it to a sample of visitors and asking questions such as: What was the main point of the text? What did this message ask you to do? Was there anything confusing or diffi-

cult in the message? What parts did you like/dislike the most? Was it believable? Did you learn anything new about "X"?

Contractors or in-house experts are engaged to assemble the program or
physical structures for public presentation. The interpretation program then is
opened to the public, and a management plan governs long-term care and
maintenance of the program. Thus the implementation phase for interpretation programs includes a number of components:

- pretest of interpretation design;
- expert review of design;
- final interpretation plan;
- strategy for implementing plan based on priority activities;
- interpretation program budget;
- staffing needs assessment; and
- interpretation program maintenance and operations.

Evaluation Phase

The interpretive program is evaluated to assess whether program goals and
objectives are being met. In *Interpreting Our Heritage* Freeman Tilden urged
interpreters to search for the gleam in a visitor's eyes to determine the effectiveness of the program. Counting gleams, however, does not provide accountability to managers and decision makers, nor does it pinpoint problem areas in
interpretive materials in order to modify them accordingly. A number of evaluation techniques that can be applied to interpretation programs are discussed
in chapters 2 and 7. Some techniques specific to interpretive activities include
collection of the following types of information:

- Impact of the interpretive materials on visitor knowledge, attitude, or
  behavior
- Long-term impact of the interpretive materials on visitors after they leave
  the site, perhaps measured through latent effects on schoolwork, home-
  owner activities, vocational interests, or repeat visits
- Feedback for designing future interpretive materials
- Cost-effectiveness studies
- Unexpected outcomes (both desirable and undesirable) that were not part
  of the original objectives
- Broad impact of the interpretive materials on the larger community, as
  measured through museum attendance or community trends
- Theoretical research on interpretive techniques

Methods used for the evaluation of interpretive materials and activities include
observational measures of behavior, surveys and questionnaires, tracking studies, interviews, focus group studies, and testing at interpretive sites. By asking

visitors questions or directly observing them, evaluators can find out whether the visitors used and learned from the interpretation.

Asking visitors questions about the interpretation determines:[13]

- whether the interpretation got its message across;
- which activities visitors found most interesting or stimulating, and why;
- what improvements and changes visitors would suggest;
- what message and information visitors remember; and
- how visitors would rate effectiveness of the interpretation.

Observing visitors at an interpretive site determines

- how many people use the interpretive materials or engage in the activity;
- what proportion of visitors approach the interpretation;
- how many visitors stay and read or do the interpretation (often measured by time spent at an activity);
- how visitors emotionally react to the interpretation (e.g., smile, frown, talk, or laugh);
- how many visitors talk to each other about the interpretation, and whether remarks are positive or negative;
- how many visitors ask questions; and
- whether visitors follow suggested activities or appropriate behaviors.

Evaluators may record comments from a suggestion box or collect long-term feedback, such as positive and negative letters commenting on the interpretation. Evaluation also can meet agency or organizational requirements for reporting and cost accounting, and provide marketing ideas to administrators who make decisions about program continuation and budgets.

Evaluation provides feedback to remedy any design or content problems that might be reducing the effectiveness of the interpretation. While problems can develop at any stage of interpretation development, many can be corrected, taking into account visitor characteristics and exhibit objectives. Fixing problems depends on good evaluation data—text cannot be worded for the interests of visitors if those interests are unknown. Major eye-contact points and visitor pathways must be observed by testing a mock-up exhibit or through observational techniques in order to design an effective exhibit.

Once the interpretive materials or activities are operational, long-term maintenance and monitoring plans ensure that the interpretation remains effective and can be updated for future visitors.

Interpretive Methods

Typical interpretive methods can be grouped into self-guided activities and personal (or person-to-person) activities. Self-guided interpretation includes exhibits, such as museum displays, signs, and kiosks; publications, such as maps, brochures, trail guides, and books; and audiovisual presentations, such as films, tapes, and computer programs. Personal services include talks and presentations, information desks, ranger help, guided hikes, campfire programs, and other guided activities. Interpretive activities in outreach programs may be either self-guided or personal. Outreach programs are discussed in other chapters (chapter 3, community events; chapter 4, mass media; and chapter 6, school activities).

Self-Guided Interpretive Activities

Personal interpretive programs are effective in educating people and influencing attitudes about conservation topics. However, agencies and organizations cannot always afford to hire staff and maintain full-blown, person-to-person interpretive programs. This is the time to turn to self-guided or nonpersonal activities in order to achieve your conservation communication goals. Both methods of interpretation offer different advantages. For example, personal interaction can increase the likelihood of making a lasting impression on a visitor to your site, yet self-guided materials may reach a much wider audience (table 5.2). This section presents the design of exhibits and brochures as models for creating your own self-guided interpretive materials.

Exhibits

The term "exhibits" is used here as a catch-all for a variety of self-guided programs. An exhibit is generally defined as a strategic presentation of ideas or themes with the intent of educating, informing, or orienting an audience. Exhibits are usually presented in informal settings such as nature centers, outdoor areas or trails, visitor centers, and building lobbies, where the majority of visitors are exposed to nonpersonal interpretation. Visits to informal facilities are self-paced, voluntary, and exploratory, so exhibits reach visitors at their own pace and level of interest. Exhibits engage an audience in nonlinear and creative kinds of learning, as opposed to the more orderly, linear, and verbal learning that goes on in classrooms and seminars.

Types of exhibits include self-guided trails, visitor center displays, educational kiosks, viewpoint markers, natural feature signs, special events displays, campground bulletin boards, regulatory signs, labeled trees or specimens, artistic statements, and three-dimensional models. Nontraditional exhibits encompass "gadgets" or devices such as quiz boards, audiovisual programs, continuous radio broadcasts, interactive CD-ROMs, talking animal displays, models, and computer simulations. Because exhibits often incorporate real objects, such as petrified wood or collections of shells, visitors get to respond to "the real thing." Many exhibits also include take-home materials, such as brochures, posters, fact sheets, or other publications, which are discussed later in this chapter.

In many cases, exhibits reach many more people than do personal approaches, making them an important part of an overall communications

TABLE 5.2. *Advantages and limitations of interpretive media*

Advantages	Limitations
EXHIBITS	
Can be viewed at visitor's pace	Are static and inflexible
Can display objects associated with the site	Require security and maintenance
Can display three-dimensional objects	Tend to compete for the visitor's attention
Can promote visitor participation	Do not work well with sequential stories
Can be complemented by publications or audiovisual programs	Can be subject to vandalism
	Are sensitive to deterioration
Can be designed for both indoor and outdoor use	
Are well suited for presenting ideas that can be illustrated graphically	
Can be always available	
Are relatively inexpensive	
Can be designed to blend with site environment	
PUBLICATIONS	
Are portable	Can discourage audience with lengthy texts
Are relatively inexpensive	Can be a source of litter
Have a souvenir value	Can dampen interest
Provide a source of reference information	Require periodic revision to remain accurate
Can be produced in foreign languages	
Allow a variety of illustrative techniques	Present poor image unless professionally written
Are suited to presenting sequential material	
Can be read at visitor's own pace	Require effort by visitor to read
Can produce income	
Complement interpersonal services	
Can be revised easily	
Can be produced at various levels of detail	
Are easy to design	
AUDIOVISUAL MEDIA	
Capture realism and provide emotional impact	Cannot be used everywhere
Communicate through images and sounds	Need equipment and electricity
Provide opportunities for dramatization	Require back-up equipment and regular monitoring
Provide visual and sound effects	
Are portable for off-site use	May be perceived as sterile or impersonal
Provide views of places, animals, plants, and seasons otherwise unavailable	May be a visual or auditory intrusion
	Cannot be modified during presentation
Create a mood or atmosphere	Difficult to change
Reach small and large audiences	Expensive to maintain
Provide a service for the sedentary	
Can illustrate space and time scales	
Can provide continuous programs	
Can ensure consistently reliable information	
PERSONAL SERVICES	
Appeal to visitors	Require trained interpreter
May be tailored to needs and interests of groups	Require close management
Use group reactions to stimulate individual interest	Limited availability
Answer visitors' questions	Are not consistently good, interpreters may "burn out" or lack skills
Prove effective during peak visitation periods	
May be monitored and changed accordingly	Are difficult to critique
May take advantage of unexpected or unusual opportunities	Require periodic revision to remain accurate
Tap diverse skills of individual interpreters	

Source: Adapted from National Park Service. 1983. *Interpretive Planning Handbook.* Government Printing Office, Washington, D.C.

plan. Because of their importance and durability, care must be taken in planning and designing exhibits to be effective channels for a conservation message. Exhibits can be effectively used in a number of settings and to accomplish a number of goals.

Museum experts use a classification system to describe the contents of indoor exhibits that also applies to outdoor displays and interpretation:

- *contemplative:* beautiful or inspiring vistas, plantings, objects, or quotations for viewers to contemplate;
- *didactic:* educational exhibits accompanied by views, demonstrations, or objects to help tell a story or deliver a message;
- *demonstrative:* an event, scene, or historic occurrence is reconstructed or demonstrated for educational purposes; and
- *exploratory:* little order or interpretation is provided, but visitors are encouraged to make their own discoveries and subtly directed to follow their own interests.[14]

Exhibits may take many physical forms. Indoor exhibits may be freestanding dividers, wall-mounted signs, objects on tables, or displays in cabinets, while outdoor exhibits may be freestanding signs or displays under weather-resistant structures. All types of exhibits may be either flat or three-dimensional, such as a model, diorama, object, or outdoor scene. Exhibits are visual, usually including illustrations, maps, graphics, charts, and other explanatory artwork. In addition, effective exhibits strive to excite more than one of the audience's senses, for example, providing an audio explanation and something to touch along with visuals and text. Some exhibits even include smell to arouse the interest of an audience, by directing them to sniff the surrounding air or a particular plant.

Self-guided tours along forest trails, bikeways, demonstration areas, and historic sites follow the same guidelines as other types of exhibits. Self-guided tours lead people sequentially along a series of interpretive stops. The tour flows from an orientation and introduction to the site through fifteen to twenty stops that elaborate on the theme. For example, the Rim Rock Trail in the Black Canyon of the Gunnison National Monument explains to visitors how the depth and sheerness of the canyon was formed and why it is a unique treasure. The first sign tells them what to expect: "You're about to embark on a short journey through geologic time. The trail is about a half-mile long and rated moderate. Remember, you're 8,000 feet above sea level. . . . Most self-guided tours are about a half-mile (one kilometer) long and take a half-hour to complete.

Research conducted on the relative effectiveness of various types of media used for self-guided interpretation shows different advantages of each. For example, self-guided trails offer the possibility of using signs, brochures, and

TABLE 5.3. *Advantages and disadvantages of various media types for interpretive trails* (● = *best,* ◐ = *fair,* ○ = *worst)*

	Brochure and marker	Sign in place	Audio (talking label)	Audio (portable cassette)
INITIAL COST	●	◐	○	◐
VANDALISM	◐	○	○	●
SUBJECT TO WEATHER	◐	●	◐	●
LITTER PROBLEMS	○	●	●	●
POTENTIAL SITE FOR DETERIORATION	◐	○	○	●
VISUAL INTRUSION	●	◐	○	●
SOUVENIR VALUE	●	○	○	○
MAINTENANCE PROBLEMS	●	◐	○	○
ILLUSTRATES PROGRESS	○	●	◐	○
EASILY MODIFIED	●	◐	◐	◐
DISTRIBUTION OF THE MEDIA	●	●	●	○
AVAILABILITY THROUGHOUT DAY	◐	●	●	○
ATTENTION SPAN OF GEARED TO VISITOR	◐	◐	●	●
SELF-PACING FACTORS	●	●	◐	○

Source: Modified from G.W. Sharpe. 1982. *Interpreting the Environment,* New York: MacMillan.

audiotapes. Table 5.3 compares the relative merits and drawbacks of these media. Based on specific characteristics of your own site, you can make practical decisions on media use and content.

Qualities of a Good Exhibit

The best exhibits attract attention and effectively communicate a message or theme within the attention span of the target audience.[15] Exhibits that use combinations of different media are stronger than exhibits that rely on a single medium (such as text), because they better reach audience members who have varied learning styles and tastes. To ensure effective exhibits, incorporate the ABCDs of exhibit design:

- *Attractive:* attention-getting exhibits that use appropriate colors and interesting graphics and visuals.
- *Brief:* well-organized and simple exhibits that contain five or fewer main ideas, only enough text to develop the theme, and graphics to help communicate with viewers.
- *Clear:* the theme of the exhibit is obvious and can be understood by the audience in two seconds or less. Additionally, the exhibit is easily visible with adequate lighting and unobstructed viewing.
- *Dynamic:* the exhibit communicates the message by arousing curiosity, inviting participation, and providing entertainment.

A clear planning process that targets these qualities is the prescription for ensuring that an exhibit will reach your audience with the essence of your conservation message.

Exhibit Development Process

Developing an exhibit involves a process similar to any communications campaign, including planning, implementation, and evaluation phases. During planning, interpreters set goals, identify and assess audiences, develop objectives, and research and conceptualize the design. Implementation includes writing text and labels, and developing and testing a mock-up exhibit. It entails working with staff or contractors to have the final exhibit produced and installed. Once the exhibit is opened to the public, an ongoing maintenance plan is instituted. Evaluation—methods of getting information to assess and improve exhibits—can be infused into almost every stage of exhibit development. The completed exhibit is assessed to determine its effectiveness and to make needed modifications. The bulk of the time for developing an exhibit is spent in the planning stage, with less time spent in each subsequent phase in the process. These stages are described here in more detail, along with specific steps that might be included in each of the exhibit development stages.[16]

Planning an Exhibit

Exhibit planning and preparation can take you a long time. It can take weeks or months to develop a small exhibit, and over a year for a major exhibit. In addition, the exhibit work plan must allow for time to test a mock-up exhibit with audience members, and for a final evaluation to find out whether the exhibit has met the interpretive objectives.

The exhibit design phase concerns the more practical and applied tasks of determining orientation, panel layouts, lighting, and other design details for the exhibit. Evaluation is used during this phase to test audience and expert opinions of exhibit design ideas. During the planning process your exhibit team must consider a number of design criteria. These describe the "powers" an exhibit should embody:[17]

- *attracting power:* does the exhibit get people to stop?
- *holding power:* does the exhibit keep people's interest and for how long?
- *teaching power:* do people learn from the exhibit?
- *motivating power:* are people motivated to find out more or take action?

The following list provides a summary of how to increase the attracting, holding, educating, and motivating powers of an exhibit:[18]

- Clear exhibit flow
- Obvious title and introductory panel
- Clear theme and structure
- Directs the visitor where to "look"
- Sense of closure at the end
- Large size graphics and text
- Strong and balanced graphic design
- Plenty of empty space, uncrowded panels
- Harmonious colors and shapes
- Consistent and clear typestyles
- Lines and angles to lead the eye
- Consistent and clear illustrations
- Main titles at or above eye level
- Short, concise, thematic text
- Fewer than twenty panels or stops, ten is better
- Fewer than eighty words per panel, fifty is better
- Short sentences and paragraphs
- Elements in motion
- Unusual, novel, rare content
- Intrinsically interesting (e.g., baby animals, not data charts)
- Engages several senses (e.g., visuals, sound, touch)
- Interactive, participatory
- Stimulates interaction between strangers
- Easily visible (adequate lighting, lack of obstacles/interference)
- Objects close to viewer
- Comfortable amenities (rails, seats, temperature, restrooms)
- Lack of sensory competition (from entrance/exit or neighboring exhibits)
- Exhibit matched to demographic characteristics and special interests of audience

- Variety, freshness within exhibit
- Perception of danger or beauty in exhibit features
- Positive perceptions based on exhibit environment (e.g., realism of display, empathy, and receptiveness from viewing animals or objects at eye level)
- Positive social pressures (e.g., attraction to crowds, walking speed adjusted to other visitors)

Getting an audience to stop and read or listen is an important function of exhibit design. People who read an exhibit learn more and spend more time looking at the exhibit. The exhibit design is what attracts people to it, but the text must keep their attention in order for them to learn something. Visitors usually stop less than one minute at an exhibit—long enough to read only a fraction of the text. Long text repels many visitors.

When preparing text, it is good to have in mind the aim of the exhibit and the characteristics of the audience. These same guidelines apply equally to any self-guided program—visitor center exhibits, trail signs, computer applications, driving tours, and audiovisual programs. Besides having accurate content, correct spelling, good grammar, and understandable language, exhibit text should convey a theme that the audience can understand, no matter what the medium.

Text preparation guidelines include writing simply, avoiding jargon and technical terms, putting the main point at the beginning, keeping it short, and using vocabulary that visitors use. Similar to guidelines for writing for the media in chapter 4, these are easier said than done. Biologists and technical staff members often have a difficult time conveying their knowledge to the public in understandable language. It is important to write as if you are a friend of the visitor, rather than as a scientist or program administrator. External interpreters, copywriters, or journalists can be hired to assist with exhibit text. An outside person also may provide a fresh and unbiased perspective of your exhibit text and design.

Most exhibits start with an introductory panel, giving the exhibit title and purpose. The audience should be able to grasp what the exhibit is about and why it is worth viewing. It also may be useful to give some information about where the exhibit or program will take the viewer—the direction of the exhibit may be obvious in a small visitor center or museum, but less obvious for a trail, discovery center, or computer simulation.

The introduction is followed by the body of the exhibit, often a series or network of panels. Section panels should follow an obvious order, such as chronology, cause and effect, problem/analysis/solution, or progress from part to whole or whole to part. Section panels should include thematic headings and give more background information about the exhibit topic.

The story told by exhibit panels is generally presented in three parts: title, subtitles, and body text (fig. 5.3). Interpretive experts note that, since most viewers only read a fraction of the text, the title and subtitles of interpretive panels must communicate the theme quickly. Instead of giving the panel a label that identifies a topic, it is better to use a title that relates the theme, uses an active voice, and is interesting and fun. Examples of topics and the theme titles that might be developed from them were discussed earlier, such as the topic of trees for which the theme was "Our Lives Depend on Forests" or the topic of medicinal plants for which the theme was "The Forest Is Your Drugstore."

Studies of exhibit titles at the Birmingham Zoo Predator House revealed theme titles that had high attracting and holding powers: "Hunter and Hunted" (attracted 40 percent of the visitors and kept them there for 27 seconds); "Animals That Eat Animals" (attracted 30 percent of the visitors for an average of 7 seconds); and "Born Killers" (attracted 30 percent for 17 seconds). Most exhibit texts were not read at all. The researchers note that, in general, only 8 percent to 15 percent of the people took time to stop and read an exhibit.[19]

As we have seen, a thematic title and strong graphic design can attract audience members to your exhibit, but it is the subtitles and body text that exert the holding power on the audience once they are near. Subtitles should

FIGURE 5.3. *An exhibit from the* Partners in Flight *kiosk of the Florida Game and Fresh Water Fish Commission shows effective placement of titles and text. (Photo by Joni Blakeslee)*

be smaller than the main title, but they must clearly relate several separate ingredients of the theme. Use fewer than five subtitles on any given exhibit panel. A coherent graphic design that physically separates the components of the theme while maintaining a consistent look will aid the viewer in finding the subtitles and understanding the theme. The body text is placed near each subtitle. More detailed text and object labels may also be added but should be placed away from the main themes and text of the exhibit panels.

Exhibit text for general, mixed audiences should be written at the 12–15-year-old level (sixth-to-eighth-grade levels), and lower for school-age audiences. Many computer software programs can test readability. In addition, simple tests of readability, such as the Fry test, can be used to see if your text meets the guidelines.

For the Fry test, use a sample of several passages of your exhibit totaling about three hundred words. Count the number of words, sentences, and syllables in the text. For text to target the 12-to-15-year age level, there should be between five and ten sentences per one hundred words (ten to twenty words per sentence) and between 120 and 150 syllables per one hundred words. It is better for text to fall at the lower end of these guidelines.[20]

In addition to these readability guidelines, other factors affect readability. The lighting and layout of the exhibit must be good, and the typeface must be large enough to read at an appropriate distance. For indoor exhibits, main titles should be a minimum of 3/4 to 1 inch (2–3 cm) tall and subtitles should be at least 1/2 to 3/4 inch (1–2 cm) tall. For outdoor exhibits, titles should be 4 to 6 inches (10–13 cm) tall and subtitles 3 to 5 inches (7–12 cm). Remember that these are *minimum* sizes—larger sizes will always be easier and more attractive for the audience to read.

Many conservation messages result in an exhibit that encourages people to seek further information or take action. Audience members may be asked to think about a question, pick up trash during their trail hike, avoid trampling an endangered species, write to a legislator, volunteer for a conservation project, take home a brochure from an exhibit, or get more information at the front desk of a visitors' center. The additional information also may take the form of a marketing device, for example, as a request for support or membership in an organization.

By following the guidelines for text development, readability, style, content, and exhibit development during the planning stage, you should be able to implement a show that has the power to attract and hold your audience and deliver your conservation message. The following style and content tips will help you attract and hold your target audience:[21]

- tell a story
- add visual images

- reword headlines, questions, and text to connect to known interests of visitors
- reposition thematic text to align with graphics
- break text into small, separate chunks to make reading easier
- reduce the number of words in text
- allow visitor control of how much information they receive, via computer controls or flip panels on exhibits
- move text closer to visitor eye level
- rewrite text to use an active voice and personal pronouns
- replace technical or abstract terms with common words
- convert some text to illustrations, graphics, or diagrams to express ideas visually
- add dramatic graphics or objects that connect exhibit themes and scenes
- place labels close to objects
- add headings that identify the theme and story line
- use questions to focus attention on key thematic objects
- use lighting to focus attention on key thematic objects
- provide an activity that can be done while viewing the exhibit, such as finding something, solving a puzzle, or making a prediction
- enlarge letter size to make exhibits more readable from a distance
- adjust exhibit panel orientation to face major visitor pathways
- add freestanding floor panels at thematic entrances to make key interest points or involve visitors in an activity
- add seating among and between exhibit areas
- remove or restrict popular interactive devices if they distract visitors or contain trivial messages

Interpretive Publications

Interpreters commonly use print media for reaching onsite and offsite audiences. Brochures, booklets, newsletters, guidebooks, and other printed material can provide a lot of information, ideas, and illustrations of concepts. Publications are easy to disseminate and can be used how and when the audience desires. Printed materials also are relatively easy to produce and revise.

Many of the guidelines for creating effective exhibits also pertain to printed materials. The design and format of publications largely dictates whether they will be picked up at all. For much of the audience, if the cover does not look inviting, few will make the effort to delve into the text, no matter how scintillating the writing. Like exhibits, qualities of attractiveness, brevity, clarity, and dynamism are crucial to hooking your audience. Then you need good content to keep their attention.

Brochures are the most commonly used written format for interpretation.

FIGURE 5.4. *A single photograph or illustration on a brochure cover is usually more effective than multiple visuals. This action illustration on a brochure of the Pecos National Historical Park has maximum attracting power.*

They are used for many purposes and disseminated in different ways: as handouts at sites, exhibits, and trails; as mailings to groups planning a site visit; and as materials for fund-raising or membership drives. Brochures also are dispensed at nearby hotels and at other public lands or agencies.

Designing a Brochure

To attract the reader, a brochure should have a catchy title, bright colors, and an inviting layout. Collect and study brochures that catch your eye from other organizations before deciding on a design for your brochure. Many of the books cited in this section offer advice and examples of brochure design to suit any purpose.

Brochure Cover

Keep the title brief and thematic. Short titles of less than ten words get more readership. Titles such as "Insects: Masters of Survival" and "Water: Lifeblood of the Everglades" give a snappy overview of the theme of the brochure. Keep your target audience in mind; if the brochure is for recreational users, mention them in the title. For example, "Insect Ecology: Key to Flyfishermen's Success" or "Boater's Guide to Seeing and Protecting Manatees." Draw readers in with an emphasis on their personal interest.

A single photograph or illustration on the cover is usually more effective than multiple visuals. Make the visual interesting by showing something happening: action shots of a bear eating berries or people hiking through a forest have more appeal than an inactive bear or a forest setting (fig. 5.4). Use bright colors or a high-contrast design to attract people. Select colors that help emphasize your theme, such as red for a brochure on prescribed fire or blue for aquatic ecology.

Body

The body of the brochure should make use of subtitles, photographs, and other graphics to break up the writing. Many people will only read the headlines, so you need to make it obvious why the reader should continue. Some tips for increasing readability include:

- Use wide margins and extra white space around the headlines and between sections to make the brochure look relaxing and easy to read. Empty areas attract the reader's attention.
- Use a simple font to make the page look inviting.
- Try using direct quotes or question-and-answer approaches. These often entice people to continue reading.
- Use bullets or check-boxes to add interest and help organize the text.
- Use simple graphics, maps, and charts.
- Put captions (in a different size or font from the text) under photos and graphics. People often read captions, second only to headlines.
- Keep sentences and paragraphs short (refer back to chapter 4 for tips on effective writing).

Many of the guidelines for designing exhibit text should be followed for brochures. A number of common mistakes in brochure design reduce readership. You would do well to avoid the "problem ABCs":[22]

Aggravation—The page is too jammed with information. The type is hard to read or too close together. Organization is poor or nonexistent. The page lacks white spaces and does not provide breathing space for the reader.

Boredom—Nothing in the brochure stands out; it looks like a page of gray. Headlines are too small. Columns are too wide. Articles are too long. Paragraphs and sentences are too long or complex.

Confusion—The reader cannot follow the flow of the text, visuals interrupt reading, or the headings and subheadings are indistinguishable.

Example: Developing a Self-Guided Interpretive Program for a Military Reserve[23]

Interpretive materials developed at Eglin Air Force Base, located in Florida's panhandle, included traditional publications such as brochures and posters, and unusual items, such as newspaper articles and signs on the base's golf courses. Audience research was key to developing materials to reach the target audience.

Eglin includes in its territory the largest remaining longleaf pine forests in the Southeast. These forests once covered much of the southeastern coastal plain and are now an endangered ecosystem. Conventional weapons testing and training programs for the military take place in Eglin's forests. Yet, the Department of Defense also manages the forests for conservation and public use. Parts of the half-million-acre base are open for public recreation, including hunting, hiking, fishing, and canoeing. In 1993, natural resource managers at Eglin Air Force Base shifted their focus from more traditional timber and game management to an ecosystem management approach that focused on the health of Eglin's entire forest ecosystem.

Eglin's ecosystem management plan called for public education in support of ecosystem management goals. The shift toward ecosystem management changed field practices at Eglin that affect the public. For example, the restoration of Eglin's longleaf pine forests includes the use of prescribed fire to mimic the regular natural fires that historically swept through the ecosystem every few years. Reaction of the public and military personnel to the renewed use of prescribed fire at Eglin was one problem to be addressed through the interpretation programs of the Natural Resources Branch.

Along with an interpretation program for Eglin's recreational users and neighboring citizens, natural resource communicators developed a program about ecosystem management for Eglin's military leaders. Military leaders were viewed as a key audience because many were on short-term assignments at Eglin and were therefore unfamiliar with Eglin's natural resources. These leaders made daily decisions about military operations that impacted Eglin's natural resources.

The goals of Eglin's interpretation programs were to build support for ecosystem management and to develop a positive agency image. The specific objectives of the interpretation program for military leaders were to improve knowledge about longleaf pine ecosystems and reinforce favorable attitudes toward ecosystem management.

Segments of the military audience targeted for the interpretation program were (1) upper-level military leaders, who set policies and make broad funding and operations decisions; and (2) unit environmental planners, the people in each division who manage day-to-day operations and submit plans to Eglin's environmental review process. All operations and military exercises proposed for Eglin undergo an environmental review, which checks for potential impacts to natural systems and endangered species, as well as for other environmental issues such as toxic hazards.

"Eglin's Natural Resources Branch normally interacts with military leaders and planners through formal meetings and reviews," said Carl Petrick, Eglin's supervisor of wildlife management. "We saw the interpretation program as another route to reach military leaders and planners with important ecosystem management information."

An interpretive communications strategy was developed using results of baseline data collection. Natural resource managers and outside experts were interviewed to gather information about key topic areas for ecosystem management interpretation efforts. Documents, such as Eglin's Natural Resources Management Plan, were reviewed for information to be included in ecosystem management interpretation efforts. Finally, military leaders and planners were surveyed to gather baseline information about their knowledge and attitudes, and about their outdoor recreational interests and other demographic characteristics.

The data identified five key content areas for the ecosystem management interpretation effort for military leaders: (1) native and endangered species, (2) fire ecology, (3) ecosystems, (4) forest resources and habitats, and (5) the compatibility of the military mission with ecosystem management. Media selected for the interpretive program included a number of self-guided interpretation options:

- A full-color poster of Eglin's main ecosystems and endangered species was coupled with a calendar to make it useful and appealing for busy military professionals (cost for printing five hundred: $1,800).

- Color brochures covered (a) Eglin's ecosystems, (b) the role of fire in the restoration and ecology of Eglin's forests, (c) Eglin's native and endangered species, and (d) a "welcome" brochure geared toward new military residents discussing how Eglin's forests serve the military mission, recreation, and wildlife habitat. All of the brochures underwent expert review before publication (cost for printing two thousand of each: $5,400).

- A 4-minute video, focusing on Eglin's ecosystem restoration efforts with vivid prescribed fire scenes, was presented on a continuous loop at an all-day, annual Eglin Open House event. (cost: $500; footage donated by local television stations).

- Interpretive signs were designed for alternating holes of Eglin's two golf courses, where 51 percent of military leaders and 33 percent of planners reported playing golf. The signs were screen-printed in four colors on aluminum for long-term durability. They described the ecosystems that occur on the golf course, the native and endangered species that inhabit those ecosystems, the role of fire in longleaf pine forest maintenance and restoration, and the compatibility of ecosystem management with the military mission (cost for eighteen silk-screened, three-color metal signs: $3,600).

- A series of three, full-length feature articles with photographs appeared in the *Eglin Eagle* base newspaper, covering (a) ecosystem management and multiple uses of Eglin's forests, (b) longleaf pine forest ecology and restoration practices, including the use of prescribed fire, and (c) native and endangered plants and animals of Eglin. Over half (52 percent) of military leaders and 57 percent of planners reported using military news sources on the baseline survey (no cost except for labor).

An evaluation showed that the interpretation for military leaders was successful in meeting program objectives. After the interpretive materials were distributed, surveys were again used to measure changes in knowledge and attitudes of the military audiences. Statistical analyses showed significantly improved knowledge and attitudes in several content areas, including attitudes toward prescribed fire, despite the high turnover in the military audiences.

Personal Interpretation

Face-to-face communication is an essential element of effective interpretation at parks and nature centers and often has more impact than the many nonpersonal approaches to communicating with the public. For example, guided walks score higher for both visitor satisfaction and increased visitor knowledge than self-guided approaches for interpreting trails.[24]

Personal delivery of interpretive messages includes one-on-one conversations at an information desk, interactions with visitors on the site, interpretive talks, and guided walks. Human contact with the audience may be brief, and limited to answering questions low on Maslow's hierarchy of needs, such as, "Where's the bathroom?" or "Where's the soda machine?" Or the contact may allow for an hour-long presentation or a morning of informal discussion while roving a nature trail.

Interpersonal communication provides direct contact between representatives of the organization and the audience, and gives basic information and orientation. Through fielding questions and volunteering assistance, staff can provide background about the interpretive site and surrounding area;

descriptions of available brochures, trails, and other activities; and emergency services.

Roving interpretation provides an opportunity for informal contacts between agency staff and individuals. Interpreters may take up positions in front of exhibits or along a popular trail in order to provide an explanation of a particular phenomenon. Interpreters may demonstrate a skill or show people how to do something in a forest, farm, or museum setting. This allows first-hand opportunities for transmitting information and conservation messages that take advantage of audience members' needs and interests. More formal interactions in the form of interpretive talks and presentations attract an audience interested in a particular subject, based on their understanding of the theme or title of your talk. Guided walks provide the opportunity to introduce your audience directly to your facilities and natural areas.

Public Presentations

Interpretive talks and presentations are delivered in a variety of settings, such as auditoriums, outdoor theaters, classrooms, extension program sites, campfire circles, park trams, botanical gardens, and almost anywhere visitors or organized groups can gather. The principles of effective public speaking apply to almost all arenas and, not surprisingly, follow the principles of effective communication. The *Golden Rule* is: Know your audience and address their needs and interest.

Giving a Talk

Psychologists report that some people are more afraid of speaking in public than of dying. Yet, much of daily life revolves around oral communication. You greet people. You ask questions and express opinions. You give and get information. Your ability to articulate your ideas often determines your happiness. Your voice, tone, body language, and appearance combine to communicate information to others. This is also true of speaking to the public. Fortunately, guidelines are available for effective public speaking, whether one is talking to small groups of people or giving formal presentations to large audiences. As with other effective interpretive communications, a good talk is entertaining, relevant to the audience, and organized around a theme.

In planning your talk, first clarify in your mind exactly what you hope to accomplish. If your goal is to inform the audience, what are the major theme and points that you want them to learn? Do you want to change the way your audience thinks or behaves? What specific actions do you want them to take?

When preparing a talk, think about the content and organization of the subject matter. But don't just think about the major points that you want to make, think about what your listeners want to hear and will pay attention to. Professional public speakers never recite only dry facts and figures to an audience. Their secret is to transform the information into a story. You can make your major point through the use of stories and follow each story with a punchy statement of fact or opinion. Facts and data are abstract and must be translated into life situations before they matter to people and make sense. For example, the statistic that 90 percent of the mortality of a threatened frog species occurs in the tadpole stage probably would mean little to most people. You can transform this fact if you allow the audience to imagine a tiny tadpole quietly feeding on algae while under attack from diving beetles, fish, and other frog larvae. Or have your audience imagine only three out of the thirty people in the room surviving to adulthood.

Good stories have inherent components, including: descriptive detail that lets the audience feel as though they are "at the scene," a focus on something meaningful and powerful, and a dramatic or surprise ending. Stories must allow the audience to relate to the situation and should be told in a conversational manner as though recounting the scene to a group of friends. For example, instead of introducing a talk on tropical plants with a dry list of species, have the audience imagine their typical morning without a drink of coffee, cocoa, or orange juice. Lead them through a whole day with no products derived from tropical plants.

The organization of a talk includes an introduction, body, and conclusion. The introduction provides a short, crisp explanation of your presentation and defines the purpose of your talk for the audience. It reveals the theme and why your subject is important. The introduction presents a road map to help your audience follow the talk. The introduction also should present the organization of the talk. Studies have shown that audiences that are given the theme at the beginning of a talk will have better recall of it later.[25]

The introduction also creates a supportive atmosphere for learning and captures the audience's attention. Acknowledge your audience and grab their attention with questions, a quotation, an illustration, a story, a picture, or an attention-getting generalization. Why should the audience listen? Tell them something that affects them directly, for example, "We all drink water from the Orange Creek watershed, but do you know where the water's been?" Or give an illustration that relates the subject to your audience. A provocative statement opening your talk may help convince the audience to stay: "Picture yourself in a situation where the only food you can eat. . . ."

The body of the speech presents the factual support for your theme. As the theme is developed, key points are made in a logical sequence and the audience follows along as you elaborate on the theme. Limit your talk to five or fewer main points to illustrate or prove your message. The amount of information you include in the body will depend on the amount of time you have. Box 5.1 suggests a method for narrating your talk to pull the audience along with you. The use of stories and anecdotes can illustrate your meaning and keep the audience's attention.

The conclusion of your speech is the climax. Reemphasize your theme or

---

Box 5.1. Some tips for giving a successful presentation are summarized here:

- Practice ahead of time. As Mark Twain said, "It takes three weeks to prepare a good ad-lib speech." Make sure your talk is the proper length of time. Thirty to 45 minutes is the maximum length for an auditorium program. Orientation presentations should be only 5 to 15 minutes long.
- Adapt your talk to your audience's background and interests. Simplify things and do not give unneeded detail. Stick to your theme.
- Talk to the audience. Do not hide behind a podium. Stand where the audience can see you and talk directly to them. If you need to write on the board, or point at a slide, stop talking while your back is turned. Then continue. Make eye contact with the audience. Some speakers like to pick out a few people in the audience in different areas of the room to focus on during their talk.
- Talk at a rate of 100 to 125 words per minute. Talk clearly and vary the pitch and tone of your voice.
- Use hand gestures and body language to help tell your story and keep the audience's attention. Put your whole body into your presentation. Facial expressions and body movements can show pleasure, enthusiasm, pain, and sorrow. Gesture with your hands and arms to show shape and location. Emphasize an important point by pounding your fist or pointing your finger. Watch politicians as they deliver speeches and see how gestures may work for you.
- Use visual aids to complement your talk. Slides, props, overhead projections, chalkboards, and other visual cues can make presentations more interesting and memorable. Make sure charts and graphs are simple and clear if you use them, and make sure the entire audience can see the visual aids you use.
- Do not worry if you are nervous. It is good to be a little nervous. Most people feel a sense of anxiety before a talk. This can make you seem enthusiastic and help you stay focused on the presentation. Your own interest in and enthusiasm for the subject will be contagious.
- End on time. Leave time for questions or discussion at the end.

---

take-home messages, and tie the conclusion back to the opening of your talk. Finish the talk in a memorable way with an anecdote, poem, visual image, or quote. If appropriate, give an appeal for a specific action and let the audience know exactly what you want them to do with the new information you have given them. Don't fade away. Conclude!

Also, do not forget to use smooth transitions between the opening, body, and conclusion of the speech. Transitions provide continuity and make the talk easy to understand. Transitions also are needed between each main point you are making. A good transition should summarize the preceding idea, establish the relationship between the preceding and following ideas, and preview the next idea.[26] For example: "Now that we know what pollinates the flower, let's see what happens to its seeds."

The best way to improve your presentation is to carefully evaluate it. You can make a videotape of your practice talk or ask a colleague to give you critical feedback. Audience feedback gathered through the use of comment forms or other methods, provides even more direct evidence of the success of your talk. The following checklists present some key characteristics of good talks and also can serve as an assessment guide.

Voice and Body
- Suitable voice volume
- Understandable speaking rate
- Varied vocal pitch
- Pleasant voice tone
- Clear articulation
- Language appropriate for audience
- Expressive body language
- Appropriate dress
- Confident manner (your audience will think you are confident if you *appear* confident)
- Good eye contact with audience

Content
- Addressed audience's needs and interests
- Attention-getting beginning
- Organized, logical flow of ideas
- Points supported by examples
- Effective transitions between points
- Effective conclusion
- Clear message
- Concrete words
- Vivid mental images
- Good use of illustrations and anecdotes
- Visual aids enhance message and points
- Visual aids clear and easily seen

Tips for Presenting a Slide Show

Slide shows are traditional interpretive presentations that illustrate a topic with a succession of slides. New computer software allows you to mix graphic images, film clips, and sound with your slide presentation. Similar to the public talks described earlier, a slide show should weave a unified story around a theme. The sequence of slide images and accompanying narration should have a cohesive beginning, middle, and end. Table 5.2 lists several advantages and limitations of audiovisual programs in comparison with other types of presentations.

It is easy to lull an audience to sleep with a slide show: just turn out the lights, speak in a monotonous tone, and show slides that are hard to see, out of focus, repetitive, or irrelevant to the theme. To avoid these hazards and to ensure a quality slide talk:

- Arrange for someone to operate the lights and projector, or computer, and to troubleshoot any problems so that you can remain in front of the audience.
- Talk to the audience before showing slides in order to establish rapport before darkening the room.
- Always preview the slides to ensure none are backward or upside down. Make sure they will show clearly in the darkened room.
- Slides should be organized in sequences to develop a single idea. If your point is to describe forest growth, a wide view of a pine forest will orient the viewer. Follow this by closer shots of pine trees, pine cones, and, finally, pine seedlings. Slide sequences are especially good at showing before and after conditions, and cause and effect images.
- Link sequences of the slides with transitions to make your presentation flow.
- Use slide sequences to reveal the complex nature of a specific topic, such as adding more details to a diagram or additional items to a list. Revealing information progressively also adds an air of intrigue and interest to your talk.
- Use high-quality slides: clear subject, in focus, with good composition and color (fig. 5.5).
- Show close-up slides so the audience can see details.
- Include people in some of your slides. People like to look at other people.
- For text slides use symbols and bullets to minimize the number of words. Use simple fonts and large lettering. Avoid crowding too much information on a slide. For a general audience, show only fifteen to twenty-five words on a slide, or ten to fifteen numbers. Graphs, like bar graphs and pie charts, are easier to read than tables.
- Vary the length of time you leave each slide illuminated, from a few seconds to a minute or more. On average, show slides at a rate of one slide per fifteen seconds, with a maximum up to a minute, depending on the text or image. Once the slide no longer pertains to your narration, change the slide. Don't let the audience contemplate the image for longer than is necessary to illustrate your particular point.
- Do not introduce each slide, for example, "This is a Florida panther."

FIGURE 5.5. *Good photography is a prerequisite for a successful slide show. Close-up images, action shots, unusual subjects, and people-nature interactions excite viewers, according to professional photographer Steve Morello. (Photo by Steve Morello)*

Instead, make your point: "Less than a hundred Florida panthers are left in the wild." The slide should enhance your narration.

- Change your voice inflection to keep the audience's attention. They cannot see your enthusiastic hand gestures in the dark.
- Your narration should anticipate the next slide and provide a smooth transition to it in advance of flashing it on the screen.
- Do not blind the audience with an empty white screen between slides or at the end of the talk. Put in blank slides if your projector does not automatically blacken the screen when no slides drop. Computer-based presentations eliminate this problem.
- Stand to the side of the screen and always face your audience (not the slide!).
- Additional equipment to add music to your narration or computer software to add film clips or Internet links can make your presentation more interesting and entertaining.
- Practice your talk. Again!

Using Other Visual Aids

Many interpretive talks occur outdoors and in informal settings where a variety of visual props can enhance the presentations. Once you have identified your theme and developed an effective talk, think about visual props to help illustrate your points. Experts have found that visual aids can increase audience understanding and retention of information by 50 to 200 percent.[27]

A variety of objects can serve as props, including actual artifacts, such as plant parts, animal specimens, soil samples, rocks, scientific equipment, or other objects that you want the audience to see. Props also can be three-dimensional models that illustrate things that are barely visible or difficult to witness. You can show an enormous model grasshopper with clearly visible chewing mouth parts, plastic components of a tree that can be taken apart to show bark and transport systems, or a diorama of the bat cave at your nature center.

Models can bring to life abstract descriptions. Dry narration can come alive with maps of a watershed, illustrations of an endangered species, photographs of your area taken during different seasons, or videotapes of the nesting behavior of resident birds.

Interpretive settings allow you to experiment in creating innovative props and programs targeted to your audiences. Some popular approaches to conveying your conservation message include the use of costumes and characterization of historic people, or even plants or animals, to give unique insight into your topic. Interpretation done in costume allows you to dress up like photographer Ansel Adams to describe the Yellowstone Valley when the park was established. Or to enliven a talk on prescribed fire, don the garb of a fire fighter to discuss the natural process of fire on forest lands.[28]

Other types of visual aids include puppetry, which uses images of creatures to make abstract ideas understandable and enjoyable. Puppets can give voice to plants, animals, and people to illustrate concepts or get across conservation messages in a nonthreatening and fun manner. Among the most popular visual aids are live animal shows. These provide memorable experiences for people to see or even touch wild creatures (fig. 5.6).

Guidelines for using visual aids are similar to those for using slides. Remember to:
- make sure the entire audience can easily see your visual aid;
- if your props are small, like a rock or leaf, have several specimens that you can quickly pass around the audience;
- maintain eye contact with the audience, not with your prop;
- use props actively, write on them, move them around, have people touch or smell them; and
- practice using your props, introducing them, holding them, and conveying your ideas about them.

Giving a Guided Walk
Guided walks and other tours offer audiences an opportunity to interact with your facilities and with natural areas, wildlife, and landscapes. Guided walks can lead visitors along a forest trail, through a zoo or botanical garden, aboard a

FIGURE 5.6. *Live animal shows provide memorable experiences for people to see or even touch wild creatures. The live Birds of Prey demonstration at the Portland Zoo attracts a crowd. (Photo by S. K. Jacobson)*

tour boat, or almost anywhere you wish to interact with an audience and a particular setting (fig. 5.7). Tours to a demonstration area can show habitat restoration efforts, such as the effects of prescribed burns or the management of rare plants or wildlife species. As mentioned in chapter 3, firsthand experiences with wildlife or wild places is an effective method for increasing people's interest and concern for conservation.

Characteristics of good guided walks have many elements in common with effective public talks. They are entertaining, relevant, meaningful, and organized around a central theme. Entertainment on a guided walk involves the audience in actively observing, searching, thinking, or doing something guided by the interpreter's narrative and theme.

Like a public talk, guided walks have an identifiable introduction, body, and conclusion. In addition, guided walks have a staging period fifteen minutes or so before the tour starts.[29] Activities for each of these periods are described below.

Staging Period

Beginning about fifteen minutes before your tour, the audience starts to gather at the departure point. This is your opportunity to greet the members of the audience, learn something about their interests and background, and answer

FIGURE 5.7. *Guided walks can lead visitors along a forest trail, through a zoo or botanical garden, aboard a tour boat, or almost anywhere you wish to interact with an audience in a particular setting, such as this ranger-led walk at Yellowstone National Park. (Photo by S. K. Jacobson)*

any questions they may have. Your friendly greeting and enthusiasm for the tour helps build rapport with the members of the audience and makes a good first impression. You can mention any physical or safety requirements, and suggestions for sun or bug protection at this time.

Introducing the Walk
Begin at the designated time and introduce your tour. Your introduction must capture the audience's attention (otherwise, they will disappear), create interest in the topic of the tour, and orient the audience. Tell them how much time the tour will take and repeat any physical or safety requirements. Most importantly, the introduction will introduce the theme of your tour and the general organization of the trip and your commentary. Set the stage for what they will be seeing along the way by giving a brief overview of the tour. As you walk along, stay in the lead and make sure that you can see the entire group behind you. As you reach each stop, make sure that you are talking to the entire group.

Body
The body of the tour is the stops that you make along the way. During this period, develop your theme by describing specific sites, plants, animals, or

objects that you pass. Organize your commentary and discussion around the theme. Do not talk about "everything." Remember, your audience will remember only about five main points.

Each stop may take one to six minutes, depending on the focus and the group. Larger groups take longer to assemble and move. Your narration generally will follow a four-step format in which you:

1. Have the group focus their attention on the specific scene or object of interest. This can be done with a question: "What do you think pollinates this white flower?"
2. Provide your explanation or description: "The white, fragrant (encourage group to take a sniff later) flower attracts bats flying at night. . . ."
3. Connect the stop with your overall theme, such as: "We depend on pollinators to maintain our landscape." This makes it clear why you stopped there and why the point was important.
4. Provide a transition sentence to the next stop. A foreshadowing of what will follow or a suggestion of what to look for along the way to the next stop will reorient the audience to the tour.

Experienced interpreters make their stops more dynamic by involving the audience at each stop in thinking or doing specific tasks. Some tour guides carry a backpack with visual aids, such as animal skins, pressed flowers, bird nests, owl pellets, binoculars, thermometers, photographs, or other objects that might not be seen or used on every tour, but would enhance or illustrate the theme at certain stops. Encouraging the use of all five senses, such as smelling tree leaves for identification or listening to frog calls, can make the audience enjoy and remember specific points.

Many interpreters rely on provocative questions to stimulate the group and encourage interaction. Asking creative questions is an art. Different types of questions solicit a variety of thoughts and answers. Questions may help compare differences and similarities between things, such as, "What do bees and people have in common?" They can stimulate the group to think about the implications of something, such as: "What will this forest look like in thirty years if timber management remains unchanged?" Follow-up questions can elicit opinions or personal feelings, such as: "What would be a fair solution to protecting the forest and forestry jobs?" Questions also may enhance problem-solving skills, such as: "What needs to happen in order to save this species from extinction?"

Like all forms of communications, your questioning techniques and descriptions will depend on your audience. Not everyone will respond to contrived objects from your backpack or want to be questioned about personal beliefs. Differences in cultural backgrounds also must be considered. For example, some foreign tourists visiting U.S. parks may find direct questions posed by young interpreters to be rude or discomforting based on their social norms.[30] Children in a group may make long stops difficult or lengthy explanations impossible.

The length of the tour also must be geared toward your audience. You may have twenty planned stops along the tour, and anticipate a few unplanned stops to take advantage of serendipitous scenes or sightings that help illustrate your theme. If you have a large audience, you will have to eliminate some stops to stay on schedule. Do not forget that the audience will probably remember only five or fewer main points and make sure that your stops do not attempt to cover more major points than can be retained.

Concluding the Walk

The conclusion is given after the last stop of your tour. Like the conclusion to a talk, it should reinforce the theme. The conclusion reminds the audience of the relationship between the stops you made and the items you discussed during the tour, and the significance of the theme. Good conclusions are brief and to the point. They reaffirm the take-home message for the audience and let them know that the tour is definitely over. Thank the group for their participation.

Last Words

Self-guided interpretive activities such as exhibits, trail signs, and publications can be an important part of your environmental communications package. They do not have to be expensive. If cost per visitor is considered, exhibits are often a good investment when compared with more intensive and expensive personal interpretive services. In cases where you are communicating conservation themes or messages with an audience on a regular and nonpersonal basis, brief, simple, and clear exhibits or printed materials are often the best environmental communications choice.

Personal interpretive activities such as public presentations and guided walks offer an opportunity to target information directly at a current audience. Social interaction can increase support and concern for conservation messages and management policies. Organizing your guided activities so that the introduction, body, and conclusion are woven around a theme can help you deliver an effective conservation message. By relating your presentation to the lives and interests of the audience, your interpretation will be both entertaining and memorable.

Chapter 6

CONSERVATION THROUGH EDUCATION

We won't forge a sustainable society until we have nurtured a
generation that is imbued by a guiding environmental ethic.*

Education programs have contributed to the conservation of wildlife and wild
areas around the world, yet a sustainable society is still beyond reach. Increasing human population and natural resource consumption encroaches on
forests, savannas, wetlands, and marine environments. Future conservation of
species and ecosystems depends on whether we are able to garner public support and participation now. Implementing successful education programs for
natural resource conservation is an essential communications tool.

Education at all levels is needed to help people understand the interrela-
tionships between humans and their environment. This chapter focuses on
programs for adults and youth conducted by teachers, environmental organizations, community groups, and resource agencies. Educational approaches
range from information and problem-oriented programs in schools to activities addressing environmental values and attitudes in communities and better technical training for resource professionals. The following descriptions of
programs aimed at various audiences provide examples of techniques for successful conservation education. Effective programs for protecting sea birds in
Canada, monitoring water quality in Michigan's rivers, and teaching ecology
in park settings showcase an array of approaches for tackling conservation
problems through education.

---

*Gaylord Nelson, former U.S. senator and organizer of the first Earth Day in 1970,
cited in J. H. Cushman Jr. 1997. Critics rise up against environmental education. *New
York Times* (22 April).

Roots of Education for Conservation

Effective educational programs are essential to finding viable solutions to the challenges of conserving wildlife and ecosystems. The clarion call by members of the World Commission on Environment and Development for a "vast campaign of education, debate, and public participation . . . if sustainable human progress is to be made," is echoed at international environmental meetings. Although education alone will not solve conservation problems, education is a prerequisite for better natural resource management and, ultimately, for safeguarding our planet.

The goals of conservation education are many and usually include:

- Increasing public knowledge, support, and skills in developing appropriate environmental management and conservation policies
- Fostering a conservation ethic that will enable people to be responsible stewards of natural resources
- Altering patterns of natural resource consumption
- Enhancing technical capabilities of natural resource managers
- Incorporating resource management concerns into private sector and government policy-making processes

Conservation education recognizes the central role of people in all nature conservation efforts. Like other communications programs discussed in this book, conservation education is designed to affect people's awareness, attitudes, and behaviors toward natural resources, but the specific aim is to develop lifelong knowledge and skills for conservation action.

The growing use of educational strategies to meet conservation goals may create a false perception that conservation education is a recent phenomenon. The diverse instructional strategies advocated by conservation educators, however, have ancient roots. The lives of early humans, for example, were connected inextricably to nature. These close interactions with the environment served as the primary vehicle for learning about the world. Educational methods used in conservation education are linked to Greek philosophers such as Socrates (ca. 470–399 B.C.), who advanced inquiry and experiential learning as a path toward knowledge, and Plato (ca. 428–348 B.C.), who emphasized the efficacy of learning by doing. The Romans also contributed to this foundation through Quintilian's (ca. A.D. 35–ca. 100) theory that components of the curriculum should be interrelated with information presented at the appropriate stage of intellectual development.[1] In the formal educational sector today, such ideas find their manifestation in support for infusing conservation education throughout a school's curriculum.

Later educational theorists shaped the direction of conservation education. For example, John Amos Comenius was an early proponent of nature education. In the 1600s, he promoted the importance of sensory learning and used a garden as a primary tool for instruction.[2] Referring to sensory learning as the "golden rule of teaching," Comenius stated: "It is when things have been grasped by the senses that language should fulfill its function by explaining it still further."[3]

Expeditions of naturalists in the 1700s and 1800s increased public awareness of natural history. From this interest emerged informative expeditions led by nature guides, such as Enos Mills, who conducted educational walks up Long's Peak in 1889 in the area now known as Rocky Mountain National Park. Education was promoted within the U.S. National Park Service with the establishment of the National Park Education Committee in 1918. Two years later, the first official nature guides were hired to lead educational programs for Yosemite National Park in California.[4]

The importance of teaching conservation was highlighted in the 1950s by a National Education Association report, "Conservation Education in American Schools."[5] Ironically, this document identified obstacles faced in the formal sector that still exist today, such as the reliance on textbooks for learning rather than hands-on experience, and the lack of appropriate training for teachers. History reminds us that the conservation education challenges of today are not new. Likewise, history provides a context for understanding successful strategies in conservation education, as reflected by the programs described in this chapter.

Evolution of Environmental Education

In the past few decades, conservation education has continued to diversify and expand. The environmental crises of the 1960s and 1970s stimulated a synthesis of educational traditions. Environmental education went beyond conservation educators' focus on natural resource management, and integrated discussion of forests and natural systems with life in the suburbs and cities.[6] Environmental education became a new approach to looking at the relationships between humans and their environment. The focus of conservation education on stewardship and problem solving was integrated with other educational traditions, such as hands-on learning. Additionally, elements from the progressive education movement, such as interdisciplinary and lifelong learning, contributed to conservation education programs.

In 1983, the North American Association for Environmental Education defined environmental education:

> Environmental education is a process which promotes the analysis and understanding of environmental issues and questions as the basis for effective education, problem solving, policy making, and management. The purpose of environmental education is to foster the education of skilled individuals able to understand environmental problems and possessing the expertise to devise effective solutions to them. In the broader context, environmental education's purpose is to assist in the development of a citizenry conscious of the scope and complexity of

current and emerging environmental problems and supportive of solutions and policies which are ecologically sound.[7]

With the growth of environmental education, conservation-focused programs expanded into new venues. Today, providers of these educational services are diverse and include:

- Formal education institutions such as schools, universities, and local/state/ federal education departments
- Governmental agencies in charge of natural resources and environmental protection
- Informal educational outlets such as nature centers, museums, zoos, camps, residential centers, scouting and youth clubs, and outdoor education organizations
- Communication outlets such as magazines, television, and other mass media
- Associations for professionals in fields such as conservation biology, environmental sciences, planning, and education
- Business and environmental associations such as conservation organizations, utility companies, and industry and labor groups

The environmentally literate citizen has been defined as someone who has ecological stewardship values, knowledge of natural systems, and the skills and desire to take action to correct environmental problems.[8] The development of environmental literacy goes beyond passive nature study. Effective conservation education programs guide individuals from awareness of problems to making the commitment, gaining the skills, and taking the actions that will eventually solve these problems. Such programs have been implemented in a diversity of settings. They use parks, schools, community organizations, resource agencies, and the mass media to reach youth and adult audiences. The examples in this chapter demonstrate that long-term communication efforts are necessary to help conserve wildlife and manage natural resources. The challenge is to expand these types of programs so that they reach many audiences in many places.

Conservation Education Programming

Although the goals of your conservation education program may be broad, similar strategic planning procedures for targeting audiences and designing effective messages apply to all communications-related programs.

Target Audiences

Audiences for conservation education are everywhere, so clearly defining the objectives and target audiences before beginning a program is critical. Program designs will differ according to whether your audience is schoolchildren, university students, consumers, family groups, business leaders, teachers, or decision makers.

Your challenge is to develop appropriate activities for specific target audiences. An effective educational intervention for hunters may be inappropriate for other groups, such as hikers or politicians. Even within these groups, subcategories based on income, education, culture, or gender influence the needs of each audience, as discussed in chapter 2.

Before beginning a program, you must analyze differences among segments of your audience. Disadvantaged students are more concerned about lack of good drinking water, acid rain, lead poisoning, and energy shortages, whereas non-disadvantaged students are more concerned about rainforest destruction and recycling.[9] Scientists are most concerned about loss of biodiversity, whereas citizens are more worried about pollution issues.[10] Understanding your target audience and enlisting their participation in program development are key to successful programs.

Designing a Program

Like all communications programs, your educational activities must address existing knowledge, attitudes, and behaviors of your target audiences. As described in chapter 3, program planning involves defining clear goals and objectives for the program, and determining resources and constraints. During implementation, you assess and refine program schedules and budgets. Through evaluation you can determine program outcomes and overall success. Let's look at how conservation education programs in parks, communities, and schools follow this model for success.

Conservation Education in Parks

Education programs associated with the conservation of natural areas can potentially have a large impact on natural resource management. Governments have established more than 3,500 reserve areas in over 120 countries. Since 1970, nations have expanded the extent of protected lands by more than 80 percent; nearly two-thirds of these are in tropical countries. Audiences for education programs associated with protected areas potentially span almost all ages, backgrounds, and cultures.

Example: Conservation Education in Parks of Malaysia and Brazil

Two examples of conservation education initiatives created for national parks in tropical countries involve programs in Malaysia and Brazil. These programs used a systematic approach to guide the development, implementation, and evaluation of their programs. Feedback from the initial stages of planning through completion of the program allowed for continuous improvement of instructional materials and strategies.

Both programs used the resources of national parks to engage local primary schools in conservation education.[11] Kinabalu Park in Malaysian Borneo not only protects a great diversity of plants and animals, from 1,500 species of orchids to clouded leopards, but also encompasses the tallest mountain in Southeast Asia. The program for Brazil's Morro do Diabo Park protects some of the last remaining Atlantic forests of interior Brazil, home to endangered species such as the black lion tamarin.

The initial stages of planning for both programs involved identifying the needs of the parks, teachers, and students. Some typical tools for data collection (described in detail in chapter 2) include:

- Survey
- Interview
- Focus group or panel
- Public meeting
- Observation
- Document review and content analysis
- Case study
- Participatory rural appraisal

Assessing program needs included an analysis of the perspectives of all stakeholder groups involved in the programs. This included techniques such as interviews with students, parents, teachers, administrators, and resource managers. The assessment also analyzed current educational programs, curricular materials, and government mandates involving education. A sample of participants and data sources is listed in table 6.1.

The objectives of the two education programs emerged from the assessment of needs. Three goals guided the programs: (1) to familiarize students with the parks and their benefits, (2) to introduce students to basic ecological principles through outdoor experiences, and (3) to enhance the interests of students in the environment and their participation in conservation activities. Measurable objectives were developed to facilitate later evaluation of the programs' impact. After completing the program, for example, students were expected to be able to describe the ecology of common plants and animals in the park and to continue activities that promoted conservation at their home and school. Other tasks essential to the planning phase involved identifying the resources, constraints, and specific target audiences for the programs.

The implementation phase for both programs involved continuous assessment of the instructional materials and methods as the educational program was formed. Baseline data were collected through questionnaires

TABLE 6.1. *Representative participants and data sources*

Formal sector	Nonformal sector
PARTICIPANTS	
Education agencies	Resource management agencies
School administrators	Environmental and nongovernmental organization
Teachers	Municipal and business leaders
Students	Resource users
Parents	Local industries
Outside organization	Museums/parks
DATA SOURCES	
Curricula	Conservation information for adults/youths
Texts	Conservation activities
Extracurricular materials	Resource-user extension materials
Student activities	Mass media involvement
Teacher pre-service training	Religious/industry/community activities
Teacher in-service training	

and tests used to survey students' attitudes and knowledge levels. Both programs began with a slide presentation, followed by small-group activities along nature trails. At Kinabalu Park, six school groups participated in a pilot program (fig. 6.1). This revealed the need for follow-up activities to reinforce student learning. A new component was added to entice the students to complete fun conservation activities at home. For the Brazilian program, follow-up activities involved adult community members through art exhibits, music festivals, and drama.

The final evaluations used a variety of assessment techniques. Students and teachers provided feedback about the programs through written evaluations. Program planners measured the impact of the programs by moni-

FIGURE 6.1. *Students participate in Kinabalu Park's conservation education program (Photo by S. K. Jacobson)*

toring changes in knowledge and attitudes about the parks and conservation based on formal baseline and post-program tests. Other assessments included documenting the percentage of students who succeeded in completing voluntary follow-up activities, such as a "Junior Ranger" list of assignments to pursue at home and school. To justify budgets, the staffs also kept records of the number of schools and students involved in the programs. Park administrators used information from the evaluation as a basis for deciding to continue the programs, which are still in operation. Chapter 7 discusses tools for evaluation in more depth.

The results of these programs expanded beyond the original objectives and included enhanced community involvement in the parks. For example, community members lobbied the government to remove a dumpsite from Morro do Diabo Park and rescued the park when a fire threatened the forest. The programs at Kinabalu Park and Morro do Diabo are concrete examples of successful conservation education built upon systematic planning and evaluation.

Field Schools Associated with U.S. Parks

Field schools associated with national parks in the United States provide educational opportunities to people seeking a deeper understanding of park resources and contribute to building support for the national park system.[12] Programs can last from an afternoon to an entire summer and may offer activities for which visitors and community members are often willing to pay, especially if recognized experts teach the courses.

Numerous field schools operate in the United States. For example, the Smoky Mountain Field School operates in Great Smoky Mountain National Park in cooperation with the University of Tennessee. Their mission statement begins with the goal of "educating public audiences about the Park's natural and cultural resources through a variety of activities, using university researchers and other professionals knowledgeable of the Park." Programs range from intensive weekend courses to thematic day hikes and family oriented activities.[13]

Mammoth Cave National Park cooperates with Western Kentucky University's Center for Cave and Karst Studies to offer a series of one-week summer courses focusing on caves and karst landscapes. These intensive field courses combine daily lectures with field observations and excursions. Visiting professors who are authorities in caving and karst science teach the classes. Some courses require previous subject knowledge, while others are designed for people merely curious about caves and caving.[14]

The Yellowstone Institute is a year-round field program offering a series of short courses in natural history, cultural history, and humanities topics where people learn about and experience the wild, natural wonders of Yellowstone National Park. Sponsored by the nonprofit Yellowstone Association in cooperation with the National Park Service, the Institute offers programs for adults of all ages as well as families. Courses typically last from two to five days and focus on a wide variety of topics such as edible plants, backpacking, photography, and geology.[15]

Another nonprofit group, the North Cascades Institute, also works in cooperation with the National Park Service to provide a variety of activities and seminars in Washington. Established in 1986, their programs have diversified to meet the needs and interests of everyone from school teachers to avid backpackers and nature poets.[16]

Some field schools operate with the assistance of a cooperating association or "friends" group. Others are self-supporting, nonprofit organizations. The Teton Science School offers a range of residential programs for school groups in the Grand Teton National Park in Wyoming. Their typical three- to five-day session includes activities such as:

- a natural history hike or ski,
- canoeing on a nearby lake,
- a lesson on animal tracks and signs,
- wildlife observation,
- assisting in ongoing field research in the park, and
- field guide use and map-reading skills.

Box 6.1. Description of one of thirty-nine courses for adults taught at the Teton Science School

Bears of Yellowstone

This three-day field trip will start at the TSS campus and then head north to Yellowstone, where students will spend two nights at Canyon Lodge in the park. We will spend time hiking in and investigating bear habitat, finding and understanding various bear sign, and visiting a bear den. Dawn to dusk will find us scouting for bears and, hopefully, observing their behavior. Field discussions will cover bear ecology, management, and the future of bears worldwide. While we will be spending time in bear country, there is no guarantee of bear sightings. Bears are magic! We might even see the reintroduced wolves. Come join us.

9 participants
Fee: $280 plus meals

Source: The Teton Science School, P.O. Box 68, Kelly, WY 83011.

Teton Science School activities for adults range from natural history seminars on bears and birds to wildlife photography and artistic explorations. Course prices range from $55 to $300, depending on activities and duration. As an example, Box 6.1 describes their Bears of Yellowstone course taught by a carnivore ecologist.

Conservation Education in Communities

We are confronted with the extinction of some 17,000 species annually.[17] Involving communities in educational programs aimed at protecting vulnerable species is one key to conserving biodiversity.

Example: Conservation Education to Reverse Population Declines in Canadian Seabirds[18]

Populations of nesting seabirds on the North Shore of the Gulf of St. Lawrence in Canada are the focus of a seabird management program that integrates education into the management agenda. During a twenty-one-year period, a nongovernmental organization—the Quebec–Labrador Foundation (QLF)—in collaboration with the Canadian Wildlife Service, designed, implemented, and tested this education and management program in order to stabilize seabird populations.

Exploitation and mismanagement have caused populations of seabirds such as the Common Murre, Razorbill, and Atlantic Puffin to fluctuate dramatically over the past two centuries. The Canadian seabird project documents the success of an educational approach to decrease human predation on seabirds and eggs by changing local residents' knowledge, attitudes, and behaviors toward seabirds. The QLF program also gives testimony to the importance of collecting baseline data on target communities, involving them in program development, and collecting data to evaluate the effects of the educational intervention.

The population declines of seabirds precipitated QLF to begin researching local hunting practices and the cultural factors affecting seabird populations. Project director Kathleen Blanchard collected data by interviewing heads-of-household in the area where the population declines were most severe. Survey results revealed a lack of knowledge among local residents concerning wildlife regulations. Responses from the residents reflected widespread illegal hunting and a utilitarian perspective regarding wildlife. These findings were not surprising, given the remote location of the North Shore and the role of the seabirds in supporting the lifestyle of the six thousand residents. Although half of the residents were employed

in cod fishing, subsistence activities such as egg gathering and berry picking supplemented the local economy.

A response to the plight of the seabirds came in 1978 with the collaborative efforts of the QLF and the Canadian Wildlife Service to develop a
seabird management plan with a local educational component. The goal of
restoring the seabird populations while respecting the local culture
resulted in several objectives:

- increasing the population levels of nesting seabirds;
- improving public knowledge, attitudes, and behaviors toward seabirds;
  and
- building avenues for greater local participation in seabird management.

The bottom line for success of the management plan depended on community participation, rather than outside enforcement of regulations,
according to Blanchard.

The educational program encompassed four primary strategies:
instruction for youth, training in leadership skills, information dissemination, and institutional support (fig. 6.2). A four-day program for youth at
the St. Mary's Islands Seabird Sanctuary provided local children with
hands-on experiences in seabird ecology and wildlife law. Instructors for
the program were local adults and university students who had received
training in experiential learning and biological sciences. The objective of
the program at St. Mary's was not to convert children to conservation
through classroom lectures, but rather to provide fun opportunities to
learn about seabirds and the effects of humans on their populations. Other
youth activities included conservation clubs, theater productions about
seabirds, and development of instructional materials about seabirds for use
in the schools.

Training activities for residents were critical to enhancing local participation. More than fifty local volunteers and staff received training in
instructional methods and field ornithology. The educational materials

FIGURE 6.2. *Common Murres
and other seabirds were the focus of
a conservation education program
on the Canadian coast. (Photo by
Steve Morello)*

were practical and relevant for community residents, and were disseminated by mass media such as Canadian radio and television. Some of the materials produced by the program included a seabird identification poster, a calendar, a nine-part radio series, a film documentary, a citizen's guide to seabird regulations, and a school newsletter. Strategies for building support for the program included study tours for leaders from national and provincial conservation groups.

The QLF documented success in achieving the goals of both the management plan and the educational program. Increases in seabird populations were recorded from 1977 to 1993. In addition, a follow-up survey revealed improvements in residents' knowledge, attitudes, and behaviors concerning seabirds. The proportion of heads-of-household that correctly stated the legal status of selected species rose from 47 percent of respondents in 1981 to 64 percent in 1988, and preliminary results of a recent survey indicate increased awareness. While community residents continued to believe that birds should be harvested, the survey results showed a shift in residents' perspectives to lower levels of harvest needed for supplemental subsistence of families.[19]

Other measures providing evidence of increased local involvement in conservation included increased memberships in conservation clubs, a waiting list for the St. Mary's Island Youth Program, increased local conservation activism, and local grant requests for environmental activities. In this case conservation education complemented legislated policy to help a community ensure the survival of its seabirds.

Conservation Education for Children

Most environmental attitudes are formed during childhood; thus children are an important target for conservation education. Children are best reached through educational programs tailored to their age and social development. For example, one of Freeman Tilden's time-honored principles of outdoor education is that: "Interpretation addressed to children . . . should not be a dilution of the presentation to adults, but should follow a fundamentally different approach."[20]

Cognitive and Social Development Theories

One way to look at how young people learn is cognitive development theory, which deals with the development of knowledge, or intelligence. The Swiss psychologist Jean Piaget described four stages of cognitive development, which loosely correspond to the age groups indicated in table 6.2. The theory holds that children, adolescents, and adults will react to educational programs according to their level of intellectual development.

As cognitive development theory suggests, children do not benefit from adult conservation education programs because they are at a different stage of development. Adults and adolescents can engage in abstract thought, using their imagination to understand a verbal presentation. Younger children, however, need concrete examples and hands-on experience to clearly understand environmental concepts. Luckily, providing experiential education is easy when addressing most conservation topics.

Theories of social maturity further predict how children interact with the people and things around them. Robert Selman outlined five stages of social development that are helpful in designing educational programs targeted at various age groups of children (table 6.2). These stages describe how a child moves through the very self-centered early years of life and develops an awareness of other perspectives and finally a broad societal view, which admits that each person has a unique perspective and way of understanding things.[21]

Learning Styles and the Learning Environment

Educators have always known that people learn in different ways—some are more visual learners, some learn better by listening, and some prefer to learn through hands-on activities. Learning-styles research suggests four types of learners:[22]

- Action-oriented learners (38 percent of U.S. population) are spontaneous, enjoy challenge and risk, and prefer hands-on activities to lectures.
- Routine learners (38 percent of U.S. population) prefer a structured learning environment and traditional techniques, such as lectures and precise instructions, in which to work.
- Research-oriented learners (12 percent of U.S. population) are excited by discovery, like to categorize things, and can focus on a specific task for an extended period of time.
- People-oriented learners (12 percent of U.S. population) understand things in terms of relationships between people and in terms of how things relate to their own personal life.

Conservation education programs should provide opportunities for all kinds of learners. Outdoor explorations are particularly useful for reaching restless, action-oriented learners, while routine and research-oriented learners may enjoy lectures or reading materials. People-oriented learners may be more interested in group activities and the politics of a conservation issue. Any audience, whether children or adults, is likely to include people with different learning styles. If learning style is taken into account during program design, educational programs will more effectively reach all program participants.

In addition, educational programs for both children and adults should incorporate findings from recent research on the dynamics of learning. For example, cognitive mapping theory suggests that, in order to be meaningful,

TABLE 6.2. *Educational techniques for different ages based on cognitive and social skills*

Age Group	Cognitive Skills	Social Skills	Educational Features and Techniques
Infancy	Organized patterns of behavior and thought Primarily sensory and motor activities Learns names of things very quickly Asks questions, Who? What? and Where?	None	Shape and color Basic words Hands-on activities Basic identification
2–6 years	Explores and masters symbols (words/language) Focuses on one idea at a time Accepts the world as it is Doesn't understand causality Asks questions, When? and Why? What does it remind me of?	Individual-based Can't differentiate between self and others Can't understand perspectives of others Forms friendships Judgment based on physical observation Realizes different perspectives exist	Guided discovery, involvement, inquiry, discussion Identification of objects Factual information Learning through repetition of others Learning distinctions (e.g., alike vs. different) Learning by analogy (e.g., role-playing and vivid images to stimulate imagination) Activities to expand youthful energy and lack of inhibitions Awareness and appreciation activities Basic ecological principles and patterns of nature Basic management and conservation information Sensational information (e.g., "biggest" or "best" Explanation through demonstration, personification, or dramatization (e.g., living history, puppetry, costumed acting, etc.) Some focus on different perspectives
7–11 years	Involved with present moment Thinks best about concrete or direct experiences Has trouble imagining that not experienced Learns through multisensory direct explorations Begins to categorize things	Influenced by peer groups Can see and assess own behavior Begins to understand other's perspective Better understanding of relationships Becomes aware of many different ideas and points of view in the world	Guided inquiry, discussion, imagery Literal interpretations Focus on different and broader perspectives Sensational information (e.g., "biggest" or "best") Sensitivity to meet societal norms Awareness and appreciation activities Intermediate ecological principles and patterns

	Grasps cause and effect Begins inductive reasoning		Intermediate management and conservation information Introduce cultural aspects of environmental issues Introduce consequences of environmental problems
Adolescent	Can use logic effectively Can think abstractly Can imagine past, present, and future Solves problems systematically Uses inductive and deductive reasoning Forms hypotheses Responds to more sophisticated and challenging materials	Can move to a neutral third-person perspective Can conceptualize a broader social system	Guided discovery, inquiry, discussion Sensitivity to and acknowledgment of adolescent feelings Structured socializing and adult treatment Meaningful and highly relevant materials Cooperative group activities Preparation for adolescent authority-testing behavior Sensational information (e.g., "biggest" or "best") Awareness and appreciation activities Advanced ecological principles and patterns Advanced management and conservation information Explore cultural aspects of environmental issues Explore consequences of environmental problems Problems to challenge new abstract thinking abilities
Adult	Same as adolescents	Broad societal perspective Understands that each person has a unique perspective and system of understanding	Same as adolescents

Source: After D.M. Knudson, T.T. Cable, and L. Beck. 1995. *Interpretation of Cultural and Natural Resource.* Venture State College, PA; A. L. Grinder and E. S. McCoy. 1985. *The Good Guide: A Source Book for Interpreters, Docents, and Tour Guides. Ironwood,* Scottsdale, AZ; J. Piaget. 1965. How children form mathematical concepts, pp. 406–414 in R. C. Anderson and D.P. Ausubel (eds.), *Readings on the Psychology of Cognition.* Holt, Rinehart, and Winston, New York; and R. Muuss. 1982. *Theories of Adolescence.* Random House, New York.

new information must relate to something already encoded in the brain of the learner.[23] This echoes the cry of communicators to keep materials relevant and understandable to the audience. This finding also emphasizes the importance of collecting background data on audiences before you embark on designing an educational program.

Other research has found that certain conditions help the human mind actively absorb information. Effective learning environments are distinguished by a lack of threat, hands-on activities, and immersion in real environments.[24] Outdoor conservation education activities go a long way toward meeting the needs of different learning styles and of incorporating learner-friendly principles into an educational program.

Basic Elements of a Program for Children

A number of basic elements characterize effective conservation education programs for children. These include activities that encourage children to use all their senses, provide them with direct hands-on experiences, and enhance the interaction between child and presenter. Techniques such as asking frequent questions, using a child's name, and standing close to a child are fundamental for a youthful audience but work well for all ages. The following elements incorporate the wisdom of cognitive and social development theories and the results of learning styles research:

- A variety of learning approaches to suit a variety of learning styles
- Exploration of the environment through all the senses to evoke sensory memories of things
- Emphasis on hands-on programs
- Absence of threat to learning or safety
- Active written and verbal communication during the learning process
- Use of higher-order thinking skills by older children to analyze issues and formulate and evaluate alternative solutions
- Use of real-world context and issues to teach concepts and skills
- Understanding of human processes and systems as they relate to natural processes and systems
- Emphasis on skills and habits that people can use throughout their lives to understand and act on conservation issues.[25]

Moving from Awareness to Action

Many educational programs fit these characteristics into a learning framework that progresses from awareness to critical thinking, and moral and attitudinal development. Models of a seven-step progression of outdoor learning[26] parallel the six-step "awareness-to-action" model shown in box 6.2.[27] These hierarchies move from early stages that emphasize basic familiarity, awareness, and comfort with the learning situation to later stages in which individuals prac-

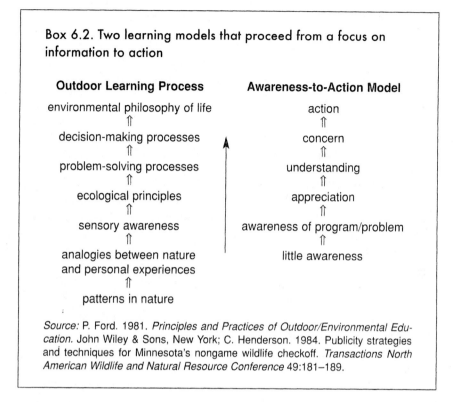

Box 6.2. Two learning models that proceed from a focus on information to action

Outdoor Learning Process	Awareness-to-Action Model

Outdoor Learning Process:

environmental philosophy of life
⇑
decision-making processes
⇑
problem-solving processes
⇑
ecological principles
⇑
sensory awareness
⇑
analogies between nature
and personal experiences
⇑
patterns in nature

Awareness-to-Action Model:

action
⇑
concern
⇑
understanding
⇑
appreciation
⇑
awareness of program/problem
⇑
little awareness

Source: P. Ford. 1981. *Principles and Practices of Outdoor/Environmental Education.* John Wiley & Sons, New York; C. Henderson. 1984. Publicity strategies and techniques for Minnesota's nongame wildlife checkoff. *Transactions North American Wildlife and Natural Resource Conference* 49:181–189.

tice critical thinking skills and develop a philosophy of life to guide conservation actions.

Learning hierarchies reflect the cognitive and social developmental theories discussed earlier. The progression of activities is loosely correlated with the maturation process, so that as children get older, activities from the higher levels may be added to educational programs. By adolescence, most youth can show concern, make decisions, and take action based on their philosophy of life. However, the first few levels of the hierarchy always should be included in educational programs, even for adolescents and adults, because the awareness phase of learning remains important and enjoyable for mature learners.

Few conservation professionals have the task of developing an entire conservation education curriculum. This entails working long hours with teachers, students, and administrators to ensure that your materials will be appropriate and useful. You may, however, be called upon to offer your expertise for a short presentation or day-long event. Interacting with children requires special techniques to stimulate their curiosity and sense of exploration. The basic elements of children's programs listed earlier provide commonsense suggestions for giving presentations to children.

A seasoned conservation educator Dan DeWolf, science director for the Needham, Massachusetts, schools, likes to enter a classroom with a provocative question. For first-graders, he instructs the students to sit in a circle on the floor. He places a box turtle in their midst and asks, "Who knows what this is?"

"A turtle!" the children usually shriek.

"How do you know?" asks DeWolf.

"It has a shell," the children say.

"How do you know it isn't a clam?" DeWolf asks. "Don't clams have shells?" A lively discussion ensues in which the students learn the characteristics of reptiles, and adaptations of their visiting turtle.

The former director of the Whale Museum in San Juan Island, Washington, Ken McCann, uses a variety of techniques to teach and inspire children. For instance, McCann designed an entertaining exercise for kids to demonstrate echolocation in toothless whales. McCann blindfolds a group of children and stands them in front of pieces of wood, carpet, and glass. Then he hands them a Ping-Pong ball. "When they throw the Ping-Pong ball at the carpet," he says, "it makes a noise, a thunk. If it hits the glass, it goes plink. If it hits the wood, bop. So they pretty much know what surface they're hitting even though they can't see. And they also know how far away they are from the object by the amount of time it takes for the ball to return."[28] Voila, an abstract lesson is made real and fun by McCann's thoughtfulness in reaching his young audience.

McCann continually searches for new ideas to hold children's interest. "Most young children would prefer to be entertained rather than educated, so the trick is to find ways of combining both." For example, when he describes the size of the blue whale, the largest creature alive, he will explain his "research," which discovered that a blue whale weighs exactly as much as four zillion, two trillion, and something M&M's. "The kids go, 'Wow, that's pretty major, dude!' They can relate to that." Like all good conservation educators, McCann's goal in working with children is to "inspire them so that when they're no longer with you, they want to continue studying on their own."

McCann emphasizes that it is not the job of conservation educators to push their opinions on the students. "When people ask me how I feel about whales in captivity, it would be so easy to go about the business of creating what I call 'false disciples' simply because I dislike the practice so intensely. I could easily say, 'I hate it, it's bad for the whale and here's why.' But I don't do that. I say to the kids, 'Okay, I want you six to come up with ten good reasons why the whales should be in captivity'—education, making worldwide advocates of people who'll never get to see whales in their natural environment—'and you six are going to come up with ten good reasons why not.' We do it around the campfire at night, and I sit back and watch them reach their own invariably correct conclusions."

TABLE 6.3. *Status of environmental education in U.S. schools* (● = *components are in place,* ◐ = *components are being developed,* ○ = *components do not exist*)

State	Master plan	Required in k–12 instruction	Teacher training requirement	Curriculum guide	State grant program	State board	State office	EE Computer network
ALABAMA	○	○	○	◐	●	◐	○	◐
ALASKA	○	○	○	○	○	○	○	○
ARIZONA	●	○	●	○	●	●	○	●
ARKANSAS	●	●	○	●	●	●	●	○
CALIFORNIA	○	◐	○	◐	●	●	●	◐
COLORADO	●	○	○	○	○	◐	●	◐
CONNECTICUT	◐	○	○	◐	●	◐	●	●
DELAWARE	○	○	●	○	●	◐	●	○
FLORIDA	◐	○	◐	◐	●	●	●	○
GEORGIA	◐	●	○	●	●	●	○	○
HAWAII	◐	○	○	●	○	○	○	◐
IDAHO	○	○	○	○	○	○	○	◐
ILLINOIS	◐	●	◐	○	◐	○	◐	◐
INDIANA	◐	○	○	○	○	◐	◐	◐
IOWA	○	●	○	●	●	◐	●	●
KANSAS	○	○	○	○	○	●	○	○
KENTUCKY	◐	○	○	○	◐	●	●	●
LOUISIANA	◐	●	○	◐	◐	○	◐	○

(continues)

Table 6.3. (Continued) (● = components are in place, ◐ = components are being developed, ○ = components do not exist)

State	Master plan	Required in k-12 instruction	Teacher training requirement	Curriculum guide	State grant program	State board	State office	EE Computer network
MAINE	○	○	○	◐	○	○	○	◐
MARYLAND	○	●	○	○	●	●	○	○
MASSACHUSETTS	◐	○	○	○	◐	●	●	◐
MICHIGAN	○	○	○	○	○	◐	○	○
MINNESOTA	●	◐	◐	●	●	●	◐	◐
MISSISSIPPI	○	○	○	○	○	○	○	○
MISSOURI	○	○	○	○	○	○	○	○
MONTANA	○	○	○	○	○	○	○	○
NEBRASKA	○	○	○	○	●	○	○	○
NEVADA	○	●	○	◐	○	○	○	○
NEW HAMPSHIRE	○	○	○	○	○	○	○	○
NEW JERSEY	●	○	○	○	○	●	◐	◐
NEW MEXICO	◐	○	○	○	○	●	○	○
NEW YORK	○	○	○	●	○	○	●	○
NORTH CAROLINA	●	○	○	○	●	●	●	●
NORTH DAKOTA	◐	○	○	○	○	○	○	◐

OHIO	○	○	●	○	●	●	○	○	●
OKLAHOMA	○	○	●	○	●	●	●	●	◐
OREGON	○	○	○	○	○	○	●	○	○
PENNSYLVANIA	●	○	●	◑	●	●	●	●	◑
RHODE ISLAND	○	○	○	◑	●	○	●	○	◐
SOUTH CAROLINA	○	○	○	●	●	○	●	○	○
SOUTH DAKOTA	○	○	○	○	○	◑	○	○	○
TENNESSEE	◐	○	○	◑	○	●	○	○	○
TEXAS	○	○	○	○	○	●	○	○	●
UTAH	◑	○	○	○	○	○	○	○	◐
VERMONT	◑	○	○	○	○	●	○	○	○
VIRGINIA	○	○	◐	●	●	●	○	●	●
WASHINGTON	●	●	●	●	○	○	●	○	●
WEST VIRGINIA	●	○	○	●	●	○	●	○	○
WISCONSIN	◑	●	●	●	●	●	●	○	●
WYOMING	○	○	○	●	○	○	○	○	○

Source: Modified from M. Kirk, R. Wilke, and A. Ruskey. 1997. A survey of the status of state-level environmental education in the U.S. *Journal of Environmental Education* 29(1):10–11; based on the 1995 National EE Advancement Project Survey.

Conservation Education in Schools

Conservation education in the formal school system varies among countries in content, scope, and disciplinary base. It often is overlooked or ignored relative to traditional subjects. For example, only thirty-one states in the United States have enacted legislation dealing with any aspects of environmental education (table 6.3). Some states provide environmental education training for their teachers and eight states currently have computer networks and databases. Twenty-seven states have a state advisory board or a state office that provides some oversight and centralization of environmental education activities. These statistics reveal that most students are not learning about the environment as part of their regular curriculum.

Many curricular supplements for conservation education are available and some are incorporated into busy school schedules. The following examples describe innovative approaches taken to increase environmental literacy in students. These programs exemplify many of the guidelines outlined in the previous section.

Example: Project WILD Curriculum Supplement

Many conservation education programs use a progression of activities that move from awareness and knowledge to skills and participation in conservation problem-solving activities. Project WILD[29] uses a seven-step learning progression as a framework for its conservation education activities.

Project WILD is an interdisciplinary, supplemental environmental education program emphasizing wildlife (fig. 6.3). WILD's primary audience is classroom teachers of all grade levels, although its activities also are often incorporated into interpretive settings. The program is distributed through teacher workshops offered primarily through state wildlife agencies throughout the United States.

"Project WILD is based on the premise that young people and their teachers have a vital interest in learning about the earth as a home for people and wildlife. The program emphasizes wildlife because of its intrinsic, ecological, and other values, as well as its importance as a basis for understanding the fragile grounds upon which all life rests. Project WILD is designed to prepare young people for decisions affecting people, wildlife, and their shared home, earth. In the face of pressures of all kinds affecting the quality and sustainability of life on earth as we know it, Project WILD addresses the need for human beings to develop as responsible members of the ecosystem." The goal of Project WILD is "to assist learners of any age in developing awareness, knowledge, skills, and commitment to result in informed decisions, responsible behavior, and constructive actions concerning wildlife and the environment upon which all life depends."[30]

FIGURE 6.3. *Project WILD, Project Learning Tree, and other supplemental curricula introduce teachers to new environmental educational education activities through a workshop format. Teachers practice the activities and learn how to facilitate the training of other teachers. (Photo S. K. Jacobson)*

Each activity includes a statement of educational objectives; descriptions and background for the teacher; a materials list; step-by-step procedures; recommendations for evaluating student learning; recommended grade level, subjects, skills, duration, group size, and setting for the activity; suggestions for extending or adapting the activity; and key vocabulary words. Activities also include a list of points that correspond to a Conceptual Framework and an outline of the concepts covered by Project WILD. Activities are divided into seven sections, with eight to twenty activities in each section. Table 6.4 lists the Project WILD sections, and samples of activities included in each section. The goal of WILD is to teach students *how* to think, not *what* to think, about conservation issues.[31]

TABLE 6.4. *Project WILD sections and representative activities and learning objectives*

Project WILD Section	Representative Activities and Grade Levels	Learning Objectives *Students will be able to . . .*
Awareness and Appreciation	Wildlife Is Everywhere! (Kindergarten–3+)	(1) State that humans and wildlife share environments; and (2) generalize that wildlife is present in areas all over the earth.
	Habitat Lap Sit (4–9+)	(1) Identify the components of habitat; (2) recognize how humans and other animals depend upon habitat; and (3) interpret the significance of loss or change in habitat in terms of people and wildlife.

(continues)

TABLE 6.4. (*Continued*)

Project WILD Section	Representative Activities and Grade Levels	Learning Objectives *Students will be able to . . .*
Diversity of Wildlife Values	Museum Search for Wildlife (3–6)	(1) Identify wildlife portrayed in an art form; and (2) Generalize that wildlife has sufficient aesthetic and spiritual value to inspire art.
	Eco-enrichers (6–12)	(1) Evaluate the importance of plant and animal matter as contributors to soil; and (2) recognize that wildlife in many forms contributes to the diversity and balance of ecological systems.
Ecological Principles	Owl Pellets (3–7)	Construct a simple food chain.
	Pond Succession (4–9)	(1) Recognize that natural environments are involved in a process of continual change; (2) discuss the concept of succession; (3) describe succession as an example of the process of change in natural environments; and (4) apply understanding of the concept of succession by drawing a series of pictures showing stages in pond succession.
Management and Conservation	Wildwork (K–6)	Name and describe three wildlife-related occupations
	Checks and Balances (6–12)	(1) Evaluate hypothetical wildlife management decisions; and (2) identify at least four factors that can affect the size of a wildlife population.
People, Culture, and Wildlife	First Impressions (K–6)	(1) Distinguish between reactions to an animal based on myth or stereotype, and those based on accurate information; and (2) recognize the value of animals' contributions to ecosystems — even those that people sometimes respond to with fear.
	Does Wildlife Sell Cigarettes? (6–12)	(1) Identify use of wildlife and other natural images in advertising; (2) critically analyze and evaluate the purposes and impacts of the use of such images in advertising; and (3) recommend appropriate uses of such nature-derived images in advertising.
Trends, Issues, and Consequences	Shrinking Habitat (4–7)	(1) Describe some effects of human development of land areas on plants and animals previously living in the area; (2) evaluate the importance of suitable habitat for wildlife; and (3) recognize that loss of habitat is generally considered to be the most critical problem facing wildlife today.

	Planning for People and Wildlife (4–12)	(1) Describe considerations that are important in land-use planning for cities and other communities of people; (2) identify means by which negative impact on wildlife and other elements of the natural environment can be reduced in developing cities; and (3) describe actions that can be taken in some contemporary cities to enhance them as places in which both people and some wildlife can live.
Responsible Human Actions	Flip the Switch for Wildlife (5–12)	(1) Trace the route of electrical energy from source to use; (2) describe impacts on wildlife and the environment derived from various kinds of energy development and uses; and (3) evaluate the impact on wildlife and the environment as a result of their own energy-use patterns.
	Can Do! (2–9)	(1) Identify a problem involving wildlife on their own school grounds; (2) suggest and evaluate alternative means by which to either solve the problem or at least improve the situation; (3) successfully undertake the project; and (4) analyze and describe the process by which they success fully solved the problem or improved the situation.

A challenge for conservation educators working in the schools is finding instructional strategies that enable students not only to learn about local and global conservation issues, but also to act in response to environmental problems. Conservation education cannot be confined to the classroom, but rather must operate within the context of the environment it seeks to conserve. One program that has met this challenge is the Global Rivers Environmental Education Network (GREEN), developed by the University of Michigan.

Example: The Global Rivers Environmental Education Network[32]

GREEN is a watershed education program that has been adopted by schools in more than 135 countries. Through participation in the program, students explore their local rivers, present their findings to government officials, and exchange data and insights with students in other cultures throughout the world.

GREEN has developed into a global communication network that includes countries such as Bangladesh, Argentina, Kenya, and the United States. While the countries differ culturally, many face similar conservation issues concerning the pollution and degradation of aquatic systems.

Through our common need for healthy rivers and watersheds, GREEN seeks to build problem-solving skills among students and increase awareness of similar conservation issues in other countries. GREEN thus works toward three interrelated goals:

- to provide students with hands-on experience in chemical, biological, and sociological research by introducing them to the environmental issues of their local watershed;
- to empower students in problem-solving skills applied to the local environment; and
- to build global and intercultural communication and understanding of cultural differences relevant to environmental concerns.

GREEN began in a Michigan high school biology class on the banks of the Huron River in 1984. Student concern about the river's water quality grew when several students contracted hepatitis A after windsurfing on the Huron River. Subsequent studies by the students and their teacher revealed that the fecal coliform counts were alarmingly high as a result of broken storm-water drains. Their interactions with city staff resulted in improved water quality. Based on this model, the University of Michigan developed a two-week water quality monitoring program appropriate for secondary students. The program included instructional materials such as maps of the local watershed, a manual outlining standards for performing nine water-quality tests, material on monitoring water for macroinvertebrates, a slide/tape presentation, and a set of water quality testing kits.[33] The two-week program followed this basic awareness-to-action schedule:

- Discuss water quality concerns in the river; view slide show (lesson 1).
- Learn nine water-test parameters (lessons 2–3).
- Monitor the water's quality (lesson 4).
- Calculate data; interpret results; derive Water-Quality Index; incorporate results into understanding of the use of the river by humans and animals (lesson 5).
- Write an action plan and take action (lessons 6–10).

GREEN has grown to include an international communication network. University of Michigan faculty and students held workshops in eighteen countries to enable educators from different countries to exchange ideas about watershed programs appropriate for different geographic areas around the world. As a result of the workshops, some national governments allocated funding to develop programs and obtain equipment, and committees were formed to prepare curriculum guides for water monitoring. The workshops also revealed that the model developed in Michigan was not appropriate for all countries, as access to both resources and equipment varied dramatically across the globe. Given this constraint, low-technology systems based on a biological index have been developed for monitoring in countries without access to the water testing kits.

The field manual has been translated into Bengali, Chinese, Czech, German, Hebrew, Hungarian, Italian, Japanese, Russian, and Spanish. As a worldwide network, GREEN distributes a semiannual, international newsletter to 2,100 educators and government officials in 125 countries. For countries with access to computers, a series of computer conferences provide an international database of water quality data and a source for exchanging ideas. The network now has more than three thousand participants from more than 135 countries. To link classrooms across countries, GREEN has established the Partner Watershed Program, which matches schools in different countries for communication via mail or computer concerning their results and experiences with water quality monitoring.

As a result of this program, GREEN participants are eager to act on real-world environmental problems and integrate this local action into a global understanding of problems faced by people of other nations. Such dissolution of cultural boundaries serves not only as a model for an effective conservation education curriculum but also as a template for solving global conservation problems in the future.[34]

Example: Engaging Students in Wildlife-Focused Action Projects in Florida[35]

For the past thirty-five years, an environmental education program in Lee County, Florida, has involved students in action-oriented projects resulting in students working to solve local conservation problems facing Florida's threatened habitats and endangered animals.

Examples of successful projects spawned by the "Monday Group" conservation education program include the Sea Turtle Research and Conservation Program, the Six-Mile Cypress Slough Acquisition, the Florida Manatee Protection Act, and the Bald Eagle Habitat Protection Ordinance. The success of these student-initiated projects attests to the instructional benefits of a community-based, problem-solving approach. Approximately 2,500 eleventh- and twelfth-grade students have participated in these action groups and classes, with an impressive 90 percent attendance rate.

The focus of the instruction is experiential learning, with wildlife issues serving as a context for "learning by doing." The primary goals of the program are as follows:

- sensitize students to human interactions within ecological systems;
- develop student knowledge and understanding of wildlife relationships in southwest Florida's ecological communities;
- empower students to be proficient at implementing positive solutions to wildlife-related issues by engaging elected and appointed decision makers in informed decision-making actions; and
- complete a wildlife-related project that directly engages students with elected public officials who have the authority to change public policy.

Students from nine high schools who elect to take the class are nominated by their principal, a teacher, or themselves. School staff have been encouraged to nominate at least half of their participants from "negative leaders," students who have discipline problems or lead other students into negative behaviors. The emphasis of the class content is based on a project selected by the students. For all classes, however, the content integrates systems models, ecological principles, and government concepts, with the intent to provide students with the necessary knowledge and skills to solve "real-world" problems in their local community. The primary instructional role played by two teachers is to facilitate learning and development of student "action skills."

Students are expected to master a set of skills, which include the following:

- effective communication by phone, letter, public speaking, and mass media;
- strategies for becoming an expert through effective research;
- techniques for effective lobbying;
- techniques for strategic planning and organizing of a group to achieve the project goal;
- strategies for team building and cooperation;
- techniques for conflict resolution; and
- techniques for public presentations and media (brochures, slide programs, exhibits, and video).

During the Monday Group classes, the students have always completed at least a significant component of an action project. As environmental issues are often complex, only nine groups have fully completed a project. One such project is the *Florida Manatee Protection Act*. Students in the program were instrumental in conducting a community awareness campaign to highlight the plight of the Florida manatee. They lobbied county officials to enforce speed limits for boats on the Caloosahatchee and Orange Rivers, home to a large population of manatees. The students soon discovered that the jurisdiction for such regulations was on a federal and state level. A local state senator who worked with the students cointroduced the nation's first Manatee Sanctuary Program, which created the first manatee sanctuary with strict speed limits for boats.

Of the "negative leaders" who have participated in the program, at least ten have earned doctoral degrees in environmental fields. Over the years, the students in the program have achieved significant conservation results.

Schools in British Columbia, Ontario, Colorado, Arizona, Oklahoma, and Indiana have adopted the problem-solving approach of the projects implemented by the Monday Group classes. The program's success has been the direct result of teachers placing control and trust in students, expecting high levels of performance, and letting students make mistakes, according to Bill Hammond, program founder. Allowing students to seek their own solutions and organize their own efforts requires adult educators to serve as facilitators, rather than as classroom leaders. Hammond preaches that only through direct hands-on experience can students develop the skills necessary to solve environmental problems as high-school students, and later as adults facing conservation dilemmas that require efforts at a community, state, or national level.

Guidelines and resources for implementing programs like the Monday Project, GREEN, and Project WILD are available.[36] These approaches have been field tested in many settings and serve as useful models for anyone faced with the daunting, but critical, task of developing programs for school children.

Programs for Adult Learners

How you communicate with adults in an educational setting depends upon the atmosphere. In an informal program, adults may be happy to observe programs aimed at their children or join in playful activities in the course of discovery. Some learning qualities that carry over from childhood to adulthood include the fascination with the superlative (the "biggest" and the "best") and the desire for hands-on, sensory exploration.[37] In some cases, adults may absorb information through their children's school-based conservation education activities, but transmission of information from kids to their parents cannot be relied on to address adult conservation education goals. Adults are an important audience because of the immediate impacts of their behaviors and their influence on policy makers through voting and public debate.

Adults engaged in formal training or personal development activities expect sophisticated approaches and do not respond to educational programs geared toward children. For example, research in North Carolina has shown that adult audiences of cooperative extension programs have definite preferences for certain modes of learning. *Doing, seeing,* and *discussing* were preferred by over 95 percent of extension clients. Other preferred modes included:

- personal visit
- meeting
- newsletter
- demonstration
- workshop
- videocassette
- bulletin/pamphlet
- field day
- on-farm test
- seminar

While adults still prefer hands-on methods, techniques such as *touching, smelling,* and *tasting* alone were not preferred. Program delivery methods that clients said they were unlikely to use to receive information from the cooperative extension service include techniques like puppetry and games, as well as computer programs. These methods were discounted by clients because they were perceived as costly (e.g., computer technologies), unavailable (e.g., teleconferencing, fax, satellite conferencing), irrelevant (e.g., cable, role-play), inappropriate (e.g., church bulletin), or considered childish (e.g., puppetry, skit, game).[38]

Whether used in training a group of Forest Service scientists in new ecosystem management strategies or a group of volunteers in preparation for serving as roving visitor guides, many techniques of adult education are useful for conservation education programming. Most adult training programs in conservation combine a number of techniques, such as lectures, discussion, and field exercises, as described in table 6.5 and the examples here.

TABLE 6.5. *Teaching techniques for adults*

Format	Description	Use	Outcomes	Limitations
Lecture	Delivery of information from speaker to group	Presents new knowledge to a group	Knowledge gains Efficient transfer of specific information	Does not reach action–oriented learners Does not provide multisensory input No audience participation No feedback from audience
Lecture/ discussion	Delivery of information from leader involving group interaction	Validating presented information with individual experiences of group members	Knowledge gains	Does not reach action–oriented learners Does not provide multisensory input
Guided discussion	Group interaction directed toward goal determined by leader	Completes task of problem solving and decision making, with some group involvement	Knowledge gains Attitudes identified	Does not reach action–oriented learners Does not provide multisensory input
Small group discussion	Group interaction with varying levels of leadership and content focus	Generates ideas for problem solving; shares feelings; helps build teams	Knowledge gains Skills enhanced Attitudes identified Involves everyone Peer-learning environment Creates sense of rapport	Talkative people dominate May stray from topic/task
Case study	Group solution to identified problem situation	Applying knowledge to relevant situations through group interactions	Knowledge gains Skills enhanced Attitudes identified	Need appropriate data and case
Role-Play	Acting out "real life" situations in a protected, risk-free environment; no scripts or rehearsals for the activity	Rehearsing behaviors and skills in realistic settings; identifying and stimulating attitude and behavior changes	Skills enhanced Attitudes identified Trainer controls content to highlight specific issues Collective exercise	Not everyone is active Anxiety among performers

(continues)

TABLE 6.5. (*Continued*)

Format	Description	Use	Outcomes	Limitations
Games/ Simulations	An extended role play or structured, experiential activity with specific rules that allows participants to learn from their own experience	Identifies behaviors and attitudes in realistic settings; generates data; identifies problems and conflicts; reinforces behavior; develops an understanding of alternative perspectives and attitudes	Attitudes identified Skills enhanced Allows for rapid feedback High participation High motivation Rapid peer learning Trainee control of learning situation Active, experiential learning	Trainees may not want to play Excitement/involvement may overshadow learning objective Can never recreate all situations
Skit	Similar to role plays except that all the parts are prescribed and rehearsed by the participants	Present information, develops practical skills, reinforces behavior, develops understanding of alternative viewpoints	Trainer controls content to highlight issues	Collective exercise Not everyone is active Anxiety among performers
Interviews	One or more people ask questions of a guest speaker or a panel of speakers. The questions may or may not be predetermined	Gathers information; develops perspective; generates ideas; evaluates situation, in-depth exploration of issues	Informal Nonthreatening for interviewers Discussion follows audience interest	Interviewer may not cover important issues
Brain-storming	A moderator presents a topic and asks for suggestions, all offerings are recorded, within a time limit, following the brainstorming the suggestions are discussed in detail	Generate ideas	Lots of information in a short period All ideas considered	Quiet people overlooked/dominated Participants afraid to give wrong or silly suggestions
Worksheets/ Handouts	Tasks are explained and completed, by individuals or groups, in writing	Develop/reinforce skills; process and retains information	Knowledge gains Individual activity Participants have something to take with them	Need resources to design and reproduce copies

Example: Training Local Naturalist Guides in Costa Rica[39]

Local people living near parks often do not realize short-term benefits from the conservation of the land around them. Spurred by the increase in ecotourism to Costa Rica, a naturalist guide training program was developed at La Selva Biological Station as a means of bringing tourism dollars to local residents and to ensure that visitors did not harm the reserve. The 1,550-hectare (630-acre) station borders Braulio Carrillo National Park and protects Central American lowland, premontane, and montane rainforests. The goal of the program was to train guides as naturalists with the skills to accompany and educate visitors interested in natural history. The program, designed by the Organization for Tropical Studies (OTS), also aimed to provide trainees with the abilities to work in a range of nature-based employment opportunities, including ecotourism and environmental education, and as assistants in ecological fieldwork.

Educator Pia Paaby and biologist David Clark developed the course with twelve thematic units.

1. Introduction to fundamental ecological concepts: individuals, populations, communities, food chains, forest ecology; field practice using binoculars and field guides
2. Conservation and environmental education
3. Plant structure and function, emphasizing aspects of interest to tourists
4. Economically valuable plants, especially medicinal and timber species
5. Introduction to ornithology and one hundred common birds of the region; field practice in finding and describing birds
6. Ecology of birds; field practice in observing bird behavior
7. Introduction to mammals, and mammals of special interest to tourists; field practice in identifying mammal signs, such as tracks, scat, and burrows; field practice in locating and identifying insects
8. Amphibians and reptiles, basic identification and ecology; poisonous and nonpoisonous snakes; field practice in locating and identifying reptiles and amphibians; night walk to observe amphibians and reptiles
9. Aquatic ecology, including common plants and animals of tourist interest along streams and rivers; field practice in identifying aquatic wildlife from boats; visit to local archaeological site
10. Ecology of tropical premontane forest; three-day field trip to nearby

Rara Avis Lodge, ending with an eight-hour hike through Braulio Carrillo National Park to La Selva

11. Scientific research and its application to tourists at La Selva; basic first aid; field guiding and group management techniques
12. Field guiding techniques taught by professional biologist guides; students practice guiding "volunteer" tourists
13. Presentation of Certificates of Participation[40]

The OTS provided logistical support with additional resources and expertise from the University of Costa Rica, the National University, the National Museum, and the Costa Rican National Park Service. Ninety-four local residents applied for the course; eighteen men and eight women were selected.

The course met for twelve weeks, with classes held all day each Saturday during the training. Meeting once a week accommodated homemakers' schedules and allowed participants with jobs to complete the training without jeopardizing their current employment. To facilitate preparation for each week, students received a written packet of materials and lectures a week in advance. In this rural area where access to books is limited, the written materials now serve as resources for naturalists who completed the program. The instructional format included a mix of strategies, including hands-on experience, lectures, oral presentations, and a three-day field trip. Paaby and Clark used the forest as the primary educational aid. A typical Saturday class schedule followed this format:

7 A.M.	Announcements and lecture
8:30 A.M.	Coffee break/preparations for field work
9 A.M.–12 P.M.	Field work
12–1 P.M.	Lunch
1–4:30 P.M.	Oral presentations by participants, followed by lecture and fieldwork
4:30 P.M.	Written quiz

The 12-week course included 40 hours in the class and 103 hours in the field. The focus on experience in the field integrated students' prior knowledge of cultural and natural history into the course. Question-and-answer sessions were an important educational strategy, replacing the traditional focus on classroom lectures. Despite the intense pace of the training, all twenty-six participants graduated from the course. The zero dropout rate represents a significant accomplishment; the dropout rate in classes in rural Costa Rican areas is usually high. Funds for the course included a $14,000 grant from the World Wildlife Fund, augmented by donated professional time and logistic subsidies from OTS. With these supplemental donations, the total budget for the course was $25,000.

To evaluate the impacts of the course, interviews were conducted with twenty-two of the students four months after the course. Twenty-one of the students said they would not have become involved in conservation activities if they had not participated in the course. As a result of the course, OTS began requiring that each group of visitors to La Selva employ one local naturalist during their visit. In addition, OTS has hired a graduate of the program as a full-time assistant to their environmental education program. The course material has been developed into a book, which was distributed to institutions in Costa Rica and individuals working in education and conservation.[41] Several years later, former participants were still involved in conservation-related work as naturalist guides, environmental educators, research assistants, and advanced students. Other guide training programs in Costa Rica have been modeled after this program.

To develop a training program, you must understand the audience and know the content of the program. You also must consider several additional factors, such as the social and economic situation in the area. The high rural literacy rate in Costa Rica resulted in a course supplemented by written materials. However, a similar course developed for adult students who are illiterate could focus on audiovisual or field materials as instructional aids. Another issue to consider is the employment market for training-program graduates. Training programs must adapt the curriculum to the needs of both the audience and the potential employers. In Costa Rica, the training and involvement of local tour guides in environmental activities generated economic benefits to the graduates and increased their support for conservation. The La Selva Biological Station provided immediate employment to many of the graduates, ensuring the success of the program. For seasoned workers, training programs can update knowledge and skills.

Example: Ecosystem Management Training for Fish and Wildlife Service Scientists

Like the Naturalist Guide training course in Costa Rica, a conservation education program targeting scientists at the U.S. Fish and Wildlife Service (USFWS) used a variety of teaching methods to address different learning styles and to keep the attention of participants. The purpose of the course was to offer an up-to-date overview of ecosystem management. Taught by well-known biologists Richard Knight, Gary Meffe, Larry Nielson, and Dennis Schenborn, the USFWS offered the five-day training course, "An Approach to Ecosystem Conservation" for their scientists.[42] The course description and the twelve topics covered read as follows:

> This course presents an integrated approach to ecosystem conservation. Guiding principles of conservation biology, particularly landscape ecology precepts and conservation planning, are discussed and developed into an implementation framework. The course integrates ecological theory and application, theory and practice of public involvement, and adaptive management. Participants learn strategic methods to implement ecological principles through comprehensive class exercises, using a hypothetical but realistic ecosystem conservation scenario.

1. Ecosystem management: What it is and what it isn't
2. Traditional and ecosystem approaches
3. Adaptive management
4. Biological diversity
5. Genetic and population diversity
6. Dealing with uncertainty
7. Population viability analysis, minimum viable populations, and meta-populations
8. Population/landscape interface
9. Landscape structure (e.g., fragmentation, edge, connectivity, matrix, size)
10. Working with stakeholders
11. Strategic thinking
12. Monitoring and evaluation

A detailed workbook accompanied the course. The workbook outlines the learning objectives for each of the twelve topics and provides a mental map to orient the participants to the goals of the course. This succinct summary helps participants anticipate and prioritize the large volume of information that they receive. For example, for the ecosystem management section, the workbook states the following learning objectives:

Ecosystem Management: What It Is and What It Isn't[43]
At the completion of this course, participants will be able to:

- Explain the pathology of traditional natural resource management.
- Contrast traditional resource management with ecosystem management.

- Define and discuss ecosystem management.
- Describe various emphases of the ecosystem approach.

The course included a session on how to work with stakeholders. This specific session had the following objectives:

Working with Stakeholders

By the end of this session, participants will be able to:

- Describe stakeholders and their interests.
- Anticipate the kinds of involvement stakeholders want and be prepared to engage in it.
- Use a practical five-step approach to help decide how to work with a stakeholder.

Providing the participants with the specific goals and learning objectives for their workshop experience helped them focus their attention on the key issues and approaches to be covered during the week. By incorporating lectures, discussions, group exercises, case studies, and group reporting into the workshop, a number of learning styles were accommodated. Evaluations revealed that workshop participants gave high marks to the interactive nature of the workshop. Participants lauded the mix of activities and the informal, problem-focused framework, according to Instructor Meffe.

Programs for Mixed Audiences

Dealing with mixed audiences, as in family-based activities, can be difficult for a conservation educator. However, programs for mixed age groups should not simply aim at the lowest cognitive levels present in the group. To deal with mixed audiences you should:

- use multiple educational techniques that fit the different levels of cognitive development and different learning styles represented in an audience;
- offer a variety of age-appropriate materials to meet the needs of all members of the group, e.g., offer several versions of a self-guided trail brochure or different age-specific versions of education exhibits; and
- aim at least some programs at children, as adults also may benefit from children's programs in informal settings.[44]

The National Wildlife Federation's NatureLink program exemplifies a strategy to cater to the young and old. This family-based program offers day-long and weekend outings to expose parents and children to the outdoors. The program makes use of volunteer mentors and collaborates with conservation organizations, camps, youth groups, and other civic groups to broaden its reach. Activities such as fishing, marsh studies, and birding are planned to appeal to all age groups, through the use of hands-on experiences targeted to different levels of skill. At the end of each program the participants sign a NatureLink pledge—a statement of their commitment to the natural world and actions to preserve it.[45]

Some activities lend themselves to audiences of all ages because of the

---

Box 6.3. Elements leading to successful conservation education programs

PLANNING
- Have clear goals
- Identify measurable objectives
- Incorporate an interdisciplinary approach
- Determine target audiences and involve them in program design
- Assess participants' social/educational/economic backgrounds
- Ensure program relevance to target populations
- Build necessary support (government/community/industry)
- Develop a budget and organizational plan
- Plan for potential problems and resolution of conflicts

IMPLEMENTATION
- Pilot test activities and materials with audience
- Use existing organizations and groups
- Encourage active/voluntary participation
- Involve reluctant participants creatively
- Provide direct contact with the environment/resource
- Use key ecosystems/resources/species in programs
- Select appropriate educational media
- Focus on economic/cultural environmental values
- Provide conservation incentives
- Maintain informality/entertainment value of the program
- Be flexible

PRODUCT EVALUATION
- Evaluate program components/monitor program
- Use more than one method of evaluation
- Collect feedback for program modification/creation of new programs
- Enhance local control and support of program
- Develop specific long-term plans for sustainability
- Disseminate program results

novelty of the experience or the pedagogical approach, such as question-and-answer formats that can target individual curiosity. The annual Reptile and Amphibian Expo held at Chinsegut Nature Center in Florida is popular among all ages. The public gets a chance to view the secretive life of a gopher tortoise deep within its burrow. A small camera is mounted on a long tube with an infrared light source attached to the end and is guided into a tortoise burrow. The camera is connected to an above ground television, allowing viewers to watch underground life. The tortoise is the key actor in this television drama, explains biologist Kristin Wood. Fleeting performances by gopher frogs, spiders, and snakes also thrill the audience. In addition, Expo attendees can tour the nature center where native reptiles and amphibians are housed in terrariums for easy viewing.

Learning about conservation is a lifelong process. Innovative educational programs can be found around the world, and the settings and activities described in this chapter offer insight into the complexity involved in the design of effective conservation education. The interdisciplinary nature and integrated solutions that are common to these programs provide an array of educational approaches for tackling conservation problems. Key elements that have led to the successful planning, implementation, and evaluation of programs are outlined in box 6.3. Factors that impact the success of a program include having clear goals and objectives, the relevance of your objectives to the target population, audience participation, the use of existing groups and organizations to sustain the program, and monitoring and evaluation to ensure activities are effective.

Challenges Facing Conservation Education

A major barrier to conservation education in schools is the fact that curricula have yet to be institutionalized in formal educational systems in most countries, including the United States. Many other constraints also limit the efficacy of conservation education in the schools. In addition to lack of time in an already crowded curriculum and lack of funding and materials, many teachers are unsure of the scope of conservation education or view it as narrowly pertaining to the sciences. Opportunities for interdisciplinary and holistic approaches are lost. Most teachers receive no training in the content or methods of conservation education, and experiential or action-oriented approaches needed for successful conservation education are not developed. Lastly, many educators do not think conservation education is a priority, and issues such as the sustainable use of natural resources or maintenance of biodiversity simply are not infused into the curriculum. The challenge lies in developing an efficient training system to provide educators with the foundation and experience to be effective teachers of conservation concepts.

Conservation education programs in the schools also face external constraints. The spread of environmental and conservation education has instigated criticisms from a variety of individuals. In some cases, critics are promoting their own ideological biases.[46] For example, one naysayer complained in a *New York Times* interview: "When you look at what is happening in environmental education, it sets any reasonable person reeling at the abuses. What the kids tend to get is the catastrophic, doomsday version of environmental problems."[47]

Opponents of environmental education claim that it is biased, unbalanced, and political. They accuse environmental educators of failing to teach children basic economics or decision-making processes, relying instead on mindless slogans, politically correct lessons, myths, and misinformation.[48]

Supporters of environmental education have countered these charges. "The attacks on environmental education are really part of the attacks on the environment we've seen over the past couple of years in Congress," says Tamara Schwarz of the Center for Commercial-Free Public Education. "If they succeed, it will undermine the quality of our nation's education system."[49]

Leaders in the environmental education field acknowledge that there is always room for improvement. Yet, the distortions of some critics have "created a public relations challenge to environmental educators" says Richard Wilke, director of the National Environmental Education Advancement Project.[50] Fortunately, the majority of U.S. citizens share basic core values about environmentally responsible behaviors such as recycling, advocating for clean water and air, and teaching children the importance of natural resources stewardship. In a recent survey, 74 percent of Americans described themselves as either "sympathetic to environmental concerns" or as an "active environmentalist."[51]

In response to criticisms that environmental education textbooks and curricula exaggerate the severity of environmental problems and the impacts of humans on the environment, the North American Association of Environmental Education (NAAEE) published *Environmental Education Materials: Guidelines for Excellence,* which presents six key characteristics for good environmental and conservation education materials:

1. *Fairness and accuracy:* Environmental education materials should be fair and accurate in describing environmental problems, issues, and conditions, and in reflecting the diversity of perspectives on them;
2. *Depth:* Environmental education materials should foster awareness of the natural and built environment; an understanding of environmental concepts, conditions, and issues; and an awareness of the feelings, values, attitudes, and perceptions at the heart of environmental issues, as appropriate for different developmental levels;

3. *Emphasis on skills building:* Environmental education materials should build lifelong skills that enable learners to prevent and address environmental issues;

4. Action orientation: Environmental education materials should promote civic responsibility, encouraging learners to use their knowledge, personal skills, and assessments of environmental issues as a basis for environmental problem solving and action;

5. Instructional soundness: Environmental education materials should rely on instructional techniques that create an effective learning environment; and

6. *Usability:* Environmental education materials should be well designed and easy to use.[52]

These guidelines address critics' charges and are helpful to keep in mind as you design conservation education materials and programs.

Last Words

Despite some successes, conservation education around the world does not always apply effective communications methods for reaching youth and adult audiences. A survey of ninth- and tenth-grade students in England, Australia, the United States, and Israel revealed that radio, television, and the press were students' most important sources of information on environmental issues.[53] Yet in disseminating information about the environment, educators typically rely on printed texts and written curriculum supplements.[54] Incorporating marketing and audience research into conservation education programs should lead to increased public awareness of the conservation message. Likewise, more widespread programs incorporating participatory, problem-solving techniques into project activities will help develop and enhance pro-conservation attitudes and behaviors among broader segments of the public. Ensuring that your content appropriately targets the age groups and learning styles of your audience, and that it works within your park, school, or community context will further enhance your chances for success.

The examples in this chapter reflect the central role possible for educational programs in the conservation agenda. Building on effective instructional strategies is critical for the growth of educational programs. Through the increased use of evaluation techniques described in the next chapter, we can substantiate and document successful education and other communications approaches and use them to develop even better programs in the future. As conservation education is infused into formal school curricula and informal programs for adults, increased public awareness, commitment, and appropriate behaviors should provide the foundation for a people "imbued by a guiding environmental ethic."

Chapter 7

EVALUATING AND MONITORING PROGRAM SUCCESS

In the beginning God created the heaven and the earth. And God saw everything that He made. "Behold," God said, "it is very good." And the evening and the morning were the sixth day.

And on the seventh day God rested from all His work. His archangel came then unto Him asking, "God, how do you know that what you have created is 'very good'? What are your criteria? On what data do you base your judgement? Aren't you a little close to the situation to make a fair and unbiased evaluation?"

God thought about these questions all that day and His rest was greatly disturbed. On the eighth day God said, "Lucifer, go to hell."

Thus was evaluation born in a blaze of glory . . . a legacy under which we continue to operate.★

After developing a communications campaign or educational project, how do you judge if your work is "very good." How do you know whether or not your program succeeded in promoting your conservation message? Have people's attitudes, knowledge, or behaviors changed as a result of your communications efforts? Once a communications program has been implemented, you will need to decide whether it is successful and make improvements if it is not. You will want to ask the following questions:

• Is the program effective?
• What are its impacts?

★From Halcolm's *Real Story of Paradise Lost,* cited in M. Q. Patton. 1981. *Utilization-Focused Evaluation.* Sage, Newbury Park, CA.

- Can the program be improved?
- Is the program cost-effective?
- Should the program be continued or modified?

Evaluation is the only systematic means of finding the answers to these questions. It is key to providing feedback for improving communications programs and to providing accountability to funding agencies, staff, and audiences. Evaluation also helps to assess secondary or unanticipated program outcomes. Ideally, evaluation should be conducted from "womb to tomb" (i.e., from beginning to end). Many program developers or administrators fail to plan for evaluation due to a perceived lack of time, experience, or money. Yet evaluation is a critical component of any successful communications program. This chapter describes the tools needed to conduct evaluations and gives examples of programs that used these tools to ensure successful communications. Detailed guidelines for each method were described in chapter 2 as data collection techniques for strategic research to plan your communications program. The information collected during planning can serve as baseline data for comparison with the results of evaluative research reviewed here.

Why Evaluate?

Each morning we look in the mirror to check our hairdo, choose among breakfast foods, and check the weather report. These evaluations help us in making daily decisions—to shampoo our hair, eat a bowl of cereal, or carry an umbrella. In a communications program, evaluation uses research techniques to make judgments or decisions regarding your activities.[1] It allows you to determine the value of your program or product and to identify areas of success and failure within a communications activity. Without evaluation, poor conservation communications can harm the natural resources that your efforts are aimed at protecting. A program may not reach the target audience, the message may be misunderstood, or the wrong behavior may be targeted. Without evaluation, hope of recognizing or improving a failed program is small. Unfortunately, many conservation professionals fail to evaluate the impacts of their communications efforts. For example, an analysis of fifty-six tropical conservation education programs from 1975 to 1990 revealed that fewer than half used some type of evaluation to assess achievement of objectives; yet, those programs that conducted evaluations reported significantly higher rates of program success.[2]

Evaluation is particularly useful in identifying problems with communications programs. One evaluation of a conservation education program in Senegal, Africa, found that local residents were *more* confused regarding the conservation objectives of the government *after* participating in their educational activities.[3] Accordingly, no conservation action ensued. A systematic evaluation was the only means of detecting the failure, the discovery of which led to immediate changes in the program.

For programs that are effective, evaluation provides the only objective method of identifying specific factors that lead to success. From the standpoint of accountability, such documentation is essential for expanding successful programs that result in real conservation gains. Key reasons for you to conduct an evaluation include the ability to:

- measure achievement of program objectives,
- assess secondary outcomes and unanticipated impacts,
- identify strengths and weaknesses in the program,
- analyze the program from a cost-benefit perspective,
- improve program effectiveness,
- collect evidence to promote future programs, and
- share experience and lessons learned with similar programs.

Internal and External Evaluations

Evaluation can use either internal or external evaluators, or a combination of both. An internal evaluator is someone who works for a program or has "inside" knowledge of the program. An external evaluator is an outsider, with no connections to the program that is being evaluated. Internal and external evaluations each have advantages and disadvantages (table 7.1).

The decision to use internal or external evaluators depends partly on the timing of the evaluation. For example, many programs use internal evaluators to assess the effectiveness of a campaign or program during its development and implementation, while an external evaluator conducts an assessment after the program has been in place for a period of time. The choice of which type of evaluation to use also depends on a program's resources and needs.

Formative and Summative Evaluations

Evaluations should be conducted both during and after implementation of your program. Formative evaluation occurs during development and implementation of a program and provides feedback for improvements in the early stages of the program. The strategic (audience) research described in chapter 2 is part of formative evaluation. It aids in making decisions about the design of a program by helping you understand the target audience. Using formative evaluation, program planners can assess the goals, objectives, resources, and constraints of a program and test alternative activities proposed. Summative evaluation is conducted at the end of a program and addresses questions about the program's worth. Both types of evaluation are vital because they provide answers to different types of questions. Program staff or project designers most often use data from formative evaluation to make decisions regarding program

TABLE 7.1. *Advantages and disadvantages of external and internal evaluators*

	External Evaluator	Internal Evaluator
Objectivity	Easy to be objective	Difficult to be objective
Understanding of program	May not understand the program, people, politics	Inside understanding of the program, people, politics
Perspective on program	Can take a fresh, outside viewpoint of the program	Knows the details of the program too well; may overlook crucial factors
Threat to program activities during evaluation	Outside "expert" may cause anxiety with participants/ staff	Insider poses no threat to daily program operations
Personal gain	No motivation of personal gain from evaluation outcomes	May have stake in evaluation outcomes
Place in power structure of program	Not a part of the power structure; hard to assure implementation of recommendations	Part of the power structure; easier to follow implementation of recommendations
Training in evaluation	Trained in evaluation methods	Little or no training in evaluation methods

Source: Adapted from M. T. Feurerstein. 1986. *Partners in Evaluation: Evaluating Development and Community Programs with Participants.* Macmillan, London.

development. In contrast, program staff, consumers, participants, and funding agencies use information from summative evaluations to answer questions regarding program impacts, continuation, termination, or expansion. Unfortunately, programs often conduct only summative evaluations, resulting in missed opportunities through formative evaluation to detect ineffective strategies before expensive and extensive implementation efforts. Table 7.2 summarizes key differences between formative and summative evaluations.

A comprehensive evaluation of a communications program to involve citizens in deer management provides an example of using both formative and summative evaluation to improve a program. The evaluation assessed a citizen task force program on deer management implemented by the New York State Department of Environmental Conservation.[4] The evaluators used two models to conceptualize decision making for deer management. The traditional model showed how deer managers typically process information from stakeholders who have no interaction with each other (fig. 7.1). Managers are stuck

TABLE 7.2. *Differences between formative and summative evaluation*

	Formative Evaluation	Summative Evaluation
Purpose	To improve a program during design, develop-ment, and implementation	To assess program effectiveness and value
Audience	Program staff/developers	Program staff, as well as con-sumers, participants, and fund-ing agencies
Frequency of data collection	Frequent	Within limited time
Sample size	Often small	Often large
Who conducts evaluation	Often an internal evaluator	Often an external evaluator, or internal and external evaluation team
Evaluation ques-tions asked	What is working? What needs to be improved? How can it be improved?	What results occurred? With whom? At what cost? Under what conditions?
Evaluation measures	Often informal	Often formal, quantitative

Source: Adapted from B. R. Worthen and J. R. Sanders. 1987. *Educational Evaluation: Alternative Approaches and Practical Guidelines.* Longman, New York, p. 36.

interpreting and weighing the disparate recommendations. In contrast, the task force model involves communication between all stakeholders, who interact and synthesize recommendations to the manager (fig. 7.2). These models served as conceptual frameworks for the formative evaluation and helped determine how to improve the exchange of information among stakeholders. During the formative evaluation, internal evaluators collected data through personal interviews, mail questionnaires, and observation techniques. They were able to change the program format and clarify task force objectives based on immediate concerns of the participants.

Later, evaluators assessed the impacts of the task force program through a summative evaluation. They distributed questionnaires before and after the program to determine changes in attitudes and knowledge of participants. They used the results to make decisions about the program and to identify fol-low-up activities needed. The use of both formative and summative evaluation

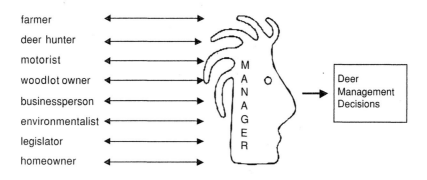

FIGURE 7.1. *The traditional model of communications between resource managers and stakeholders involves no interaction or consensus among stakeholders.*

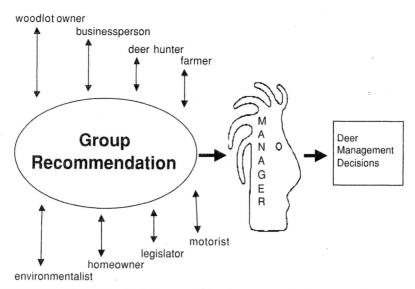

FIGURE 7.2. *The Citizen Task Force model involves communication among all stakeholders who interact and synthesize recommendations to the managers.*

enhanced program success, and facilitated interaction between the various interest groups such as farmers, environmentalists, deer hunters, and legislators.

Types of Information Collected during Evaluations

Evaluation involves collecting two general types of information: quantitative and qualitative data. Some evaluations focus primarily on quantitative data—data measured in numbers, or quantities. For example, you may count the number of people who read an environmental newsletter, or measure the change in scores on a survey of recycling knowledge before and after a recycling communications campaign. Other evaluations focus on factors that lend themselves to qualitative measurement techniques, such as interviews or photographs. For example, visitors' understanding of a tree nursery exhibit at a nature center may be measured by a survey (quantitative), but open-ended interviews or comments from a suggestion box may reveal more information (qualitative).

Evaluators debate the relative importance of quantitative and qualitative data collection tools.[5] Quantitative tools provide objective, replicable data, while qualitative measures give in-depth information impossible to glean from numbers. Evaluations that successfully integrate both quantitative and qualitative inquiry result in a more complete assessment. Table 7.3 outlines some key differences between quantitative and qualitative methods in evaluation.

Planning an Evaluation

Models exist for almost any type of evaluation context. Techniques range from management-oriented approaches that address the needs of administrative decision makers to participatory approaches that involve stakeholders in the evaluation process. An evaluation model that has been effective in the context of conservation communication approaches is the Planning-Process-Product (P-P-P) model, which corresponds to the three phases of program activity.[6] This model emphasizes evaluation as a continuous process in the life of a communications program. Figure 7.3 outlines the steps involved in the P-P-P model, which uses formative evaluation to improve the development and implementation of a program and summative evaluation to assess the final outcomes.

The Planning Evaluation

A communication program's needs, goals, opportunities, target audiences, resources, and constraints are evaluated during the planning stages. Involvement of stakeholders at this phase in the evaluation process is critical. Information generated from the planning evaluation provides direction for identifying specific objectives and choosing among alternative methods. Planning

TABLE 7.3. *Comparison of quantitative and qualitative evaluation methods*

	Quantitative Methods	Qualitative Methods
Role of evaluator	Evaluator tries to stay removed from the process as "objective" outsider	Evaluator often *is* the main measurement instrument
Data collection and analysis	Data collection and analysis are distinct phases; data collection precedes analysis	Data collection and analysis are interactive and interdependent
Theoretical basis	Positivism (world is a concrete reality that can be measured scientifically)	Constructivism (world exists as multiple realities, as viewed by the observer)
Research design	Structured research design; standardized data collection tools and statistical analysis	Flexible research design; conceptual framework guides emergent research design
Evaluator's concerns	Measurement, causality, generalization, replication, control	Description, contextualism, process, multiple perspectives, flexibility
Data collection tools	Experimental and quasi-experimental designs; structured surveys; tests; analysis of previously collected data (e.g., enrollment, program statistics); content analysis	Interviews; participant observation; case studies; naturalistic inquiry; focus groups; mapping exercises; photography; drawing and discussion
Disadvantages	Concern with measurement may miss data not reflected by numbers	Time-consuming; difficulty of analysis
Advantages	Precision; parsimony; ease of analysis from large number of subjects	Understanding of context and program complexities; in-depth data from fewer subjects

Sources: A. Bryman. 1988. *Quantity in Social Research.* Unwin Hyman, London; M. M. Mark and R. L. Shotland. 1987. *Multiple Methods in Program Evaluation.* New Directions in Program Evaluation, no. 35. Jossey-Bass, San Francisco; M. Q. Patton. 1990. *Qualitative Evaluation and Research Methods,* 2nd ed. Sage, Newbury Park, CA.

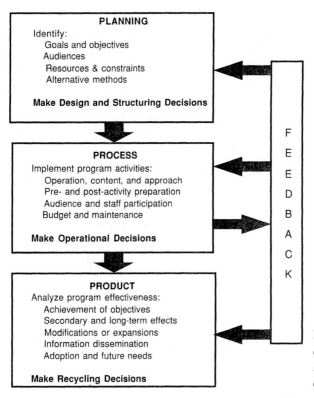

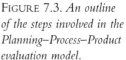

FIGURE 7.3. *An outline of the steps involved in the Planning–Process–Product evaluation model.*

evaluation also provides baseline data that can be used at the end of your program to assess success.

The planning evaluation for a conservation education program at the Monteverde Cloud Forest Reserve in Costa Rica identified needs, audiences, resources, and constraints at a regional level and set the stage for defining specific objectives for a school program.[7] One environmental problem faced in the area was unsustainable agricultural practices. A school curriculum promoting home gardens was developed to address the problem. The objective for the program was that 75 percent of the participants would plant new crops in their home gardens following the school activities. At this stage community members helped to review alternative strategies and selected the most appropriate program design for their region. Educational strategies included classroom lectures, field trips, garden construction, workshops, theater programs, and newsletters. Review of existing programs in Costa Rica allowed program staff to adapt many existing materials for their own use, rather than wasting time and resources reinventing activities.

The Process Evaluation

Throughout implementation, process evaluation involves pilot testing of all facets of the campaign to allow for ongoing modification and improvement. Feedback from participants provides staff with information to enhance the efficiency of the program. In the Monteverde garden program, for example, the education director realized the need for additional input from farmers in order to produce a newsletter with a useful content and format for the agricultural audience. The communications staff organized discussion groups with farmers to solicit this information and review trial materials. Content of programs, roles of staff, adequacy of funding, methods of dissemination, and audience participation are all components of the assessment during program implementation.

The Product Evaluation

The product, or summative, evaluation addresses the efficacy of the overall program and its impacts. Were your objectives achieved? What were the secondary and long-term effects? Was the program cost-effective? Should the program be modified or expanded? Various evaluation tools exist for assessing impacts, including written tests, performance tests, surveys and questionnaires, direct interviews, attendance records and number of activities conducted, participant observation, and role playing. The data from the product evaluation can be compared to baseline information collected during the planning stages described in chapter 2.

In addition to measuring outcomes based on the achievement of the program's objectives, identification of unexpected or secondary outcomes is important. In the Costa Rican school program, 75 percent of the students not only planted gardens, they also increased their attendance at school-sponsored activities—an unanticipated benefit of the program.

The product evaluation measures program success or failure by revealing discrepancies between program objectives and outcomes. Results of the evaluation also provide feedback for program improvement. In the Costa Rican program, product evaluation documented significant increases in knowledge and attitudes among participants. Systematic evaluation—from a project's beginning to end—can justify the use of communications approaches and provide an objective means of improving programs.

Evaluation Design

Designing an evaluation may seem like an overwhelming task, but a good plan serves as a roadmap for actually conducting an evaluation. The following five steps are useful for conceptualizing the design of any type of evaluation:

1. Decide what to evaluate and develop evaluation questions.
2. Select who will conduct the evaluation.

3. Determine evaluation design and data collection instruments.
4. Collect, analyze, and interpret findings.
5. Report findings and use results for program improvement or decision making.

These steps can serve as a helpful guide in planning an evaluation. They structure evaluation activities around the central evaluation questions or objectives, which guide subsequent evaluation activities.[8] Completion of an evaluation plan requires an input from the evaluator, project staff, and stakeholders. The indicators of success should be linked directly to program objectives or evaluation questions.

Planning an evaluation requires making choices regarding the evaluation design; data collection, analysis, and dissemination; and the use of evaluation results. The answers to the key questions on the worksheet are derived from planning and negotiation among the evaluator, program staff, and administrators.[9]

1. Planning an evaluation

   • What are the evaluation questions or objectives?
   • What are the evaluation criteria or indicators of success?
   • Who will be involved in the evaluation? If an experimental design is selected, how will random assignment to control and treatment groups be done?
   • How will the results from the evaluation be used?

2. Data collection

   • What are the information sources?
   • What data collection tools and methods are most appropriate for the evaluation questions?
   • How large is the sample? What sampling methods, if any, are needed?
   • How will the quality of the data be ensured?
   • Will data collection instruments need to be pilot tested?
   • Who will collect the data?
   • When will the data be collected?

3. Data analysis

   • How should the data be analyzed?
   • Are computers, software, and expertise available for statistical analyses, if needed?
   • What is the most useful format for the data?

4. Reporting and using evaluation results

- What do the findings reveal for making programmatic decisions and recommendations?
- To whom should the results be reported?
- How should the evaluation findings be presented for different groups?
- What follow-up measures can assess implementation of recommendations?

Evaluation Techniques

Evaluation techniques range from experimental and quantitative methods, such as before-and-after tests, to informal measurement indices, such as observation and direct interview techniques. Familiarity with a wide range of tools is helpful to communicators. Each tool is appropriate for collecting specific types of information, from specific target audiences, and in specific situations. The type of evaluation questions you are asking will guide your data collection. For example, the level of detail in your evaluation will be based on your communication objectives. You may need to assess one or more of the three potential levels of impact of your communications program.[10]

Level 1

The first level of impact simply measures the activities and products of the communications campaign. At this most basic level you may want to measure the outputs of your communications. How much exposure did your communications receive? How many events, press releases, and publications were produced? Were they likely to have reached your target audience? To measure these outputs, you can use content analysis techniques to count the number and focus of press reports. Or you can conduct public opinion polls to find out if your target audience has been exposed to your conservation message.

Level 2

The second level of impact is more complex. Measurements attempt to determine whether or not the target audience received, paid attention to, understood, and retained your conservation message, and in what form. Data collection tools such as focus groups, in-depth interviews, and extensive polling of target audiences are necessary to assess these types of evaluation questions.

Level 3

The final level of impact seeks to measure changes in target audiences' opinions, attitudes, and behaviors. To determine these outcomes, you may use techniques such as surveys, experimental designs, unobtrusive collection methods such as observation and role playing, or a variety of other multifaceted measurement methods. Monitoring of the environment or conservation problem that your communications address can reveal ultimate changes in your audiences' behaviors.

Data Collection for an Evaluation

The following section describes useful tools for collecting data to answer evaluation questions. Examples of programs that have used each tool as an evaluation method follow the summary of each technique. These methods have been described in detail in chapter 2 as approaches for collecting baseline data to help in program design. The endnotes for chapter 2 and this chapter also give you plenty of references to consult as you devise your own evaluation tools.

Tests of Attitudes, Knowledge, Skills, and Behavior

This method measures a sample of the target population with attitude surveys, knowledge/skills tests, or behavioral observations that address the objectives of the conservation communications program. The evaluator tests the sample before implementation and then after program completion to measure specific impacts of the communications intervention. Such evaluation designs can involve experimental or quasi-experimental design. In an experimental design, subjects are randomly assigned to a treatment (i.e., communications activity) or a control group. The results of their tests can be compared statistically to determine any changes resulting from the communications program.

A quasi-experimental design does not have a control group. Instead a comparison group is used that is as similar as possible to the treatment group on all potentially confounding variables, such as age, education level, and income. Evaluations often use quasi-experimental designs when random assignment is impractical. For example, all visitors to a park expect to be able to participate in a program. They would be sorely disappointed to be assigned to a control group that could not participate. One type of quasi-experiment is the time series design, in which the evaluator measures subjects on some indicator before program implementation and at several data collection points during and after the program. As the name implies, time series designs assess changes over a period of time.

Example: An Experiment Testing Knowledge and Attitudes about Ecosystem Management

An evaluation of an ecosystem management education program by the Department of Defense at Eglin Air Force Base in Florida used a baseline survey to measure knowledge, attitudes, and interests of targeted audi-

ences—recreational users and neighboring citizens. The baseline survey
focused on endangered species, fire ecology, forest resources, and ecosystem management. These surveys revealed that the target audiences held
neutral to slightly positive attitudes toward these content areas, but lacked
basic ecological knowledge. Educational materials included posters,
brochures, youth activity booklets, a public display, and print, radio, and
television spots. Respondents to the baseline survey, as well as new subjects, were randomly assigned to treatment and control groups in an experimental design. Both groups were surveyed at the end of the education
program. The treatment group increased their knowledge levels and held
more positive attitudes after exposure to the communications program
(fig. 7.4).[11] By randomly assigning people to the control or treatment
group, variation in educational levels, income, ethnic background, or
recreation habits should be fairly evenly mixed between the two groups.
Therefore changes in knowledge or shifts in attitudes should be a result of
the communications program.

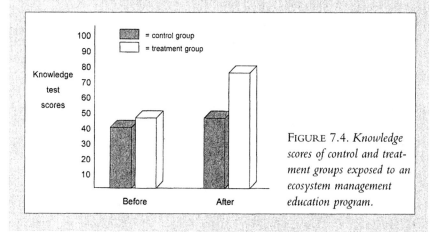

FIGURE 7.4. *Knowledge
scores of control and treatment groups exposed to an
ecosystem management
education program.*

Example: A Quasi-experimental Design Assessing a Bluebird Box Campaign

A local birders club launched a communications campaign to convince
homeowners in their county to mount bird boxes in their yards that would
be suitable for nesting bluebirds. The bird club launched a two-week
media blitz, including a press conference, direct mailings to large landowners, and free placement of public service announcements on local radio

and television shows. In order to evaluate the success of their program, the bird club counted the number of bird boxes mounted along roads in their county before and up to several months after their communications activities (the treatment). They compared these numbers with a neighboring county where no activities had occurred (fig. 7.5). Their results indicated that the impact of the program was substantial—hundreds of boxes were nailed to fence posts in their county. The lack of boxes in the comparison county suggested that other influences had not tainted their results.[12]

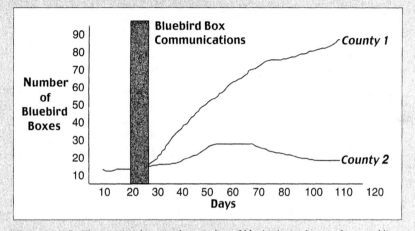

FIGURE 7.5. *Time series data on the number of bluebird nest boxes after a public communications program on the decline of bluebirds and their nesting cavities in County 1. County 2 serves as a comparison group with no exposure to the program.*

Questionnaires and Surveys

Questionnaires and surveys provide a direct, inexpensive method of receiving written feedback from target audiences for evaluation. Questionnaires and surveys can be conducted on site, through the mail, or via telephone or the Internet. Refer to chapter 2 for guidelines and examples of each type of survey research.

Example: A Survey Evaluating a Park Management Course

The International Seminar on National Parks and Equivalent Reserves brought together thirty-eight participants from thirty countries to study park management in a forum coordinated by the U.S. Park Service, Parks Canada, and the University of Michigan.[13] Every week during the month-long program, participants completed a one-page anonymous survey. The survey asked respondents to rate the program activities during the previous week, as well as complete five open-ended questions about the content and pedagogical methods of the course. Feedback from the survey was used to modify the seminar as it was being conducted to address immediate concerns and interests of the participants. This continuous monitoring helped instructors fine-tune the course to ensure that it was as effective as possible for their international participants.

Interviews with Participants

In an evaluation, interviews provide immediate data regarding program effectiveness. The personal contact between the evaluator and the interviewee allows for collection of more detailed information than a written questionnaire. Participants in interviews can provide data on the strengths and weaknesses of a program and suggestions for improvement. Common interview questions you might ask participants include:

- What did you like most about the program?
- What did you like least about the program?
- How would you improve the program for the future?

Interviews also may focus on other stakeholders besides the target audience, such as funders, program staff, parents, government officials, and community members. Interviews can be structured or unstructured, either following a preset interview guide or allowing the interviewee to digress from the initial questions. Interviews provide in-depth information, as opposed to written surveys and other techniques that limit feedback.

One specialized interview technique makes use of photographic documents. Photo-interviewing is an evaluation tool that involves taking photographs of participants engaged in an activity, and then using the photographs as interview prompts with participants. Showing photographs to participants cues them to their attitudes and receptivity toward an activity at various points in the program.[14] Chapter 2 describes personal interview techniques.

Example: Participant Interviews for Assessing a Guide Training Course

Trainers of the ecotourist guide-training course in Costa Rica described in chapter 6 used interviews to assess their program.[15] Conducted four months after the training course, the interviews revealed that twenty of the twenty-six participants were working in conservation-related fields. The interviewees reported they would not have been involved in conservation activities before the course, whereas they were currently employed as guides or research assistants. The interviews also provided feedback about which components of the course were most helpful and what was lacking.

Example: Photo-Interviewing to Enhance Data Quality

U.S. Peace Corps volunteer Mallory McDuff used photo-interviews to document the impacts of an environmental education program that she designed in the Central African Republic. She used photographs of participating children engaged in educational activities as a means of evaluating the programs from the children's perspective. McDuff interviewed individual children by showing them photos of themselves engaged in different activities that had occurred in the past six months, from nature walks to community gardening projects. The photos served as a recall cue for the children, helping them to remember and describe their attitudes and reactions to the activities. McDuff combined these results with data obtained from teachers and parents to gain a full understanding of the impact of her program.

Focus Groups and Other Group Interviews

Focus groups are an effective tool for immediate feedback from a target audience regarding the efficacy of a communications strategy for conservation. Participants in a focus group include seven to twelve people who represent a homogeneous group, such as urban high school students or retirees in Arizona. The use of focus groups requires a trained facilitator to moderate the discussion. For evaluation, focus groups can be most beneficial during formative evaluation, as the results can allow modification of communications materials or strategies being developed. An example of a focus group targeting children's perceptions of hunting was provided in chapter 2, demonstrating the use of a discussion guide.

Other group interview techniques involve drawing and mapping exercises. These are most appropriate when evaluating community or individual perceptions of a program with visually oriented cultures or children. Drawings produced by individuals or a group can facilitate discussion, as well as provide comparison for later drawings. Maps produced by community members are useful tools for monitoring land use and perceptions of land use change.[16] Maps drawn by different groups of people can serve as baseline and comparison data before and after a conservation program is conducted.

Example: A Focus Group to Determine Citizen Opinions about the Florida Everglades

Researchers at the University of Florida used focus groups to determine public opinion about management goals and restoration of the Everglades National Park.[17] Restoration of the Everglades represents a billion dollar task whose success depends on public support. Focus groups served as a means of assessing public attitudes toward this restoration project. They provided data to assess public opinion of current management practices and helped in evaluating objectives for future policies. Results of the focus groups pinpointed participants' lack of understanding of the restoration process and agency goals. At the same time, their concerns and desires for restoring the Everglades were articulated. The focus groups also provided a forum by which residents surrounding the Everglades could begin to participate in developing indicators for the success of the project.

Example: Drawing Techniques Used to Assess Conservation Programs

A conservation program in Ecuador used drawings of water resources drawn by local men and women to depict gender differences in perceptions of available resources.[18] The drawings were used at the beginning of the program as the basis for discussions with the target audience about community needs regarding water conservation. New drawings made upon completion of the program were used to evaluate changes in audience satisfaction and perceptions of impacts.

An evaluation of a schoolyard ecosystem program designed in Florida as a teaching tool and habitat restoration activity used student drawings to help assess program impacts.[19] Students were asked to draw their schoolyard habitats before and after the habitats were planned and restored. Researchers analyzed the drawings to determine students' perceptions and knowledge of the flora, fauna, and natural processes taught through the program activities. The evaluators devised specific measures, such as the complexity of the images and the diversity of the wildlife depicted, to understand the students' changing ecological knowledge and views of the schoolyard program (fig. 7.6).

FIGURE 7.6. *Evaluators used student drawings as an assessment tool to measure ecological knowledge after exposure to a schoolyard ecosystem program.*

Observation

Observational techniques provide a useful evaluation tool, especially for assessing behavior. The method involves observing participants before, during, and after a conservation program. Some evaluations use behavioral checklists for recording presence, absence, and frequency of behaviors (fig. 7.7). Observers must be properly trained to ensure reliable results. If it is impossible to observe the actual program, evaluators can record and analyze audience behaviors from the observation of videotapes. Photographs also can be used to document changes before and after a program. For example, photographs of an interpretive area can document a reduction in the amount of litter following a public awareness campaign on littering. Chapter 2 describes a variety of methods and examples of observational research.

Other forms of systematic observation of behavior involve role playing or simulation games, in which participants enact "theoretical" situations of interest to the evaluator. Such dramatics can provide insight into the impact of a program, as participants often express attitudes that would be concealed in an interview or survey.

Example: Observational Techniques to Improve Interpretive Materials for a Wetlands Tour

An evaluation of a brochure for a self-guided tour through Alabama wetlands used unobtrusive observation to assess visitors' use of the interpretive materials.[20] Following a map of the tour, the researcher observed and recorded visitors' comments, location, and frequency of use of the brochure along the trail. The unobtrusive observations revealed that the majority of visitors only read the brochure at the beginning of the trail, not at the stops provided along the way. These findings revealed brochure design problems to the project staff. The result was a newly modified brochure that was attractive and useful to the target audience.

FIGURE 7.7. *The behavior of visitors to the Mt. Mitchell interpretive trail is observed at each marker to determine their interest and use patterns. (Photo by S. K. Jacobson)*

Production of Activities and Participant Counts

Other measurements useful for program evaluation include monitoring the number of products and activities produced, as well as number of participants. Such documentation provides a simple and inexpensive, yet often ignored, means of recording activities. Baseline data from such indicators can provide comparison for measuring increases in program products, audience size, and new activities.

Example: Participant Counts of a School Program

The Monday Group Environmental Education Program described in chapter 6 carefully documented environmental action projects undertaken by groups of eleventh and twelfth graders since the program's inception.[21] Over twenty-four years, 875 students participated in environmental community projects, including protection of loggerhead sea turtles on Sanibel Island, acquisition of the Six-Mile Cypress Slough System east of Ft. Myers, and passage of the Florida Manatee Protection Act. The attendance rate during the twenty-four years was over 90 percent. Recording such basic data is essential to measuring the growth and continuity of a program.

Content Analysis and Document Review

Content analysis represents an efficient and objective tool for evaluating the text of communications documents or other materials. To conduct a content analysis, you must first determine which documents to evaluate and define the unit of analysis. For example, you may wish to review all U.S. Park Service brochures from 1989 to 1999 for Smoky Mountain National Park. Your variable of interest could be references to bear management or some other subject area that you wish to research. After coding the references to bears from each brochure, the evaluator calculates the frequency of bear-related information over the years. To evaluate conservation communications in the mass media, content analysis can be used to quantify frequency of press releases on a specific topic, placement within the newspaper, number of people reached, messages expressed, and attitude conveyed toward the topic or organization. More detailed discussion and examples of content analysis are provided in chapter 2.

Example: Content Analysis Using Mass Media in Australia

A content analysis of environmentalism in the print media analyzed news articles published in June at five-year intervals between 1967 and 1992 in the *Courier-Mail* in Australia.[22] The researcher coded environmental articles into ten categories: food production, energy, global warming, land degradation, oceans, plants, animals, radioactive poisoning, toxic chemicals, and water. A measure also was taken of column length of each article, as well as page number, location on page, and size of headline. The content analysis revealed an increase in the variety and amount of environmental news in the *Courier-Mail* over the period.

Case Study

A case study is a tool for qualitative evaluation that focuses on an in-depth portrayal of one program, participant, institution, or community. The results of a case study provide detailed insight into a particular program and its outcomes. The specific context and impacts are analyzed in detail for a specific situation. Based on the results of a case study, evaluators make recommendations concerning methods, tools, audiences, and impacts of a communications program.

Example: A Case Study of the Communications Program for the Yellowstone Wolves

A case study of the communications program for the reintroduction of the gray wolf to Yellowstone National Park is provided in appendix 1. The case study uses interviews and document analysis to evaluate the communications activities on behalf of wolf reintroduction by the U.S. Fish and Wildlife Service and Yellowstone National Park. Like most case study approaches, this detailed report pertains only to a particular situation and suggests to communicators which activities worked and ways to improve their efforts in the future. The lessons revealed might be useful to others involved in similar, controversial conservation activities, such as reintroduction of panthers in Florida or bobcats to the Georgia islands, but different contexts for these reintroductions do not allow direct comparisons.

Using Multiple Methods

Using several tools for evaluation will strengthen your analysis and findings by capitalizing on the strengths of different methods and minimizing the weaknesses inherent in single strategies. By using several methods, you combine multiple data sources, multiple perspectives, and multiple investigators or participants in data gathering. This provides cross-checks to validate your findings. Knowledge and use of the range of quantitative and qualitative tools for gathering data should result in more efficient and effective communications programming. Chapter 2 provided a detailed summary of the advantages and constraints of the various evaluation tools described here.

Example: Multiple Methods to Assess a Park-School Program

An evaluation of the park-school program developed by the Yale School of Forestry and Environmental Studies used a number of evaluation techniques to assess the project, which engaged inner-city students in environmental field activities at a neighborhood park.[23] Yale students taught forty-six fifth graders about natural resources and local ecology. They used qualitative and quantitative evaluation techniques to document the impacts of the program. Some of the results included the following:

- Portfolios of the children's research projects provided feedback on the quality of information received and retained.
- Pre- and post-test scores showed significant gains in children's knowledge of ecology.
- Pre- and post-test scores of the children's environmental attitudes were inconclusive.
- A user-satisfaction survey revealed high satisfaction with the program.
- Structured interviews with teachers and parents revealed enthusiastic support for the program and specific benefits to at-risk students.
- A videotape of the program documented activities and helped secure future funding.

The evaluation of the program provided suitable documentation of the changes in student knowledge, attitudes, social interactions, and communication skills. It also validated the program's goals and objectives through feedback from teachers, parents, and community representatives. One of the unanticipated outcomes was an improvement in the students' classroom behavior, reported by both teachers and students. This comprehensive evaluation helped promote the expansion of the park-school program.

Reporting and Using Evaluation Results

The main reason for doing evaluations is to improve programs and learn from mistakes. The results of an evaluation should lead to sound decisions regarding the success and future of the communications program. Guidelines for reporting on evaluation results depend on the audience and purpose of the evaluation.

Stakeholders in the results of an evaluation include the communications staff as well as administrators, funding sources, target audiences, and the public. Evaluation results can be presented in a variety of formats, from a simple oral briefing for participating stakeholders to a fifty-page report for a funding agency.

Like all forms of communication, the scope and format of the evaluation findings should match the interests and needs of the intended audiences. The responsibility for effectively reporting the results falls on the evaluators. Often results need to be reported in several formats. Periodic briefings by the evaluator are often more effective at disseminating key information to busy program staff than mailing them a detailed report. Videotapes or brochures summarizing the results may best serve a general audience. Oral briefings and an executive summary highlighting recommendations for future actions may be most useful for decision makers.

Formats for reporting evaluation results include:

- draft and interim progress reports,
- written or oral briefings,
- fact sheets,
- meeting presentations,
- question-and-answer sessions,
- internal memos,
- videotapes or slide-shows,
- informal communications,
- press releases or speeches,
- brochures,
- computerized presentations,
- policy papers,
- conference presentations,
- articles in professional journals or newsletters, and
- the Internet or mailing lists.

The evaluation process generally includes the input and involvement of evaluation sponsors, program staff, outside experts, participants, and others as needed. Providing draft summaries or regular briefings while the evaluation is being conducted can help tailor the presentation of the final evaluation results to your audience.

Successful reporting of evaluation findings follows a series of logical steps:

1. Early in the evaluation, establish an outline that explains the purpose, contents, planned length, timeline, and style of reporting the evaluation findings to be agreed upon by all evaluation stakeholders.
2. Partway through the evaluation, develop a concise and graphic briefing package that covers how each section of the evaluation will be reported.
3. As soon as possible, develop a draft of the interim or final report/materials for review and approval by advisers and sponsors.

4. When final reports are required, include a one- to two-page executive summary. Your report will be most effective if you use appealing graphics; present the most important information first; give real-life details— short case studies, direct quotes, and photographs; and provide clear guidance and recommendations for the future based on the findings.
5. Revise and polish the report/materials to a level appropriate for the final audience.
6. Disseminate the findings to potentially helpful audiences.[24]

This process ensures that the report and recommendations reflect the goals of the project and that the evaluation receives endorsement through the approval of draft materials. This will help you avoid presenting an evaluation report at the end of all your hard work that is deemed irrelevant, unfair, sloppy, or incomprehensible. By involving stakeholders early in the process, you will reduce surprises and your evaluation findings are more likely to be used and disseminated. This process also ensures that evaluation staff and sponsors have a briefing package so that they can tell others about the goals and preliminary results of the evaluation when seeking recognition, funds, budgetary preferences, or other public or organizational attention.

Reporting evaluation findings effectively requires keeping the needs of intended audiences in mind. The final results can be presented in writing or orally. Reporting evaluation findings in face-to-face meetings may be difficult to schedule on short notice and could be undermined by a poor presentation. These disadvantages, however, can be outweighed by the benefits of direct communication. Oral reporting can have a great impact when key stakeholders are assembled for discussion of the evaluation issues. The meeting can stimulate action by fitting the communications mode of many managers, who prefer direct communication and rarely sit and read lengthy documents.[25]

Effective Use of Evaluation Findings

A study by UNICEF revealed that the majority of evaluation reports devote 97 percent of the text to findings and only 3 percent to recommendations or specific program modifications suggested by the evaluation results.[26] Framing the evaluation questions around the needs of the intended users of the results provides more useful assessments. Such a strategy, however, demands early interaction between the evaluator and program stakeholders to focus the evaluation questions for relevant results. For example, a participatory evaluation was conducted in Canada to assess a teacher-training program in the Yukon. The evaluation team developed an ongoing written narrative with the targeted stakeholders. The evaluators periodically disseminated progress notes and invited written feedback from key players, such as teachers, administrators, and pupils in the program. These comments were incorporated into future progress notes and served to shape and disseminate the evaluation findings.[27]

The results of an evaluation must be disseminated in such a way that they are pertinent and practical for the intended audience. To help ensure that the results of your evaluation will be valuable and that your recommendations will be implemented:

- gain the interest and support of policy makers, managers, and users by meeting needs identified by your agency or organization staff;
- communicate results and recommendations clearly in an understandable form for all stakeholders in a timely manner;
- provide opportunities for stakeholder discussions about evaluation results to increase consensus about findings and actions;
- specify actions needed to improve your communications programs and emphasize their value to policy makers and the public;
- make recommendations that are realistic within organizational and resource constraints, directed at the appropriate person or entity, easily understood, and specific. For example, provide data in sufficient detail that staff and decision makers can identify areas for improvement under their power (using programmatic, geographic, or demographic data);
- integrate results into organizational management; and
- develop information databases to track information or clients over time to provide regular monitoring systems for future evaluations.[28]

Perhaps the most difficult aspect of evaluation is turning the objective findings into more subjective recommendations—turning the results into action. Because evaluation is about change and action, it may be disquieting in some organizational settings. However, the feedback provided by evaluation is extremely important as it can help a program or agency to excel in future communications endeavors. Over the long term, evaluations can be used to propose target levels of performance or outcome measures that can be reviewed annually to set goals.

In conservation communications programs, the sponsors of an evaluation are often in the same organization or even the same office as the evaluators. Having a coherent evaluation reporting process is just as important in small organizations or for small projects as it is in larger agencies. In fact, a strong evaluation process may provide more direct benefits to smaller organizations, because results can immediately be put to work for raising funds, marketing programs, or communicating critical conservation information.

Last Words

Evaluation is a process of collecting and weighing information to make decisions about the merits of a program. Decisions can be based on whether the program meets identified needs or achieves specific objectives. Limited funds available for conservation communications demand the use of evaluation to ensure programs are as effective as possible. Evaluation provides feedback with which to improve a program and verify its worth to funding agencies, participants, and other groups. Evaluation also uncovers unanticipated program outcomes.

Ideally, program evaluation should be conducted from start to finish. It is a valuable tool for gathering feedback on audiences and program design as described in chapter 2 and for assessing final outcomes as summarized in this chapter. Evaluation techniques range from quantitative methods such as before-and-after tests to qualitative observations or in-depth interviews. Table 7.4 outlines the strengths and weaknesses of common evaluation techniques. Guidelines presented in this chapter for compiling and disseminating the results of your evaluation will help you learn from your mistakes and make the most of your triumphs.

TABLE 7.4. *Strengths and weaknesses of common evaluation tools*

Evaluation tool	Strengths	Weaknesses
Before and after tests	Easy to administer Can obtain a large sample Quick scoring and processing	May be threatening to participants Cannot measure unexpected outcomes Possible cultural biases
Surveys	Good for large, homo-geneous groups Easy to analyze Cost-effective Good for factual, unambiguous data	Unknown bias from nonrespondents Cannot probe for complex information Need complete list of population Must deal with item non-response
Interviews	Provide in-depth information Allow probing Can reveal individual perceptions Allow open-ended responses	Time-consuming Costly Can be difficult to analyze Possible subjectivity of interviewer "Response effects" (tendency of respondent to give inaccurate information)
Focus groups	Socially oriented Allows moderator to probe Low costs Quick results Reasonable sample size	Can be difficult to analyze Require trained moderator Groups can vary considerably Less controlled than individual interview

(continues)

TABLE 7.4. (*Continued*)

Evaluation tool	Strengths	Weaknesses
Observation	Nonthreatening to participant Effective way to measure behavior changes	Require trained observers May be disruptive Often unreliable
Products/audience numbers	Useful for long-term monitoring of activities and audiences Inexpensive Easy	Do not measure actual impacts May be misleading
Case studies	Provide in-depth understanding of situation Easy to conduct	Results cannot be generalized Dependent on data available

Appendix

CASE STUDY OF PUBLIC COMMUNICATIONS FOR THE GRAY WOLF REINTRODUCTION TO YELLOWSTONE NATIONAL PARK

Populations of the endangered gray wolf are naturally expanding in Minnesota, Michigan, Wisconsin, and Montana. Yet the gray wolf is the only living large mammal absent from the greater Yellowstone ecosystem where it once was the top predator on deer and elk herds.[1] Under the Endangered Species Act (ESA), the 1987 Gray Wolf Recovery Plan calls for a continuation of the species' natural expansion and the reintroduction of wolves as a step toward recovery of populations in Yellowstone National Park and central Idaho. The reintroduction of wolves to Yellowstone was surrounded by controversy. Effective public communications efforts on behalf of the wolf reintroduction were crucial for success.

This case study explores the goals, objectives, target audiences, and activities of the communications programs for the gray wolf. The lead agency in wolf recovery efforts is the U.S. Fish and Wildlife Service (USFWS) of the U.S. Department of Interior, in cooperation with the National Park Service (NPS), U.S. Forest Service (USFS), tribal organizations, and state fish and game agencies in Idaho, Wyoming, and Montana. These agencies undertook a large number and variety of communications activities and approaches, many of which have been discussed throughout this book. This case study was compiled from a review of documents (listed in the endnotes) and oral interviews and written comments from the following sources:

- Edward Bangs, Western Gray Wolf Recovery coordinator, U.S. Fish and Wildlife Service
- Steve Fritts, chief scientist for Grey Wolf Recovery, U.S. Fish and Wildlife Service, Denver Region

- Cheryl Matthews, Public Affairs, Yellowstone National Park
- Rick McIntyre, Wolf Interpretation, Yellowstone National Park
- Ellen Petrick-Underwood, Interpretation/Environmental Education, Yellowstone National Park
- Sharon Rose, External Affairs, U.S. Fish and Wildlife Service, Denver Region

A lack of time and resources precluded additional research techniques to be used for this case study, such as direct observation of program activities or interviews with audience members. Yet, even the limited data collected demonstrate the value of a case study approach to analyze program components and make recommendations for future activities. The organization of this case study follows the natural steps of program planning by reviewing the mission and goals, problem and audience identification, determination of objectives and strategies, and implementation and evaluation of the communications initiative.

Mission and Campaign Goals

Resource agencies launched public communications efforts to support the mission of reintroduction and establishment of viable populations of the endangered gray wolf. Communication goals were to keep the public informed before, during, and after the reintroduction period about gray wolf status and management, and to inform and involve the public through the formal Environmental Impact Statement process mandated by Congress. Although a number of nongovernmental organizations were involved in promoting or opposing wolf reintroduction, this case study focuses on the activities of the lead agencies in the effort to reintroduce wolves to Yellowstone National Park (YNP).

Interviews with wolf recovery team members, agency statements, and documentation in the form of unpublished reports and published accounts of the reintroduction effort helped in identifying the communications goals.[2] Biologists associated with the project viewed communications leading to supportive public attitudes and interagency cooperation as key elements of the successful reintroduction of gray wolves.[3] "The key to wolf survival is human attitudes," said recovery team leader Ed Bangs. "People, especially local rural residents, don't need to like wolves, but they need to be tolerant of them in order for wolves to survive."

The philosophy of the gray wolf recovery program was simple. First, program leaders recognized that success depended on public support because people could prevent wolf recovery through illegal killing of animals. The USFWS believed that an emphasis on public outreach through a well-conceived communications program was vital to the success of the program

Second, agencies hoped to avoid unnecessary restrictions on human activ-

ities in order to accomplish wolf recovery. Biologists believed that the reintroduced wolves would reproduce and live near people as long as they were not
killed, and that few, if any, restrictions on private land uses would be necessary.
A survey of hunters and rural residents of northwestern Montana had indicated that respondents, although supportive of gray wolf recovery, were not
willing to tolerate restrictions on commercial or recreational activities to facilitate recovery efforts.[4] "Imposing restrictions on grazing, logging, and mineral
extraction would likely alienate the rural public and might actually result in
greater wolf mortality rates," said Steve Fritts, the chief scientist for gray wolf
recovery. "We felt that wolves really didn't need additional restrictions because
of their reproductive potential and willingness to live in more disturbed areas."

Problem Identification and Audience Targeting

The idea of gray wolf recovery had been evolving since the middle of the
twentieth century, but it was not an official concept until the 1987 Gray Wolf
Recovery Plan was published. Some public opposition to the process was well
known—agency personnel realized that they must address general public attitudes and concerns, as well as specific concerns of stakeholder groups.

Academic research carried out from the late 1970s to early 1990s documented attitudes of residents and interest groups toward gray wolf reintroduction well in advance of actual reintroduction efforts. This social research
detailed local, regional, and national attitudes and the attitudes of special interest groups toward gray wolf reintroduction.

Social research specifically measured levels of public support for wolf reintroduction and levels of public knowledge about gray wolves. For example,
research showed that residents of the Northern Rocky Mountains (NRM) in
Montana, Wyoming, and Idaho (fig. A.1) had mixed but overall positive attitudes toward wolves and wolf recovery:

- Fifty percent of the public in the NRM liked wolves, while 30 percent dis-
  liked wolves.[5]
- Support for wolf reintroduction was strongest in Idaho and weakest in
  Montana.[6]

In addition, researchers showed that visitors to YNP and the regional and
national public favored wolves and wolf recovery:

- A majority of visitors to YNP supported wolf reintroduction in the park:
  74 percent said the presence of wolves would enhance the Yellowstone
  experience and 82 percent agreed or strongly agreed that wolves still had a
  place in modern Yellowstone; 60–70 percent of visitors remained positive
  even when asked questions about personal fear of wolves and wolf predation on livestock or big game; overall 81 percent of respondents were "pro
  wolf."[7]

FIGURE A.1. *Map of the Northern Rocky Mountain region and Yellowstone National Park.*

- Regional and national surveys revealed the public held high levels of support for wolf reintroduction.[8]

Researchers also found that both opponents and supporters of wolf recovery had low levels of ecological knowledge concerning wolves. Residents of Wyoming, Montana, and Idaho had knowledge levels of only 37–40 percent out of a possible 100 percent score on a random mail survey of residents.[9]

Through this body of research, well in advance of the public outreach portion of the recovery program, social science researchers had identified:

- target audiences,
- appropriate media and important content areas, and
- strategic messages.

Target Audiences

The survey research provided clearly defined target audiences for wolf education efforts by identifying the subgroups of the public that felt most strongly for or against wolf reintroduction as:

- Hunters
- Nonconsumptive outdoor users
- Members of environmental groups
- Members of industry groups, such as livestock growers
- Residents of counties near YNP[10]

Organizations known to oppose reintroduction of wolves in the Yellowstone area included agricultural interests, some sport hunting groups, and groups who represented substantial economic uses of natural resources and public lands. "We knew that hunters and livestock growers were the most likely to carry guns in the woods and had the greatest chance to illegally kill wolves if they were upset enough," explained Ed Bangs.

Unfortunately, the surveys revealed that the people most likely to encounter wolves or to perceive being affected by wolves (hunters, livestock growers, and rural residents) also held the least favorable attitudes toward wolves. Wolf recovery team members experienced the unfavorable attitudes of target audiences when conducting public outreach activities during the course of the reintroduction effort. "In giving up to five hundred public talks, the team had firsthand experience in hearing and 'feeling' what the public concerns and issues were and what the agency responses should be," said Ed Bangs. "This constant interaction gave managers direct knowledge of the community pulse."

Appropriate Media, Important Content Areas, and Strategic Messages

Preliminary research suggested appropriate media for disseminating information to the public about wolf reintroduction efforts. Surveys revealed that newspapers, magazines, and television were the main information sources for key audiences such as hunters, but that public meetings and direct interactions with biologists were important sources of information for residents of remote rural areas.[11] In addition, social scientists recommended that the agency involve the public in a negotiation process to improve understanding among different constituencies and to publicize the willingness of wolf recovery proponents to compromise and compensate for wolf damages.[12]

The social survey research identified the primary reasons, based on truth and fiction, why people were for or against wolf reintroduction. The main reasons for public opposition to reintroduction were:

- Cost of the program
- Fear of wolves as dangerous based on family stories and myths
- Fear of wolves spreading outside the experimental area
- Concern over possible livestock losses
- Concern over possible restrictions on commercial and recreational use of public lands
- Concern over possible declines in game animal populations
- Concern that wolf management and control would be restricted by the ESA
- Wolf recovery as symbolic of the larger issue of government or "outside" control in the West[13]

The main reasons the public supported the reintroduction were:

- Wolves are an important member of the ecosystem.
- Wolves have a historic presence.[14]
- Wolves are magical and charismatic creatures.[15]

These areas of opposition and support provided an outline of potential content areas for public wolf education materials. However, very few real issues surrounding wolf recovery efforts had to do with the wolves themselves, according to Ed Bangs.

"Wolves are very symbolic and the 'wolf issue' was more about rural versus urban values and trust in government," said Bangs. "We knew that more 'wolf information' could not resolve these issues." A content analysis conducted of public testimony at Environment Impact Statement (EIS) hearings confirmed that public comments fell into three categories—risks/benefits of wolf reintroduction, local/national sovereignty issues, and trust/mistrust of government—and that testimonies at rural and urban sites differed in the frequency of mention of these issues.[16]

The social survey research provided a number of recommendations upon which to base public information programs. The key messages the public communications programs could convey were:

- the willingness of wolf recovery proponents to pay increased taxes in support of wolf recovery—important because the primary reason stated by respondents against wolf recovery was the high cost of the program
- the growing national awareness, interest, and financial commitment to wolf recovery
- the willingness of proponents of wolf reintroduction to compromise on issues of wolf management
- the fact that members of the Wyoming Wildlife Federation, a hunting-based group, did not believe that wolves would reduce big game numbers to unacceptable levels
- the unwillingness of wolf recovery opponents to compromise[17]

Not all these messages were thought to be effective with various target audiences. Ed Bangs points out that some local residents were angered by national support for wolf recovery. "That was *the* issue," said Bangs. "New York telling Montana what to do. It also would have been a big mistake to criticize local opponents of wolf recovery for their unwillingness to compromise—it would have made some people more willing to take illegal actions. The whole issue revolved around illegal killing and how strong the local opposition to reintroduction was. At a certain point, the strength of national support was irrelevant. All politics are local."

Lead wolf recovery scientist Steve Fritts agreed. "A focus on national support for wolves just wouldn't have helped," said Fritts. "In fact, I talked to a bunch of ranchers who just couldn't believe that anyone would actually want wolves because they've never actually talked to anyone with that viewpoint."

Bangs noted that USFWS had been strategically communicating with local audiences for several years. "For example, in 1988 a major focus in our programs was to let people know the high rate of wolf population increases and that wolves would soon expand into Idaho and YNP areas as fully protected endangered species," said Bangs. "This message shifted the debate from whether or not to have wolves to how to manage wolves when they get here." As a result, there was some improved local support for reintroduction of an experimental population of wolves, so that troublesome wolves could be removed or killed.

Research also provided specific selling points for the benefits of wolf reintroduction to affected communities around YNP. An economic analysis included in the Environmental Impact Statement projected benefits of about $23 million per year through increased wolf-related tourism in the Yellowstone region.[18]

Measurable Objectives and Strategic Planning

Much strategic social information was available before and during the wolf reintroduction effort, from academic studies and firsthand experiences of wolf recovery team members. Although no strategic plan or objectives were written for communications efforts associated with gray wolf reintroduction, much thought went into information and education efforts surrounding wolf recovery, according to Ed Bangs. "Although there is some truth to the lack of comprehensive planning," said Steve Fritts. "We had many facets of reintroduction to deal with. I think Ed Bangs summed it up in a planning document from 1988 that said we were seeking 'not acceptance, but tolerance.'"

The USFWS and NPS wolf reintroduction effort passed through three communications phases. These included public education and information programs before and during the EIS process, public meetings required by the federal government during the EIS process, and extensive media contact at the time of the captures and actual reintroduction.

According to wolf recovery leader Ed Bangs, education and outreach programs of the USFWS before and during the EIS process primarily targeted rural residents in those communities most likely to be affected by wolf reintroduction. The main media channels employed were public presentations, dialogue, and one-on-one conversations. They attempted to identify and target individuals who might be sympathetic to wolf recovery efforts. Earlier research in northwest Montana had shown that people expressing the strongest opinions about wolves, both positive and negative, were the most likely to have attended public meetings where wolves were discussed.[19]

In addition, team leaders focused on local newspaper coverage and continually worked to develop and nurture media contacts. "The key to media coverage was doing something worth reporting, getting reporters to cover the story, and arranging interviews with representatives of our team," said Bangs. "In addition, media for wolves always involved getting good visual images. Wolves make their own story because they are beautiful. So with every story, good or bad, we tried to offer great pictures, because people remember images more than words."

USFWS public affairs specialist Sharon Rose said that a lack of staffing—only four biologists working on wolf recovery—and a lack of funding often hampered planning efforts. However, during July and August of 1994, NPS public affairs specialists were able to take time to plan for reintroduction events at YNP through an *Incident Command System* originally designed for handling wildfire episodes.

"The process calls for an incident commander to oversee logistical, public affairs, and biological aspects of an incident, in this case the reintroduction of wolves," explains Cheryl Matthews, public affairs specialist for YNP (box A.1.). Through this protocol, YNP public affairs staff was able to

- predict what would happen with the reintroduction and plan public affairs events;
- coordinate logistics with other team members; and
- hold practice sessions of media relations activities.

The process also included regular briefings of staff on key topics and incorporated an assessment of the information needs of mass media news organizations and a media plan for the release of gray wolves at YNP.

Implementation Activities
Following federal approval of the Gray Wolf Recovery Plan in 1987, NPS implemented a public opinion poll and education program in YNP. Concurrent with this effort, USFWS engaged in a 1989–1992 public information and education program. Then the USFWS engaged in the EIS process mandated by federal law for major government actions with environmental impacts. Finally, both agencies participated in the capture, transport, and release of wolves into the Yellowstone ecosystem.

The Public Education Program
Activities of the 1988–1992 public education campaign conducted by the USFWS included:

- 260 presentations to more than thirteen thousand people, including businesses, livestock grower groups, outdoor sports groups, educators, conservation groups, and school groups
- Wolf education booths at state and county fairs

Box A.1. Media, information, and education planning document for Yellowstone National Park Wolf Reintroduction.

INFORMATION OFFICER
• Act as liaison with management and project leaders
• Assemble resources, money, commitments
• Perform media relations
• Direct planning with group leaders
• Inform group leaders in three areas

    1. Media group leader
        • Arrange media tours, press conferences
        • Assemble and train event information team
        • Prepare press releases
        • Inform other agency public affairs officers
        • Handle phone inquiries from public, press
        • Prepare for big event days

    2. Information/education group leader
        • Direct environmental education programs
        • Direct onsite interpretation programs
        • Prepare publications
        • Work with outside groups on publications
        • Prepare special programs
        • Advise support group on courses, books

    3. Resource liaison
        • Acquire scientific references
        • Prepare biological fact sheets
        • Talk with specialist groups
        • Act as liaison with field staff
        • Inform resource managers
        • Arrange journal articles

Source: Adapted from C. Matthews. 1994. *Wolf Reintroduction: Media/Information and Education Plan.* Public Affairs Office, Yellowstone National Park Service, Unpublished Document, Yellowstone National Park, WY.

• Films and pamphlets on correctly identifying wolves/dogs/coyotes
• Numerous informational meetings with an internal working group and other agencies, conservation organizations, journalists, television and radio talk shows, and telephone and personal interviews

- Hundreds of newspaper and magazine articles, books, and other public media about wolves and wolf recovery
- Twenty wolf education trunks on traveling rotation in schools, containing wolf and coyote hides and skulls; wolf, coyote, dog, and elk scat; wolf, coyote, lion, and elk tracks (plaster casts); an elk skull; pieces of hide from common wolf prey; audiotape of wolf howling; four wolf education videotapes; K–12 lesson plan binder; and other materials (prepared by National Wildlife Federation with USFWS support)
- Wolf posters requesting individuals to report wolf sightings displayed by agencies, sporting goods stores, schools, and other establishments.[20]

USFWS educational programs addressed a number of content areas. They provided a factual view of the wolf and the biological and legal rationale for recovery. They stated USFWS's position on gray wolf recovery, warning that some wolf control must accompany recovery and emphasizing that few restrictions on public land use would accompany wolf recovery. They also pointed out the differences between wolves and other canids.[21]

The official recovery plan had four major elements: (1) monitoring, (2) wolf and ungulate research, (3) public information, and (4) control of problem wolves, but public communications were by far the most important element around Yellowstone because there were yet no wolves to monitor or study in the area. During this time, USFWS wolf project staff spent 60 percent of their time on education and outreach efforts, 25 percent on monitoring, 5 percent on research, 5 percent on control, and 5 percent on other activities (fig. A.2).[22]

· "Because public education was incorporated into all of our activities, we probably spent more like 80 percent of our time on public outreach," said Ed Bangs, wolf recovery coordinator. "This includes not only things like presentations to groups and taking reporters along on wolf monitoring activities, but also lots of one-on-one interactions with people on their front porches or over coffee," explains Bangs. "Word of mouth is how information spreads in rural areas."

According to Ellen Petrick-Underwood, environmental educator for YNP, NPS public education programs that took place up to five years before and during wolf reintroduction included:

- Summer wolf interpretive programming at YNP, including campfire programs, slide shows, and walks, and covering topics including wolf recovery status, legal basis for wolf recovery, history of wolves in YNP, etc.
- Getting to Know the Wolf, an NPS curriculum supplement for grades 4–6, part of a "wolf pac" of free materials for teachers, which included a variety of publications
- Outreach programs throughout Greater Yellowstone Ecosystem for adult

FIGURE A.2. *Chief Scientist for Gray Wolf Recovery, Steve Fritts, carefully transports an anesthetized gray wolf. (Photo by David Mech)*

and student groups, led by district naturalists, biologists, and resource interpreters
- Responding to information and program requests
- Onsite naturalist wolf-watching assistance in YNP's Lamar Valley
- Onsite, 3–5-day, adult group courses at the Yellowstone Institute, YNP's nonprofit natural history association
- Several different posters distributed through YNP visitor centers
- Wolf books and publications distributed through YNP visitor centers

In addition, a variety of public education programs were conducted by conservation groups and volunteers, including National Wildlife Federation, Defenders of Wildlife, Wolf Fund, Wolf Education and Research Center, Wolf Haven International, Mission Wolf, and others. For example, prior to 1995 Defenders of Wildlife (DOW) engaged in the following educational activities targeted at ranchers and small communities:

- A traveling booth and literature display presented in YNP, regional malls, and small communities

- Numerous public meetings and talks
- A hands-on youth education program

DOW engaged in strategic use of communications targeted at their membership, such as:

- Regular Website updates, including a chronology of wolf recovery activities to date and a summary of Defenders' activities (e.g., press releases)
- Regular *WolfPrints* newsletter.

Other nonprofit organizations published a variety of posters, activity guides, and books before and during wolf reintroduction.[23] USFWS wolf recovery leaders said that they appreciated any accurate outside education programs, but noted that a few groups distributed materials that included distorted information, only presenting an unbalanced negative or positive view of wolves.[24]

The Environmental Impact Study Phase

From late 1991 to 1994, the USFWS engaged in the EIS process requiring full public review. Although public education was ongoing, the USFWS shifted into high gear during the EIS process. USFWS public affairs specialist Sharon Rose emphasized that much of the public outreach associated with wolf recovery was done under the aegis of the EIS process. The EIS process included (1) an issues scoping stage, (2) an alternatives definition stage, and (3) public hearings and a comment period on the draft EIS before the final EIS was prepared. During the issues scoping stage:

- 2,500 groups or individuals previously interested in wolf recovery were contacted.
- Over 1,730 people attended thirty-four open house meetings held in April 1992 in Wyoming, Idaho, Montana, and seven other U.S. locations.
- Nearly four thousand comments were received from every state and several other countries
- Thirty-nine issues were identified, eighteen of which were addressed as part of one or more of the alternatives, six of which were analyzed in depth as potentially impacted by wolf recovery (big game, hunting harvest, domestic animal depredation, land use restrictions, visitor use, local economics), and fifteen of which were not significant to the decision.[25]

During the alternatives definition stage:

- Over two thousand people attended twenty-seven open houses and six formal hearings held in August 1992 in Wyoming, Montana, Idaho, and three other U.S. locations.

- Five thousand comments were received on the five alternatives.
- Alternatives scoping brochures were sent to thirty-two thousand individuals or groups on the list of interested parties and were inserted into 230,000 Sunday newspapers in Wyoming, Montana, and Idaho
- At the end of the process nearly forty thousand people were on the EIS mailing list.[26]

During the draft EIS comment period:

- The draft EIS was released at a July 1993 press conference in Washington, D.C.
- News releases requesting comments were sent to over five hundred newspaper, radio, and television media contacts.
- 1,700 copies of the 397-page draft EIS were mailed to government agencies, public libraries, special interest groups, and other requesters.
- Forty-two thousand copies of the draft EIS summary were mailed to the list of interested parties.
- A flier requesting reports of wolf sightings was inserted into 230,000 Sunday papers in Montana, Idaho, and Wyoming.
- Twelve formal public hearings were held in Idaho, Montana, and Wyoming, and four hearings were held in other U.S. locations during August and September 1993.
- Presentations were given to interested groups in Montana, Wyoming, and Idaho throughout the comment period.[27]

Comment response was so overwhelming that the comment deadline was extended from October 15 to November 26, 1993. In all, 160,254 comments were received and seven hundred people testified at hearings. A summary of public comments and requests to report wolf sightings were mailed to the forty-three thousand people on the list of interested parties in March 1994. For the entire thirty-two-month EIS comment period, there were approximate totals of:

- 130 public meetings,
- 750,000 documents distributed, and
- 170,000 comments received from the public in all the states and forty foreign countries.[28]

"The USFWS did a lot of outreach through the EIS process," said Hank Fischer, leader of Defenders of Wildlife's wolf reintroduction support campaign. "They held town meetings in dozens of communities with videos and publications. This effort was beyond what was required by the EIS. Before there were even concrete options or proposals on the table, USFWS was targeting rural communities with wolf recovery information."

The Reintroduction Phase

Public affairs specialists Sharon Rose of the USFWS and Cheryl Matthews of YNP described the public communications activities carried out during the gray wolf capture and reintroduction:

- Advance media advisories described media access and wolf reintroduction processes.
- Public affairs specialists from USFWS (2) and NPS (2) were on hand during capture/transport and release phases.
- Press releases were disseminated for the capture, transport, placement in pens, placement in enclosures, and three releases of gray wolves.
- Media representatives were given access to every phase of the operation (provided activities did not interfere with safety of wolves and project personnel) through open arrangements during wolf capture in Canada and through a press pool arrangement during wolf release in YNP.
- Daily trips were provided to Canadian capture sites for all media and for pool media during wolf releases in YNP.
- Press conferences were held twice daily by USFWS on location during wolf capture efforts in Canada and daily by NPS at YNP media centers during release efforts.
- Satellite links from wolf capture sites in Canada were provided to all U.S. media.
- Regular news releases were distributed about the status of gray wolf reintroduction and recovery.
- Biological, veterinary, and zoological experts were available at daily news briefings to describe capture details and explain the dart fatality that occurred during capture.
- Still photos and video footage of the operation were provided to the news media by cooperating agencies and contracted specialists during some operations.
- The wolf project leader remained in Helena, Montana, to coordinate overall effort and serve as spokesperson for the project, so that USFWS always had an expert available to talk to the media.
- At the capture sites there were over twenty-thousand national, international, and Canadian media present in 1995, and several local, Canadian, and U.S. media in 1996.
- Capture coverage was featured in three Canadian wildlife magazines and hundreds of news media outlets from the United States as well as Great Britain, Japan, and Australia.
- At the release sites there were over sixty major news organizations present, including all of the major U.S. television networks (e.g., CNN, ABC, NBC, CBS).
- Wolf reintroduction news coverage was international in scope.

"Because the wolf reintroduction effort was such a massive and contentious issue, the role of agencies has been mostly a matter of responding to preexisting media interest rather than launching a strategic campaign to generate public interest," explained Defenders of Wildlife's Hank Fischer. Although the overwhelming media interest had many benefits for the gray wolf recovery effort, it also has occupied a major amount of agency time to handle requests and demands. "Our defense was on the field too much of the time," said Steve Fritts. "We got an onslaught of media attention after every event and we handled a number of Freedom of Information requests. It just didn't leave us much time for planning or catching up on the business of keeping the media informed."

Throughout the capture and release operation, biologists felt strongly about the importance of providing full information to the media and the public. "We were well aware that any mistakes would be publicized and public perception of poor planning or animal care would result in criticism of the program or calls for its termination."[29] In addition to public information, the NPS produced a monthly internal *Wolf Tracker* newsletter for the first few years of wolf reintroduction to keep its employees up to date on the status of wolf recovery efforts.

USFWS's Sharon Rose notes that intense media interest in the wolves continues to this day. Many USFWS and NPS education and information programs are ongoing, including regular updates to the media on gray wolf status and recovery, and USFWS also provides regular media updates on wolf activities in general for the entire NRM region. "Current media messages focus on the wolf population as a whole, not individual packs or animals," said YNP's Cheryl Matthews. "We talk about it as a recovered population in all public relations materials now."

Wolf interpretation efforts at YNP have accelerated since the successful reintroduction. A full-time wolf interpreter, supported by private funds, now provides formal talks, guided walks, and roving interpretation all summer at YNP. In 1996, a public gray wolf information hotline was launched by biologists. And YNP has been flooded with volunteers wanting to help with wolf-related programs.

Since the reintroduction, several nongovernmental organizations have specialized in ongoing public outreach and education about gray wolves. Leading examples are the Wolf Education and Research Center, and Wild Sentry, which takes an ambassador wolf and biologist to rural communities for youth education.

Evaluation Plan

No formal evaluation has been conducted of the communications program of the wolf recovery effort. Informal observations provide insight into the impact of the public outreach efforts to date. Wolf recovery leader Ed Bangs sums up the project succinctly: "The wolves got reintroduced and are doing great!"

"Humble in success is the key," explained Bangs. "Because many local people felt they 'lost,' boasting would be like rubbing their noses in it. We knew that if we humiliated them, the only way they could show their anger would be to illegally kill wolves. However, the local culture has decided that killing wolves is wrong, and while some people feel angry, killing wolves is still not a locally acceptable outlet for that anger." As if to confirm this evaluation, a local Montana jury recently convicted a rancher of illegally killing a wolf.

USFWS's Sharon Rose said that there have been discussions with agency staff in Washington, D.C., about what did and didn't work, and that both USFWS and NPS think the effort was successful. "We think that getting as many local groups and communities as informed as possible made a major difference in the success of the program," Rose said. "Rural residents said 'we don't want wolves, but we're glad you're talking to us.' And people who didn't like wolves were still very respectful of Ed Bangs and Laird Robinson [USFS public affairs] and other agency staff."

"Most of the people who were strongly opposed to wolves are still strongly opposed to wolves," Rose added. "But some people have shifted their view because they've seen that wolves aren't killing livestock after all. This sort of looking for cooperative solutions is what's best for ranchers and endangered species."

"There's absolutely nothing that could have been done to win over all the public," said Steve Fritts. "There were a lot of minds changed, but there are some that will never change because of the symbolism of the wolf. This was borne out by research that showed that some ranchers were opposed to any and all possible scenarios."

Analysis of Public Communications for Wolf Reintroduction

Wolf biologists have applauded the amazing shift toward public acceptance of gray wolves compared to the days when wolves were shot, poisoned, and trapped all across the West. National public support for wolf recovery was described as "the clamor of a whole culture that echoes constantly. I cannot believe that it will stop until it is finally replaced by the clamor of wolf packs in the park."[30]

Yet the continuing local contention and controversy surrounding gray wolf reintroduction has not subsided. Comments on the draft EIS reflected the public polarization that had characterized the entire reintroduction process. The majority of those who commented (many of whom lived in urban areas or outside of the potentially affected areas) wanted immediate reintroduction and protection of reintroduced wolves. The minority (primarily rural residents living near YNP) did not want wolves to be recovered or wanted the least possible legal protection and liberal management and control guidelines for reintroduced wolves. They also wanted assurances that the presence of wolves would not further restrict consumptive uses of public lands.[31]

Biologists commenting on the process have concluded that "many recovery issues are perceptional, having more to do with deeply held personal values about government, outside influences, people's relationship to 'nature,' and the political role of special interest groups than to wolves themselves."[32] Even after the successful reintroduction of gray wolves to YNP, pending court cases on both sides of the issue threaten the ongoing process.[33]

Outcomes such as the continuing opposition to gray wolf recovery suggest that some aspects of the public communications program associated with gray wolf recovery may have been problematic. Nor are communications a panacea for all resource management conflicts. "There will always be some opposition to controversial resource management programs," said YNP's Cheryl Matthews. "To believe that public information would turn that around is unrealistic."

There are many positive outcomes of the public communications efforts associated with the wolf recovery effort. The challenges and successes associated with the wolf recovery program can be analyzed within the framework of a communications program design.

Achieving the Mission and Goals
The overall mission—the reintroduction of endangered gray wolves to YNP—has been met, with the wolf population growing more rapidly than expected. Communications in support of this mission met the goal of keeping the public informed before, during, and after the gray wolf reintroduction, and throughout the extensive EIS process. The recovery team stated up front that the success of gray wolf reintroduction depended on public support, and some level of acceptance, or at least tolerance, has developed in the YNP area, as evidenced by the lack of illegal killing of wolves. In addition, agencies have been able to avoid restrictions on human activities and private land uses in wolf recovery areas, a secondary goal of the wolf recovery project.

Targeting the Audience
Large amounts of baseline social data were available to resource managers in the form of a number of published surveys dealing with public attitudes and knowledge about gray wolves. Many biological projects that involve public controversy have no social research upon which to base communication strategies. Of particular interest in this case are the research results that show the clear subgroup differences that have resulted in the ongoing controversy over wolves and livestock in the region. This mass of social research data also

is available to guide future program improvement and for comparison to future social survey measurements to identify ongoing communication needs.

The official gray wolf recovery plan called for targeted information and education programs and careful analysis of potential points of controversy. Despite the large quantity of research, wolf recovery agencies did not use all of the existing data or recommendations in creating communications programs. One public affairs specialist noted never having seen the background literature on public attitudes and knowledge about wolves. The incomplete use of baseline research may have contributed in part to the continued controversy over gray wolves in the reintroduction area.

However, some of the social data available may not have been useful for on-the-ground wolf recovery communications purposes. Ed Bangs questions the underlying and unexpressed attitudes behind some of the published research results. "One survey found that 20 percent of the people fear wolves for human safety reasons, despite all the publicity to the contrary. I think this really is because 20 percent of the people don't trust the government, not because they actually believe wolves are a threat," said Bangs. "The issues have to do with basic life philosophy and mistrust of government. These are core values and not wolf issues."

"Because the issues didn't have anything to do with wolves, they were not under control of the wolf recovery team," added Bangs. Yet biologists continue to lament the high incidence of "misperceptions that have no basis."[34] Wolf recovery leader Ed Bangs said, "We did a *lot* of public relations work. We banged our heads against the wall to keep everyone informed, but we still felt stabbed in the back by some folks who would never admit that there was anything good about this project."

Baseline research showed moderate levels of public support in the YNP region and high levels of support throughout the United States for gray wolf recovery. Comments to the draft EIS confirmed general public support for gray wolf reintroduction. No guidelines exist for acceptable levels of public opposition. Although the staff would feel better if opposition to wolf recovery diminished, some level of opposition to controversial biological conservation activities is inevitable. Communications efforts based on strategic research and careful planning can help sway public opinion and may mean the difference between success and failure of a program.

Determining Objectives and a Strategy

Measurable Objectives

While public attitudes toward wolves in the YNP region have apparently shifted, the change is modest and subtle. YNP wolf interpreter Rick McIntyre notes "a marked drop off in anti-wolf letters to the editor of the local

Billings Gazette." And a recent letter to the editor from northwest Montana rancher Leo Hargrave notes that the main causes for livestock mortality in his area were disease, weather, poor management, or respiratory and digestive problems. "As a rancher, I have a great deal more to worry about than the wolves in my valley," Hargrave said. Hargrave's letter closes: "I encourage Wyoming ranchers to have an open mind about wolf recovery. Wolves are back, and we ought to learn to live with them. This is an issue where people with common sense and good intentions should be able to work together."[35]

Editors of the *Helena Independent Record* are publicly congratulating the agencies for their quick action on problem wolves: "Opponents of the wolves' return aren't reaching for their gun racks because the feds have shown they will respond to problem wolves themselves." The editorial continues: "We love to know that once again wolves are living in Montana's wilds. The idea of shooting any of them is repugnant. But doing what it takes to prevent widespread livestock predation will, in the long run, do a lot more to protect the species than giving wolves an open season on cattle."[36]

This published evidence of gray wolf acceptance is remarkable, but without a set of measurable objectives or a survey to compare to baseline measurements, it is difficult to scientifically assess these changes in public attitudes toward wolf reintroduction. Social survey research conducted in the YNP region in coming years will be able to measure public attitudes and compare them to the results of past surveys to provide documentation of shifts in attitudes.

Strategic Planning

Getting the message out about gray wolf recovery certainly was a difficult job for the agencies: "In view of the pro-wolf and anti-wolf campaigns in progress, getting accurate information, and the USFWS' position on recovery out to the public has been a major challenge."[37] Although an earlier and more comprehensive strategic communications planning effort might have addressed some of the issues that continue to contribute to the controversy surrounding gray wolves, any reintroduction of predators is going to involve controversy and a certain level of intransigent opposition.

Wolf biologists describe the preintroduction public education program designed by USFWS as having an emphasis on "building the trust of local citizens through one-on-one contact and presenting balanced accurate information. This approach is labor intensive, and the payoff is usually not immediately seen; nevertheless, long-term change in public attitudes and acceptance of wolves is vital."[38] Although time intensive, this personal approach to public outreach was effective in developing local tolerance for gray wolves and local support for the wolf recovery team.

Baseline research showed mass media, particularly network television, as the primary source of information for key audiences, but television was too expensive for tight agency budgets, according to USFWS's Sharon Rose. Therefore, the second main focus of wolf recovery communication efforts was local newspaper and television media. This resulted in a huge amount of local media coverage of topics such as wolf capture and life history, in addition to national media attention on the gray wolf reintroduction event. Other researchers have found that mass media are effective in influencing public knowledge and attitudes about conservation issues.[39]

The public meeting format employed by USFWS during the EIS is a traditional mechanism for involving the public; other techniques may foster more participation. By the time the EIS process began, the wolf reintroduction effort had already attained a high level of controversy and polarization of attitudes among local people. Research has shown that public involvement mechanisms such as citizen task forces can result in the same biological recommendations that wildlife managers reach through traditional citizen input processes. However, the participation process itself is valuable in increasing public awareness and acceptance of management objectives and programs and in increasing public appreciation of the management agency.[40] Such mechanisms for public involvement are particularly useful where conflicts arise between stakeholder groups. University of Wyoming researcher James Thompson contends that stakeholders were not fully consulted about wolf reintroduction, that stakeholders were not allowed to participate in defining the important issues before reintroduction became controversial, and that public involvement was interpreted as simply keeping the public "informed" after the issues had already been selected.[41] However, Ed Bangs points out that agencies and tribal organizations throughout the three-state area were involved in developing reintroduction plans and that some stakeholder groups, like stock growers, absented themselves from this planning process.

In 1994, YNP public affairs staff engaged in a comprehensive communications planning effort for events surrounding the actual reintroduction of gray wolves to the park. This effort included complete plans for media relations, public education, and overall goals and objectives. This plan was effective and was put into practical and successful use as media representatives flooded the park during the reintroduction and release events. As good as this plan was for the reintroduction phase of wolf recovery efforts, a similar interagency plan unfortunately was not available to guide earlier education and information efforts before and during the EIS process.

The lack of an overall strategic plan for message content, media, public involvement, and communications in general posed a challenge for the wolf recovery effort. However, wolf recovery team members used public input to intuitively develop a public communications effort. "We did hundreds of local meetings so *we* could learn what worked and what didn't work," said Ed Bangs.

Interagency Cooperation

Interagency cooperation was identified early in the wolf recovery process as a key to success. Unfortunately, factors such as uncertainty about whether a reintroduction would occur, growing controversy, lack of clear direction to the affected agencies, and the unwieldy involvement of three states, two national parks, and six national forests (in three USFS districts) in the recovery region contributed to the difficulty of interagency cooperation.

While agencies in the YNP region did not establish a formal multiagency force to coordinate the communications aspects of wolf recovery as has been done in the other wolf recovery regions of Montana and Idaho,[42] agencies did work well together and openly communicated with each other as necessary. "All of the agencies were there with us, but because of politics it was the USFWS's job to be out in front and take the high profile heat," explained Ed Bangs. "The whole EIS process was strongly interagency. Wyoming and Idaho wildlife agencies had representatives assist with all meetings, so the public saw them there as well." Bangs explained that the Idaho game agency was hired to write the EIS, and that tribal, state, and federal Animal Damage Control agencies were closely involved. "The final rule [of the EIS] is the Wyoming state recommendation," Bangs noted.

The reintroduction effort was an enormous coordinated effort between state, tribal, and other agencies, and across international borders, according to Ed Bangs. This coordination continued after wolves were reintroduced. "When a wolf wandered outside of the park, we immediately contacted the state game officials, local leaders, news media, and affected landowners," said Cheryl Matthews. "Everyone was kept informed of the status of the wolves."

The same informal cooperative relationship was maintained with the many nongovernmental organizations involved in supporting or opposing wolf reintroduction. "Publicity really wasn't coordinated with NGOs [nongovernmental organizations], but they did honor biologists' recommendations to wait to release information when it was necessary to protect the health of the animals or the confidentiality of the operation," Sharon Rose noted. "NGOs cooperated in the transport of the wolves [Wolf Education and Research Center] and in setting up livestock damage compensation funds [Defenders of Wildlife]. This help was critical in completing the gray wolf reintroduction effort." Cheryl Matthews added, "There was no formal coordination with NGOs, but as an example, DOW was there at the release site media center. They were provided space, and they had press kits and did interviews with the media present."

Implementing Activities

Public Education

The broad public education efforts undertaken by the agencies working on gray wolf recovery were timely and appropriate for a regional predator reintroduction action. Although strategies for content and media use were not always clearly delineated, public affairs staff designed materials for adult and youth audiences throughout the region.

Materials incorporated informational messages about wolf biology and reintroduction. While messages to report wolf sightings may have been somewhat confusing to area citizens because there were not yet any wolves reintroduced into the area, this particular message was designed to "find out who might be sympathetic to wolf recovery," said Ed Bangs. "The people who turn in reports are usually rural residents, they are out in the woods, they are perhaps sympathetic to the cause of wolf recovery, and they are willing to talk to a 'fed.' In return they got a follow-up call and a handwritten note with published information about gray wolf recovery. This process established 'local authorities' in every little community scattered throughout the vast rural zone of wolf recovery—people who got inside information and then shared it with their peers over beer or at the next softball game," said Bangs. This public communications approach rewarded sympathetic audience members and also provided managers with information about where wolves might be in the vast Rocky Mountain landscape.

The Environmental Impact Statement Process

The USFWS encouraged and accommodated public interest through the open-house and face-to-face format used at the multitude of public meetings. Thousands of people were involved in commenting on wolf reintroduction, and agency personnel involved in the wolf recovery effort went out of their way to expand the EIS process beyond what is required by law to reach as many people as possible for meetings and discussions early in the process. Wolf biologists stated that a basic principle of the public outreach program was "the importance of gaining the interest and involvement of the maximum number of citizens and agency personnel."[43] Although the EIS process by its nature is designed primarily to *inform* the public of a governmental action and not to *involve* the public in meaningful discussion of the action being planned, the biologists involved in gray wolf recovery extended the process into a public forum on wolf recovery. Researchers cite the wolf recovery program as a rare example of local concerns being addressed within the confines of the ESA.[44]

Media Coverage

Local news media covered gray wolf issues for years leading up to the reintroduction. During actual reintroduction, the agencies used heightened media interest to gain a high level of national and international coverage for wolf recovery efforts. Expecting very high media interest, USFWS and NPS officials had public affairs representatives and media information on hand at a media center throughout the entire wolf reintroduction process. Agencies allowed as much media access as possible during all phases of the reintroduction, either through open access or through media pool arrangements.

"Our success was due to the biologists being open and honest about the process and in allowing people to 'watch' through the media at the capture and release sites," said USFWS public affairs specialist Sharon Rose about the coverage of gray wolf reintroduction. NPS public affairs specialist Cheryl Matthews echoed these sentiments: "The keys to our success were our honesty, our openness, our full provision of information, and our quick response when problems or concerns arose. We did our best to dispel misinformation and were very open about what was happening."

Evaluating the Results

Biologically, the reintroduction of gray wolves in the YNP and central Idaho regions has been very successful. Reintroduced wolves have reproduced well and reintroduction will continue until viable populations of the endangered predator have been established in the region. "The fact that during the first five months no wolves killed livestock and none were known to travel outside the experimental population areas intended for them was contrary to the predictions of program opponents and favorable for continuous public approval of the program."[45]

Much of the success of wolf recovery efforts has resulted from the team's straightforward approach to communications. "We didn't try to convince anybody of anything," said Ed Bangs. "It really made people angry if we were viewed as biased." That there has been very little illegal killing of wolves is a sign that tolerance for the predators has developed among local rural residents.

In parallel with public acceptance of gray wolf reintroduction were high levels of public approval for the lead wolf recovery biologist, Ed Bangs. Both USFWS's Sharon Rose and DOW's Hank Fischer cited the high public approval ratings of Bangs as a success factor, even among people who were staunchly opposed to wolf reintroduction. Integrity of the agency personnel and respect for the information source is a positive factor in communications.

Although the reintroduced gray wolves have been tolerated and there are signs of greater local acceptance of wolves, the significance of these changes is undocumented. The lack of a formal evaluation of communications efforts limits feedback for improvement of future public communications and education efforts, and changes in public opinion have not been measured over the course of the wolf reintroduction effort.

Baseline research had predicted a positive economic impact of wolves in YNP. In 1996, over ten thousand visitors to Yellowstone National Park saw the wolves.[46] Defenders of Wildlife now reports that visitors to YNP rate wolves as the number one animal they want to see.[47] YNP wolf interpreter Rick McIntyre estimates that he led 2,800 visitors on extended wolf walks in 1995 in groups of up to 165 people per walk, by far the highest attendance on any hikes in Yellowstone, perhaps the entire national park system. McIntyre also spoke to forty-thousand visitors in 1995 in YNP's Lamar Valley wolf-viewing area. Yellowstone-area newspapers have reported that local businesses are profiting from the growing interest in wolves.[48]

Future Needs

Amidst all of the indicators of success, agency representatives continue to express frustration with public opposition to reintroduction efforts. While the biological success of wolf reintroduction seems to be certain, success in the realm of public communications and public acceptance is unsure, particularly with several lawsuits still pending. Biologists predict that the controversy over wolf reintroduction will continue for years to come. "[We] expect public interest in wolves to remain high. The only prediction that we consider absolutely safe is that extreme controversy will continue to characterize wolves and wolf recovery in the NRM for years to come."[49] "Future reintroduction planners can expect sociocultural issues to pervade the effort, but can be optimistic that from a biological standpoint, reintroduction of wolves has strong potential as a restoration technique."[50]

Biologists have identified several new issues of wolf management and control that are expected to become controversial in the future. "We predict that controversy will continue well beyond the time when wolves are recovered and removed from federal protection, although the focus will shift from whether and how wolves should be restored to how wolves should be managed, particularly in relation to state-regulated ungulate hunting programs."[51] Biologists say that wolves will thrive, and that eventually wolf populations will require some kind of control, which will lead to opposition from those who were originally strong supporters of wolf recovery. Of these future problems, wolf biologist David Mech has said that "public education is probably the most effective way to minimize the problem and maximize wolf recovery, but the effort must begin immediately."[52]

This case study suggests that future communications efforts must build on the successes of the public communications associated with the early stages of gray wolf recovery in Yellowstone National Park and the NRM region. "That effort has already begun," says Ed Bangs. More formal evaluation of the communications programs would provide lessons learned for other controversial conservation initiatives, such as reintroduction of panthers into north Florida. This case study also suggests that a sound understanding of effective planning, implementation, and evaluation phases of a communications program would make ongoing communication activities more efficient and would help ensure the success of future conservation efforts.

Notes

Chapter 1. Communications for Conservation

1. Mel Sunquist, Florida Panther Technical Advisory Council.
2. Times Mirror Magazines. 1994. *National Environmental Survey.* Times Mirror Magazines, New York.
3. National Opinion Research Center. 1995. *Environmental and Scientific Knowledge around the World.* National Opinion Research Center, University of Chicago, Illinois.
4. *ABC News/Washington Post.* 1995. *ABC News/Washington Post Poll,* May 11–14. Unpublished data. *ABC News,* New York.
5. Gigliotti, L. M. 1990. Environmental education: What went wrong? What can be done? *Journal of Environmental Education* 21(2):9–12.
6. Case, D. J. 1989. Are we barking up the wrong trees? Illusions, delusions, and realities of communications in the natural resource management mix. *Transactions North American Wildlife and Natural Resource Conference* 54:630–639.
7. Olson, E. C., M. L. Bowman, and R. E. Roth. 1984. Interpretation and nonformal environmental education in natural resources management. *Journal of Environmental Education* 15(4):6–10.
8. Jacobson, S. K., and R. Robles. 1992. Ecotourism, sustainable development, and conservation education: Development of a tour guide training program in Tortuguero, Costa Rica. *Environmental Management* 16(6):701–713.
9. For example, Cable, T. T., and D. M. Knudson. 1983. Interpretation as a management tool—the manager's view. *Proceedings of the 1983 National Association of Interpreters Workshop: Advances in Interpretation.* West Lafayette, Indiana; Jacobson, S. K. 1990. A model for using a developing country's park system for conservation education. *Journal of Environmental Education* 22(1):19–25. Sharpe G. W., and G. L. Gensler. 1978. Interpretation as a management tool. *Journal of Interpretation* 3(2):3–9.
10. The Nature Conservancy. 1995. Focus on Biodiversity: Balancing People, Community and Habitat. Unpublished document.

11. Blum, A. (1987) Students' knowledge and beliefs concerning environmental issues in four countries. *Journal of Environmental Education* 18(3):7–13.

12. For example, see Cutlip, Scott M., Allen H. Center, and Glen M. Broom. 1985. *Effective Public Relations,* 6th ed. Prentice-Hall, Englewood Cliffs, NJ.

13. Stout, R. J., D. J. Decker, B. A. Knuth, J. C. Proud, and D. H. Nelson. 1997. Comparison of three public-involvement approaches for stakeholder input into deer management decisions: A case study. *Wildlife Society Bulletin* 24(2):312–317.

14. Jacobson, S. K., and S. B. Marynowski. 1997. Public attitudes and knowledge about ecosystem management on Department of Defense Lands in Florida. *Conservation Biology* 11(2):1–13.

15. U.S. Department of Agriculture, Forest Service. 1984. *"Remember Only You . . ." 1944 to 1984, Forty Years of Preventing Forest Fires, Smokey's 40th Birthday.* USDA Forest Service Publication, Washington, DC.

16. Seitel, F. P. 1995. *The Practice of Public Relations,* 6th ed. Prentice-Hall, Englewood Cliffs, NJ.

17. Seitel, F. P. 1995. *The Practice of Public Relations.*

18. For more details, see: Brown, L. A. 1981. *Innovation Diffusion: A New Perspective.* Methuen, New York; Rogers, E. M. 1962. *Diffusion of Innovations.* Free Press, New York.

19. Smith, B. L. 1995. Education to promote male-selective harvest of grizzly bear in the Yukon, pp. 156–174 in Jacobson, S. K. (ed.), *Conserving Wildlife: International Education and Communication Approaches.* Columbia University Press, New York.

20. Smith B. L. 1995. Education to promote male-selective harvest of grizzly bear in the Yukon.

21. Ibid.

22. Nixon, R. 1978. *The Memoirs of Richard Nixon.* Grosset & Dunlop, New York.

23. Fritts, S. H., and L. N. Carbyn. 1995. Population viability, nature reserves, and the outlook for gray wolf conservation in North America. *Restoration Ecology* 3(1):26–38.

24. Quoted from Denny Griswold of *Public Relations News,* cited in Seitel, F. P. *The Practice of Public Relations,* p. 7.

25. Cantril, H. 1972. *Gauging Public Opinion.* Princeton University Press, Princeton.

26. Maslow, A. H. 1954. *Motivation and Personality.* Harper & Row, New York.

27. Lasswell, H. D. 1971. *A Pre-view of Policy Sciences,* Elsevier, New York. For further discussion of conservation values, see: Meffe, G. K. 1997. Biodiversity and base values. *Oryx* 31(2):78–80.

28. For example, Henderson, C. 1984. Publicity strategies and techniques for Minnesota's nongame wildlife checkoff. *Transactions North American Wildlife and Natural Resource Conference* 49:181–189.

29. Hines, J. M., H. R. Hungerford, and A. N. Tomera. 1986–87. Analysis and synthe-

sis of research on responsible environmental behavior: A meta-analysis. *Journal of Environmental Education* 18(2)1–8.

30. For details, see Smith, W. A. 1995. Behavior, social marketing and the environment, pp. 9–20 in Palmer, J., Goldstein, W., and Curnow, A. (eds.), *Planning Education to Care for the Earth.* International Union for Conservation of Nature and Natural Resources, Gland, Switzerland; Byers, B. A. 1996. *Understanding and Influencing Behaviors in Conservation and Natural Resources Management.* African Biodiversity Series, no. 4. Biodiversity Support Program, Washington, DC.

31. Fishbein, M., and I. Ajzen. 1975. *Belief, Attitude, Intention and Behavior: An Introduction to Theory and Research.* Addison-Wesley, Reading, MA; Byers, B. A. 1996. *Understanding and Influencing Behaviors in Conservation and Natural Resources Management.*

32. Graeff, J., J. P. Elder, and E. Mills. 1993. *Communication for Health and Behavior Change: A Developing Country Perspective.* Jossey-Bass, San Francisco.

33. Fazio, J. R., and D. L. Gilbert. 1981. *Public Relations and Communications for Natural Resource Managers.* Kendall/Hunt, Dubuque, IA.

34. U.S. Department of Agriculture, Forest Service. 1984, *"Remember Only You. . . ."*

35. U.S. Department of Agriculture, Forest Service. 1984, *"Remember Only You. . . ."*

36. Jacobson, S. K., and S. B. Marynowski. 1997. Public attitudes and knowledge about ecosystem management on Department of Defense Lands in Florida.

37. Reid, T. R. 1987. When the press yelled "fire." *Journal of Forestry* 87:36–37.

38. *Gainesville Sun,* July 12, 1998, pp. 1, 12.

39. Daniel, T. C. 1990. Social/political obstacles and opportunities in prescribed fire management. *U.S. Forest Service General Technical Report* 191:134–138; Taylor, J. G., and R. W. Mutch. 1986. Fire in wilderness: Public knowledge, acceptance, and perceptions. In Proceedings of a National Wilderness Research Conference, Ogden, UT, *U.S. Forest Service General Technical Report* 212:49–59.

40. A sample of members of the Florida prescribed fire council includes: U.S. Fish and Wildlife Service, Florida Division of Forestry, U.S. Forest Service, Florida Department of Environmental Protection, Florida Game and Fresh Water Fish Commission, Water Management Districts, Georgia Pacific, Container Corporation, and large ranch and forest landowners.

41. U.S. Forest Service and Florida Division of Forestry. *The Natural Role of Fire.* Forestry Report R8-FR 15.

42. USDI, USDA. 1995. *Federal Wildland Fire Policy and Program Review: Implementation Action Plan Report.* National Interagency Fire Center, Boise, ID.

43. Sources: Daniel, T. C. 1990. Social/political obstacles and opportunities in prescribed fire management; Taylor, J. G., and R. W. Mutch. 1986. Fire in wilderness: Public knowledge, acceptance, and perceptions; Manfredo, M. J., M. Fishbein, and G. E. Haas. 1990. Attitudes toward prescribed fire policies. *Journal of Forestry* 88:19–23; Taylor, J. G., and T. C. Daniel. 1984. Prescribed fire: Public education and perception. *Journal of Forestry* 82(6):361–365; McCool, S. F. 1985. *Visitor Atti-*

tudes Toward Wilderness Fire Management Policy—1971–84. U.S. Department of Agriculture, Forest Service, Intermountain Research Station, Ogden, UT.

44. *Mark Trail Tells How Prescribed Fire Can Be Helpful to Southern Ecosystems: A Book to Color.* USDA Forest Service Publication, Washington, DC.

45. U.S. Department of Agriculture, Forest Service. 1984, *"Remember Only You. . . ."*

46. Marynowski, S. B., and S. K. Jacobson. (1999). Ecosystem management education for public lands. *Wildlife Society Bulletin* 27(1): in press Manfredo, M. J., M., Fishbein, and G. E. Haas. 1990. Attitudes toward prescribed fire policies; Taylor, J. G., and T. C. Daniel. 1984. Prescribed fire: Public education and perception; McCool, S. F. 1985. *Visitor Attitudes toward Wilderness Fire Management Policy—1971–84;* Carpenter, E. H., J. G. Taylor, H. J. Cortner, and P. D. Gardner. 1986. Targeting audiences and content for forest fire information programs. *Journal of Environmental Education* 17(3):33–41.

47. Manfredo, M. J., M. Fishbein, and G. E. Haas. 1990. Attitudes toward prescribed fire policies.

48. Seitel, F. P. 1995. *The Practice of Public Relations.*

Chapter 2. Research for Conservation Communications

1. Communications Consortium Media Center. 1994. *An Analysis of Public Opinion on Biodiversity and Related Environmental Issues:1990–1994.* Communications Consortium Media Center, Washington, DC.

2. Beldon and Russonello. 1995. *Communicating Biodiversity: Focus Group Research Findings Conducted for the Consultative Group on Biological Diversity.* Beldon and Russonello Research and Communications Report, Washington, DC.

3. Kellert, S. R. 1996. *The Value of Life: Biological Diversity and Human Society.* Island Press, Washington, DC; Kellert, S. R. 1980 Americans' attitudes and knowledge of animals. *Transactions of the North American Wildlife and Natural Resources Conference* 45:111–124.

4. Jacobson, S. K., and S. B. Marynowski. *1994 Fact Sheet on Hunters and Hunting at Eglin Air Force Base.* Eglin AFB Publication, Niceville, FL.

5. Kellert, S. R. 1985. Public perceptions of predators, particularly the wolf and the coyote. *Biological Conservation* 31:167–189.

6. Kellert, S. R. 1996. *The Value of Life: Biological Diversity and Human Society.*

7. Fishbein, M., and I. Ajzen. 1975. *Belief, Attitude, Intention and Behavior: An Introduction to Theory and Research.* Addison-Wesley, Reading, MA.

8. Jacobson, S. K., and M. Jurado. 1995. Environmental education through park interpretation in Guatemala, pp. 143–145 in L. Hay-Smith and J. Harvey (eds.), *Nature Tourism and Conservation in Central America.* Paseo Pantera Publication, U.S. Agency for International Development, Washington, DC.

9. Joint project with the University of Florida and the Wildlife Conservation Society, funded by the U.S. Agency for International Development.

10. Cantrell, D. C. 1993. Alternative paradigms in environmental education research:

The interpretive perspective, pp. 81–101 in R. Mrazek (ed.), *Alternative Paradigms in Environmental Education Research*. North American Association for Environmental Education, Troy, OH; Patton, M. Q. 1990. *Qualitative Evaluation and Research Methods*. 2nd ed. Sage, Newbury Park, CA.

11. Stout, R. J., D. J. Decker, B. A. Knuth, J. C. Proud, and D. H. Nelson. 1997. Comparison of three public-involvement approaches for stakeholder input into deer management decisions: A case study. *Wildlife Society Bulletin* 24(2):312–317.

12. Many books on survey research provide in-depth information on surveys and sampling. See: Lake, C. C. 1987. *Public Opinion Polling: A Handbook for Public Interest and Citizen Advocacy Groups*. Island Press. Washington, DC; Dillman, D. A. 1978. *Mail and Telephone Surveys: The Total Design Method*. John Wiley & Sons, New York; Rossi, P. H., J. D. Wright, and A. B. Anderson (eds). 1985. *Handbook of Survey Research*. Academic Press, San Diego; Salant, P. and D. A. Dillman. 1994. *How to Conduct Your Own Survey*. John Wiley & Sons, New York.

13. Lake, C. C. 1987. *Public Opinion Polling: A Handbook for Public Interest and Citizen Advocacy Groups*.

14. Duda, M. D. 1987. *Floridians and Wildlife: Sociological Implications for Wildlife Conservation in Florida*. Technical Report No. 2. Florida Game and Fresh Water Fish Commission, Tallahassee, FL.

15. Dillman, D. A. 1978. *Mail and Telephone Surveys: The Total Design Method*.

16. Marynowski, S. B., and S. K. Jacobson. (1999). Ecosystem management education for public lands. *Wildlife Society Bulletin* 27(1): in press.

17. Cramer, P. 1995. *The Northeast Florida Panther Education Program: Final Report to the Florida Advisory Council on Environmental Education*. University of Florida, Gainesville.

18. Cramer, P. 1995. *The Northeast Florida Panther Education Program: Final Report to the Florida Advisory Council on Environmental Education*, pp. 103–106, 108–109.

19. Fiallo, E., and S. K. Jacobson. 1995. Local communities and protected areas: Attitudes of rural residents toward conservation and Machalilla National Park, Ecuador. *Environmental Conservation* 22(3):241–249.

20. DiCamillo, J. A. 1995. Focus groups as a tool for fish and wildlife management: A case study. *Wildlife Society Bulletin* 23(4): 616–620; reprinted with permission.

21. Stout, R. J., D. J. Decker, B. A. Knuth, J. C. Proud, and D. H. Nelson. 1997. Comparison of three public-involvement approaches for stakeholder input into deer management decisions: a case study.

22. Ewert, A. 1990. Decision-making techniques for establishing research agendas in park and recreation systems. *Journal of Park and Recreation Administration* 8(2):1–13. Fox, W. 1987. *Effective Group Problem Solving*. Jossey-Bass, San Francisco.

23. Delbecq, A., and A. Van de Ven. A Group Process Model for Problem Identification and Program Planning. *Journal of Applied Behavioral Science* 7:466–492. Creighton, J. L. 1980. *Public Involvement Manual: Involving the Public in Water and*

Power Resources Decisions. United States Department of the Interior Water and Power Resources Service. U.S. Government Printing Office, Washington, DC.

24. Johnson, D. W., and R. Johnson. 1987. *Learning Together and Alone: Cooperation, Competition, and Individualistic Learning.* Prentice Hall, Englewood Cliffs, NJ.

25. Ewert, A. 1990. Decision-making techniques for establishing research agendas in park and recreation systems.

26. Moore, C. 1988. *Group Techniques for Idea Building.* Sage, Newbury Park, CA.

27. Fox, W. 1987. *Effective Group Problem Solving.*

28. Modified from: Creighton, J. L. 1980. *Public Involvement Manual: Involving the Public in Water and Power Resources Decisions.*

29. Creighton, J. L. 1980. *Public Involvement Manual.*

30. Henderson, K. 1991. *Dimensions of Choice: A Qualitative Approach to Recreation, Parks, and Leisure Research.* Venture, State College, PA.

31. Source: Smith, W. A. 1995. Behavior, social marketing and the environment, pp. 9–20 in J. Palmer, W. Goldstein, and A. Curnow (eds.), *Planning Education to Care for the Earth.* IUCN, Gland, Switzerland; used with permission.

32. Henderson, K. A. 1995. *Evaluating Leisure Services: Making Enlightened Decisions.* Venture, State College, PA.

33. For more details, see: Burrus-Bammel, L., G. Bammel, and K. Kopitsky. 1988. Content analysis: A technique for measuring attitudes expressed in environmental education. *Journal of Environmental Education.* 19(4):32–37; Berelson, B. 1952. *Content Analysis in Communication Research.* Free Press, Glencoe, IL.

34. Pomerantz, G. A., and K. A. Blanchard. 1992. Successful Communication and Education Strategies for Wildlife Conservation. *Transactions of the North American Wildlife Natural Resource Conference* 57:156–163.

35. For more details, see: Seitel, F. P. 1995. *The Practice of Public Relations.* 6th ed. Prentice Hall, Englewood Cliffs, NJ.

36. Stankey, G. H. 1972. The use of content analysis in resource decision making. *Journal of Forestry* 70(3):148–151.

37. Stankey, G. H. 1972. The use of content analysis in resource decision making.

38. Henderson, K. A. 1995. *Evaluating Leisure Services;* Yin, R. 1984. *Case Study Research: Design and Methods.* Sage, Beverly Hills.

39. Case, D. J. 1989. Are we barking up the wrong trees? Illusions, delusions, and realities of communications in the natural resource management mix. *Transactions of the North American Wildlife and Natural Resources Conference* 54:630–639.

40. Personal Communication, Suzana Padua, IPE, Brazil.

41. Case, D. J. 1989. Are we barking up the wrong trees?

42. Horwich, R. H., and J. Lyon. 1995. Multilevel conservation and education at the community baboon sanctuary, Belize, pp. 235–253 in S. K. Jacobson (ed.), *Conserving Wildlife: International Education and Communication Approaches.* Columbia University Press, New York.

43. Chambers, R. 1994. The origins and practice of participatory rural appraisal. *World Development* 22(4):953–969.

44. Institute of Development Studies. 1996. *The Power of Participation*. Policy Briefing Issue 7. Sussex, U.K.

45. Source: Kohl, John, and Indra Candanedo. 1997. Recruiting a PRA team that works. *TRI News. Journal of the Tropical Resources Institute,* Yale School of Forestry and Environmental Studies, New Haven, pp. 3–5. Used with permission.

46. Lincoln, Y. S., and E. G. Guba 1985. *Naturalistic Inquiry.* Sage, Beverly Hills. Guba, E. G. 1987. What have we learned about naturalist evaluation? *Evaluation Practice* 8(1):23–43.

47. Sources: Chenery, M. F., and R. V. Russell. 1987. Responsive evaluation: An application of naturalistic inquiry to recreation evaluation. *Journal of Park and Recreation Administration* 5(4):30–38; Smith, L. J. 1985. *Nature of the Resident Camp Experience As Perceived by Counselors.* Ph.D. diss., Indiana University.

48. Chenery, M. F., and R. V. Russell. 1987. Responsive evaluation: An application of naturalistic inquiry to recreation evaluation. *Journal of Park and Recreation Administration* 5(4):30–38; Smith, L. J. 1985. *Nature of the Resident Camp Experience As Perceived by Counselors.*

49. For more details, see: Henderson, K. A. 1995. *Evaluating Leisure Services.*

Chapter 3. Designing a Public Communications Campaign

1. NWF. 1997. *National Wildlife Federation 1996 Annual Report*. Washington, DC.

2. For details see http://www.nwf.org

3. Save the Manatee Club, Inc. (SMC) *Annual Report*. 1995. Maitland, FL.

4. http://www.nbs.gov, 1997.

5. Berkowitz, E. N., R. A. Kerin, S. W. Hartley, and W. Rudelius. 1994. *Marketing.* Richard D. Irwin, Burr Ridge, IL.

6. California Wilderness Coalition, 2655 Portage Bay East, Suite 5, Davis, CA 95616.

7. "100 leading national advertisers," *Advertising Age,* January 4, 1993, p. 16.

8. Judy Gillon, director of education, Florida Game and Fresh Water Fish Commission, personal communication.

9. *Save the Manatee Club Handbook,* 1996. Maitland, FL.

10. *Save the Manatee Club Handbook,* 1996.

11. According to the online issue of NRDC's Earth Action Newsletter for Environmental Activists, http://www.nrdc.org/nrdc, 1997.

12. *Nature Conservancy,* January 1997.

13. Personal communications, Manley Fuller, director, Florida Wildlife Federation.

14. http://www.cmc-ocean.org

15. Gluckman, C., and D. Gluckman. 1987. *Citizen's Handbook to the Local Government Comprehensive Planning Act,* Florida Audubon Society, 1101 Audubon Way, Maitland, FL 32751; used with permission.

16. Susan K. Hughes. 1997. *Population and Habitat Update* (March): 2–3; used with permission.

17. http://www.wwf.org

18. Carl Ross, Save America's Forests, personal communication.

19. U.S. Environmental Protection Agency Office of Public Affairs. 1972. *Don't Leave It All to the Experts: The Citizen's Role in Environmental Decision Making.* U.S. Government Printing Office, Washington, DC, pp. 14–15.

20. For additional ideas, see: Kendall, R. 1996. *Public Relations Campaign Strategies: Planning for Implementation.* HarperCollins, New York.

21. Landfried, S. E., M. Malik, A. Ahmad, and A. Chaudhry. 1995. Integrated crane conservation activities in Pakistan: Education, research, and public relations. S. K. Jacobson (ed.), pp. 121–173 in *Conserving Wildlife: International Education and Communication Approaches.* Columbia University Press, New York.

22. http://www.virtuallynw.com/~vnw/stories/1997/Jun/15/s244733.html

23. Faris, D. E. 1995. *Mass Media Strategies of Interest Groups: Profiles of Education and Environmental Organizations.* Ph.D. diss., Columbia University, pp. 55–56.

24. Salzman, J. 1995. *Let the World Know: Make Your Cause News.* Rocky Mountain Media Watch, Denver, CO.

25. World Resources Institute. 1994. *Teacher's Guide to World Resources: Citizen Action.* Washington, DC.

26. Salzman, J. 1995. *Let the World Know.*

27. Susan Boghosian, National Wildlife Federation, personal communication.

28. Sievert, R. C., Jr. 1988. Public awareness and urban forestry in Ohio. *Journal of Arboriculture* (February): 48–51.

29. Sievert, R. C., Jr. 1988. Public awareness and urban forestry in Ohio.

30. Ritchie, B. 1996, CD stirs passions about environment, *Gainesville Sun* (24 December), p. 1D.

31. Beamish, R. 1995. *Getting the Word Out in the Fight to Save the Earth.* Johns Hopkins University Press, Baltimore.

32. Described in detail in Beamish, R. 1995. *Getting the Word Out in the Fight to Save the Earth.*

33. *The Environmental Grantmaking Foundations Directory* is published by Environmental Data Resources, Inc., Rochester, NY, and is updated regularly.

34. For more details on writing grant proposals, see Tilt, W. 1996. Moving beyond the past: A grant-maker's vision for effective environmental education. *Wildlife Society Bulletin* 24(4):621–626; Howe, F. 1991. *The Board Member's Guide to Fund Raising.* Jossey-Bass, San Francisco.

35. Public Relations, Store Tie-Ins Launch "Green" Cosmetics Line. 1991. *Public Relations Journal* (April):24–25.

36. http://www.foacadia.org

37. For details on the establishment of environmental partnerships see: Management Institute for Environment and Business. 1993. *Conservation Partnerships: A Field Guide to Public–Private Partnering for Natural Resource Conservation.* National Fish and Wildlife Foundation, Washington, DC; Roche, L., and S. K. Jacobson (1999) Partnerships for Conservation in Brazil. *Wildlife Society Bulletin.*

38. See http://www.esri.com/conservation

39. Andy Lyons, Internet consultant, personal communication.

40. North Cascades Institute, 2105 State route 20, Sedro-Woolley, WA 98284.

41. See http://www.nps.gov/roc

42. Jim Covel, interpretive program manager, Monterey Bay Aquarium, personal communication.

43. http://www.wwf.org

44. http://www.learner.org/jnorth

45. http://www.zooweb.net

Chapter 4. Using Mass Media

1. National Center for Education Statistics, cited in the *Gainesville Sun* (1 September 1998), p. 2A.

2. Farhar-Pilgrim, B., and F. F. Shoemaker. 1981. Campaigns to affect energy behavior, p. 166 in R. Rice and W. Paisley (eds.), Public Communications Campaign. Sage, Beverly Hills.

3. Interview with Lynn Bowersox, media relations manager of the National Wildlife Federation, June 4, 1991, Washington, DC; cited in Faris, D. E. 1995. *Mass Media Strategies of Interest Groups: Profiles of Educational and Environmental Organizations.* Ph.D. diss., Columbia University, p. 32.

4. Grunig, J. E., and T. Hunt. 1984. *Managing Public Relations.* Holt, Rinehart & Winston, New York.

5. Patterson, B. R. 1986. *Write to Be Read.* Iowa State University Press, Ames.

6. Beamish, R. 1995. *Getting the Word Out in the Fight to Save the Earth.* Johns Hopkins University Press, Baltimore.

7. Maslow, A. H. 1954. *Motivation and Personality.* Harper & Row, New York.

8. Green, R., and D. Shapiro. 1987–88. A video news release primer. *Public Relations Quarterly* (Winter):10–13.

9. Beamish, R. 1995. *Getting the Word Out in the Fight to Save the Earth.*

10. Interview with Mark J. Rovner, vice president for public affairs at the World Wildlife Fund, July 24, 1991, Washington, D.C. Cited in Faris, D. E. 1995. *Mass Media Strategies of Interest Groups: Profiles of Educational and Environmental Organizations,* p. 66.

11. Interview with Jennifer Beck, office manager at the Greenhouse Crisis Foundation, June 27, 1991, Washington, D.C. Cited in Faris, D. E. 1995. *Mass Media Strategies of Interest Groups.*

12. For more examples of words that convey feelings, see Jones, C. 1983. *How to Speak TV: A Self-defense Manual When You're on the News.* Video Consultants, Marathon, FL.

13. Wilke, A. W. 1997. Adam Werbach: The youngest Sierra Club president is aiming for the Grassroots and MTV. *E* (September–October):10–13.

14. Moseley, B. 1993. Daniel Janzen. *Omni* (April):73–78.

15. Carving up tomorrow's planet: Interview with John G. Robinson. 1994. *International Wildlife* (January–February):31–36.

16. McKibben, B. 1996. More than a naturalist. *Audubon* (January–February):92–97.

17. Mandese, J. 1993. Super Bowl '94 has tough act to follow. *Advertising Age* (8 February), p. 34.

18. Busch, A. M. 1990. What media hold student interest. *Advertising Age* (5 February), S-4, S-5.

19. Tucker, K., and D. Derelian. 1989. *Public Relations Writing: A Planned Approach for Creating Results.* Prentice Hall, Englewood Cliffs, NJ.

20. Smith, J. 1995. *The New Publicity Kit.* John Wiley and Sons, New York.

21. Media Report and Selected Clips (February–May 1991), Conservation International, Washington, DC.

22. Faris, D. E. 1995. *Mass Media Strategies of Interest Groups,* p. 37.

23. Cited in Patterson, B. R. 1986. *Write to Be Read,* p. 10.

24. Patterson, B. R. 1986. *Write to Be Read.*

25. Interview with Kristen Merriman, media relations director at the Izaak Walton League of America, June 26, 1991, Washington DC. Cited in Faris, D. E. 1995. *Mass Media Strategies of Interest Groups,* p. 51.

26. A Media Guide to Experts in Marine Conservation, the Center for Marine Conservation, July 1990. Cited in Faris, D. E. 1995. *Mass Media Strategies of Interest Groups,* p. 66.

27. Forn, J. A., and B. S. Glenn. 1989. *Lake Michigan Sport Fish: Should You Eat Your Catch?* Great Lakes Natural Resource Center, Ann Arbor, MI. Cited in Faris, D. E. *Mass Media Strategies of Interest Groups,* p. 95; interview with Lynn Bowersox, media relations manager at the National Wildlife Federation, June 4, 1991, Washington, DC. Cited in Faris, D. E. 1995. *Mass Media Strategies of Interest Groups,* p. 95.

28. Smith, J. 1995. *The New Publicity Kit.*

29. http://www.commerce.net

30. GVU (Graphics, Visualization, and Usability Center), 1996. http://www.cc.gatech.edu/gvu

31. GVU, 1996.

32. See http://members.aol.com/SJAudubon.

33. For the results, see http://eelink.umich.edu/wild.

34. PDF stands for Portable Document Format. It's a common format for documents on the Web because it can save pictures, different fonts, columns, etc. PDF files can be viewed or printed with Acrobat Reader, a free program available from Adobe, http://www.adobe.com. However, to create the PDF files you must purchase software from Adobe.

35. See http://dnr.state.il.us

36. GVU 1996.

37. Do a keyword search on "Web promotion," Yahoo, or one of the other search engines to see a list of these useful sites.

38. http://eelink.net/

39. GVU, 1996.
40. such as Listserv, Listproc, or MajorDomo
41. for example, http://www.liszt.com/

Chapter 5. Methods and Materials for Interpreting the Environment

1. Tilden, F. 1977. *Interpreting Our Heritage,* 3rd ed. University of North Carolina Press, Chapel Hill.

2. Refined from Tilden's definition and cited in Veverka, J. 1994. *Interpretive Master Planning.* Falcon, Helena, MT.

3. Veverka, J. 1994. *Interpretive Master Planning.*

4. Falk, J., and L. Dierking. 1992. *The Museum Experience.* Whalesback Books, Washington, DC.

5. National Park Service. 1988. *Management Policies,* U.S. Dept. of the Interior, Washington, DC, cited in Knudson, D. M., T. T. Cable, and L. Beck. 1995. *Interpretation of Cultural and Natural Resources.* Venture, State College, PA.

6. For examples, see: Spears, C. J. 1991. Using the press in controversial issues, pp. 295–296 in *Proceedings, National Interpreters Workshop,* NAI. Vail, CO; Dillon, C. 1991. Interpretation and the protection of Zambia's wildlife, pp. 65–68 in *Proceedings, National Interpreters Workshop,* NAI. Vail, CO; Clark, R. N., R. L. Burgess, and Hendee. 1972. The development of anti-litter behavior in a forest campground. *Journal of Applied Behavior Analysis* 5(1):1–5; Marynowski, S. B., and S. K. Jacobson. (1999). Ecosystem management education for public lands. *Wildlife Society Bulletin* 27(1): in press.

7. Knudson, D. M., and M. E. Vanderford. 1980. Participation in interpretive programs by state park visitors. *Journal of Interpretation* 5(2):20–23.

8. For details, see: S. H. Ham. 1992. *Environmental Interpretation: A Practical Guide for People with Big Ideas and Small Budgets.* North American Press, Golden, CO; Tilden, F. 1977. *Interpreting Our Heritage;* Knudson, D. M., T. T. Cable, and L. Beck. 1995. *Interpretation of Cultural and Natural Resources.*

9. For more examples, see: Ham, S. H. 1992. *Environmental Interpretation.*

10. Actually people generally can recall five to nine main ideas, see Ham 1992 for discussion; the number five or fewer is recommended here to address the majority of people.

11. For more discussion on thematic interpretation, see: Ham, S. 1992. *Environmental Interpretation.* 2nd ed. Macmillan, New York.

12. For details, see: Sharpe, G. W. 1982. *Interpreting the Environment.* 2nd ed. Macmillan, New York. Veverka, J. 1994. *Interpretive Master Planning.*

13. For further discussion, see: Ambrose, T., and C. Paine. 1993. *Museum Basics.* International Council of Museums (ICOM) supported by the Cultural Heritage Division of UNESCO and Paine, New York and London; Piper, J. 1988. Writing Pan-

els in "People English," pp. 204–215 in Proceedings of the 1988 National Inter-preters Workshop. San Diego, CA. Writing panels in "People English"; Screven, C. G. 1986. Exhibitions and information centers: Some principles and approaches. *Curator* 29(2): 109–137.

14. Adapted from Ambrose, T., and C. Paine. 1993. *Museum Basics,* p. 86.

15. For details, see: Fazio, J. R. and D. L. Gilbert. 1981. *Public Relations and Communications for Natural Resource Managers.* Kendall/Hunt, Dubuque, IO; Miller, G. A. 1990. Developing exhibits that communicate, pp. 100–104 in D. L. Kulhavy, and M. H. Legg (eds.) in *What Past Is Prologue: Our Legacy—Our Future.* Proceedings of the 1990 National Interpreters Workshop. National Association for Interpretation, Ft. Collins, CO.

16. Sources for exhibit planning information: Knudson, D. M., T. T. Cable, and L. Beck. 1995. *Interpretation of Cultural and Natural Resources;* Ambrose, T., and C. Paine. 1993. *Museum Basics;* Miller, G. A. 1990. Developing exhibits that communicate; Screven, C. G. 1986. Exhibitions and information centers: Some principles and approaches; Ham, S. H. 1992. *Environmental Interpretation.*

17. Bitgood, S., and D. Patterson. 1987. Principles of exhibit design. *Visitor Behavior* 2(1):4.

18. Modified from Bitgood, S., and D. Patterson. 1987. Principles of exhibit design; Miller G. A. 1990. Developing exhibits that communicate; Piper, J. 1988. Writing panels in "People English"; Ham, S. H. 1992. *Environmental Interpretation: A Practical Guide for People with Big Ideas and Small Budgets.*

19. Bitgood, S., T. Finlay, and D. Woehr. 1987. Design and evaluation of exhibit labels. *Evaluation and Design of Zoos* (1)1:1–7.

20. For details, see: Ambrose and Paine, 1993. *Museum Basics.*

21. Modified from Bitgood, S., and D. Patterson. 1987. Principles of exhibit design; Screven, C. G. 1990. Uses of evaluation before, during, and after exhibit design. *ILVS Review: A Journal of Visitor Behavior* 1(2):36–66. Screven, C. G. 1986. Exhibitions and information centers.

22. For more details on brochure design, see Brigham, N. 1991. *How to Do Leaflets, Newsletters, and Newspapers.* PEP, Detroit.

23. See Jacobson, S. K., and S. B. Marynowski. (In press). Interpreting ecosystem man-agement on military lands. *Journal of Interpretation Research.*

24. Jacobson, S. K. 1988. Media effectiveness in a Malaysian park system. *Journal of Environmental Education* 19:22–27.

25. Thorndyke, P. 1977. Cognitive structures in comprehension and memory of nar-rative discourse. *Cognitive Psychology* 9(1):77–110.

26. Lewis, W. J. 1980. *Interpreting for Park Visitors.* Eastern Acorn Press, Eastern National Park and Monument Association, Philadelphia.

27. Bunnell, P., and T. Mock. 1990. *A Guide for the Preparation and Use of Overhead and*

Slide Visuals. Forestry Canada, B.C. Ministry of Forests, Research Branch publication.Victoria, British Columbia, Canada.

28. For more about these techniques, see: Regnier, K., M. Gross, and R. Zimmerman 1992. *The Interpreter's Guidebook: Techniques for Programs and Presentations.* UW-SP Foundation Press. University of Wisconsin, Stevens Point.

29. Ham, S. H. 1992. *Environmental Interpretation.*

30. For a discussion of sociological implications of interpretation see: Machlis, G., and D. Field (eds.). 1984. *On Interpretation: Sociology for Interpreters of Natural and Cultural History.* Oregon State University Press, Corvallis.

Chapter 6. Conservation through Education

1. Freeberg, W. H., and L. E. Taylor. 1961. *Philosophy of Outdoor Education.* Burgess Publishing, Minneapolis.

2. Freeberg, W. H., and L. E. Taylor. 1961. *Philosophy of Outdoor Education.*

3. Freeberg, W. H., and L. E. Taylor. 1961. *Philosophy of Outdoor Education,* p. 185.

4. Sharpe, G.W. 1982. *Interpreting Our Environment.* Macmillan, New York.

5. Freeberg, W. H., and L. E. Taylor. 1961. *Philosophy of Outdoor Education.*

6. Kirk, J. J. 1980. The quantum theory of environmental education. *Nature Study* 33(4):2–3.

7. North American Association for Environmental Education. 1983. *Defining Environmental Education: The NAAEE Perspective.* North American Association for Environmental Education, Troy, OH. This definition builds on earlier definitions of environmental education, such as the 1977 *Tbilisi Declaration,* developed at the first international conference on environmental education:

    • to foster clear awareness of, and concern about, economic, social, political, and ecological interdependence in urban and rural areas;

    • to provide every person with opportunities to acquire the knowledge, values, attitudes, commitment, and skills needed to protect and improve the environment;

    • to create new patterns of behavior of individuals, groups, and society as a whole toward the environment.

8. Roth, C. E. 1991. *Environmental Literacy: Its Roots, Evolution, and Directions in the 1990s.* ERIC/SMEAC, Columbus, OH; Capra, F. 1993. What is ecological literacy? *Guide to Ecological Literacy,* pp. 4–8. The Elmwood Institute, Berkeley.

9. Roper-Starch. 1996. *NEETF Environmental Attitudes and Knowledge Survey.* Roper-Starch Worldwide, New York.

10. Hart. 1993. *Highlights from a National Public Opinion Study on Biodiversity.* Defenders of Wildlife, Washington, DC; Communications Consortium Media Center (CCMC). 1994. *An Analysis of Public Opinion on Biodiversity and Related Environmental Issues: 1990–1994.* Communications Consortium Media Center, Washington, DC.

11. Jacobson, S. K., and S. M. Padua. 1995. A systems model for conservation educa-

tion in parks: Examples from Malaysia and Brazil, pp. 3–15, in S. K. Jacobson (ed.), *Conserving Wildlife: International Education and Communication Approaches.* Columbia University Press, New York.

12. National Parks and Conservation Association. 1988. *Interpretation: Key to the Park Experience.* NPCA, Washington, DC.

13. http://www.ce.utk.edu/Smoky

14. http://www2.wku.edu/www/geoweb/karst

15. http://www.yellowstoneassociation.org

16. http://www.ncascades.org/nci

17. Wilson, E. O. 1988. *Biodiversity.* National Academy Press, Washington, DC.

18. Blanchard, K. A. (1995). Reversing population declines in seabirds on the north shore of the Gulf of St. Lawrence, Canada, in S. K. Jacobson (ed.), *Conserving Wildlife,* pp.51–63.

19. For more details, look for a new book by Kathleen Blanchard entitled, *Signs, Fines, Hearts, and Minds: The Power of Community-Based Bird Conservation.* Contact the QLF-Atlantic Center for the Environment, 39 South Main Street, Ipswich, MA 01938.

20. Tilden, F. 1977. *Interpreting Our Heritage,* 3rd ed. University of North Carolina Press, Chapel Hill.

21. Muuss, R. 1982. *Theories of Adolescence.* Random House, New York; Knudson, D. M., T. T. Cable, and L. Beck. 1995. *Interpretation of Cultural and Natural Resources.* Venture, State College, PA.

22. For example, Kiersey, D., and M. Bates. 1978. *Please Understand Me: An Essay on Temperament Styles.* Prometheus Nemesis Books, Del Mar, CA; Golay, K. 1982. *Learning Patterns and Temperament Styles.* Manas-Systems, Newport Beach, CA; Knudson, D. M., T. T. Cable, and L. Beck. 1995. *Interpretation of Cultural and Natural Resources.*

23. Hammitt, W. 1981. A theoretical foundation for Tilden's interpretive principles. *Journal of Environmental Education* 12(3):13–16

24. Hart, L. 1991. The "brain" concept of learning. *The Brain-Based Education Networker* 3(2):1–3

25. For example, Knudson, D. M., T. T. Cable, and L. Beck. 1995. *Interpretation of Cultural and Natural Resources;* North American Association for Environmental Education. 1996. *Environmental Education Materials: Guidelines for Excellence.* NAAEE, Washington, DC.

26. Ford, P. 1981. *Principles and Practices of Outdoor/Environmental Education.* John Wiley & Sons, New York.

27. Henderson, C. 1984. Publicity strategies and techniques for Minnesota's nongame wildlife checkoff. *Transactions North American Wildlife and Natural Resource Conference.* 49:181–189.

28. This interview is excerpted from Adams, E. 1995. *San Juan Islands Wildlife.* The Mountaineers/The San Juan Preservation Trust, Seattle, WA.

29. Council for Environmental Education (CEE). 1992. *Project WILD K–12 Activity Guide.* CEE, Gaithersburg, MD.

30. CEE, 1992. *Project WILD K–12 Activity Guide.*

31. For more information see also http://eelink.umich.edu/wild

32. Stapp, W. B., M. M. Cromwell, and A. Wals. 1995. The global rivers environmental education network, pp.177–197, in S. K. Jacobson (ed.), *Conserving Wildlife.* Columbia University Press, New York.

33. Mitchell, M. K., and W. B. Stapp. 1992. *Field Manual for Water Quality Monitoring: An Environmental Education Program for Schools.* 6th ed. Thomson-Shore Printers, Dexter, MI.

34. See http://www.igc.apc.org/green

35. Source: Hammond, W. C. 1995. Engaging students in wildlife-focused action projects in Florida: A thirty-five year perspective, pp. 198–218, in S. K. Jacobson (ed.), *Conserving Wildlife.* Columbia University Press, New York.

36. See notes 31–34.

37. Tilden, F. 1977. *Interpreting Our Heritage.*

38. Richardson, J. G. 1994. Selecting program delivery methods effectively. Paper presented at the Agricultural Communications Section, Southern Association of Agricultural Scientists, February 1994, Nashville, TN.

39. Source: Paaby, P., and D. B. Clark. 1995. Conservation and local naturalist guide training programs in Costa Rica, pp. 263–276, in S. K. Jacobson (ed.), *Conserving Wildlife.*

40. Source: Paaby, P., and D. Clark. 1995. Conservation and local naturalist guide training programs in Costa Rica, p. 266, in S. K. Jacobson, *Conserving Wildlife.*

41. Paaby, P., and D. B. Clark. 1995. Conservation and local naturalist guide training programs in Costa Rica.

42. For more information about the course, contact: U.S. Fish and Wildlife Service, National Conservation Training Center, Rt. 1, Box 166, Sheperdstown, WV 25443.

43. U. S. Fish and Wildlife Service. 1998. *An Apporach to Ecosystem Conservation, Course Book.* USFWS, Washington, DC.

44. For example, Knudson, D. M., T. T. Cable, and L. Beck. 1995. *Interpretation of Cultural and Natural Resources.*

45. http://www.nwf.org/naturelink

46. For example, Center for Commercial-Free Public Education (CCPE). 1997. Right-wing think tanks, corporate polluters behind recent attacks on environmental education: Major new report reveals attack aim to de-fund environmental education. Press Release (9 April); Clearinghouse of Environmental Advocacy and Research (CLEAR). 1997. Assault on environmental education. *A CLEAR View: Special Issue* (27 January): vol. 4, p. 2.

47. Clearinghouse of Environmental Advocacy and Research (CLEAR). 1997. Assault on environmental education.

48. Clearinghouse of Environmental Advocacy and Research (CLEAR). 1997. Assault on environmental education.

49. Center for Commercial-Free Public Education (CCPE). 1997. Right-wing think tanks, corporate polluters behind recent attacks on environmental education.

50. Wilke, R. 1996. Director's corner. *Environmental Education Advocate* (fall).

51. National Environmental Education Training Foundation (NEEFT). 1996. *Report Card: Environmental Attitudes and Knowledge in America.* NEEFT, Washington, DC.

52. North American Association for Environmental Education. 1996. *Environmental Education Materials Guidelines for Excellence,* Washington, D.C.

53. Blum, A. 1987. Student's knowledge and beliefs concerning environmental issues in four countries. *Journal of Environmental Education* 18(3):7–13.

54. Archie, M., L. Mann, and W. Smith. 1993. *Partners in Action: Environmental Social Marketing and Environmental Education.* Academy for Educational Development, Washington, DC.

Chapter 7. Evaluating and Monitoring Program Success

1. For more details, see Worthen, B. R., and J. R. Sanders. 1987. *Educational Evaluation: Alternative Approaches and Practical Guidelines.* Longman, New York.

2. Norris, K., and S. K. Jacobson. 1998. Content analysis of tropical conservation education programs: Elements of success. *Journal of Environmental Education* 30(1):39–44.

3. International Institute for Environment and Development (IIED). 1994. *Whose Eden Is It Anyway?* IIED Publication, London.

4. Stout, R. J., D. J. Decker, and B. Knuth. 1992. Evaluating citizen participation: Creating communication partnerships that work. *Transactions of the Fifty-seventh North American Wildlife and Natural Resources Conference,* pp. 135–140.

5. For example, Smith, J. K., and L. Heshusius. 1986. Closing down the conversation: The end of the quantitative–qualitative debate among educational inquirers. *Educational Researcher* 15(1):4–12.

6. Jacobson, S. K. 1991. Evaluation model for developing, implementing, and assessing conservation education programs: Examples from Belize and Costa Rica. *Environmental Management* 15(2):143–150.

7. Jacobson, S. K. 1991. Evaluation model for developing, implementing, and assessing conservation education programs.

8. For more details, see: Worthen, B. R., and Sanders, J. R. 1987. *Educational Evaluation: Alternative Approaches and Practical Guidelines.* Longman, New York.

9. For more details, see: Wholey, J. S., H. P. Hatry, and K. E. Newcomer. 1994. Planning and managing evaluation for maximum effectiveness, pp. 489–491 in Wholey, J. S., H. P. Hatry, and K. E. Newcomer (eds.), *Handbook of Practical Program Evaluation.* Jossey-Bass, San Francisco.

10. For more details, see: Lindemann, W. 1993. An "effectiveness yardstick" to measure PR success. *Public Relations Quarterly* (Spring):7–9.

11. Marynowski, S. B., and S. K. Jacobson. (1999). Ecosystem management education for public lands. *Wildlife Society Bulletin* 27(1): in press.

12. For statistical analyses of quasi-experimental designs, see: Langbein, L. I. 1980. *Discovering Whether Programs Work.* Scott, Foresman, Glenview, IL.

13. Nowak, P. F. 1984. Direct evaluation: A management tool for program justification, evolution, and modification. *Journal of Environmental Education* 15(4):27–31.

14. Tucker, S., and J. Dempsey. 1991. Photo-interviewing: A tool for evaluating technological innovations. *Evaluation Review* 15(5):639–653.

15. Paaby, P., and D. B. Clark. 1995. Conservation and local naturalist guide training programs in Costa Rica, pp. 263–275 in S. K. Jacobson (ed.), *Conserving Wildlife: International Education and Communication Approaches.* Columbia University Press, New York.

16. Davis-Case, D. 1990. *The Community's Toolbox: The Idea, Methods, and Tools for Participatory Assessment, Monitoring, and Evaluation in Community Forestry.* Food and Agriculture Organization of the United Nations, Rome, Italy.

17. Personal communications, Alan Hodges, University of Florida.

18. Personal communications, Mallory McDuff and McIlvaine-Newsad.

19. Personal communications, Joe Schaefer and Linda Jones, University of Florida.

20. McDuff, M. D. 1995. External evaluation report: Weeks Bay National Estuarine Research Reserve. Fairhope, AL. (Unpublished).

21. Hammond, W. C. 1995. Engaging students in wildlife-focused action projects in Florida: A thirty-five-year perspective, pp. 198–218 in S. K. Jacobson (ed.), *Conserving Wildlife.*

22. Kidman, G. 1992. Analysis of environmentalism in the print media. Master's thesis, Griffith University, Australia.

23. Milton, B., E. Cleveland, and D. Bennet-Gates. 1995. Changing perceptions of nature, self, and others: A report on a park/school program. *Journal of Environmental Education* 26(3):32–39.

24. See Bell, J. B. 1994. Managing evaluation projects step by step, pp. 510–533 in Wholey, J. S., H. P. Hatry, and K. E. Newcomer (eds.), *Handbook of Practical Program Evaluation*; Hendricks, M. 1994. Making a splash: Reporting evaluation results effectively, pp. 549–575 in Wholey, J. S., H. P. Hatry, and K. E. Newcomer (eds.), *Handbook of Practical Program Evaluation*; Sonnichsen, R. C. 1994. Evaluators as change agents, pp. 534–548 in Wholey, J. S., H. P. Hatry, and K. E. Newcomer (eds.), *Handbook of Practical Program Evaluation*; Kossecoff, J., and A. Fink. 1982. *Evaluation Basics: A Practitioner's Manual.* Sage, Newbury Park, CA.

25. For more details, see: Hendricks, M. 1994. Making a splash.

26. Hursh-Cesar, G. 1991. Eight ways to make communication evaluation more useful. *Development Communication Report* 72:23–24.

27. Hart P., M. Taylor, and I. Robottom. 1994. Dilemmas in participatory enquiry: A case study of method-in-action. *Assessment and Evaluation in Higher Education* 19(3):201–204.

28. For more details, see: Sonnichsen, R. C. 1994. Evaluators as change agents; Who-ley, J. S., H. P. Hatry, and K. E. Newcomer. 1994. Planning and managing evalua-tion for maximum effectiveness; Carter, R. 1994. Maximizing the use of evalua-tion results, pp. 576–589 in Wholey, J. S., H. P. Hatry, and K. E. Newcomer (eds.), *Handbook of Practical Program Evaluation*; Hatry, H. P., K. E. Newcomer, and J. S. Wholey. 1994. Conclusion: Improving evaluation activities and results, pp. 590–602 in Wholey, J. S., H. P. Hatry, and K. E. Newcomer (eds.), *Handbook of Practical Program Evaluation.*

Appendix. Case Study of Public Communications for the Gray Wolf Reintroduction to Yellowstone National Park

1. Mech, L. D. 1995. The challenge and opportunity of recovering wolf populations. *Conservation Biology* 9(2):270–278.

2. Jacobson, S. K., and S. B. Marynowski, unpublished case study.

3. Fritts, S. H., and L. N. Carbyn. 1995. Population viability, nature reserves, and the outlook for gray wolf conservation in North America. *Restoration Ecology* 3(1):26–38.

4. Tucker, P. A., and D. H. Pletscher. 1989. Attitudes of hunters and residents toward wolves in northwestern Montana. *Wildlife Society Bulletin* 17:509–514.

5. Kellert, S. R. 1985. Public perceptions of predators, particularly the wolf and the coyote. *Biological Conservation* 31:167–189.

6. Bath, A. J., and T. Buchanan. 1989. Attitudes of interest groups in Wyoming toward wolf restoration in Yellowstone National Park. *Wildlife Society Bulletin* 17:519–525. Bath, A. J. 1991. Public attitudes in Wyoming, Montana, and Idaho toward wolf restoration in Yellowstone National Park. *Transactions of the North American Wildlife and Natural Resources Conference* 56:91–95. Thompson, T., and W. Gasson. 1991. *Attitudes of Wyoming residents on wolf reintroduction and related issues.* Wyoming Game and Fish Department, Cheyenne; Bath, A. J. 1992. Identification and documenta-tion of public attitudes toward wolf reintroduction in Yellowstone National Park, pp. 2–3 to 2–30 in Varley, J. D. and W. G. Brewster (eds.), *Wolves for Yellowstone? A Report to the United States Congress. Vol. IV. Research and Analysis.* U.S. National Park Service, Yellowstone National Park, Mammoth, WY.

7. McNaught, D. A. 1987. Wolves in Yellowstone National Park? Park visitors respond. *Wildlife Society Bulletin* 15:518–521.

8. Bath, A. J. 1992. Identification and documentation of public attitudes toward wolf reintroduction in Yellowstone National Park; Fritts, S. H., and L. N. Carbyn. 1995. Population viability, nature reserves, and the outlook for gray wolf conservation in North America; Mech, L. D. 1995. The challenge and opportunity of recover-ing wolf populations.

9. Bath, A. J. 1991. Public attitudes in Wyoming, Montana, and Idaho toward wolf restoration in Yellowstone National Park.

10. Fritts, S. H., E. E. Bangs, J. A. Fontaine, W. G. Brewster, and J. F. Gore. 1995. Restoring wolves to the Northern Rocky Mountains of the United States, pp. 107–125 in L. D. Carbyn, S. H. Fritts, and D. R. Seip (eds.), *Ecology and Conservation of Wolves in a Changing World.* Occasional Publication No. 35. Canadian Circumpolar Institute, Edmonton, Alberta.

11. Tucker, P. A., and D. H. Pletscher. 1989. Attitudes of hunters and residents toward wolves in northwestern Montana. *Wildlife Society Bulletin* 17:509–514; Fritts, S. H., E. E. Bangs, J. A. Fontaine, W. G. Brewster, and J. F. Gore. 1995. Restoring wolves to the Northern Rocky Mountains of the United States.

12. Bath, A. J. 1989. The public and wolf reintroduction in Yellowstone National Park. *Society and Natural Resources* 2:297–306; Bath, A. J. 1991. Public attitudes about wolf reintroduction in Yellowstone National Park, pp. 367–376 in Keiter R.B. and M. S. Boyce (eds.), *The Greater Yellowstone Ecosystem: Redefining America's Wilderness Heritage,* Yale University Press, New Haven; Thompson, J. G. 1993. Addressing the human dimensions of wolf reintroduction: An example using estimates of livestock depredation and costs of compensation. *Society and Natural Resources* 6:165–179.

13. Bath, A. J. 1991. Public attitudes about wolf reintroduction in Yellowstone National Park; Mech, L. D. 1991. Returning the wolf to Yellowstone, pp. 309–322 in R. B. Keiter, and M. S. Boyle (eds.), *The Greater Yellowstone Ecosystem: Redefining America's Wilderness Heritage.* Yale University Press, New Haven; Thompson, T., and W. Gasson. 1991. *Attitudes of Wyoming residents on wolf reintroduction and related issues;* Fritts, S. H., E. E. Bangs, J. A. Fontaine, W. G. Brewster, and J. F. Gore. 1995. Restoring wolves to the Northern Rocky Mountains of the United States.

14. Thompson, T., and W. Gasson. 1991. Attitudes of Wyoming residents on wolf reintroduction and related issues.

15. Rick McIntyre, personal communication.

16. Wicker, K. J. 1996. An analysis of public testimonies on the reintroduction of wolves to the Greater Yellowstone Ecosystem. Master's thesis, Texas A&M University.

17. Bath, A. J. 1991. Public attitudes about wolf reintroduction in Yellowstone National Park.

18. USDI Fish and Wildlife Service. 1994. *Notice of Record of Decision and Statement of Findings for the Reintroduction of Gray Wolves to Yellowstone National Park and Central Idaho.* USDI Fish and Wildlife Service, Washington, DC.

19. Tucker, P. A., and D. H. Pletscher. 1989. Attitudes of hunters and residents toward wolves in northwestern Montana.

20. Fritts, S. H., E. E. Bangs, J. A. Fontaine, W. G. Brewster, and J. F. Gore. 1995. Restoring wolves to the Northern Rocky Mountains of the United States.

21. Fritts, S. H., E. E. Bangs, J. A. Fontaine, W. G. Brewster, and J. F. Gore. 1995. Restoring wolves to the Northern Rocky Mountains of the United States.

22. Fritts, S. H., E. E. Bangs, J. A. Fontaine, W. G. Brewster, and J. F. Gore. 1995. Restoring wolves to the Northern Rocky Mountains of the United States.

23. Such as: an art poster depicting a wolf family at YNP's geysers produced by the National Wildlife Federation; *Wolf Recovery in the Northern Rocky Mountains,* a scientific report prepared by the National Audubon Society and National Fish and Wildlife Foundation; *Looking at the Wolf,* a publication of the Wyoming-based Teton Science School for audiences of all ages; *Twilight Hunters* natural history booklet, *The Wolf Video,* and *A Howling in America's National Parks* art poster published by the Wolf Education Task Force; an issue of the youth periodical *Zoo-Books* on wolves, put out by Wildlife Education, Inc. of San Diego; and *The Wonder of Wolves,* a youth activity booklet published by the Denver Museum of Natural History.

24. Sharon Rose, External Affairs, U.S. Fish and Wildlife Service, Denver Region, personal communication.

25. Fritts, S. H., E. E. Bangs, J. A. Fontaine, W. G. Brewster, and J. F. Gore. 1995. Restoring wolves to the Northern Rocky Mountains of the United States; Fritts, S. H., E. E. Bangs, J. A. Fontaine, M. R. Johnson, M. K. Phillips, E. D. Koch, and J. R. Gunson. 1997. Planning and implementing a reintroduction of wolves to Yellowstone National Park and central Idaho. *Restoration Ecology* 5(1):7–27.

26. Fritts, S. H., E. E. Bangs, J. A. Fontaine, W. G. Brewster, and J. F. Gore. 1995. Restoring wolves to the Northern Rocky Mountains of the United States. Fritts, S. H., E. E. Bangs, J. A. Fontaine, M. R. Johnson, M. K. Phillips, E. D. Koch, and J. R. Gunson. 1997. Planning and implementing a reintroduction of wolves to Yellowstone National Park and central Idaho.

27. Fritts, S. H., E. E. Bangs, J. A. Fontaine, W. G. Brewster, and J. F. Gore. 1995. Restoring wolves to the Northern Rocky Mountains of the United States; Fritts, S. H., E. E. Bangs, J. A. Fontaine, M. R. Johnson, M. K. Phillips, E. D. Koch, and J. R. Gunson. 1997. Planning and implementing a reintroduction of wolves to Yellowstone National Park and central Idaho.

28. Fritts, S. H., E. E. Bangs, J. A. Fontaine, W. G. Brewster, and J. F. Gore. 1995. Restoring wolves to the Northern Rocky Mountains of the United States; Fritts, S. H., E. E. Bangs, J. A. Fontaine, M. R. Johnson, M. K. Phillips, E. D. Koch, and J. R. Gunson. 1997. Planning and implementing a reintroduction of wolves to Yellowstone National Park and central Idaho.

29. Fritts, S. H., E. E. Bangs, J. A. Fontaine, M. R. Johnson, M. K. Phillips, E. D. Koch, and J. R. Gunson. 1997. Planning and implementing a reintroduction of wolves to Yellowstone National Park and central Idaho.

30. Mech, L. D. 1991. Returning the wolf to Yellowstone.

31. Fritts, S. H., E. E. Bangs, J. A. Fontaine, M. R. Johnson, M. K. Phillips, E. D. Koch, and J. R. Gunson. 1997. Planning and implementing a reintroduction of wolves to Yellowstone National Park and central Idaho.

32. Fritts, S. H., E. E. Bangs, J. A. Fontaine, W. G. Brewster, and J. F. Gore. 1995. Restoring wolves to the Northern Rocky Mountains of the United States.

33. Cases included: *Wyoming Farm Bureau Federation et al. vs. Bruce Babbitt, Secretary of the Interior et al.; National Audubon Society et al. vs. Babbitt et al.;* and *James R. and Cat D. Urbigkit vs. Babbitt et al.*

34. Fritts, S. H., E. E. Bangs, J. A. Fontaine, W. G. Brewster, and J. F. Gore. 1995. Restoring wolves to the Northern Rocky Mountains of the United States.

35. *Billings Gazette* (26 January 1997).

36. Editors. 1997. Dealing with problem wolves. *Helena Independent Record* (9 July 1997).

37. Fritts, S. H., E. E. Bangs, J. A. Fontaine, W. G. Brewster, and J. F. Gore. 1995. Restoring wolves to the Northern Rocky Mountains of the United States.

38. Fritts, S. H., E. E. Bangs, J. A. Fontaine, W. G. Brewster, and J. F. Gore. 1995. Restoring wolves to the Northern Rocky Mountains of the United States.

39. For example, Marynowski, S. B., and S. K. Jacobson. (In press). Ecosystem management education for public lands. *Wildlife Society Bulletin.*

40. Stout, R. J., D. J. Decker, B. A. Knuth, J. C. Proud, and D. H. Nelson. 1997. Comparison of three public-involvement approaches for stakeholder input into deer management decisions: A case study. *Wildlife Society Bulletin* 24(2):312–317.

41. Thompson, J. G. 1993. Addressing the human dimensions of wolf reintroduction: An example using estimates of livestock depredation and costs of compensation. *Society and Natural Resources* 6:165–179.

42. Fritts, S. H., E. E. Bangs, J. A. Fontaine, W. G. Brewster, and J. F. Gore. 1995. Restoring wolves to the Northern Rocky Mountains of the United States.

43. Fritts, S. H., E. E. Bangs, J. A. Fontaine, W. G. Brewster, and J. F. Gore. 1995. Restoring wolves to the Northern Rocky Mountains of the United States.

44. Keiter, R. B., and P. K. Holscher. 1990. Wolf recovery under the Endangered Species Act: A study in contemporary federalism. *Public Land Law Review* 11:19–52.

45. Fritts, S. H., E. E. Bangs, J. A. Fontaine, M. R. Johnson, M. K. Phillips, E. D. Koch, and J. R. Gunson. 1997. Planning and implementing a reintroduction of wolves to Yellowstone National Park and central Idaho.

46. Rick McIntyre, Wolf Interpretation, Yellowstone National Park, personal communication.

47. Brooke, J. 1996. Yellowstone wolves get an ally in tourist trade. *New York Times* (11 February), 10.

48. Bangs, E. E., and S. H. Fritts. 1996. Reintroducing the gray wolf to central Idaho and Yellowstone National Park. *Wildlife Society Bulletin* 24(3):402–413.

49. Fritts, S. H., E. E. Bangs, J. A. Fontaine, W. G. Brewster, and J. F. Gore. 1995. Restoring wolves to the Northern Rocky Mountains of the United States.

50. Fritts, S. H., E. E. Bangs, J. A. Fontaine, M. R. Johnson, M. K. Phillips, E. D. Koch,

and J. R. Gunson. 1997. Planning and implementing a reintroduction of wolves to Yellowstone National Park and central Idaho.

51. Bangs, E. E., and S. H. Fritts. 1996. Reintroducing the gray wolf to central Idaho and Yellowstone National Park.

52. Mech, L. D. 1995. The challenge and opportunity of recovering wolf populations.

Index